# Prehistoric Cultural Change at
# Kitselas Canyon

## Gary Coupland

Canadian Museum of Civilization
National Museums of Canada

© National Museums of Canada 1988

**Canadian Cataloguing in Publication Data**

Coupland, Gary, 1953-
    Prehistoric cultural change at Kitselas Canyon

(Mercury series, ISSN 0316-1854)
(Paper/Archaeological Survey of Canada, ISSN
0317-2244; no. 138)
Includes abstract in French.
Bibliography: p.
ISBN 0-660-10781-3

1. Paul Mason Site (B.C.)—Antiquities. 2. British
Columbia—Antiquities. 3. Kitselas Canyon
(B.C.)—Antiquities. 4. Paleo-Indians—British
Columbia—Kitselas Canyon—Antiquities. 5. Indians of
North America—British Columbia—Antiquities. 6.
Excavations (Archaeology)—British Columbia.
I. Canadian Museum of Civilization. II. Archaeological
Survey of Canada. III. Title. IV. Series. V. Series:
Paper (Archaeological Survey of Canada); no. 138.

E78 B9 C68 1988        971.1'01        C88-099104-6

Printed and bound in Canada

Published by
Canadian Museum of Civilization
National Museums of Canada
Hull, Quebec
K1A 0M8

ASC Papers Coordinator
*Richard E. Morlan*

Cover  photograph by George F. MacDonald

## OBJECT OF THE MERCURY SERIES

The Mercury Series is designed to permit the rapid
dissemination of information pertaining to the
disciplines in which the Canadian Museum of
Civilization is active. Considered an important
reference by the scientific community, the Mercury
Series comprises over three hundred specialized
publications on Canada's history and prehistory.

Because of its specialized audience, the series consists
largely of monographs published in the language of the
author.

In the interest of making information available quickly,
normal production procedures have been abbreviated.
As a result, grammatical and typographical errors may
occur. Your indulgence is requested.

Titles in the Mercury Series can be obtained by writing
to the

> Mail Order Services
> Publishing Division
> Canadian Museum of Civilization
> Hull, Quebec
> K1A 0M8

> (613) 957-9905

## BUT DE LA COLLECTION MERCURE

La collection Mercure vise à diffuser rapidement le
résultat de travaux dans les disciplines qui relèvent des
sphères d'activités du Musée canadien des civilisations.
Considérée comme un apport important dans la
communauté scientifique, la collection Mercure
présente plus de trois cents publications spécialisées
portant sur l'héritage canadien préhistorique et
historique.

Comme la collection s'adresse à un public spécialisé
celle-ci est constituée essentiellement de monographies
publiées dans la langue des auteurs.

Pour assurer la prompte distribution des exemplaires
imprimés, les étapes de l'édition ont été abrégées. En
conséquence, certaines coquilles ou fautes de
grammaire peuvent subsister : c'est pourquoi nous
réclamons votre indulgence.

Vous pouvez vous procurer la liste des titres parus dans
la collection Mercure en écrivant au :

> Service des commandes postales
> Division de l'édition
> Musée canadien des civilisations
> Hull (Québec)
> K1A 0M8

> (613) 957-9905

National Museums    Musées nationaux
of Canada           du Canada

Canada

## Abstract

This study investigates the prehistoric transition from egalitarian to ranked social structure at Kitselas Canyon, Skeena River, British Columbia. It contributes to archaeological theory by developing and testing a model of the evolution of cultural complexity. A culture historical contribution is also made in the development of a prehistoric local sequence for Kitselas Canyon.

The theoretical model argues that cultural change at Kitselas Canyon occurred as a deviation amplifying process. Beginning with an initial condition of environmentally limited access to the critical salmon resource, the cultural response was to impose further access restriction by placing control of the resource in the hands of fewer and fewer individuals. An important stage in this process is the formation of corporate groups, initially organized along egalitarian lines. It is argued that ranked corporate groups emerged from egalitarian corporate groups, not as a response to subsistence-related stress, but rather as a means of consolidating control over the most productive resource locations.

This model is tested against archaeological data from Kitselas Canyon. The historic period is described to elucidate the ethnographic model, which represents the comparative base for the study of prehistoric social change. Data from the Paul Mason Site at Kitselas Canyon is presented. Three cultural components at this site are identified through multivariate quantitative analysis. These results are then integrated with the existing sequence from the nearby Gitaus site to establish a five-phase prehistoric cultural sequence for Kitselas Canyon. This constitutes the temporal framework for the investigation of prehistoric social change.

Social change is investigated in terms of a series of variables - residential permanency, storage, population aggregation, household variability, and status goods. Much of the investigation focusses on the Paul Mason Phase, dated at ca. 3000 B.P. This phase represents the development of salmon intensification, residential permanency, large-scale storage, and substantial population aggregation. However, there is no evidence of ascribed status differentiation, as seen historically among the Skeena River groups. This pattern is attributable to the formation of egalitarian corporate groups.

This study demonstrates the importance of egalitarian corporate groups in the evolution of Northwest Coast society. Identification of such a group at Kitselas Canyon during the Paul Mason Phase supports the proposition that social ranking evolved as a deviation amplifying process with respect to resource access.

# Résumé

La présente étude se penche sur la transition entre société
égalitaire et société hiérarchique, qui a marqué l'époque
préhistorique au canyon Kitselas, sur la rivière Skeena, en
Colombie-Britannique.  Par l'élaboration et la vérification d'un
modèle de l'évolution de la complexité culturelle, l'étude pousse
plus avant les recherches théoriques en archéologie.  En nous
présentant un segment de la période préhistorique du canyon
Kitselas, elle contribue, d'autre part, à faire connaître
l'histoire culturelle de cette région.

Suivant le modèle théorique, les changements culturels
survenus dans cette région sont le résultat d'un procédé de
déviation croissante.  Il semblerait que, au départ, la
communauté ait eu un accès limité au saumon, qui constituait en
fait une des ressources de base.  Face à cet état de choses, un
nombre de plus en plus restreint d'individus s'est vu confier le
contrôle de cette source d'approvisionnement, ce qui eut pour
effet d'en limiter encore davantage l'accès.  La formation de
groupes individualisés, constitués à l'origine sur une base
égalitaire, représente une étape importante dans ce procédé de
déviation.  Les groupes hiérarchiques seraient, selon nous, issus
des groupes égalitaires, non pas en réponse à des problèmes de
subsistance, mais plutôt pour assurer un plus grand contrôle des
lieux les plus riches en approvisionnement.

Le  modèle est mis à l'épreuve en fonction de données
archéologiques relevées au canyon Kitselas.  Quant à la
description de la période historique, elle vise à éclaircir le
modèle ethnographique qui constitue la base comparative de
l'étude des changements sociaux de cette époque particulière.

Des données recueillies au site Paul Mason, au canyon Kitselas, sont également présentées. L'analyse quantitative multivariée permet par ailleurs d'identifier trois composantes culturelles propres à ce site. Les résultats sont ensuite intégrés dans la chronologie du site Gitans avoisinant, afin de bien camper l'organisation culturelle en place pendant la période préhistorique du canyon Kitselas dans un cadre temporel réparti en cinq phases. Notre étude des changements sociaux qui se sont manifestés à l'époque préhistorique s'inscrit dans ce cadre.

Ces changements sont examinés, d'autre part, en fonction d'une série de variables, soit la résidence permanente, l'entreprosage, la concentration de la population, la variabilité des ménages et les biens de prestige. Une partie importante de l'étude porte sur la phase Paul Mason, qui date d'environ 3 000 ans avant nos jours. Cette phase correspond à l'accroîssement de la pêche au saumon, à la sédentarité du groupe, à l'entreposage à grande échelle ainsi qu'à une concentration élevée de la population. Toutefois, aucune transformation du statut social n'y est attestée, à l'opposé de ce qui est observable chez les groupes de la rivière Skeena. Ce fait serait attribuable à la formation de groupes égalitaires.

Bref, l'étude démontre l'importance des groupes égalitaires dans l'évolution de la société de la côte nord-ouest. La présence d'un tel groupe au canyon Kitselas, au cours de la phase Paul Mason, semble confirmer que la hiérarchie sociale est issue du procédé de déviation croissante susmentionné, procédé intimement lié à l'accès aux ressources.

## Acknowledgements

As with any dissertation, there are many people to thank. I would like to start by expressing my gratitude to two people, without whose assistance and interest, this project would have fallen short of the mark. Professor R.G. Matson, chairman of my advisory committee, has guided my interest in prehistoric social organization. What words of wisdom exist in the following pages are attributable to his demands for thoughtfulness and thoroughness. It has been my pleasure to study under someone who I consider both teacher and friend. Dr. George MacDonald, Director of the National Museum of Man, and a member of my committee, first introduced me to the Skeena River and Kitselas Canyon. He is in many ways the "father of north coast archaeology". Without his support, both scholarly and financial, the Kitselas Project could never have been undertaken.

Professor Donald Mitchell of the University of Victoria has helped me to understand some of the finer points of Northwest Coast ethnography, as well as providing valuable archaeological insights. Professor Richard Pearson has contributed greatly to my understanding of complex societies, and has pushed me to consider the reader of this dissertation. Professor David Pokotylo offered constructive theoretical and methodological criticisms, and did a thorough editorial job. To the above members of my committee, I am greatly indebted.

The National Museum of Man through the auspices of Professor MacDonald, and the British Columbia Heritage Trust provided financial support for the project. I am thankful for their assistance. The Kitselas Band administered the Heritage Trust funds. I would like to take this opportunity to acknowledge their friendship and support of the project. To Paul Mason, Ralph Wright, Roy Bolton and Wilfred Bennett, I owe a special debt of gratitude.

The University of British Columbia provided me with financial support from 1981 to 1984 through the Charles and Alice Borden Fellowship in Archaeology. For this, I am most grateful.

Moira Irvine, the most acknowledged person in B.C. archaeology, prepared the graphs, figures and photos with her usual speed and accuracy.

Three seasons were spent in the field at Kitselas Canyon. For their work, often under adverse conditions, I thank David Archer, Al Mackie,

Jenny Johnston, Jennifer Hayman, Colleen Rudy, Keith Johnston, Gwyn Langemann, Andrea Burbidge, Irene Hayman, Ruth Murdoch, Eric Hotz, Diva Vinceguerra, Debbie Thayer, Susan Reynolds, Glenn Bennett, Edison Bolton, Paul Mason Jr., Francis Wright, Kjerstin Smith, James Amos, Elaine Moore and Mason Hersey. Special thanks to Richard Mackie, Dave Walker and Jack Heppelwhite.

For their help along the way, I thank Marty Magne, Deanna Ludowicz, Dana Lepofsky, Linda Roberts, Mike Broderick, Ann Underhill, Linda Burnard and Diana Alexander.

I would also like to take this opportunity to thank my family, whose support has been of a more personal nature. To my parents, Donald and Elizabeth, and my sisters Kathy and Laurie, go my thanks for their unflagging support every step along the way. They were always there when I needed them. I am fortunate to be married to a woman, Carol, who has given me only encouragement and support in this endeavour. This dissertation could not have been completed without her. I dedicate this study to Carol and our children, Michael and Arran.

TABLE OF CONTENTS

ABSTRACT                                                        iii

ACKNOWLEDGEMENTS                                                vii

CHAPTER 1:   INTRODUCTION                                       1

    Orientation                                                1

    Format of the dissertation                                 2

    History of archaeological research on the north coast      4
    Research objectives                                        14

CHAPTER 2:   CORPORATE GROUPS AND SOCIAL RANKING:
             THE EVOLUTION OF CULTURAL COMPLEXITY              16

    Definitions                                                16

    Deviation amplification                                    16

    The deviation counteracting argument: a critical review    19

    Social ranking as deviation amplification:
    the Northwest Coast                                        23

CHAPTER 3:   KITSELAS CANYON: THE NATURAL ENVIRONMENT          42

    General geographic setting                                 42

    Surficial geology                                          46

    Climate                                                    48

    Hydrology                                                  49

    Natural flora and fauna                                    51

    Paleoenvironment                                           67

    Recent environment                                         69

    Summary                                                    74

CHAPTER 4:   KITSELAS CANYON: THE CULTURAL SETTING             76

    Introduction                                               76

Part 1 - Regional Ethnography                                  76

    Cultural and linguistic affiliation                        76

    Settlement pattern and yearly round                        77

    Kitselas villages and territories                          83

    Subsistence technology and material culture                93

    Demography                                                 97

    Social organization                                        99

    Summary                                                    102

CHAPTER 4
Part 2 - Regional Culture History                                    103
   Early evidence                                                     103
   Prehistory of the lower Skeena                                     108

CHAPTER 5:   THE PAUL MASON SITE                                      128
   Introduction                                                       128
   Site description                                                   128
   Sampling methodology                                              131
   Stratigraphy at the Paul Mason Site                               135
   Dating                                                            144
   Artifact descriptions                                             148
   Summary                                                           187

CHAPTER 6:   THE PREHISTORIC SEQUENCE AT THE PAUL MASON SITE          188
   Lithic analysis of Excavation H                                   192
   Lithic analysis from the Floor 2 excavation                       201
   Lithic analysis of Floor 9                                        212
   Lithic analysis of Excavation J                                   220
   Summary of the Paul Mason Site lithic analyses                    227

CHAPTER 7:   THE PREHISTORIC SEQUENCE AT KITSELAS CANYON              230
   The Bornite Phase                                                 230
   The Gitaus Phase                                                  232
   The Skeena Phase                                                  234
   The Paul Mason Phase                                              237
   The Kleanza Phase                                                 237
   The Historic Period                                               241
   Summary                                                           242

CHAPTER 8:   PREHISTORIC SOCIAL ORGANIZATION AT KITSELAS CANYON       243
   Residential permanency                                            243
   Storage                                                           248
   Population aggregation and village formation                      262
   Household variability                                             271
   Status goods                                                      280
   Summary: Prehistoric social organization at Kitselas Canyon       285

CHAPTER 9:  SUMMARY AND CONCLUSIONS                            289

REFERENCES                                                     302

APPENDIX I:  EXCAVATIONS                                       329

APPENDIX II:  ARTIFACT TYPE DESCRIPTIONS                       344

APPENDIX III:  FAUNAL ANALYSIS (Linda Roberts)                381

## LIST OF FIGURES

1.1  Archaeological sites and localities from the north coast area.                                                5

2.1  Schematic of change in resource diversity and niche width without and with intensification (after Christenson 1980).   26

2.2  Variable states related to the control of resource locations.                                               29

2.3  Deviation amplifying model of the evolution of status inequality: the Northwest Coast example.          40

3.1  Skeena drainage of northwestern British Columbia.          43

3.2  Kitselas Canyon.                                           45

3.3  Surficial geology of the Kitselas Canyon area.            47

3.4  Biogeoclimatic zones of the middle Skeena area.           52

4.1  Tsimshian linguistic divisions (from Duff 1965).          78

4.2  Schematic of Coast Tsimshian seasonal round.              80

4.3  Kitselas Canyon archaeological sites.                     84

4.4  Gitlaxdzawk.                                              86

4.5  Gitsaex.                                                  89

4.6  Kitselas territories of the Skeena Valley.                92

4.7  Prince Rupert Harbour Sites.                              109

5.1  The Paul Mason Site, GdTc 16.                             129

5.2  The Paul Mason Site: house floors and excavations.        133

5.3  Schematic matrix profile of the Paul Mason Site.          136

5.4  Schematic profile showing slope transformation during the occupation of the Paul Mason Site.              138

5.5  Cross-sectional schematic of house floor transformation.  139

5.6  Plan of floor 2 (depth = 70 cm).                          140

5.7  Plan of floor 9 (depth = 70 cm).                          141

5.8  Particle size of Paul Mason Site soils.                   143

5.9  Radiocarbon dates from the Paul Mason Site plotted against depth of sample.                               147

5.10 Implements with varying edge angles.                      149

5.11 Implements showing different types of edge wear.          149

5.12 Implements with varying quality of edge retouch.          150

5.13 Modified cobble flake with platform cortex.               156

5.14 Utlized spall with smooth edge.                           159

5.15 Saw and sawn fragment.                                    164

5.16 Implement with ground, bifacially bevelled edge.     168

5.17 "Pencil" showing blunted end.     168

5.18 Scraper re-sharpening flake.     179

5.19 Pieces Esquilleess (a) and bipolar core (b).     179

5.20 Microblades and microcore rejuvenation flakes.     179

5.21 Element spectre for Anahim I and Mt. Edziza III obsidian.     185

6.1 Unconstrained clustering of Excavation H stratigraphic units.     195

6.2 Constrained clustering of Excavation H stratigraphic units.     196

6.3 Artifact profiles for Excavation H clusters.     198

6.4 Multidimensional scaling of Excavation H stratigraphic units - dimensions 1 x 2.     199

6.5 Unconstrained clustering of floor 2 stratigraphic units with Excavation H clusters.     203

6.6 Constrained clustering of floor 2 stratigraphic units.     205

6.7 Artifact profiles of floor 2 clusters and Excavation H clusters.     206

6.8 Multidimensional scaling of floor 2 and Excavation H clusters - dimensions 1 x 2.     210

6.9 Unconstrained clustering of floor 9 stratigraphic units with Excavation H clusters.     214

6.10 Constrained clustering of floor 9 stratigraphic units.     216

6.11 Artifact profiles for floor 9 and Excavation H clusters.     217

6.12 Multidimensional scaling of floor 9 stratigraphic units - dimensions 1 x 2.     219

6.13 Unconstrained clustering of Excavation J with Excavation H clusters.     222

6.14 Constrained clustering of Excavation J stratigraphic units.     224

6.15 Artifact profiles of Excavation J and Excavation H clusters.     225

6.16 Multidimensional scaling of Excavation J stratigraphic units - dimensions 1 x 2.     226

6.17 Artifact profiles for the three components of the Paul Mason Site.     228

7.1 Artifact proportions for the five phases at Kitselas Canyon.     231

8.1 Cache pits on the east side of Kitselas Canyon.     251

8.2 "Box and dot" plot of between-floor spacing for the Paul Mason Site and Gitsaex.     267

8.3 "Box and dot" of house floor areas for Kitselas Canyon sites.     274

8.4   Gitsaex: house floor 2.                                           277

8.5   Gitsaex: house floor 6.                                           278

I.1   Profile of Trench A: south wall.                                  330

I.2   Profile of Trench B: south wall.                                  331

I.3   Profile of Excavation E units 1, 4, Excavation B unit 2,
      Excavation D units 1, 4: north wall.                              332

I.4   Profile of Trench C: south wall.                                  334

I.5   Profile of Trench G: east wall.                                   335

I.6   Profile of Excavation H: east wall.                               338

I.7   Profile of Excavation J: east wall.                               340

# LIST OF TABLES

1.1  Summary of the North Coast Prehistory Project.          9

3.1  Climate of the lower and middle Skeena area.          50

3.2  Food plants available in the Kitselas Canyon vicinity.          53

3.3  Mammalian fauna of the middle Skeena area.          59

3.4  Avian fauna of the middle Skeena area.          61

3.5  Ichthyofaunal species indigenous to the Skeena River.          63

3.6  Salmon escapement through Kitselas Canyon.          66

5.1  Radiocarbon dates from the Paul Mason Site.          146

5.2  Element peaks for five obsidian samples from the Paul Mason Site.          186

6.1  Artifact frequencies and proportions for Excavation H stratigraphic units.          193

6.2  Excavation H distance matrix.          196

6.3  Artifact frequencies and proportions for floor 2 stratigraphic units.          202

6.4  Floor 2 distance matrix.          205

6.5  Artifact frequencies and proportions for floor 9 stratigraphic units.          213

6.6  Floor 9 distance matrix.          216

6.7  Artifact frequencies and proportions for Excavation J stratigraphic units.          221

6.8  Excavation J distance matrix.          224

7.1  The prehistoric cultural sequence at Kitselas Canyon.          242

8.1  Cache pit measurements for Gitsaex.          255

8.2  House floor measurements and household estimates for Gitsaex.          257

8.3  Cache pit measurements for the Paul Mason Site.          258

8.4  Housefloor measurements and household estimates for the Paul Mason Site.          259

8.5  Dwelling spacing for the Paul Mason Site and Gitsaex.          267

8.6  Artifact density for Component IV.          269

8.7  Housefloor measurements and household estimates for Gitlaxdzawk.          270

8.8  Summary statistics of dwelling size for Kitselas Canyon sites.          274

II.1 Artifact type distribution at the Paul Mason Site.          377

III.1  Faunal samples and provenience.          382

## LIST OF PLATES

I cobble tools                                             153

II cobble choppers                                         154

III cobble tools                                           155

IV spall and flake tools                                   158

V spall and flake tools                                    160

VI stone saws and slate fragments                          163

VII ornamental/decorative objects                          166

VIII projectile points and bifaces                         167

IX pencils and other gropundstone implements               170

X abraders                                                 172

XI grinding stones                                         174

XII chipped bifaces                                        176

XIII unifaces and retouched flakes                         178

XIV cores                                                  182

XV microblades and rejuvenation flakes                     183

Chapter 1

INTRODUCTION

Orientation

This is a study of change in prehistoric social organization at
Kitselas Canyon, a small canyon on the Skeena River, 145 km upriver from
the coast at Prince Rupert. The primary objective is to develop a model of
the evolution of cultural complexity; specifically, the transition from
egalitarian to non-egalitarian or ranked society. A second objective is to
develop a prehistoric sequence for the area, to be used as a framework for
the investigation of cultural change. The evolutionary model is then
evaluated against archaeological data from Kitselas Canyon and the lower
Skeena River. In short, this is a study in "social" archaeology (Redman et
al) 1978:1).

There is a famous cartoon in which two scientists are closely studying
a complex formula on the chalkboard. The first scientist, who obviously
developed the formula, is explaining it to the second scientist. There is
a large blank space with numerous question marks at a critical point near
the end of the formula. The second scientist is puzzled, and asks what
happens here. The first scientist says, "A miracle occurs".

For many years, archaeologists approached the origin and development
of cultural complexity on the Northwest Coast in the manner of the above
cartoon. Developing regional chronologies, based on sequences of phases,
archaeologists were aware that the social organization of prehistoric
Northwest Coast cultures changed fundamentally from egalitarian to
hierarchical. They could even suggest when this change occurred. However,
analysis of the process of this change was considered beyond the bounds of
archaeological research; simply, "a miracle occurred". Social
anthropologists have long been fascinated by the rich and complex cultures
of the Northwest Coast. A large body of ethnological research now exists,
aimed at understanding the evolution and integration of these cultures.
Until recently, however, archaeologists contributed little of value to this
research.

Over the years, as the methods and techniques of archaeology were
continually refined, the focus of archaeological investigations shifted
from the materials of culture to the process of culture; from understanding

1

prehistoric artifacts to understanding how prehistoric people lived.

This study is concerned with the prehistoric people of Kitselas Canyon. It seeks to understand their relationships with each other, and how these relationships changed through time.

In order to investigate this problem, data from two sites at Kitselas Canyon, Gitaus (GdTc 2) and the Paul Mason Site (GdTc 16), are analyzed. These sites are critical to an understanding of the evolution of cultural complexity at Kitselas Canyon. Together, their dated occupation was from 5000 to ca. 2000 B.P. (see Allaire 1979; Chapter 5, this volume). Most archaeologists agree that ranked societies evolved on the Northwest Coast during this time (see, for example, Ames 1981).

Cultural change at Kitselas Canyon did not occur in isolation. Data from two other important localities on the lower Skeena River--Prince Rupert Harbour and Hagwilget Canyon--are compared to the Kitselas Canyon material. This places Kitselas Canyon in the larger context of the lower Skeena River. I argue, contrary to an existing model, that Kitselas Canyon and the two localities mentioned above have existed as part of a cultural interaction system for the past 4300 years. A quantitative analysis of lithic artifacts from the Kitselas Canyon sites is employed to establish a cultural sequence for the area.

This sequence is then used as a temporal framework for the investigation of social change. Specifically, we seek to establish stages of development in the transition from egalitarian to ranked society at Kitselas Canyon. A series of variables, sensitive to change in social organization, are selected and tested against the data (stone tools and other cultural features) to determine how the transition to cultural complexity occurred.


Format of the Study

The study is organized into nine chapters. The present chapter gives an overview of the history of archaeological research on the north coast to elucidate the current state of knowledge of the prehistory of the area. Herein, the rationale for the present study is given, and the general problem orientation, including specific research objectives is presented.

Chapter 2 presents the research design of the study. Previous arguments for the evolution of ranked society on the Northwest Coast are examined, and a new model of the evolution of cultural complexity is developed.

In Chapter 3, an overview of the natural environment of the Kitselas Canyon area is presented, including the general geographic setting, geology and geomorphology, climate, modern flora and fauna, and paleoenvironmental history.

The cultural setting of Kitselas Canyon is reviewed in Chapter 4. This chapter is in two parts. Part 1 is an ethnographic overview of the Kitselas people, emphasizing aspects of settlement, subsistence economy, material culture and social organization. Archaeological data pertaining to the early historic period at two sites in Kitselas Canyon are used to supplement ethnographic information, and to provide a data base from which comparisons to the prehistoric record are made. Part 2 is a review of the regional culture history of the north coast, with special attention to previous archaeological investigations at Prince Rupert Harbour, Kitselas Canyon and Hagwilget Canyon. Existing models of prehistoric cultural change are examined in this chapter.

The present archaeological research conducted at Kitselas Canyon is discussed in Chapter 5. The Paul Mason Site is introduced, and the substantive results of the excavation and survey fieldwork are presented.

Chapter 6 presents multivariate analyses of the Paul Mason Site lithic assemblages to identify discrete temporal components.

Chapter 7 integrates the Paul Mason Site components with those from Gitaus, a prehistoric site at Kitselas Canyon previously analyzed by Allaire (1978, 1979), to establish a prehistoric cultural sequence for Kitselas Canyon.

Chapter 8 examines the evidence for the evolution of cultural complexity at Kitselas Canyon. Expectations derived from the model developed in Chapter 2 are compared to the data from Kitselas Canyon to focus the investigation of social evolution.

The concluding chapter discusses the efficacy of the model developed in Chapter 2 with respect to archaeological evidence from Kitselas Canyon. An interpretive statement concerning social evolution on the lower Skeena is presented, and comparisons are made to other areas of the Northwest

Coast.

## History of Archaeological Research on the North Coast

> The Northwest Coast so well studied by ethnographers
> and linguists, has been grievously neglected as a
> field for archaeological research (Drucker 1943:23).

Despite Drucker's lament, further archaeological investigations in
the area of northwestern British Columbia were not immediately
forthcoming. In the southern part of the province, archaeologists led by
C.E. Borden were quick to take up Drucker's challenge, and initiated
research in the Gulf of Georgia and lower Fraser Valley regions. Another
quarter of a century passed, however, before intensive archaeological
investigations began to shed new light on the human prehistory of the north
coast.

In this review, the north coast is defined as the coast and adjacent
inland areas from Milbanke Sound at the southern extent of Tsimshian
territory to Yakutat Bay on the north (see Figure 1.1). It includes the
north coast of British Columbia and the Alaska Panhandle. "Adjacent inland
areas" refer to the lower drainages of the major rivers of the area; the
Skeena, Nass and Stikine Rivers. Historically, this area is commensurate
with the territories of the three northern ethnolinguistic groups: Haida,
Tlingit and Tsimshian.

The history of archaeological research on the north coast mirrors an
archaeological construct that has served many researchers in the past.
Following Willey and Sabloff (1974:21-87), there was a "Descriptive Period"
and an "Historical Period". The Descriptive Period covers the first half
of the twentieth century, and was characterized by speculations about
recent population migrations and trait diffusions. The ensuing Historical
Period, beginning in the mid-1960's, was marked by more intensive research
and the establishment of local cultural sequences, extending in some areas
to the end of the Pleistocene. Evidence of an "Explanatory Period" in
north coast archaeology is limited (see Ames 1981). The north coast is the
land that the "new archaeology" forgot.

4

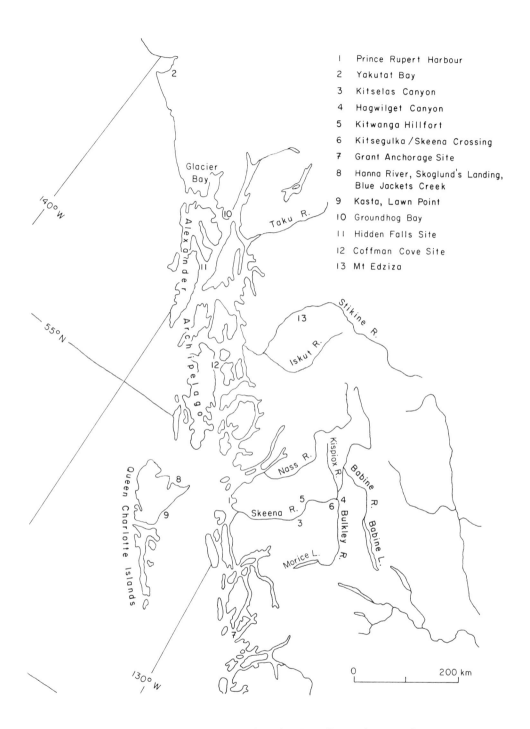

1   Prince Rupert Harbour
2   Yakutat Bay
3   Kitselas Canyon
4   Hagwilget Canyon
5   Kitwanga Hillfort
6   Kitsegulka /Skeena Crossing
7   Grant Anchorage Site
8   Hanna River, Skoglund's Landing,
    Blue Jackets Creek
9   Kasta, Lawn Point
10  Groundhog Bay
11  Hidden Falls Site
12  Coffman Cove Site
13  Mt Edziza

Figure 1.1  Archaeological sites and localities from the north coast area.

5

**The Descriptive Period (1900-1965)**

Early Research in the Tsimshian Area

The first archaeological research in the area was conducted by Harlan
Smith during the first decade of this century, as part of the Jesup North
Pacific Expedition under Franz Boas. Smith's work on the north coast was
unfortunately more cursory than his investigations in southern British
Columbia, but he was the first archaeologist to record shell midden sites
in Prince Rupert Harbour and Metlakatla Pass (see Smith 1909).

Later, Smith (1930) documented 18 sites for the National Museum of
Canada along the Skeena River and its tributaries, as far upriver as
Kitwanga. These included historic and protohistoric village sites at
Kitselas Canyon (Gitlaxdzawk and Gitsaex), and at the mouth of the
Kitsumkalum River. There were no excavations. Smith's primary effort was
to record and preserve standing and fallen structural remains. Inglis and
MacDonald (1979:10) suggest that Smith's research was one of the first
attempts at heritage conservation on the west coast.

Smith was also concerned with obtaining archaeological evidence from
upriver that might indicate that the Tsimshian had only recently migrated
to the coast. According to MacDonald (1969a:242), Smith spent much time
searching, in vain, for the interior village of Temlehem, the mythical
homeland of the Tsimshian.

In 1938, Philip Drucker (1943) conducted archaeological survey and
test excavations along the northern Northwest Coast from Venn Passage, near
Prince Rupert, south to Rivers Inlet, with the general objective of
accumulating data that might lead to an understanding of the origin of the
ethnographic cultural pattern. Three sites in the Prince Rupert Harbour
area were tested and from these excavations, Drucker (1943:112-13)
concluded that the area had been only recently settled. This
interpretation is not surprising as Drucker, using the Direct Historic
Approach, only tested sites with historic surface remains.

Like Smith, Drucker subscribed to the theory of recent, interior
origins of the Coast Tsimshian (Drucker 1943:34, 111). He stated that
there appeared to be little difference between the archaeological and
ethnographic cultures, and that the earliest components explored were
essentially "coast cultures" similar to those of the historic period

(Drucker 1943:112-13). Unfortunately, these "early" components probably date to the late prehistoric period.

It was Drucker's (1943:125) contention that the distinctiveness of the northern culture was attributable in large part to the exertion of influences from the east and from the north.

The decades of the 1940s and 1950s were marked by a paucity of archaeological research in the northwest. In 1954, C.E. Borden made a brief reconnaisance into the area, where he recorded and test excavated a possible prehistoric village site (GdTd 1) at the canyon on the Kitsumkalum River. In a recent re-visit to this site, J. MacDonald (1982) recorded a series of elliptical house depressions (not noted by Borden) on a terrace overlooking the river, and cache pits which Borden apparently mistook for house post depressions.

James Baldwin, working with Borden in 1954, conducted excavations at the Co-op Site (GbTo 10) on Kaien Island in Prince Rupert Harbour. This work was not reported, however, until much later (Calvert 1968), when renewed archaeological investigations at Prince Rupert Harbour were underway.

Early Research in the Tlingit Area

In 1949, Frederica de Laguna began archaeological and ethnological research at Yakutat Bay in southeastern Alaska (de Laguna, Riddell, McGeein, Lane and Freed 1964; de Laguna 1972). A student of Boas, de Laguna's approach was particularistic. The prehistoric Yakutat culture was considered in terms of its artifact traits, with the objective of determining the origin of these traits. Comparison of the Yakutat material to excavated assemblages from southwest Alaska (de Laguna 1934, 1956) led de Laguna et al. (1964:207-10) to argue that northern Northwest Coast culture was "built on a foundation" of long-standing Aleut-Pacific Eskimo contact.

This Northwest Coast/Eskimo link was not only expounded by de Laguna. Borden (1962), for example, postulated that this Eskimo contact may have extended to the south coast of British Columbia during the Locarno Beach Phase.

The early archaeological research of Smith, Drucker and de Laguna was

7

heavily influenced by the anthropology of Franz Boas. Their approach was
that of historical particularism applied to archaeology. Prehistoric
cultures were seen as a series of diverse traits (artifact types), and the
objective of archaeological research was to document the place of origin of
these traits. In so doing, archaeologists could infer the directions of
influence, in the form of trait diffusion and population migration, that
shaped the prehistoric culture in question. Unfortunately, there was
little attempt to explain how this implied interaction led to the
development of Northwest Coast culture. Trait diffusions and population
migrations were simply seen as explanations in themselves. There was
little or no effort to understand the process of cultural change.

**The Historical Period (1966-1981)**
Research in the Tsimshian Area
    The North Coast Prehistory Project, one of the largest archaeological
investigations undertaken on the Northwest Coast, was initiated in 1966 by
the National Museum of Man under the direction of G.F. MacDonald. With
little previous research (Smith 1909; Drucker 1943) on which to base the
study, the initial problem was essentially exploratory; to locate and test
sites with sufficient time depth to detail the development of the elaborate
cultural pattern known historically (MacDonald and Inglis 1981:37).
    The magnitude of the North Coast Prehistory Project makes a detailed
review here difficult. Analysis of cultural material is ongoing, and much
of the written material, particularly pertaining to the critical area
around Prince Rupert Harbour exists only in manuscript draft form. The
geographic scope of the project covered an area ranging from Kisgegas, at
the junction of the Skeena and Babine Rivers, to Kiusta on the northwest
Queen Charlotte Islands. The history of work undertaken by the project has
been outlined by MacDonald and Inglis (1981:37-43), and is summarized in
Table 1.1.
    The investigations focused on Prince Rupert Harbour. Although the
data have not yet been fully analyzed or published, MacDonald (1969a), in a
preliminary report, was able to delineate a three-period chronolgy covering
the last 5000 years. The time frame of this scheme was later altered, but
not radically so, by MacDonald and Inglis (1981). The culture history at

Prince Rupert Harbour, as presented by MacDonald, and the data on which it is based are reviewed in greater detail in Chapter 4.

### Table 1.1
### Summary of the North Coast Prehistory Project

|                  | Prince Rupert | Skeena River | Queen Charlottes | Total |
| ---------------- | ------------- | ------------ | ---------------- | ----- |
| recorded sites   | 200           | 25           | 40               | 265   |
| excavated sites  | 11            | 4            | 3                | 18    |
| radiocarbon dates| 121           | 4            | 2                | 127   |
| artifacts        | 18350         | 3450         | 100              | 21900 |

source: MacDonald and Inglis 1981:37-43.

The antiquity and continuity of this occupation presented a strong argument against the "recent migration hypothesis" advanced by Smith and Drucker.

Upriver from Prince Rupert, the North Coast Prehistory Project conducted archaeological investigations at two locations along the Skeena River: Kitselas Canyon and Hagwilget Canyon. Investigations at Kitselas Canyon included excavations at Gitaus (GdTc 2) in 1968 (Allaire 1978; 1979) and at the historic site, Gitlaxdzawk (GdTc 1), in 1971 (Allaire and MacDonald 1971; Allaire, MacDonald and Inglis 1979). There is also a brief report of petroglyphs at Kitselas Canyon (Walker 1979). Ames (1971, 1973) has reported the results of a site survey in the middle Skeena Valley above Kitselas Canyon.

Allaire's work at the deeply stratified Gitaus site resulted in the development of a three-component sequence, beginning ca. 4000 B.P.

In 1970, Ames (1979a) excavated GhSv 2 at Hagwilget Canyon on the Bulkley River, near its confluence with the Skeena River. The site had been previously tested by MacDonald in 1966, and a carbon sample from this test produced an early age estimate of 3430 ± 200 B.P. (GSC 746) (MacDonald 1969a:249). Results of the Gitaus and Hagwilget investigations are discussed in greater detail in Chapter 4.

In 1979, MacDonald (1979) conducted excavations at the Kitwanga hillfort, near the modern village of Kitwanga. This site included a small village or defensive refuge (five house floors) on top of a steep hill. This had apparently served as a fort for the warrior chief Nekt, during the

9

early historic period.

This excavation, and the ethnohistorical research conducted at Gitlaxdzawk (Allaire and MacDonald 1971) were important because they focussed on the practice of aboriginal warfare and the use of defensive fortifications along the Skeena. Both sites were occupied during the early historic period when the fur trade was operative, and an active struggle for control of the Skeena River trade route was occurring (see Mitchell 1983a).

Elsewhere along the Skeena, Acheson (1977) test excavated GgSw 5 at Gitsegukla/Skeena Crossing. The importance of this investigation was the recovery of two chert microblades. At the time, these were the only microblades recovered from Skeena Valley. Unfortunately, the deposit was undated.

In 1969 and 1970, Simonsen (1973) conducted archaeological investigation in the Hecate Strait-Milbanke Sound area, as part of the North Coast Prehistory Project. Of the 108 sites recorded, 55 were habitations, and 40 were tidal stone fish traps. Excavations were conducted at one site in Higgins Passage, the Grant Anchorage Site (FcTe 4). Simonsen (1973:73-75) identified an early and a late component at this site. The late component has two radiocarbon dates of ca. 2100 B.P. Simonsen (1973:74) notes that the principal difference between the components was the increased emphasis placed on sea mammal hunting and foreshore resources in the late component.

Research in the Haida Area

Another centre of archaeological investigation on the northern Northwest Coast is the Queen Charlotte Islands. Smith (1927) made a brief early reconnaisance to the islands as part of the Jesup North Pacific Expedition, describing a single earthwork site. Much later, Duff and Kew (1957) recorded a number of historic Haida sites during a brief survey.

Initial archaeological investigations were conducted by G.F. MacDonald in 1966 and 1967, again as part of the North Coast Prehistory Project. Three Haida burial sites were excavated, including the Gust Island shelter (FhUb 1), Skungo Cave (GbUf 1), and a mass burial site at Tanu (FeTv 1) (MacDonald 1973).

10

One non-burial site was excavated on the Queen Charlottes by the
North Coast Prehistory Project, near the mouth of Honna River (FhUa 1).
This was a shell midden site with basal dates of 3040 ± 100 B.P. (Gak 1870)
and 3300 ± 100 B.P. (Gak 1871) (MacDonald 1969a:249).  An assemblage of
bone and ground stone tools was recovered which were similar in form to
artifacts of the same time period at Prince Rupert Harbour.

In 1969, Fladmark (1970) conducted archaeological investigations at
Skoglund's Landing (FlUa 1).  Excavation of this site recovered a lithic
assemblage from a non-shell context, dated to ca. 4000 B.P., constituting
mainly retouched flakes and modified cobbles.  Fladmark (1970:39) noted
that this assemblage, lacking pecked and groundstone artifacts and chipped
stone points, was unlike contemporaneous assemblages from Prince Rupert
Harbour.  On the basis of this dissimilarity, he suggested that early
cultural developments on the Queen Charlottes occurred without mainland
contacts until at least 4000 B.P. (Fladmark 1970:39).

In 1970, Fladmark (1971, 1979a) excavated two Queen Charlotte Islands
sites, Lawn Point (FiTx 3) and Kasta (FgTw 4).  Two other sites, at
Skidegate Landing (FhUa 7) and Honna River (FhUa 15) were surface
collected.  The importance of these excavations was the recovery of early
Holocene assemblages (pre-dating 5000 B.P.) that included a microcore and
blade industry.

The possibility of earlier habitation (perhaps as early as 10,000
B.P.) of the Queen Charlotte Islands was examined by Hobler (1978) during a
survey of Moresby Island conducted in 1974 and 1975.  Hobler recorded 10
sites from the intertidal zone, which he interpreted as relating to a time
of lowered sea levels at the end of the Pleistocene.

In 1973, Severs (1974) excavated at Blue Jackets Creek (FlUa 4), near
Skoglund's Landing.  A lithic and bone tool assemblage was recovered in
shell context, and radiocarbon dated between 4000 and 2000 B.P.

Research in the Tlingit-Tahltan Area

In southeastern Alaska, at Groundhog Bay II, Ackerman (1968) and
Ackerman, Hamilton and Stuckenrath (1979) have added to the record of early
microblade components, with radiocarbon dates ranging from 9200 to 4200
B.P.  The late component at this site has been assigned to the

11

protohistoric period (Ackerman 1968:62) and appears to relate to the development of Tlingit culture in the area.

In 1978, Davis (1979) excavated the Hidden Falls site in southeastern Alaska. He identified five components spanning the last 9000 years. The early assemblage included obsidian microblades. Lightfoot (1983) analyzed the Component 2 assemblage (4000 to 3000 B.P.) from this site. It was characterized primarily by groundstone and chipped stone tools. A similar assemblage was recorded by G. Clark (1979) at the nearby Coffman Cove Site.

In 1969 and 1970, J.W. Smith surveyed and excavated in the Stikine-Tahltan region, in the area of Telegraph Creek, east of the Coast Range. Six sites were tested (Smith 1970), and five cultural components were established, based on the presence or absence of obsidian, microblades, and projectile points. The dates for the sequence, beginning at earlier than 9000 B.P. and ending at 500 B.P. were based on the obsidian hydration technique (Smith 1971:201). The main contribution of this research was the definition of the Ice Mountain Microblade Industry (Smith 1971, 1974), and the recognition of similarities in manufacturing technique to west-central Alaska (D. Clark 1972) and Asia (Morlan 1967).

Fladmark re-visited the Mt. Edziza area in 1982, where he surface collected and test excavated three localities. This research resulted in a full description of the lithic complex associated with microblades (not done by Smith), and a refinement of Smith's terminal dates for the sequence. Fladmark (1982b:347) placed the end of the microblade sequence at 4000 to 3000 B.P., substantially earlier than the 500 B.P. date given by Smith (1971:201).

Summary

In this review of the history of archaeological research on the north coast, a number of points are apparent. The first, and perhaps most important, is that archaeology in this part of the world has lagged behind archaeological advances in method and theory elsewhere in the Americas (see Willey and Sabloff 1974). The early research of H.I. Smith, Drucker, and De Laguna was primarily aimed at determining what, if any, archaeological record existed in the area, and where the origins of prehistoric Northwest Coast culture lay. Their work was exploratory. Smith made no attempt at

reconstruction. Drucker's model of a north coast prehistoric culture with
little time depth has long since been laid to rest. De Laguna's
"normative" approach to Yakutat archaeology focused on artifact
descriptions, and failed to explain satisfactorily how or why classic
Tlingit culture evolved in the area.

Moreover, it is now clear that the archaeology of the Decriptive
Period dealt only with the late manifestation of north coast prehistory
(see MacDonald 1969a:242, 246). Following Smith, Drucker and de Laguna,
most intensive archaeological research on the north coast has been
conducted within the last twenty years. The primary effort of this
research was to establish local chronological sequences, and it met with
limited success. Chronological frameworks have been proposed for three
areas along the Skeena River--Prince Rupert Harbour (MacDonald 1969a;
MacDonald and Inglis 1976, 1981), Kitselas Canyon (Allaire 1979),and
Hagwilget Canyon (Ames 1979a)--and a provisional sequence exists for the
Queen Charlotte Islands (Fladmark 1975, 1979a). However, in each
framework, the components are broadly defined temporally, and their
relationship to aspects of cultural change, especially in the social realm,
is not always clear. Other areas including the southeast Alaska coast, the
mainland coast south of Prince Rupert, and the Stikine River-Mt Edziza area
have been investigated and have yielded prehistoric cultural remains, but
regional sequences for these areas have not been proposed. Still, many
other areas including the Nass and Kitsumkalum drainages are virtually
unknown archaeologically.

At this time, there is no single culture historical framework for the
entire region, other than a basic early/late division. Indeed, Fladmark
(1982a:101) has recently noted that the cultural and environmental
diversity of British Columbia may eventually defy simple generalizations on
a macro-regional level.

Systematic regional studies of settlement-subsistence patterns are
almost wholly lacking for the area, although the extensive shell midden
excavations at Prince Rupert Harbour have provided an enormous body of data
for future study. The main problem in undertaking regional settlement
studies has been archaeological visibility. Systematic surface survey in
the dense, temperate, rain forest environment covering the region is

extremely difficult. Moreover, ground moss or humus covers many small sites (lithic scatters, temporary camps), making recording difficult without shovel-testing or random test-pit excavation. Both procedures are costly in terms of time and money, and not often productive in terms of finding sites. As a result, most archaeological research on the north coast has tended to concentrate on the excavation of deeply stratified and intensively occupied shell midden sites in fairly accessible locations. Archaeological research on the north coast has generally precluded consideration of regional assemblage variability, despite the fact that it is well known that seasonal movement inland was an important aspect of the aboriginal lifestyle. Most regional sequences developed to date fail to control for (or even consider) functional variability as a factor affecting artifact assemblage composition. Thus, when apparently differing artifact assemblages have been recovered from two or more nearby localities, they have generally been thought to reflect separate, localized populations, rather than discrete tool kits of a single population.

Finally, with respect to changes in prehistoric social organization in northwestern British Columbia, some attempt has been made to document the development of classic Northwest Coast culture (MacDonald 1969a; MacDonald and Inglis 1976, 1981), but these efforts have primarily been aimed at describing different stages of development. There has been little attempt to formulate models to explain how or why these social changes occurred (but see Ames 1981). It is to the process of the evolution of cultural complexity that we must now turn our attention.

## Research Objectives

Although gaps exist in all lines of archaeological research on the north coast, one of the least understood areas is prehistoric social organization. With the wealth of archaeological data from the lower Skeena River area, specifically Kitselas Canyon and Prince Rupert Harbour, we are now able to turn our attention to this important area of research.

The primary objective of this study is to determine the nature and mechanism of change in prehistoric social organization at Kitselas Canyon. The critical focus is on the nature of social integration during early village life at the canyon.

14

In addition, another objective of this study is the development of a chronological sequence for Kitselas Canyon. This provides a temporal framework for the investigation of social change.

Chapter 2
## CORPORATE GROUPS AND SOCIAL RANKING: THE EVOLUTION OF CULTURAL COMPLEXITY
Definitions

As the primary objective of this study is understanding the transition from egalitarian to ranked society, it is important at this point to formally define these terms. I use the definitions given by Fried (1967).

> An egalitarian society is one in which there
> are as many positions of prestige in any given
> age-sex grade as there are persons capable of
> filling them (Fried 1967:33).

This definition allows for considerable status differentiation. The critical point is that in egalitarian societies, status is achieved, not ascribed. Leadership is transient. It rests on authority and competence, rather than power; it is situational, rather than personal (Fried 1967:83).

> A ranked society is one in which positions
> of valued status are somehow limited so that
> not all those with sufficient talent to occupy
> such statuses actually achieve them (Fried 1967:109).

In ranked societies, status differences are rigidly defined, usually according to a clearly distinguished principle of descent. Unlike egalitarian societies, status is ascribed, although there is generally some room for mobility. Leadership is regular and repetitive, and to the extent that a chief redistributes food and wealth, there is unequal access to resources.

Deviation Amplification

In order to conceptualize the evolution of cultural complexity at Kitselas Canyon, this chapter presents a model that explains how and why social hierarchies evolve. The model examines the relationship between resources (food and wealth) and human social organization. It is argued that access to resources will become increasingly restricted (to members of the population at large) as social organization becomes more complex. When the point is reached at which ascribed status inequalities exist, access to certain resources will not only be restricted to all non-group members of the population, but also to the majority of members within the community. In this sense, the evolution of status inequalities is a process of continually restricting access to resources to more and more people within the society. The process is morphogenetic rather than morphostatic; it amplifies deviation

(Maruyama 1963).

We are probably familiar with situations of deviation amplification in the form of "vicious circles" - those problems that only seem to compound themselves as events unfold. Maruyama (1963:164) defines deviation amplification as "...all processes of mutual causal relationships that amplify an insignificant or accidental initial kick, build up deviation and diverge from the initial condition". He offers the geological example of the weathering of rock. A crack in the rock collects water which freezes and expands the crack. More water collects, which further expands the crack, and the process continues until it is possible for a tree to take root. The roots expand the crack even more. Thus, beginning with an initial condition (a crack in the rock) and an initial kick (collection of water), a series of deviation amplifying mutual causal processes are set in motion which have the effect of continually expanding the crack.

Deviation amplifying systems function differently from deviation counteracting systems. In the former, change results from mutual **positive** feedbacks among the elements of the system, while in the latter, change results from mutual **negative** feedbacks.

The application of the deviation amplifying model in archaeology has been discussed in general terms by Wood and Matson (1973), who include it as part of their "complex adaptive systems" model. The model was used in a specific archaeological case by Flannery (1968), who was concerned with the evolution of agriculture in Mesoamerica. Flannery argued that chance genetic changes in wild grasses, including teosinte, ultimately lead to maize intensification. The wild grass system was, according to Flannery, one of a number of wild procurement systems in highland Mesoamerica around 7000 B.P. Scheduled and seasonal use of each system served to maintain a high level of procurement efficiency, but prevented intensification of any one system. In this sense, seasonality and scheduling functioned as regulators in a deviation counteracting procurement system. This was the initial condition. The initial kick that changed the system to one of deviation amplification was the direct result of early "experiments" with the wild grasses to increase yield (Flannery 1968:81-82). Wild grasses had been a relatively minor procurement system, but the combination of genetic changes and human interaction caused it to increase in importance out of proportion

17

to the other systems. At this point, deviation amplification took over. Cultivation lead to further favourable genetic crosses and back crosses which increased the yield even more. This promoted population increase and ever more intensive cultivation. The constraints of seasonality and scheduling were diminished under the demands of prolonged planting and harvesting seasons. Ultimately, the old wild procurement systems became secondary to the new system of domestication.

On the northern Northwest Coast, the initial condition was similar to that proposed by Flannery for Mesoamerica. Around 3500 B.P., a number of resources were being used along the lower Skeena River, including land mammals (which may have been the single most important resource), sea mammals, intertidal species, a variety of plant foods, and fish including salmon. Further, it is likely that the constraints of seasonality and scheduling were operative. These resources were exploited when and where they were available. At times of the year when the availability of two or more of these resource systems overlapped, harvesting time was probably divided in varying proportions among each of the systems, rather than concentrated on one system. This pattern of broad-spectrum or generalized procurement minimized the risk involved if one resource system failed in a given year. We may expect that social group size fluctuated in accordance with seasonal fluctuations in resource availability (see Smith 1981). It is unlikely that permanent social groups larger than the nuclear family would form. Fluidity of group membership was probably more important than group solidarity.

Now let us consider one resource in particular--salmon. Like the wild grass system of Mesoamerica, salmon was probably not the critical resource for the early inhabitants of the lower Skeena area (ca. 5000 to 3500 B.P.) that it later became. Like wild grass, part of the reason for this had to do with scheduling constraints. The time for salmon harvesting is late summer which conflicts with the optimal time for land mammal hunting and plant gathering. Here, a critical difference exists. Wild grasses were readily available to the early Mesoamericans, but the potential of this system as a subsistence staple was low until genetic changes increased the yield. Salmon, on the other hand, had the potential of being a subsistence staple on the Northwest Coast from at least 5000 B.P., and probably much earlier (see

18

Chapter 3). The problem was not the lack of abundance of salmon for the early inhabitants of the lower Skeena, but the lack of availability or access to the resource. Salmon was both abundant and predictable by 5000 B.P., but it was only seasonally available, and the access points or extractive locations were limited in number.

Further, in order to make intensification worthwhile, salmon requires intensive processing and storage (see Schalk 1977; Matson 1983:134). In turn, this requires changes in technology and organization of labour.

The basic argument here is that the minor importance of salmon to the early inhabitants of the lower Skeena had little to do with the productivity of the resource, but was rather a factor of the temporal and spatial restrictions of access, and the difficulty of processing and storing the resource for winter consumption.

In this model, deviation amplification is seen in any ensuing process that has the effect of placing progressively tighter retrictions on access to the resource.


## The Deviation Counteracting Argument: A Critical Review

In order to develop the model more fully, I will argue against an existing model of the evolution of cultural complexity among hunter-gatherers. Reference here is to the concept, popular among functional-ecologists, that non-egalitarian societies evolve as regulating or equilibrating systems. Essentially, this argument sees the evolution of cultural complexity as a deviation counteracting process.

While the functional-ecological argument has been modified and refined over the years (see Orans 1975), many recent archaeological attempts to explain the evolution of status inequalities still rely on the deviation counteracting concept. For example, in his model of the evolution of cultural complexity in the Gulf of Georgia region, Burley (1979, 1980, 1983) postulates that a migration of salmon fishing specialists from the Hope/Yale locality at the end of the Baldwin Phase (ca. 2500 B.P.) was directly responsible for the rise of social ranking in the Marpole culture. Here, we see the deviation counteracting approach. Burley (1979:136) describes the demographic condition of the pre-Marpole culture (Locarno Beach culture) as being in "established density equilibrium", and as being a "closed system" (Burley 1979:140).

19

Population influx from the lower Fraser Canyon upset this equilibrium, creating demographic stress. Social ranking, economically based on the newly introduced salmon specialization, was the mechanism adopted to restore the system to a state of equilibrium. At the risk of over-simplifying, Burley argues that a system, originally in a state of equilibrium, is subsequently forced out of equilibrium by some process (in this case, population influx). A new trait is then adopted (social ranking) which functions to restore equilibrium. It is implicit in Burley's argument that social ranking is need-serving and that ranking will not be adopted until the appropriate need arises. But how do we know that the proposed population influx from the canyon, if indeed it did occur, represented the appropriate need? Further, is social ranking the only response to a "disequilibrating" process such as population influx? Is there no less costly response?

In another recent archaeological example from the Northwest Coast, Ames (1979b, 1981, 1983) has considered ranking in terms of environmental monitoring and information flow within a proposed framework of stable and resilient systems. Ames (1983:183) states that social hierarchies will evolve "whenever circumstances constrain the capacity of the system to adapt internally", and "strategies which maintain internal values in the face of external changes will be positively selected. Ranking is such a strategy". Here again it is argued that the system in its present form cannot maintain internal stability because of external pressures. Restructuring is required and hierarchical restructuring is selected. Ames (1981:792) states that "ranking acts as a homeostatic mechanism maintaining the equilibria of systems". Again, at the risk of over-simplifying, ranking is presented as a need-serving or deviation counteracting response. The efficiency of hierarchies at processing information in state level societies has been well demonstrated (e.g., Wright and Johnson 1975). But in these bureaucracies there is a real need for information processing because the hierarchical elite control vast territories and oversee the activities of large populations dispersed in many communities. To what extent are hierarchies more efficient than egalitarian groups at processing information, when group size rarely exceeds one hundred people, and territories are controlled by household groups?

The basic premise of the deviation counteracting argument for social ranking is that hierarchies function to counteract subsistence related stress.

20

In light of the above review, there is reason to question this premise. Did the ethnographic societies of the Northwest Coast counteract resource stress?

One of the clearest explications of the deviation counteracting argument is that of Suttles (1960, 1962, 1968), later expanded by Vayda (1961), Piddocke (1965) and Weinburg (1965). The core of the argument is that the prestige system, which included the rank structure, was adaptive; it facilitated the adjustment of the population as a whole to its environment. The function of the system was to maintain high levels of food production and to equalize food consumption (Suttles 1960:304). Balancing resources was important because, according to Piddocke (1965:245), "scarcity of food was an ever-present threat... and without the distribution of food from wealthier local groups to poorer ones, the latter would often have died of hunger".

The Suttles/Vayda/Piddocke model has been reviewed in detail on more than one occasion (see Drucker and Heizer 1967; Rosman and Rubel 1971; Ruyle 1973; Orans 1975), so my comments here will be brief. Suttles et al argued that while great surplus abundance may have characterized Northwest Coast economy in general, this picture was less than true for individual local groups who occasionally faced food shortages due to fluctuations in resource productivity. Support for this claim is drawn from relevant ethnographic sources, particularly Boas (1921, 1935), in which accounts of starving people are given.

Suttles (1960:298-301) argues that the principle means by which unbalanced food resources were equalized was through food-for-wealth exchange, which preceeded potlatching. In this exchange, a man would bring food usually to an affinally related house. The latter was obliged to "thank" the donor with articles of wealth. As Suttles (1960:303) states, this type of exchange could lead to accumulation of wealth, since local inequities in resource productivity could be transformed into inequities in wealth. Less productive communities would be at a disadvantage, as they would soon be "unable to give back wealth in exchange for ...food" (Suttles 1960:303). Suttles argues that this potential inequity was **regulated** by the potlatch. At a potlatch, the host validated his claim to status by giving away wealth to guests. For Suttles, the function of the potlarch was the distribution of wealth, which "restored the purchasing power" of other communities.

A critical question with respect to the food-for-wealth exchange is

21

whether the food-receiving household was actually in need of food. Piddocke, Vayda and Weinburg all argue that the food-receiving households were being saved from hunger, even possible starvation. In reality, this seems to have rarely been the case. Suttles (1960:298) states, " a man could **at any time** take food to a co-parent-in-law and expect to receive wealth in return" (emphasis mine). In other words, the exchange had little to do with starvation or temporary scarcity. In fact, one might expect the donor to take food to his affine during "good times", not "bad times", when the affine would likely have the most amount of wealth on hand.

The food-receiving household typically consumed the food by holding a feast with other members of their community (Suttles 1960:298). The food received in the exchange was generally consumed in one sitting. This seems a very strange thing for "starving" people to do.

If the food-receiving household was indeed facing scarcity, why would they not initiate the exchange? Suttles (1960) is very explicit that this is a food-for-wealth exchange, but it should be a wealth-for-food exchange. I think it is unlikely that people who are hungry, and who also have wealth, would wait for food to be brought to them.

Others (Drucker and Heizer 1967; Ruyle 1973; Orans 1975) have noted that individuals in wealthy, powerful households, capable of feasting or potlatching, would probably be affinally related to individuals in other wealthy, powerful households, given the preference for marriages between people of roughly equal status (Suttles 1960:297; Jorgensen 1980:164-68). Similarly, affinal relationships would exist between poorer, less fortunate households. Thus, exchange and potlatching assured that resources circulated only among high status households, those very households that had the least to gain in terms of subsistence from the acquisition of food or wealth. Those households that could have benefitted in terms of subsistence from exchange or potlatching had no access to it. This much is admitted by Suttles (1973:622) who states, "the separate lower class settlements probably suffered most precisely because they had fewer extra-village affines", and we might add "poorer" extra-village affines.

Examples of shortages and starvation presented by Suttles (1968:59, 1973:622) and Piddocke (1965:247), which in itself seems to contradict the food-equalizing hypothesis, may not be overstated, Drucker and Heizer to the

22

contrary. The important point is that some households faced privation far more often than others, and these people, because of their lack of surplus food and wealth, would not have benefitted from the potlatch or food-for-wealth exchange. Thus, we have the apparently contradictory situation in which potlatching and feasting are characterized by gormandizing and excess in the name of individual or family prestige, while households, and even entire communities of lower status often faced the prospect of food scarcity. Such disparity would not (could not) exist in an egalitarian society where access to resources is, by definition, free and equal. It is only in non-egalitarian societies that surplus (of food and wealth) and starvation can co-exist.

There is good reason to argue that the prestige system did not function to counteract or balance resource stress, but rather, amplified it, by concentrating food, wealth and prestige in the hands of the status elite.

The purpose of the preceding discussion has been to demonstrate that there is room for re-interpretation of the functional-ecological model of ranked societies as regulating or equilibrating systems. On the contrary, it may be argued that the pre-contact socioeconomic system of the Northwest Coast functioned in such a way that the rich got richer while the poor got poorer. Rather than re-distributing resources, the system concentrated resources (food and wealth) in the hands of powerful households. This cannot be seen as a homeostatic process.

## Social Ranking as Deviation Amplification: the Northwest Coast
### The Initial Condition

Let us now consider social ranking in terms of the deviation amplifying model. On the Northwest Coast, most archaeologists trace the origin of the development of "classic" Northwest Coast culture to about 5000 B.P. Fladmark (1982a:110) refers to the last 5000 years as the "Developmental Stage" in Northwest Coast prehistory. The initial economic condition at this time was one of resource diversity. A variety of resources were exploited, including salmon, but as Mitchell (1971:57-58), Burley (1979:136), and Matson (1981:83) have argued for the south coast, there is little evidence for intensive salmon production until about 2500 B.P. This date also seems to hold for the north coast (see Chapter 4).

23

The elements of salmon ecology (abundant, predictable, but localized) were critical to the ensuing developments of cultural complexity on the Northwest Coast. As Matson (1981, 1983) argued in his intensification model, salmon abundance made it possible to harvest a surplus, and reliability made control of the resource economical because of its consistent return. Since the resource is predictable, technology can be developed to utilize it fully (Matson 1983:138). It is also important that access to the resource is restricted, so that control of a particular access location would be worthwhile because it would ensure access year after year. Access to the river or to salt water did not necessarily ensure good access to the fishery. There were only certain discrete access points at which fish could be taken, given the available procurement technology. Moreover, all locations were not equally productive, as Suttles, Vayda and Piddocke have shown. Offshore reefs, estuarine zones, and river narrows or canyons were areas of high productivity. Other areas, such as heads of inlets or river sections lacking shallows or back eddies, would have had relatively low productivity. Other factors being equal, salmon procurement locations near the beginning of the run are more desirable than locations near the end of the run for two reasons. First, salmon stop feeding entirely when they re-enter fresh water, and thus lose caloric value during upriver migration (Idler and Clemens 1959). Initially, this involves the loss of oil and fat content, which is not critical to the human consumer. In fact, this loss may be beneficial because preservation by smoking or drying is facilitated when the oil and fat are removed. Ultimately, however, the nutritional value of the meat is depleted as the salmon continue to expend energy in the upriver migration. Thus, locations near the beginning of the runs, in salt water or the lower river sections, would be more productive once the necessary technology for preservation was in place, since fewer fish would have to be taken to achieve a given caloric level (Kew 1976:8). Second, peak density occurs as the salmon enter fresh water, but this changes as breeding populations branch off into tributary spawning streams. The size of the run steadily decreases as the run moves upriver. Therefore, to exploit the maximum abundance of the runs, the most important procurement locations are those at the entrance or on the lower course of the main river in the system.

The size of the runs also varies for different rivers. On smaller rivers, even ideal locations did not always ensure good catches. This variability among locations was important in terms of human demography and social structure. In an example from the Interior, Sneed (1971) has shown that salmon abundance and human population size were strongly correlated. On the central coast, Donald and Mitchell (1975) demonstrated that salmon abundance was integrally related to population size and inter-group prestige.

### The Initial Kick

Why become salmon specialists in the first place? Why would a population with a diversified economy change their strategy to resource specialization? Christenson (1980) argued that this change may occur as a result of changes in resource diversity and food niche width. Resource diversity refers to the number of different resources consumed, regardless of their proportional contribution. Niche width refers to the differing proportions or "eveness" in which food resources are consumed (Christenson 1980:34). According to Christenson (1980:37), low density populations will typically have low resource diversity and low niche width. Resource selection will be a function of two variables: cost of procurement and maximum yield. Low cost resources with high yield will be selected first, and higher cost or lower yield resources will be added on in an agglomerative manner. The addition of high cost resources will usually be associated with some form of technological change. In addition, there might be some experimentation with improving the yield of certain resources, either through chance genetic changes (Flannery 1968:81-82), or by improving growing conditions (e.g., adoption of irrigated rice paddies in Indonesia (Geertz 1963:29-31)). If intensification is not possible (or not successful) resource diversity, niche width and human population size will increase to a maximum point and then stop (see Figure 2.1a). If intensification is possible, resource diversity and niche width will increase to a certain point at which labour efficiency will begin to favour the intensification of one or more resources. At this point, niche width will decline as the non-intensified resources are exploited less often. Resource diversity will level off or perhaps even decline (see hatched line, Figure 2.1b) as high cost, low yield resources that conflict with the intensified resource are dropped altogether. Human population will continue to grow, however, as long as intensification improves resource yield.

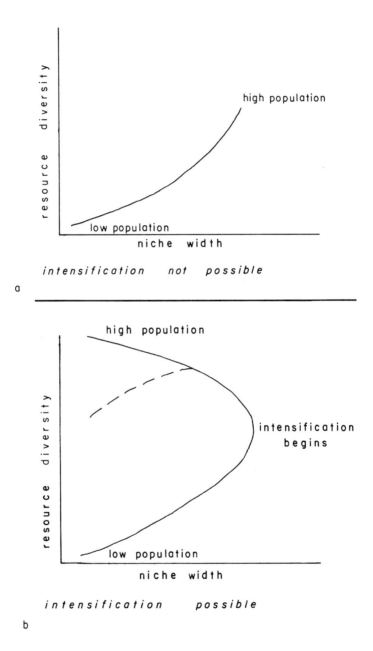

Figure 2.1   Schematic of change in resource diversity and niche width
without and with intensification (after Christenson 1980).

26

Christenson's model was aimed at explaining the evolution of agriculture in areas such as the Tehuacan Valley and the mid-western United States (see Christenson 1980:39-52), but it also has applicability to the intensification of salmon on the Northwest Coast. For example, in the Gulf of Georgia area, land mammal hunting predominated in the Old Cordilleran Culture until about 5000 years ago (see Matson 1981:80). Resource diversity and niche width were low at this time. In the ensuing St. Mungo Phase, resource diversity and niche width increased, with the most notable increase seen in the exploitation of shellfish and fish. Matson (1981:81) states that bay mussel and salmon may have been the most important single resources at this time. Seal hunting also increased in importance during the St Mungo Phase, and it is likely that maximum resource diversity and niche width were reached by the St. Mungo/Locarno Beach interface (R.G. Matson, pers. comm., March 1985).

The increase in shellfish exploitation, beginning about 4300 B.P. (Matson 1981:83), was particularly important. Shellfish are a low cost, low yield resource. They were not completely ignored during the Old Cordilleran Culture at Glenrose, but they were not intensively exploited (see Matson 1981:80). Recently, Croes and Hackenberger (1984:28) cogently argued that in pre-storing economies on the Northwest Coast, the limiting factor on population size was the winter resource base. Shellfish are the only coastal resource that is abundant in winter, and can be intensively exploited throughout the year. The increase in shellfish exploitation (ca. 4000 B.P.) seen at Glenrose and other sites is suggestive of an increase in coastal population at this time. Croes and Hackenberger (1984:37) even suggest that exponential population growth may have resulted in the over-exploitation of shellfish resources between 4000 and 3000 years ago. Even if the point of shellfish over-exploitation was not reached--and it seems unlikely that this happened all over the Northwest Coast--the intensive exploitation of a low yield resource such as shellfish as the primary means of supporting a large population through winter would ultimately favour the adoption of a new economic strategy. It is at this point that intensification of a resource such as salmon may be adopted, including preservation and storage for winter consumption.

## Intensification and Resource Control

What are the correlates of developing resource specialization? One possibility is increasing control of specific resource extraction locations. This lies at the intersection of two variables: procurement technology and resource access (see Figure 2.2). If the procurement technology requires mobility and access to the resource is not restricted by the number of extraction locations available for use, then control of a specific location is unlikely (Figure 2.2, cell A). An example is seen in the aboriginal fishery of the middle Fraser drainage, including upper Fraser Canyon and the long series of rapids and canyons above it. The area, occupied by the Thompson, Lillooet, and Shuswap, extends from Yale to Soda Creek (Kew 1976:12). Here, dip-netting was the main procurement technology. Dip-netting is a mobile technology that can be practised by a single individual. The necessary equipment is minimal and portable, and this allows the fisherman to move up and down the river from one fishing location to another. The best dip net locations were back eddies and areas of slack water along the river shoreline, where water turbidity was high, so that the salmon could not see the nets (Kew 1976:12). Dip nets were operated from natural stands such as rock ledges or boulders, or from wooden platforms. These finite locations along the middle Fraser exist in sufficient number so that dependable access to the resource was not a problem. Some of the more productive locations may have been "owned" by individuals (especially among the Lillooet - see Kennedy and Bouchard 1978:40), but it is not known to what extent this was practised prior to white contact. Not all middle Fraser groups recognized ownership, and it is apparent that many fishing locations in this region were open to common access. One could be assured of returning to the river year after year to good fishing locations, if not always the same ones.

If access to the resource is restricted, in terms of a limited number of extraction locations, then control of specific locations will be important, and adoption of fixed procurement technologies will be favoured. Fixed technologies or permanent "facilities" (see Oswalt 1976:105-07) often require considerable labour efforts in construction and maintenance, but usually the high initial cost is offset by the yield. Accordingly, groups involved in the construction of fixed technologies will have a vested interest in their continual use. Cove (1982:4) argued that the use of fixed technologies such

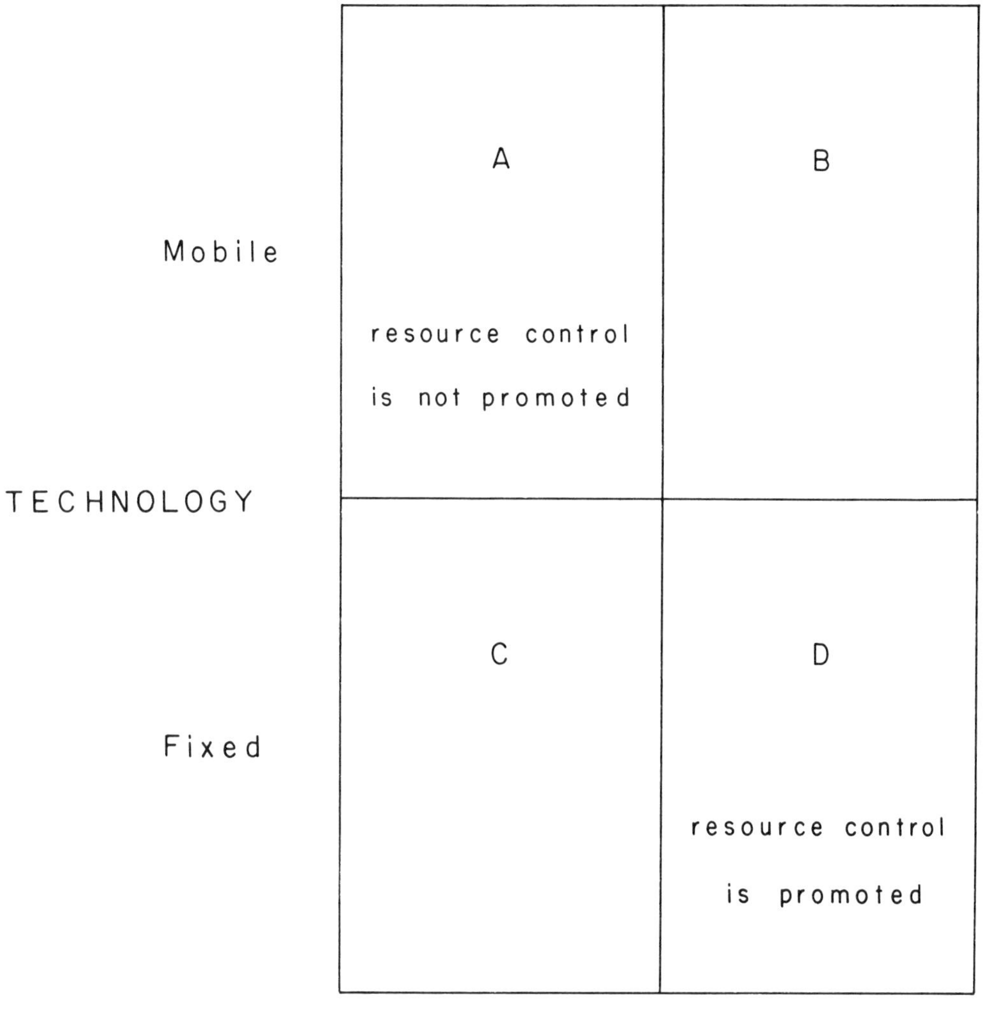

```
┌─────────────────┬─────────────────┐
│                 │                 │
│        A        │        B        │
│                 │                 │
│   resource control                │
│                 │                 │
│   is not promoted                 │
│                 │                 │
├─────────────────┼─────────────────┤
│                 │                 │
│        C        │        D        │
│                 │                 │
│                 │   resource control
│                 │                 │
│                 │      is  promoted
│                 │                 │
└─────────────────┴─────────────────┘
```

Mobile

TECHNOLOGY

Fixed

Unrestricted          Restricted

RESOURCE  ACCESS

Figure 2.2  Variable states related to the control of resource locations.

as weirs and traps by the Gitksan was an important factor in the
establishment of lineage ownership of these locations. Ultimately, control of
fishing locations can form the basis of more complex notions of territoriality
(see Dyson-Hudson and Smith 1978), with a spawning stream or river section
as the territorial locus.

Further, Cove (1982:4) argued that the combination of fixed
technologies and restricted access led to the adoption of residential
permanency by the Gitksan. The implication here is that sedentary settlement
is one way of controlling access to important resource locations.

Another likely correlate of increasing resource specialization is change
in domestic organization as a result of change in the type of production.
Wilk and Rathje (1982:622-23) posit two basic types of production: linear and
simultaneous. Linear production involves a series of activities that are
scheduled to occur consecutively rather than at the same time. Among
hunter-gatherers, linear production is typically associated with residential
mobility. People move from one location to the next as resources in those
locations become available. Although large households and base camps may
occur on a temporary seasonal basis, linear production usually promotes small
population aggregates for two reasons. First, resources tend to be dispersed
rather than localized, which favours small dispersed social groups. Second,
resources are often unreliable. Abundance may fluctuate from year to year,
and small mobile groups are an adaptation to this uncertainty.

Simultaneous production involves a number of people acting at the same
time (Wilk and Rathje 1982:622). Large nucleated social groups are likely to
develop when simultaneous tasks must be performed (see Pasternack, Ember
and Ember 1976) if resources are localized and reliable. These conditions
generally prevail for agriculturalists; rarely for hunter-gatherers. An
exception is the Northwest Coast, where salmon meets the conditions of a
localized and reliable resource. Here, salmon specialization is an example of
simultaneous production. Coast Salish reef-netting is a case in point (Suttles
1951:161-62). Boat captains, fishermen and fish processors all came together
for brief periods during the salmon runs to engage in intensive and complex
simultaneous labour.

On the northern Northwest Coast, task simultaneity was even more
pronounced. The availability of salmon and other resources is attenuated here

compared to the south coast because of environmental constraints (see Schalk 1977). Salmon runs in northern rivers are of shorter duration than the Fraser and Columbia River runs, and intensive simultaneous labour is required to extract the maximum amount of the resource. Places like Kitselas Canyon, the first canyon of the Skeena River, thus became probable localities for simultaneous production.

Permanent households would be promoted here because they facilitated the need for complex divisions of labour and more efficient completion of simultaneous tasks. In addition, Kitselas Canyon is only 2 km long. Once a prehistoric village was established, it would be unlikely to give up such a strategic location. Permanent occupation became a means of controlling the resource, and simultaneous production facilitated permanent residence.

Returning to the deviation amplifying model, a critical level has now been reached. By engaging in simultaneous production and controlling resources at specific locations through permanent residence, social groups effectively impose greater access restrictions by limiting access to resources only to group members. In this sense, the cultural response to the initial condition of environmentally restricted access is to impose further access restrictions by bringing critical resource locations under the control of the resident group. In turn, this can create a positive feedback chain. As favourable locations come under control, it becomes important for other groups to establish control over remaining locations, further amplifying access restrictions.

**The Formation of Egalitarian Corporate Groups**

How may these resource controlling groups be characterized? Are they in fact corporate groups? Recently, Hayden and Cannon (1982) considered the corporate group as an archaeological unit of analysis. They outlined four essential characteristics: 1) closed or restricted membership, 2) residential coherency, 3) internal hierarchical structure, 4) economic pressure as the underlying cause of corporate group formation.

It is important to note here that these criteria were aimed at identifying prehistoric corporate groups in the archaeological record. Not all are defining characteristics. For example, residential coherency can include substantial variability. Hayden and Cannon (1981:141-47) indicate that

31

corporate group members need not live in the same dwelling or even in the same community. They may be widely dispersed in a number of communities. With respect to hierarchical structure, Hayden and Cannon (1981:148) state, "there is always some sort of administrative or authoritative hierarchy which directs major decisions concerning the corporate group". Here, it is important to know how roles of authority are defined, and what decision-making powers a leader or leaders will have. In some societies, such as chiefdoms, corporate groups may exist in which the authoritative elite have absolute decision-making power over life, death and the redistribution of wealth. In other cases, corporate groups may exist in which ultimate decision-making powers are entrusted to the mutual agreement of all group members. Here, leaders may exist, but only in an advisory capacity or as managers of wealth and resources. An example of this type of leadership is the Melanesian "big man" (Sahlins 1963:289). Such a case is likely to develop when the corporate group is small and localized. This obviates the need for a complex system of centralized information-processing, which some authors have suggested as a cause of social stratification (e.g., Wright and Johnson 1975).

Indeed, most other definitions of corporate groups cited by Hayden and Cannon (1982:133-35) stress the importance of group solidarity and control or ownership of resources **by the group** rather than by a centralized authority figure. For example. Honigmann (1959:360) listed a number of criteria as definitive of corporate groups including enduring, selective, stable membership, conferring specific rights and duties, **group** ownership of wealth (emphasis mine), clear group identity and leadership. Weber (1947:45) defined a corporate group as "a social relationship which is either closed or limits the admission of outsiders by rules". Nadel (1951:160) stressed the sharing of rights and duties as definitive of corporate groups. Goodenough (1959:30-31) defined corporate groups as "groups that function as individuals in relation to property".

Returning to Hayden and Cannon's definition, "some sort of hierarchy" is a vague concept. In a sense, all societies have some sort of hierarchy, even egalitarian societies. It is interesting that Hayden and Cannon (1982:142-43) suggest the Iroquois, who were stridently egalitarian (see Trigger 1969:85), as an example of a society with corporate group structure.

32

In considering the above definitions, two characteristics stand out: 1) closed, stable membership, 2) mutual desire to achieve a common purpose. Residential coherency and centralized authority may be two ways of increasing the efficiency of the corporate group (i.e. achievement of a common purpose), but according to the above definitions, neither characteristic is definitive or even critical to the existence of a corporate group.

It is apparent that corporate groups may be organized along egalitarian lines. To clarify this concept, we may draw a comparison to Matson's (1983) model of the evolution of cultural complexity on the Northwest Coast. The core of Matson's model, "is that ranked society, sedentariness, and large scale use of salmon resources should all be tied tightly together and that, initially, one should not occur without the other two".

In the model developed in this study, it is argued that sedentism (related to resource control) and salmon intensification can occur in the absence of ranked society. In effect, social ranking is replaced in this triumvirate by egalitarian corporate groups.

An abundant, reliable, localized resource (salmon) makes complex simultaneous production possible. This promotes sedentism for two reasons. First, complex simultaneous production requires a steady, dependable labour force. Secondly, permanent residence promotes ownership or control of critical resource locations (i.e., where groups may engage in complex simultaneous production). Under these conditions, egalitarian corporate groups will form if all members of the resident group have equal rights of access to the resource.

As resource specialists, egalitarian corporate groups would have engaged co-operatively in complex simultaneous production and controlled specific resource locations in such a way that unrestricted access to the resource was available to group members (those who co-resided permanently), while access to non-members (non-residents) would be severely curtailed or even denied, as a result of the limited number of extractive locations, and the establishment of usufruct over each location by the existing corporate group.

It does not seem unreasonable that egalitarian corporate groups could exercise control over critical resource locations because there is no reason to expect that outside groups would be any larger or better prepared to wrest control for themselves.  If anything, it may be expected that outside groups would be smaller and more loosely organized.

This concept of group ownership of resources is not at all inconsistent with ethnographic evidence from the northern Northwest Coast.  The Tsimshian, Haida and Tlingit had a well-developed concept of resource ownership, and it is generally argued that ownership was vested in the corporate lineage (Cove 1982:4 refers to this group as the "House"), with the lineage or "House chief" functioning as a "steward" (Drucker 1939:59) or "manager" (Richardson 1982:97-99) of resources.  In Cove's (1982) analysis of Gitksan land ownership, it is clear that title to resources belonged to the House.  The House chief gained (or lost) prestige on his ability to manage the resources of the House, and to represent the House at ceremonial gatherings.

The concept of group ownership has been contested by some (e.g., Ruyle 1973) who argue that at the time of contact an incipient form of social stratification had developed on the Northwest Coast, with chiefs having clear title to resources.  If this was the case, might we not expect the emergence of "village" or "regional" chiefs, commensurate with fully developed chiefdoms?  If ownership was vested in the individual, rather than the House, what would prevent a chief from extending his power and authority beyond his own kin group?  Yet, in a study of Hudson's Bay Company post journals from Fort Simpson, Mitchell (1983a:64) indicated that Tsimshian chiefs at Metlakatla held no real authority beyond their own group, "and even there his hold seems fragile".  Halpin (pers. comm., May 1985) stated that although chiefs enjoyed certain rights and privileges that tended to set them apart from others in their House, they were not above being replaced by their followers if their work was deemed unsatisfactory.  The ethnographic concept of group ownership of resources on the northern Northwest Coast may be a fundamental holdover from an earlier time, when corporate groups were organized along egalitarian lines.

## Egalitarian corporate groups: some ethnographic examples

To further elucidate the concept of egalitarian corporate groups, some specific ethnographic examples are offered here.  One example is the Hopi. Although transient leadership may exist within Hopi villages, they conform to Fried's definition of an egalitarian society.  The Hopi household, the smallest

unit of society, is an example of an egalitarian corporate group. Households
may consist of numerous nuclear families organized in adjacent or quite
separate dwelling units (Titiev 1944:51; Connelly 1979:545). Connelly
(1979:549) identifies these as "management groups" that function as
cooperative work units. This organization "provided a stabilizing effect,
making possible production for survival" (Connelly 1979:549). On a larger
scale, Hopi villages also function as egalitarian corporate groups. These are
permanent, co-operative units for defense and production. "Each village is
autonomous and has its own land" (Kennard 1979:554).

The Huron provide another example of egalitarian corporate groups.
There is some debate about whether the Huron were truly egalitarian at the
time of European contact. Clan segments had "chiefs", but it is likely that
these individuals were better defined as "big men". Civil chiefs were **chosen**
from a number of qualified candidates (Heidenreich 1978:371), which suggests
that their status was achieved rather than ascribed. There is no indication
that Huron "chiefs" had unequal access to wealth or prestige through
redistributive exchange. Hoarding or control of resources by an individual
met with strong disapproval, and could lead to expulsion from the village
(Trigger 1969:40-41). Undoubtedly, status differences existed within Huron
society, but the above evidence is consistent with Fried's definition of an
egalitarian society.

Corporate identity existed among the Huron on many levels. The most
basic corporate unit was the "fireside" group, consisting of two families that
shared a hearth within a dwelling (Fenton 1978:303). This was the day-to-day
producing unit. Huron longhouses were commensurate with the extended
family. In terms of corporate identity, Heidenreich (1978:377) states:

> the longhouse represented the physical
> manifestation of their social and economic
> system. It was at this level... that the
> Huron values of family solidarity, economic
> co-operation, and rule by the mutual agreement
> of adults found their basic expression.

On an even larger scale, the Huron village represented a corporate unit for
defense, and was often strongly fortified.

These two examples indicate the nature and extent to which corporate
identity may be expressed in egalitarian societies.

## The Transition from Egalitarian to Ranked Corporate Groups

The next step in the model is the restriction of access to resources to members within the group. This marks the transition from egalitarian to non-egalitarian or ranked corporate groups. Egalitarian corporate groups are unlikely to persist if two conditions exist:

1) variability exists in the amount that can be produced from one location or territory to another.

2) competition develops within the corporate group for household access to specific locations within the controlled territory.

Egalitarian societies engage in "practical" production, intended to meet subsistence needs. Since there is no central hierarchy, there is no individual control of wealth, and no effort to produce a surplus beyond perceived subsistence needs ("social" production).

In many cases, egalitarian social organization will be maintained because there is an upper limit to production. For example, on the Northwest Coast shellfish harvesting could not be the basis of surplus production because of the danger of over-exploitation and depletion of the resource (see Croes and Hackenberger 1984).

The situation with salmon was clearly different. Given aboriginal technology, there was no upper limit to the amount of salmon that could be caught, provided one had access to a productive location. Moreover, a larger, hierarchically organized labour force could improve the efficiency of complex simultaneous production. This might mean the incorporation of new complex techniques of extraction and processing, or the use of a variety of different techniques in different locations at the same time. It might also mean that some group members functioned primarily as subsistence producers, while others specialized in craft production, trade or warfare.

The question still remains, however; why would egalitarian corporate groups re-organize hierarchically? The answer is not because hierarchies function to balance fluctuating resources. Rather, the answer has to do with a fundamental change in the transmission of rights to property, which results from intra-group competition among households for continued rights of access to prime extraction locations.

As long as numerous extractive locations exist, the rights to use these locations are transmitted by village residence (Murdock 1949:80-81; Goody

1972:121).  Inheritence is likely to be partible (divided among heirs) (Goody 1972), or new families may simply leave the village to establish use of new locations in other territories.  This latter example of fissioning may be one way in which non-localized clans develop.

As more and more extractive locations come under corporate control, the transmission of rights of access will eventually shift from the larger village group to the household group (Goody 1972; see also Wilk and Rathje 1982:627-28).  For example, in Luzon, where land for swidden farming is plentiful, it is managed by village patrilineages, but rice paddies, which are at a premium, are owned and managed by households (Drucker 1977:9).  This fundamental change in the transmission of rights to resources is stated by Wilk and Rathje (1982:627): "As property becomes more difficult to gain access to, the group that controls the resources becomes more and more strictly defined, eventually being reduced to the household itself".

At this point the emergence of a leader or chief may become important.  Questions regarding household membership can be settled by this individual, and more important inheritance of resources will tend to be reckoned through his line as a means of ensuring that ownership of resources continues to be vested in the same household from one generation to the next.  In a sense, the chief functions as a hereditary "yardstick".  Rather than partible inheritance, the corporate group is now practising impartible inheritance (Goody 1972).

This fundamental change in the transmission of rights to resources is not intended to balance or even-out a fluctuating resource base, but rather it is a strategy for ensuring control of critical resource locations by small, vested interest groups.

For his part, the emerging chief is now in an advantageous position to encourage a change from "practical" production to "social" production within his corporate group.  Since there is disparity in productive capacity from one resource territory to another, some households will be able to out-produce others.  This can result in an increase in the size of the most competitive households (see Donald and Mitchell 1975) or in the expansion of household control to include new territories, or both.  The surplus production resulting from this expansion is controlled by the chief, and he uses it to finance his political activities.  Earle (1977:217) argued that the complex redistributive

37

system of the Hawaiian chiefdoms at the time of contact functioned in this capacity. He demonstrated that, contrary to Service's (1962) model, the small, localized socioeconomic units in Hawaii, the **ahupua'a**, were not resource specialists dependent upon regional redistribution, but were instead essentially self-sufficient. The redistributive system, based on social production, existed to channel the flow of wealth into the hands of a few elite individuals within society.

I think that a similar situation existed prehistorically on the Northwest Coast. I suggest that as the forerunner to ranked society, the egalitarian corporate group formed the basic socioeconomic unit. These groups would have controlled critical resource locations such as Kitselas Canyon, where simultaneous production was possible. As more and more resource locations came under corporate control, it became increasingly important that access to resources be more rigidly defined (as postulated by Goody 1972). A shift from partible to impartible inheritence would ensure household rights of access to specific locations from one generation to the next.

For his part, the emerging leader could encourage a shift from practical to social production through expansion and hierarchical re-organization of corporate labour. The surplus could be transformed into wealth for feasting and potlatching. It is important to recall that among the northern coastal groups, prestige was conferred on the House, not the individual (see Cove 1982), so that in theory, all members of the corporate group would benefit, although in practice, it seems clear that the House chief was the greatest beneficiary.

There is no shortage of evidence that Northwest Coast chiefs had differential access to wealth accrued through social production. For example, Boas (1921:1333-34) states that a Kwakiutl numaym chief could appropriate a certain portion of a hunter's catch. Meares (1790:258) states that among the Nootka, whaling and sea otter hunting were limited to chiefs (perhaps because only chiefs could organize the necessary labour force). Among the Coast Tsimshian, Mitchell (1983a:60) states that the Gispaxloats chief, Legaic, gained control of Skeena River trade, during or shortly after the establishment of Fort Simpson. Over a 13 year period, after 1836, the Hudson's Bay Company journals record 32 trading excursions, with Legaic personally acting as trader on at least 15 expeditions.

The third and most critical level in the deviation amplifying model has now been reached. Not only does restricted access to resources exist on the inter-group level (level 2; see Fig 2.3), but there is also differential access within groups. House chiefs controlled direct access to wealth through control of trade and potlatching. In addition, chiefs took an active role in activities related to increasing household (i.e. labour) size. Slavery and the establishment of marriage alliances were means by which household size could be increased, and this in turn could increase the amount of surplus produced, and the potential for conversion to wealth. Warfare was another important means of direct acquisition of wealth from rival groups, and may also have been important in terms of competition between groups for control over critical resource locations (see Donald and Mitchell 1975:341-42; Ferguson 1983; Mitchell 1984).

Thus, there were numerous ways in which wealth and prestige could be increased, and while low status or non-titled household members may have benefitted vicariously from their association with a powerful chief, it was clearly the chief who controlled access to resources within the household, and benefitted most from the conversion of surplus into wealth.

### Summary

The deviation amplifying model of the evolution of status inequality, based on increasingly restricted access to resources, is summarized in Figure 2.3. Initially, access to critical resources is restricted by spatial and temporal environmental constraints. The second level of access restriction is cultural - the formation of egalitarian corporate groups, who control productive resource locations, denying access to outsiders. The third level of access restriction is also cultural--the transformation of egalitarian corporate groups into ranked corporate groups. At this level, access to resources is not only denied to outsiders, but there is also unequal access within the group. This formed the basis of ascribed status inequality on the Northwest Coast.

In conclusion, it is difficult to perceive of social ranking as part of a deviation counteracting system on the one hand (cf. Burley 1979; Ames 1981), while it creates differential access to resources on the other hand. In the model presented here, it is argued that social ranking evolves as a process of amplifying, rather than counteracting access restrictions. In addition, I have

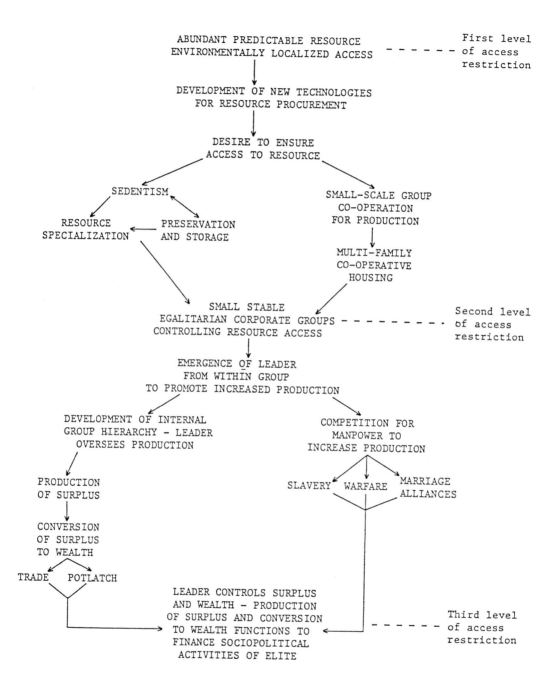

Figure 2.3  Deviation amplifying model of the evolution of status inequlity:
the Northwest Coast example.

argued that a critical sub-stage in the evolution of ascribed status inequality for some societies is the formation of corporate groups, initially organized along egalitarian lines.

On the northern Northwest Coast, these were likely small, household and village groups, exhibiting some degree of sedentism at or near a key resource location, specializing in the production of that resource, and capable of meeting subsistence requirements on a co-operative basis. This is an essentially stable form of socioeconomic organization in a number of societies (e.g., Iroquois; Trigger 1969:85). On the northern Northwest Coast however, egalitarian corporate groups were eventually replaced by internally ranked corporate groups. The reason for this hierarchical re-structuring was to further consolidate control of territories and expand and re-organize the existing labour group to create surplus production, which in turn served to finance the sociopolitical activities of an emerging elite.

This model of the development of cultural complexity on the Northwest Coast will now be tested against the archaeological data from Kitselas Canyon and the lower Skeena River.

Chapter 3

KITSELAS CANYON: THE NATURAL ENVIRONMENT

In the preceding chapter, it was argued that the initial condition for the formation of corporate groups was the presence of an abundant, reliable, localized resource. The chapter examines the natural environment of Kitselas Canyon. It is demonstrated that the canyon meets the initial condition. In addition, it is shown that that the unique location of Kitselas Canyon provides ready access to a wide variety of other resources in numerous biogeoclimatic zones. This further enhances Kitselas Canyon as a prime potential location for the formation of corporate groups.

General Geographic Setting

Kitselas Canyon is located on the Skeena River, 16 km east of Terrace, British Columbia, and approximately 150 km inland from the mouth of the Skeena. The canyon is situated at 54° 36′ north latitude, and 128° 25′ west longitude. It is located within the Kitselas Indian Reserve Number 1.

Kitselas Canyon lies within the Canadian Cordillera, one of the major physiographic divisions of Canada. The Canadian Cordillera of British Columbia has been divided by Holland (1964:27) into three major sub-divisions or "systems", including the Western, Interior and Eastern systems. These systems, oriented along a northwest to southeast alignment, conform to the Coast Mountain, Intermontane and Rocky Mountain regions respectively.

Kitselas Canyon is situated roughly on the boundary between the Coast Mountains and the Intermontane system (Figure 3.1). It is located in the extreme western flanks of the Hazelton Mountains of the Interior system, and is bordered on the west by the Kitimat Ranges of the Coast Mountains.

The Kitimat Ranges (Holland 1964:41) comprise mainly granitic rocks and crystalline gneisses (Farley 1979:28), and extend from the Nass Range southward to the Bella Coola River. Peaks range in elevation from 1200 to 3000 metres, and the mountains are crossed by major rivers in valleys that are less than 100 metres above sea level, creating maximum relief of over 2500 metres. The higher peaks and ridges are sharp-crested, and have cirque glaciers and permanent snowfields. Streams and rivers are deeply cut into canyon-like gorges (Duffell and Souther 1964:7).

42

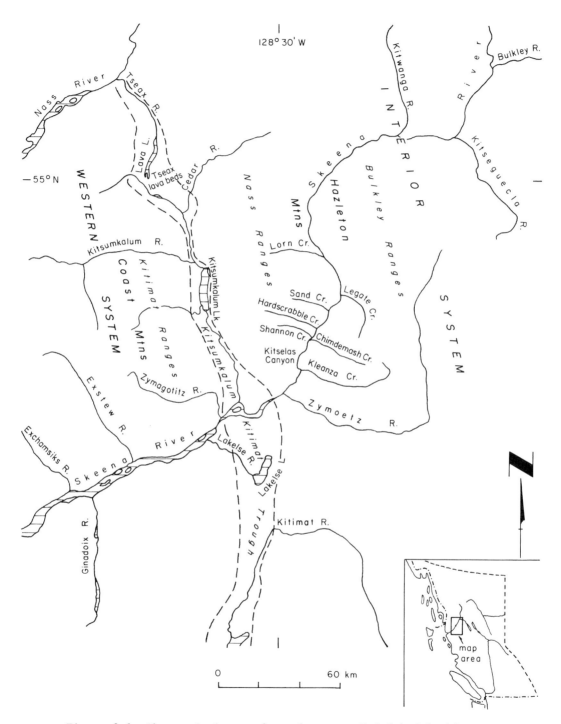

Figure 3.1  Skeena drainage of northwestern British Columbia.

43

The Hazelton Mountains of the Interior System are quite distinct from the Coast Mountains. Comprising mainly folded and faulted sedimentary strata, the Hazelton Mountains are much less steep than their coastal counterparts. Peaks are serrate to rounded, and the higher peaks have cirque glaciers.

Two interesting physiographic features, in addition to Kitselas Canyon, are located between the Kitimat Range and the Hazelton Mountains. A surficial lava plain is located in the Nass Basin, south of the Nass River at Canyon City. The source of the lava is in the Tseax River in the Nass Ranges (Holland 1964:58). Perhaps the most spectacular physical feature of the area is the broad drainage valley or trough that extends from Kitimat Arm north across the Skeena River at Terrace, up the Kitsumkalum and Cedar River, ultimately meeting with the Nass River at Canyon City. The valley floor is unusually wide and flat for the area, ranging from 3 to 9 km in width. South of Terrace, the valley drains into the Skeena system via Lakelse Lake and Lakelse River. North of the Skeena, the valley roughly divides the Coastal Mountain System from the Intermontane System. South of the Skeena, this division runs for some distance along Zymoetz River, a tributary of the Skeena, just below Kitselas Canyon (Duffell and Souther 1964:8).

Kitselas Canyon cuts a deep gorge through the westernmost extent of the Hazelton Mountains (Figure 3.2). The canyon is 1.7 km long, and is oriented approximately north/south. On the west side of the canyon, steep slopes rise abruptly from the river in most places. The highest peak on this side is Kitselas Mountain at 1488 metres. One exception to this steep relief is at mid-canyon, where a rocky promontory cuts into the river. The site of Gitlaxdzawk (the "Fortress") (GdTc 1) is located on this promontory. On the east side, the canyon walls rise vertically to a height of 20 to 30 metres, but then level on to a series of flat upper terraces. Behind these terraces, Bornite Mountain in the Bulkley Range rises to a height of 1751 metres.

The Skeena Valley bottom elevation at Kitselas Canyon is 100 metres above sea level. A number of islands are exposed in the river, in the upper half of the canyon, depending on water level. These cut the river into numerous narrow, deep channels that are marked by rapids, boils and

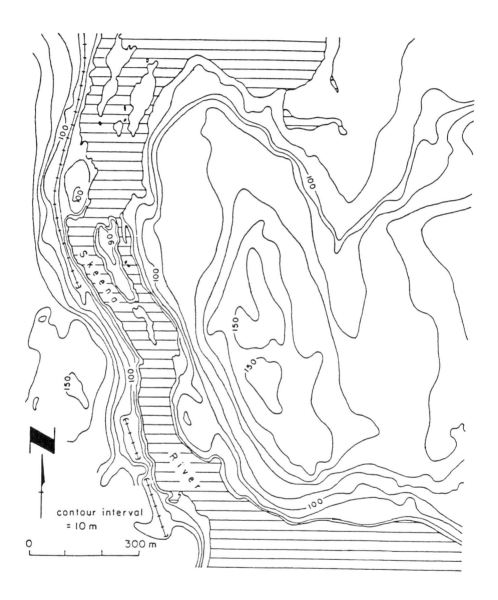

Figure 3.2  Kitselas Canyon.

whirlpools. Shallow back eddies are located in numerous locations on both sides of the river. Immediately below Kitselas Canyon, Kleanza Creek empties into the Skeena River from the Bulkley Range. The larger Zymoetz River, fed by McDonnel Lake also in the Bulkley Range, empties into Skeena River about 7 km below Kitselas Canyon. Above Kitselas Canyon, a number of small rivers and creeks cut the Hazelton Mountains on either side of the Skeena. These include Shannon, Chimdemash, Hardscrabble, Sand, Legate, and Lorn Creeks.

## Surficial Geology

The surficial geology of the Kitselas Canyon area is characterized primarily by glaciofluvial deposits, laid down during glacial retreat up the Skeena Valley (Clague 1984). On the east side of the canyon, this deposit is a glaciofluvial veneer of sand and gravel ranging in depth from 0.5 to 1.0 metres. The west side of the canyon, within one hundred metres of the shoreline, is covered by a thicker glaciofluvial blanket of 1.0 metre or more in depth (see Figure 3.3). This narrow strip widens perceptibly below the canyon. As the steep slope rises from the west side of the canyon, the glaciofluvial material yields to exposed bedrock and a colluvial veneer.

Bedrock exposures on both sides of the canyon are of metamorphosed sedimentary and volcanic rock, ranging in age from late Paleozoic to early Cretaceous times.

Erosional and depositional processes in Kitselas Canyon are generally not important due to the high, steep canyon walls that rise immediately from the river. However, at the upper end of the canyon, small river terraces are located on either side, and a narrow terrace exists just below the canyon on the east side. The site of Gitaus (GdTc 2) is located on the latter terrace. Erosion from river undercutting is extensive here, and it is likely that some of the site has been washed away.

The terrain on the east side of the canyon is quite uneven, due mainly to the bedrock outcroppings, numerous deadfalls and small stagnant ponds in this coniferous rainforest environment.

Large river terraces and floodplains exist just above Kitselas Canyon on the east side of Skeena River, and below the canyon at the mouth of

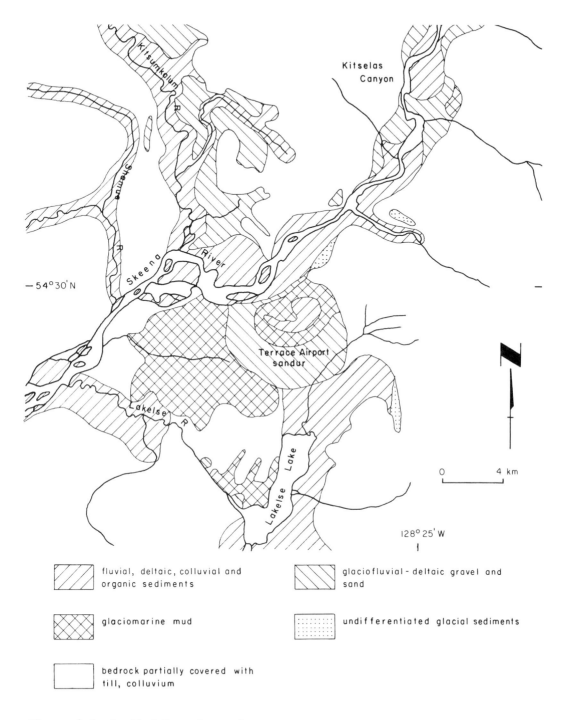

Kitselas
Canyon

Kitsumkalum R.

Skeena R.

— 54° 30' N

Skeena    River

Terrace Airport
sandur

Lakelse  R.

Lakelse  Lake

0          4 km

128° 25' W

| | |
|---|---|
| fluvial, deltaic, colluvial and organic sediments | glaciofluvial - deltaic gravel and sand |
| glaciomarine mud | undifferentiated glacial sediments |
| bedrock partially covered with till, colluvium | |

Figure 3.3  Surficial geology of the Kitselas Canyon area.  (sources:
Duffell and Souther 1964; Clague 1984)

47

Kleanza Creek. The latter is flanked by remnant deltas on either side. Colluvial sediments predominate on the steep west side of the canyon.

An unusual feature is the presence of an active sand and gravel slide just below Kitselas Canyon on the east side. Gitaus is located in the area below the slide. It is not known if the slide was active when the site was occupied.

The local soil of Kitselas Canyon is derived from the glaciofluvial parent material and from colluvium. The soil type is mainly humo-ferric podosol, well-drained and very acidic (Valentine, Sprout, Baker and Lavkulich 1981). Leaching is extreme. This is to be expected, as the area is characterized by coarse-textured, acidic parent materials, high rainfall and dense coniferous forest.

## Climate

Kitselas Canyon is influenced by two major climatic divisions: coastal and continental (Inglis and MacDonald 1979:4). As one proceeds up the Skeena Valley from the canyon, the effect of the coastal climate, characterized by small seasonal variation in temperature, cold summers and mild wet winters, diminishes. It is steadily replaced by the continental climate with abrupt seasonal temperature changes, reduced precipitation and longer frost periods.

Although the Coast Mountain range generally impedes the flow of Pacific maritime air into the interior, two gaps through the Coast Mountains, one by way of the Skeena Valley, and the other extending north from Kitimat to Terrace via the Kitimat-Kitsumkalum Valley, provide interior access for this moisture laden air. This influence is felt most noticeably at Terrace, but as distance from the coast increases, the maritime influence steadily weakens. At Hazelton, at the confluence of the Bulkley and Skeena Rivers, the climate is significantly cooler and drier than at Terrace (British Columbia Lands Service 1969:63).

At Terrace, during the period from April to September, precipitation averages 365.8 mm. During the period from October to March, precipitation, often in the form of snow, averages 947.4 mm. The wettest months of the year are October through December, and the driest months are May through July (Atmospheric Environment Service 1982: 234). This summer/winter

48

variation in precipitation, with the winter average being significantly higher, is generally consistent with the coastal climatic regime.

Terrace and Kitselas Canyon have moderately warm summers and mild winters. January is the coldest month of the year with a mean daily temperature of -5.9°C. The warmest month is July with a mean daily temperature of 16.1°C. Terrace experiences an average of 134 frost-free days per year (British Columbia Lands Service 1969:64).

By contrast, Prince Rupert is wetter and temperature variation is less extreme; Hazelton is drier and temperature variation is more extreme (see Table 3.1). This reflects the general upriver gradient of coastal to continental climate.

In addition to the coast/inland trend, altitudinal changes account for some climatic variation in the Kitselas Canyon area. Meteorological data on precipitation and temperature fluctuations do not exist to reflect these changes, but changes in vegetation (see Table 3.2) from valley bottom coastal species that thrive on moderate temperatures to high elevation species adapted to alpine tundra conditions do indicate considerable variability in temperature.

The important point here is that Kitselas Canyon is strategically located, so that one need travel only short distances from the canyon to experience a range of environmental conditions from coastal to interior, and from valley bottom to alpine tundra.

Hydrology

The area is drained by the Skeena River, and south of Terrace by the Kitimat-Kitsumkalum Valley below Lakelse Lake (Clague 1984), via the Kitimat River into Kitimat Arm. The Skeena River accounts for most of the drainage in the area. The Skeena is one of the major rivers of Canada's west coast, draining an area of 42,217 km$^2$ (Farley 1979:39).

Many of the rivers and streams tributary to the Skeena drain large lakes. Babine Lake feeds the upper and lower Babine River; Morice Lake feeds the Bulkley system; McDonnel Lake feeds Zymoetz River; Kitsumkalum Lake feeds Kitsumkalum River; and Lakelse Lake feeds Lakelse River.

**Table 3.1**
Climate of the lower Skeena area

| | | JAN | FEB | MAR | APR | MAY | JUN | JUL | AUG | SEP | OCT | NOV | DEC | YEAR |
|---|---|---|---|---|---|---|---|---|---|---|---|---|---|---|
| average mean daily temperature in °C | P.R. | 1.7 | 2.9 | 3.8 | 6.1 | 8.9 | 11.3 | 13.3 | 13.5 | 11.7 | 8.5 | 5.0 | 2.6 | 7.4 |
| | T. | -5.9 | -1.4 | 1.5 | 5.7 | 9.9 | 13.7 | 16.1 | 15.8 | 11.9 | 6.4 | 0.3 | -3.4 | 5.9 |
| | H. | -10.7 | -4.8 | -0.1 | 5.2 | 10.2 | 13.6 | 15.9 | 15.5 | 11.2 | 5.4 | -1.9 | -7.7 | 4.3 |
| total rainfall in mm | P.R. | 184.8 | 217.2 | 168.9 | 175.0 | 120.5 | 110.4 | 112.9 | 143.7 | 231.2 | 352.4 | 276.8 | 241.1 | 2334.9 |
| | T. | 50.1 | 56.4 | 41.0 | 49.1 | 42.8 | 42.5 | 56.6 | 63.6 | 98.5 | 211.0 | 131.8 | 90.9 | 943.3 |
| | H. | 15.6 | 10.1 | 17.2 | 16.8 | 32.5 | 56.0 | 55.8 | 53.4 | 56.5 | 74.0 | 28.7 | 13.4 | 430.0 |
| total snowfall in mm | P.R. | 23.3 | 15.8 | 16.2 | 5.1 | 0.1 | 0.0 | 0.0 | 0.0 | 0.0 | 0.2 | 3.8 | 19.6 | 84.1 |
| | T. | 116.3 | 71.6 | 44.2 | 12.1 | 0.4 | 0.0 | 0.0 | 0.0 | 0.0 | 3.9 | 48.9 | 105.6 | 403.0 |
| | H. | 56.5 | 30.4 | 13.7 | 3.1 | 1.0 | 0.0 | 0.0 | 0.0 | 0.2 | 2.1 | 25.7 | 50.1 | 172.8 |
| total precipitation in mm | P.R. | 210.1 | 215.8 | 185.4 | 180.6 | 120.6 | 110.4 | 112.9 | 143.7 | 231.2 | 352.5 | 281.3 | 258.6 | 2403.1 |
| | T. | 153.7 | 123.0 | 83.1 | 61.3 | 43.3 | 42.5 | 56.6 | 63.6 | 98.5 | 214.9 | 180.3 | 192.4 | 1313.2 |
| | H. | 76.5 | 36.2 | 30.2 | 20.2 | 33.7 | 56.0 | 55.8 | 53.4 | 56.7 | 77.9 | 57.0 | 71.0 | 624.6 |
| number of days with precipitation | P.R. | 20 | 19 | 21 | 18 | 17 | 16 | 16 | 16 | 18 | 24 | 22 | 22 | 229 |
| | T. | 18 | 17 | 15 | 14 | 13 | 12 | 12 | 13 | 16 | 22 | 19 | 21 | 192 |
| | H. | 16 | 11 | 10 | 10 | 11 | 13 | 14 | 15 | 16 | 18 | 16 | 17 | 167 |
| number of frost free days (monthly figures not available) | P.R. | | | | | | | | | | | | | 200 |
| | T. | | | | | | | | | | | | | 134 |
| | H. | | | | | | | | | | | | | 69 |

P.R. = Prince Rupert, T. = Terrace, H. = Hazleton

source: Atmospheric Environment Service 1982.

These lakes are of economic importance for their sockeye salmon runs.

The Skeena and its tributaries are permanent, year-round streams and rivers fed directly by lakes or mountain freshets from permanent snow fields and snowcaps. At Usk, on the Skeena 2 km upriver from Kitselas Canyon, the mean annual discharge is 900 m$^3$ per second, while in June at the height of the runoff, discharge can reach 3000 m$^3$ per second (Farley 1979:39). The increased summer discharge coincides with the annual salmon runs, and was important to the aboriginal fishing technology. Higher summer water turbidity made techniques such as dip-netting and basket trapping more efficient (see Kew 1976:12).

<u>Natural Flora and Fauna</u>

This section outlines the animal and plant resources available in the Kitselas area. As suggested by its physiographic and climatological position, Kitselas Canyon is in a unique location. The immediate canyon area is located within the Coastal Western Hemlock biogeoclimatic zone (Krajina 1973, 1976). This zone predominates on the north coast of British Columbia, and stretches up the Skeena Valley and adjacent Nass Valley to the middle regions of both rivers. The area surrounding Kitselas Canyon, however, is not entirely homogeneous. Major biogeoclimatic zones change with elevation, and more subtle zonal changes occur as distance from the coast increases.

On the forested slopes flanking Kitselas Canyon, at elevations from 300 to 900 metres above sea level, the Subalpine Mountain Hemlock biogeoclimatic zone exists. At higher elevations, (1000 to 1700 metres ASL), the Subalpine Engelmann Spruce-Subalpine Fir biogeoclimatic zone occurs. Above the treeline, the Alpine Tundra zone exists. These zones all occur in patches on the middle and upper slopes flanking Kitselas Canyon.

In the valley bottom, Coupe, Ray, Comeau, Ketcheson and Annas (1982:7) indicate a zonal change to a more interior orientation at a point about 30 km upriver from Kitselas Canyon. This marks the beginning of the Interior Cedar Hemlock biogeoclimatic zone, and coincides with a gradual widening of the valley bottom (see Figure 3.4). This diversity results in a wide variety of natural flora and fauna in the Kitselas Canyon area.

51

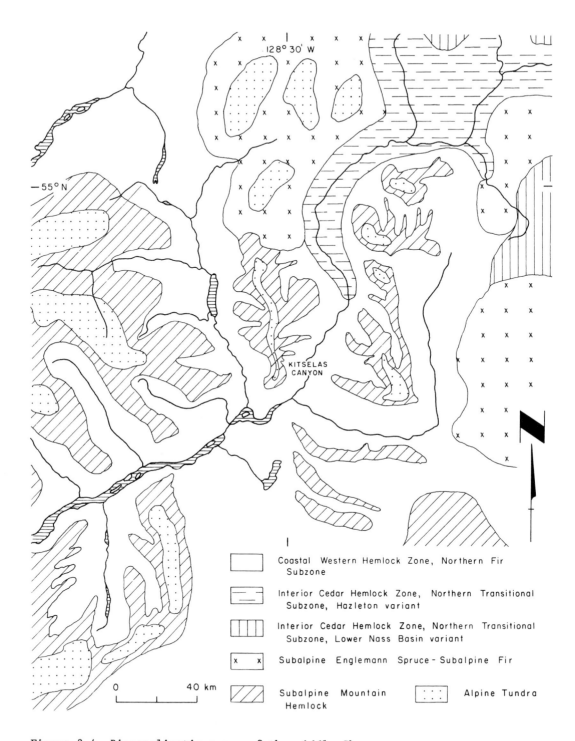

Figure 3.4  Biogeoclimatic zones of the middle Skeena area.
(source: Coupe et al. 1982; Krajina 1973, 1976)

52

Table 3.2
Food Plants Available in the Kitselas Canyon Vicinity

| Species | Habitat | Zone |
|---------|---------|------|

Edible berries

| | | |
|---------|---------|------|
| beaked hazelnut (Corylus cornuta) | valley bottoms, lower slopes | (2)* |
| coast red elderberry (Sambucus pubens) | riparian, streamside | (3) |
| common snowberry (Symphoricarpos albus) | thickets, open slopes | (3) |
| high-bush cranberry (Viburnum edule) | swamps, stream banks, alluvial sites | (2) |
| soapberry (Shepherdia canadensis) | dry open woods | (2) |
| crowberry (Enpetrum nigrum) | various | (3) |
| kinnikinnick (Arctostaphylos uva-ursi) | dry, open woods | (2) |
| creeping snowberry (Gaultheria hispidula) | bogs, sphagnum hummocks | (2) |
| salal (Gaultheria shallon) | streamside, thickets | (1) |
| Labrador tea (Ledum groenlandicum) | streamside, swamps | (3) |
| Alaskan blueberry (Vaccinium alaskaense) | coastal forests, humus | (1) |
| dwarf huckleberry (Vaccinium caespitosum) | mountain slopes | (3) |
| blue huckleberry (Vaccinium membranaceum) | mountain slopes | (3) |
| oval-leaf huckleberry (Vaccinium ovalifolium) | streamside to mountain slopes | (3) |

**Table 3.2** (continued)

| Species | Habitat | Zone |
|---------|---------|------|
| wild cranberry (<u>Vaccinium oxycoccos</u>) | sphagnum bogs | (3) |
| red blueberry (<u>Vaccinium parvifolium</u>) | valley bottom forests | (3) |
| bog blueberry (<u>Vaccinium uliginosum</u>) | sphagnum bogs | (3) |
| mountain cranberry (<u>Vaccinium vitis-idaea</u>) | dry bogs, thickets | (3) |
| stink currant (<u>Ribes bracteosum</u>) | riparian | (1) |
| prickly gooseberry (<u>Ribes lacustre</u>) | riparian to sub-alpine | (3) |
| trailing black currant (<u>Ribes laxiforum</u>) | riparian to sub-alpine | (3) |
| northern gooseberry (<u>Ribes oxyacanthoides</u>) | dry, open valley bottom | (3) |
| serviceberry (<u>Amelanchier alnifolia</u>) | open mountain slopes | (2) |
| western crabapple (<u>Malus fusca</u>) | swamps, bogs to mountain slopes | (1) |
| bitter cherry (<u>Prunus emarginata</u>) | riparian to wet slopes | (1) |
| choke cherry (<u>Prunus virginiana</u>) | dry, exposed sites | (2) |
| nootka rose (<u>Rosa nutkana</u>) | thickets to open woods | (3) |
| red raspberry (<u>Rubus idaeus</u>) | riparian to open woods | (2) |
| thimbleberry (<u>Rubus parviflorus</u>) | open woods | (3) |

**Table 3.2** (continued)

| Species | Habitat | Zone |
|---------|---------|------|
| salmonberry (Rubus spectabilis) | riparian, swamps | (1) |
| cloudberry (Rubus chamaemorus) | sphagnum bogs | (2) |
| strawberry bramble (Rubus pedatus) | forested slopes | (3) |
| red blackberry (Rubus pubescens) | riparian, moist woods | (3) |
| Canadian bunchberry (Cornus canadensis) | moist humic soil, riparian to mid-slopes | (3) |
| blueleaf strawberry (Fragaria virginiana) | open exposed sites | (3) |

**Non-berries**

| | | |
|---------|---------|------|
| cascade mountain ash (Sorbus scopulina) | mid-slopes to sub-alpine | (3) |
| sitka mountain ash (Sorbus sitchensis) | open mid-slopes to sub-alpine | (3) |
| horsetail (Equisetum arvense) | open woods | (3) |
| lady fern (Athyrium filix-femina) | moist woods | (3) |
| spiny wood fern (Dryopteris assimilis) | moist woods | (3) |
| male fern (Dryopteris filix-mas) | moist woods, talus slopes | (3) |
| sword fern (Polystichum munitum) | wet, shaded woods | (3) |
| bracken fern (Pteridium aquilinum) | dry, open sites | (3) |

Table 3.2 (continued)

| Species | Habitat | Zone |
|---------|---------|------|
| nodding onion (Allium cernum) | open, exposed sites | (3) |
| rice root (Fritillaria camschatcensis) | moist, open, mountain slopes | (3) |
| Solomon's seal (Smilacina stellata) | riparian, moist woods | (3) |
| fairy slipper (Calypso bulbosa) | moist, shaded woods | (3) |
| wild sarasparilla (Aralia nudicaulis) | moist, shaded woods | (2) |
| fireweed (Epilobium angustifolium) | open exposed sites | (3) |
| cinquefoil (Potentilla palustris) | swamps, bogs | (3) |
| stinging nettle (Urtica dioica) | moist, shaded valley bottom | (3) |

* (1) coastal
  (2) interior
  (3) coast and interior
  Sources: Turner (1978); Coupe et al. (1982)

It is convenient to consider three main altitudinal zones in the vicinity of Kitselas Canyon: alpine, middle slopes/subalpine, and valley bottom. Each offers different resources. The alpine zone was probably of least economic importance to the inhabitants of Kitselas Canyon. Mountain goat (<u>Oreamnos americanus</u>), marmot (<u>Marmota monax</u>) and cougar (<u>Felis concolor</u>) are found seasonally at these high elevations. Mule deer (<u>Odocoileus hemionus hemionus</u>), kermody black bear (<u>Ursus americanus kermodei</u>), and grizzly bear (<u>U. arctos horriblis</u>) also range into the alpine zone during the summer and early fall months (see Table 3.3). J. MacDonald (1984: Table 1) lists a small mountain caribou (<u>Rangifer tarandus montanus</u>) population in the alpine zone adjacent to the Kitsumkalum Valley. The range of this population may also include the Kitselas area. Cowan and Guiguet (1964:384) indicate that mountain caribou inhabit the eastern slopes of the Coast Range and the Bulkley Mountains.

The middle slope/subalpine zone is characterized by mountain hemlock (<u>Tsuga mertensiana</u>) with lodgepole pine (<u>Pinus contorta contorta</u>), (<u>P. c. latifolia</u>) and american green alder (<u>Alnus viridus</u>) also present. A number of important food plants occur in this zone (see Table 3.2), including one or more species of shrubs with edible fruits (<u>Betulaceae</u>, <u>Caprifoliaceae</u>, <u>Empetraceae</u>, <u>Ericaceae</u>, <u>Grossulariaceae</u>, <u>Roseaceae</u>), horsetails (<u>Equistaceae</u>), ferns (<u>Polypodiaceae</u>), lilies (<u>Liliaceae</u>), orchids (<u>Orchidaceae</u>), and other herbaceous plants (<u>Apiaceae</u>, <u>Araceae</u>, <u>Araliaceae</u>, <u>Cornaceae</u>, <u>Fabaceae</u>, <u>Onograceae</u>, <u>Orobanchaceae</u>, and <u>Urticaceae</u>). Of these, the edible berries of the various shrubs (especially <u>Vaccinium</u> and <u>Rubus</u>) and other herbaceous plants were probably of greatest aboriginal economic importance.

In addition, most fur-bearing animals of economic importance could be found in this zone through much of the year.

The valley bottom was the richest and most varied ecological zone in terms of aboriginal economic importance. Major vegetation in this zone includes red cedar (<u>Thuja plicata</u>), yellow cedar (<u>Chamaecyparis nootkatensis</u>), western hemlock (<u>Tsuga heterophylla</u>), white spruce (<u>Picea glauca</u>), black spruce (<u>P. mariana</u>), and sitka spruce (<u>P. sitchensis</u>). In addition, broad leaf deciduous species, including black cottonwood (<u>Populus balsimfera</u>), common paper birch (<u>Betula papyrifera</u>), bog birch

(B. glandulosa), and small trees including douglas maple (Acer glabrum), trembling aspen (Populus tremuloides) and red alder (Alnus rubra) all occur in this zone, especially in swampy, marshy or streamside locations. All of the food plant families listed for the middle slopes/subalpine zone (see Table 3.2) occur in the valley bottom in greater or less abundance, although there are often differences in the time of ripening between these two zones. Two families not present on the middle slopes, Nymphaeceae and Typhaceae occur in swampy or marshy locations.

Most mammalian species of the lower Skeena occur in the valley bottom zone (except the alpine species). Duffell and Souther (1964:3) report that coast deer (Odocoileus hemionus columbianus) are found occasionally in the lower Skeena Valley, although Cowan and Guiguet (1965:369) indicate that mule deer and sitka deer (O. h. sitchensis) may also be found here. Sitka deer are generally regarded as a coastal species, whereas mule deer are more common in the interior. In fact, Kitselas Canyon is situated roughly on the distributional boundary between these latter two sub-species, so it is likely that both are indigenous to the area (see Cowan and Guiguet 1965:371).

Table 3.3 lists all mammalian species whose present range includes the Kitselas Canyon area. Avian species found in the Kitselas area are listed in Table 3.4.

As stated previously, Kitselas Canyon roughly straddles the coastal-interior boundary. The importance of this in terms of the variety of edible species--both plant and animal--cannot be underestimated. The ameliorated coastal climate of Kitselas Canyon means that a variety of coastal food plants, such as salal, salmonberry, crabapple and Alaskan blueberry are common in the Kitselas Canyon valley bottom area (Coupe et al 1982:32, 37, 45, 49). A short distance upriver, the effect of the wet coastal climate is attenuated. Drier, more open conditions exist; food plants that are rare or absent on the coast are more abundant here. These include kinnikinnick, high-bush cranberry, serviceberry and choke cherry (Coupe et al 1982:25, 29, 45, 46). In addition, mule deer, mountain caribou and mountain goat, all found at or near Kitselas Canyon, are rare or absent on the coast.

# Table 3.3
## Mammalian Fauna of the Middle Skeena Area

| Species | Zone |
|---|---|
| **Insectivores** | |
| Cinerus shrew (<u>Sorex cinerus</u>) | 1* |
| wandering shrew (<u>Sorex vagrans longicauda</u>) | 3 |
| navigator shrew (<u>Sorex palustris navigator</u>) | 1 |
| little brown myotis (<u>Myotis lucifugus alascensis</u>) | 3 |
| yuma myotis (<u>Myotis yumanensis saturatus</u>) | 1 |
| | |
| **Lagomorphs** | |
| varying hare (<u>Lepus americanus</u>) | 2 |
| | |
| **Rodents** | |
| marmot (<u>Marmota monax petrensis</u>) | 2 |
| northwestern chipmunk (<u>Eutamias amoenus</u>) | 2 |
| red squirrel (<u>Tamiasciurus hudsonicus picatus</u>) | 1 |
| flying squirrel (<u>Glaucomys sabrinus zaphaeus</u>) | 1 |
| american beaver (<u>Castor canadensis belugae</u>) | 1 |
| (<u>C. c. sagittatus</u>) | 2 |
| white-footed mouse (<u>Peromyscus maniculatus</u>) | 3 |
| northern bog-lemming (<u>Synaptomys borealis wrangeli</u>) | 1 |
| (<u>S. b. dali</u>) 2 | |
| boreal redback vole (<u>Clethrionomys gapperi caurinus</u>) | 1 |
| (<u>C. g. saturatus</u>) | 2 |
| long-tailed vole (<u>Microtus longicaudus littoralis</u>) | 3 |
| muskrat (<u>Ondrata zibethica osoyoosensis</u>) | 3 |
| meadow jumping mouse (<u>Zapus hudsonius hudsonius</u>) | 3 |
| western jumping mouse (<u>Zapus princeps saltator</u>) | 3 |
| american porcupine (<u>Erithizon dorsatum</u>) | 3 |
| | |
| **Carnivores** | |
| coyote (<u>Canis latrans inoculatus</u>) | 3 |
| wolf (<u>Canis lupus fuscus</u>) | 1 |
| (<u>C. l. columbianus</u>) | 3 |
| red fox (<u>Vulpes fulva abietorum</u>) | 3 |
| black bear (<u>Ursus americanus kermodei</u>) | 3 |
| grizzly bear (<u>Ursus arctos horriblis</u>) | 3 |
| marten (<u>Martes americana caurina</u>) | 3 |
| fisher (<u>Martes pennanti columbiana</u>) | 3 |
| short-tailed weasel (<u>Mustela erminea richardsoni</u>) | 3 |
| mink (<u>Mustela vison</u>) | 3 |
| wolverine (<u>Gulo luscus luscus</u>) | 3 |
| striped skunk (<u>Mephistis mephistis</u>) | 3 |
| Canadian river otter (<u>Lutra canadensis</u>) | 3 |
| cougar (<u>Felis concolor missoulensis</u>) | 3 |
| Canada lynx (<u>Lynx canadensis</u>) | 2 |

Table 3.3 (continued)

|                      Species                                          | Zone |
|-----------------------------------------------------------------------|------|
| Pinnipeds                                                             |      |
|   hair seal (_Phoca vitulina richardi_)                               |   1  |
|                                                                       |      |
| Artiodactyls                                                          |      |
|   mule deer (_Odocoileus hemionus hemionus_)                          |   2  |
|                 (_O. h. sitkensis_)                                   |   1  |
|   moose (_Alces alces_)                                               |   3  |
|   mountain caribou (_Rangifer tarandus montanus_)                     |   2  |
|   mountain goat (_Oreamnos americanus americanus_)                    |   3  |

\* (1) coastal
  (2) interior
  (3) coast and interior
source: Cowan and Guiguet (1965)

**Table 3.4**
**Avian Fauna of the Middle Skeena Area**

Waterfowl
  common loon (<u>Gavia immer</u>)
  red-throated loon (<u>Gavia stellata</u>)
  red-necked grebe (<u>Podiceps gricenga</u>)
  horned grebe (<u>Podiceps auritus</u>)
  great blue heron (<u>Ardia herodius</u>)
  Canada goose (<u>Branta canadensis</u>)
  mallard duck (<u>Anas platyrhynchos</u>)
  pintail duck (<u>Anas acuta</u>)
  green-winged teal (<u>Anas carolinensis</u>)
  blue-winged teal (<u>Anas discors</u>)
  American widgeon (<u>Mareca americana</u>)
  shoveler (<u>Spatula clypeata</u>)
  common goldeneye (<u>Bucephela clangula</u>)
  Barrow's goldeneye (<u>Bucephela islandica</u>)
  harlequin duck (<u>Histrionicus histrionicus</u>)
  surf scoter (<u>Melanitta perspicillata</u>)
  hooded merganser (<u>Lophodytes cucullatus</u>)
  common merganser (<u>Mergus merganser</u>)
  sora (<u>Porzana carolina</u>)
  American coot (<u>Fulica americana</u>)
  black oystercatcher (<u>Haematopus bachmani</u>)

Upland Game Birds
  blue grouse (<u>Dendragapus obscurus</u>)
  Franklin grouse (<u>Canachites franklini</u>)
  ruffed grouse (<u>Bonassa umbellus</u>)
  spruce grouse (<u>Canachites canadensis</u>)
  sharp-tailed grouse (<u>Pediocetes phasianellus</u>)
  rock ptarmigan (<u>Lagopus lupestris</u>)
  willow ptarmigan (<u>Lagopus lagopus</u>)
  white-tailed ptarmigan (<u>Lagopus leucurus</u>)
  band-tailed pidgeon (<u>Columba fasciata</u>)

**Table** 3.4 (continued)

Birds of Prey
   goshawk (<u>Accipter gentilis</u>)
   sharp-shinned hawk (<u>Accipter striatus</u>)
   red-tailed hawk (<u>Buteo jamaicensis</u>)
   bald eagle (<u>Haliaetus leucocephalus</u>)
   marsh hawk (<u>Circus cyaneus</u>)
   osprey (<u>Pandio haliaetus</u>)
   pigeon hawk (<u>Falco columbarius</u>)
   sparrow hawk (<u>Falco sparverius</u>)

sources: Godfrey (1966); Guiguet (1961, 1968).

## Table 3.5
## Ichthyofaunal Species Indigenous to the Skeena River

Anadromous
  river lamprey (<u>Lampetra ayresi</u>)*
  green sturgeon (<u>Acipenser medirostris</u>)*
  white sturgeon (<u>Acipenser transmontanus</u>)
  longfin smelt (<u>Spirinchus thaleichthys</u>)
  coastal cutthroat trout (<u>Salmo clarki clarki</u>)
  steelhead trout (<u>Salmo gairdneri</u>) (marine)
  Dolly Varden trout (<u>Salvelinus malma</u>) (marine)
  pink salmon (<u>Oncorhynchus gorbuscha</u>)
  chum salmon (<u>Onchorhynchus keta</u>)*
  coho salmon (<u>Oncorhynchus kisutch</u>)
  sockeye salmon (<u>Oncorhynchus nerka</u>)
  chinook salmon (<u>Oncorhynchus tshawytscha</u>)

Adfluvial
  longnose sucker (<u>Catostomus catostomus</u>)
  white sucker (<u>Catostomus commersoni</u>)
  largescale sucker (<u>Catostomus macrocheilus</u>)
  rainbow trout (<u>Salmo gairdneri</u>) (freshwater)
  Dolly Varden (<u>Salvelinus malma</u>) (freshwater)

Fluvial-Lacustrine
  western brook lamprey (<u>Lampetra richardsoni</u>)
  longnose dace (<u>Rhinichthys cataractae</u>)
  redside shiner (<u>Richardsonius balteatus</u>)
  threespine stickleback (<u>Gasterosteus aculeatus</u>)
  coastrange sculpin (<u>Cottus aleuticus</u>)
  prickly sculpin (<u>Cottus asper</u>)
  peamouth (<u>Mylocheilus caurinus</u>)
  lake whitefish (<u>Coregonus clupeaformis</u>)
  mountain whitefish (<u>Prosopium williamsoni</u>)
  northern squawfish (<u>Ptychocheilus oregonensis</u>)
  lake trout (<u>Salvelinus namaycush</u>)
  burbot (<u>Lota lota</u>)

* rare in Kitselas Canyon
sources: Rostlund (1952); Carl, Clemens and Lindsey (1967);
         Nolan (1977).

The single most important resource to the aboriginal economy was fish. Nolan (1977:401-11) has listed 293 ichthyofaunal species indigenous to the north coast area. Most of these spend their entire lives in salt water. Only 31 species spend part or all of their lives in the fresh water of the Skeena or Nass systems. These include 14 anadromous species, which spend most of their adult lives in the sea or estuaries, but enter fresh water to spawn in streams, rivers or lakes; 5 adfluvial species, which spend most of their adult lives in large river or lakes, ascending smaller streams to spawn; and 12 fluvial-lacustrine species which spend their entire lives in fresh water, but are not adfluvial. The species included in these three general categories are listed in Table 3.5.

Most, but not all 31 species may be found in Skeena River at Kitselas Canyon. Eulachon (_Thaleichthys pacificus_) run in Skeena River, but not in great abundance, and spawn below Kitselas Canyon. The major eulachon run occurs in the Nass River, and a smaller run occurs in the Kitimat River. Two other anadromous species, river lamprey (_Lampetra ayresi_) and green sturgeon (_Acipenser medirostris_), are both very rare in Skeena River, and it is not known if they occur as far upriver as Kitselas Canyon (Carl Clemens and Lindsey 1967:30, 33; Hart 1973:23, 82; Scott and Crossman 1973:56, 91).

Thus, of the 293 species of fish occurring in or near north coastal waters, less than 10 percent (N=28) can be found in the Skeena system in the vicinity of Kitselas Canyon. In addition, seven of these species achieve a maximum size of less than 20 cm. With the possible exception of longfin smelt (_Spirinchus thaleichthys_), it is unlikely that any of these were of aboriginal economic importance.

Although ichthyofaunal diversity is minimal at Kitselas Canyon (relative to the coast), this does not mean that ichthyfaunal biomass is minimal. Quite the opposite is the case, primarily due to the presence of one genus of fish--_Onchorhynchus_ (salmon). All five species of North Pacific salmon that migrate into North American river systems occur at Kitselas Canyon. Four of these--sockeye (_Oncorhynchus nerka_), pink (_O. gorbuscha_), coho (_O. kisutch_), and chinook (_O. tschawytscha_)--occur in large numbers in Kitselas Canyon. In fact, high proportions of the Skeena runs of each of these species pass through Kitselas Canyon on their way to upriver spawning beds (see Table 3.6). The fifth species, chum (O. keta), occurs in Kitselas Canyon, but in unknown abundance. Chum generally run a short distance in fresh water before spawning, and according to Aro and Shepard (1967:286), the Skeena is only a minor producer of chum.

Sockeye and coho run long distances upriver before spawning. Sockeye only spawn in streams that are fed and flushed by lakes (Forester 1968). The major sockeye runs are in the upper and lower Babine Rivers and Fulton River (Milne 1955) (see Table 3.6). The major coho run is in Lakelse River, just below Kitselas Canyon (see Table 3.6). Chinook or pink may run long or short distances, depending on the breeding population. The major pink run is in Kispiox River in odd years, and in Lakelse River in even years.

The major chinook runs are in Bear River, lower Babine River, Kispiox River and Morice River. Aro and Shepard (1967:296-99) indicate that approximately 83.4 percent of all spawning sockeye, coho, pink and chinook pass through Kitselas Canyon annually.

Chinook may be present year round in Kitselas Canyon, but the major run, along with the sockeye run, begins in June. Both species occur in the canyon in abundance as late as August or September, as successive breeding populations run through the canyon. Pink and coho begin to run through the canyon in early July. The runs of pink are short; spawning usually occurs in September. The coho run lasts longer, with spawns occurring into November.

Other ichthyofaunal species occurring in Kitselas Canyon include the anadromous and adfluvial varieties of trout: cutthroat (Salmo clarki), steelhead (S. gairdneri), and Dolly Varden (Salvelinus malma). These species do not approach the abundance or predictability of salmon, but were undoubtedly important nonetheless in the aboriginal economy. This is especially true of steelhead and cutthroat which spawn in late winter and early spring, a time when other resources are depleted.

The adfluvial species are similar to the anadromous species in that spawning is a cyclical event that occurs at the same time each year, and takes place in shallow creeks and streams. These fish are most predictable and accessible at this time.

## Table 3.6
## Salmon Escapement Through Kitselas Canyon

| Spawning Location | Escapement (X 1000 fish) | | Spawn Start | Peak | End |
|---|---|---|---|---|---|
| **Sockeye** | | | | | |
| Upper Babine River | 116.0 | | Sept. | Oct. | Oct. |
| Lower Babine River | 84.0 | | Sept. | Oct. | Oct. |
| Bear Lake | 5-10 | | Sept. | Oct. | Oct. |
| Falls Creek | 2-5 | | Sept. | Sept. | Oct. |
| Pinkut Creek | 29.0 | | Aug. | Sept. | Sept. |
| Four Mile Creek | 2.3 | | Aug. | Aug. | Sept. |
| Fulton River | 86.0 | | Sept. | Oct. | Oct. |
| Grizzly Creek | 9.9 | | Aug. | Sept. | Sept. |
| Pierre Creek | 23.7 | | July | Sept. | Sept. |
| Tachek Creek | 2.2 | | Aug. | Sept. | Sept. |
| Twin Creek | 7.9 | | July | Aug. | Sept. |
| Williams Creek * | 5-10 | | Aug. | Aug. | Sept. |
| **Pink (odd and even years)** | **Odd** | **Even** | | | |
| Lower Babine River | 28.1 | 15.7 | Aug. | Sept. | Sept. |
| Kispiox River | 475.5 | 59.0 | July | Sept. | Sept. |
| Kitwanga River | 158.8 | 71.3 | Aug. | Sept. | Sept. |
| Lakelse River * | 206.3 | 273.5 | Aug. | Sept. | Oct. |
| Skeena River | 165.0 | 25.5 | Aug. | Sept. | Sept. |
| **Chum** | | | | | |
| Skeena River | unknown | | | | |
| **Coho** | | | | | |
| Lower Babine River | 2-5 | | Sept. | Oct. | Nov. |
| Upper Babine River | 2-5 | | Sept. | Oct. | Nov. |
| Upper Bulkley River | 2-5 | | Oct. | Nov. | Dec. |
| Lower Bulkley River | 1-2 | | Oct. | Nov. | Dec. |
| Gosnell Creek | 2-5 | | Sept. | Sept. | Nov. |
| Kispiox River | 5-10 | | Sept. | Oct. | Nov. |
| Lakelse River * | 20-50 | | Sept. | Oct. | Nov. |
| MacDonell Lake | 1-2 | | Sept. | Oct. | Nov. |
| Morice River | 5-10 | | Aug. | Sept. | Nov. |
| **Chinook** | | | | | |
| Lower Babine River | 5-10 | | Sept. | Sept. | Sept. |
| Bear River | 10-20 | | Sept. | Sept. | Oct. |
| Upper Bulkley River | 0.5-1 | | Aug. | Sept. | Sept. |
| Cedar River | 0.5-1 | | Aug. | Sept. | Sept. |
| Kispiox River | 5-10 | | Aug. | Sept. | Sept. |
| Morice River | 5-10 | | Aug. | Sept. | Oct. |

* depart Skeena River just below Kitselas Canyon
source: Aro and Shepard (1967)

The disadvantage of adfluvial and fluvial lacustrine fish is their reduced abundance relative to anadromous species. Without access to the productive marine biocycle, the amount of exploitable ichthyobiomass in spawning adfluvial and fluvial lacustrine fish is much less than among anadromous fish. Fluvial lacustrine species have the additional disadvantage of being unpredictable and generally inaccessible. They do not spawn in large numbers or at predictable times, and spend most of their time in deep water (large rivers or lakes).

Paleoenvironment

The paleoenvironmental conditions of Kitselas Canyon, and surrounding area are not well known at this time. Two studies of late Quaternary environmental change have been conducted in the Terrace area (Duffell and Souther 1964; Clague 1984). These studies focussed primarily on the history of late Pleistocene glaciation and de-glaciation in the Kitimat-Kitsumkalum Valley, and in the Skeena Valley below Terrace. The data from these studies can be extrapolated to provide a general picture of the late Quaternary environment of the larger area of the lower Skeena including Kitselas Canyon.

At the climax of the late Wisconsinan Fraser glaciation (ca. 14,500 B.P.), a massive ice sheet covered much of British Columbia. Along the north coast area, three major ice lobes projected down Nass Valley, Skeena Valley and the Kitimat-Kitsumkalum Valley. They coalesced over eastern Hecate Strait (Clague 1984:41), and a complex of confluent ice tongues enveloped all valleys and lowlands in the area. Clague (1984:6-7) suggests that during the climax of the Fraser glaciation, peaks and ridges above 1500 to 2000 metres in the Coast and Hazelton Mountain ranges probably projected above the surface of the ice to form nunataks.

De-glaciation began about 13,000 years ago, and occurred by a combination of downwasting and complex frontal retreat (Clague 1984:2). The outer coast became ice-free first, in response to destabilization of the western periphery of the Cordilleran ice sheet by eustatically rising seas. By 12,500 to 12,000 B.P., the western margin of the Cordilleran ice sheet had disintegrated in Hecate Strait leaving discrete lobes at the present day mouths of the Nass and Skeena Rivers, and at the base of

Douglas Channel. At this time, glaciers were retreating rapidly by calving, and were soon confined to fjords and mountain valleys. Clague (1984: Figure 9) indicates that by 11,000 B.P. the Skeena Lobe had retreated about 70 km up Skeena Valley from the present river mouth. At the same time, the Kitimat Lobe had almost completely retreated from Douglas Channel, remaining only in Kitimat Arm. By 10,500 to 10,000 B.P., these two piedmont lobes had split in Skeena Valley at Terrace. From here, the Skeena glacier continued to retreat westward up Skeena Valley, while the Kitimat-Kitsumkalum glacier retreated northward up Kitsumkalum Valley. Kitselas Canyon was probably ice-free by 10,000 B.P. or shortly thereafter.

During the period of deglaciation, Skeena Valley and other valleys and lowlands in the area were isostatically depressed. As the glaciers retreated the sea closed in, often in contact with the ice front. At about 10,000 B.P., Skeena Valley existed as an arm of the sea to a point well above Kitselas Canyon. Marine shell collected from mud near Terrace yielded a radiocarbon age of 10,200 ± 100 B.P. (GSC 2306) (Clague 1984:15). Similar marine flooding, in contact with the retreating glacier, also occurred in the Kitimat-Kitsumkalum Valley. It halted where Kitsumkalum Valley narrows north of Pine Lake, and constructed a large delta sandur complex graded to a shoreline about 200 metres above present sea level (Clague 1984:20).

Clague's (1984) study, which is the first detailed analysis of the de-glaciation of this area of the north coast of British Columbia, focuses on these deltas, and on the large ice-frontal delta sandur complexes in particular. There are two in the Kitimat Valley, and both mark periods of stagnation or stabilization during the ice retreat. One is located 5 km south of Lakelse Lake; the other is 17 km north at Terrace airport. The Lakelse sandur is the largest, stretching completely across the valley, and covering an area of 60 km$^2$. Both sandurs graded to shorelines about 200 metres above the present. Despite the presence of these stillstands, Clague (1984:18) argues that deglaciation from Kitimat to Terrace took no more than 1000 years. Radiocarbon dates on glaciomarine sediments in this part of the valley range from 9900 to 10,800 B.P., and do not become systematically younger towards the north (i.e., the direction of retreat). This suggests that the outwash plain probably formed in a relatively short time period, and that around these stillstands glacial retreat was very rapid.

Marine transgressions culminated in the Skeena Valley (including Kitselas Canyon) and Kitimat-Kitsumkalum Valley about 10,500 B.P. (Clague 1984:24; Clague, Harper, Hebda and Howes 1982), when the sea was 200 metres higher relative to the land than at present. Isostatic rebound at the close of the Pleistocene and during the early Holocene lead to rapid emergence of Skeena Valley and Kitimat-Kitsumkalum Valley. Clague et al (1982) indicate that shorelines had fallen to about 120 metres above present by 10,000 B.P., and to +35 metres by about 9300 B.P. Glacial retreat was diachronous, so the timing of emergence probably differed locally. Clague (1984:26) states that the sea in the Skeena and Kitimat-Kitsumkalum Valley areas had fallen to its present level relative to the land by 8000 B.P. He indicates no major sea level fluctuations after this time.

The Recent Environment

This section examines the potential for human occupation of Kitselas Canyon and the lower Skeena during the late Pleistocene and Holocene. The seminal research on late Pleistocene and Holocene environments on the north coast of British Columbia was conducted by Heusser (1960, 1965) as part of a larger study of North Pacific North America. The north coast area studied was Prince Rupert, where cores from three peat bogs were taken. Heusser's (1960:181-89) four phase climatic scheme, covering the period from the late Pleistocene to the present remains the yardstick for measuring late Quaternary climatic change, although it is thought by some to be overly simplistic (e.g., Bryson, Barreis and Wendland 1970) for an area stretching from California to western Alaska. However, in the absence of any more detailed post-Pleistocene environmental recontruction for the area pertinent to Kitselas Canyon, Heusser's generalized scheme is adopted here with some modification (cf. Miller and Anderson 1974).

Heusser's reconstruction is as follows: 1) late glacial, 2) early Postglacial, 3) hypsithermal, 4) late Postglacial. Each phase is characterized by climatic change from its predecessor, and by distinctive floral communities.

The late glacial phase in northern British Columbia, beginning about 11,000 years ago was significantly colder and drier than the modern climate. At Prince Rupert, willow, alder and lodgepole pine dominated. Sedges and the Polypodiceae were present as ground cover, but ferns were present only in small amounts. Alpine tundra conditions were present at considerably lower elevations than today.

The Kitselas Canyon area may have been inhabitable for man at this time, but it would have been a harsh environment, with river valleys clogged by ice, and minimal ground cover to support animal species.

The early Postglacial phase in northern British Columbia began about 10,000 years ago, and lasted until about 8000 B.P. Heusser (1960:183) indicates that a cool, moist climate continued to prevail on the north coast, although somewhat warmer than that which dominated the final interval of the late glacial phase. At some time during the early Postglacial, climatic conditions were similar to those that exist today. Lodgepole pine, alder and sedges and ferns were the principal members of the vegetation community. Sitka spruce and western and mountain hemlocks became established at this time, but only in small numbers (Heusser 1960:183).

In the area of Kitselas Canyon, east of the Coast Mountains, it is not clear whether wet climatic conditions existed during the early Postglacial, as they did on the coast. Miller and Anderson (1974) have compared pollen cores from the Taku district in the Alaska panhandle (after Heusser 1952, 1960) with samples from Atlin in northwestern British Columbia, east of the Coast Mountains. This contrast is analogous to that between Prince Rupert Harbour and Kitselas Canyon.

During the early Postglacial, the lodgepole pine maximum occurred at Taku about 9000 B.P. (Miller and Anderson 1974:46), indicating cool, wet conditions, as suggested by Heusser (1960:183). However, inland at Atlin, Miller and Anderson (1974:46) state that a spruce woodland environment, indicative of a cool dry climate, existed at this time. They relate this to an east-west shifting across the Coast Mountain ranges of the Arctic Front--the line of demarcation between high pressure anti-cyclonic continental weather, and low pressure, cyclonic maritime conditions--throughout the Holocene. When this front was located west of the Coast Mountains, the associated storm path would produce cool, wet conditions on the coast, and cool, dry conditions inland. When the front was situated east of the Coast Mountains, relatively warmer and drier conditions would have existed on the coast, while warm, wet conditions would have existed inland (Miller and Anderson 1974:54).

The implications of this inverse pattern for Kitselas Canyon are not clear. If the Taku/Atlin climatic pattern held for Prince Rupert/Kitselas Canyon, then a cool, dry early Postglacial climate may have existed at Kitselas Canyon. However, two additional factors exist to further confuse the picture. First, Taku/Atlin are much farther north than the lower Skeena. Therefore, latitudinal change as a factor affecting climatic variability cannot be ignored. Secondly, the Skeena Valley allows maritime air to penetrate to Kitselas Canyon. No similar condition exists at Atlin, where today semi-arid conditions prevail. Given this evidence, climatic conditions at Kitselas Canyon during the early Postglacial may have been cooler and somewhat drier than on the coast, as is the case today.

The question of sea level fluctuations at the end of the early Postglacial remains contentious. Heusser (1960:194) and Fladmark (1975:151-52) both argue that as late as 7500 B.P., sea level in the Prince Rupert area may have been 40 to 50 metres higher than at present. Fladmark (1975:152) indicates that sea level at Prince Rupert did not stabilize to present conditions until shortly before 5000 B.P. This model of continued sea level fluctuations into the middle Holcene was important for Fladmark because it served as the basis for his "salmon climax productivity" model (Fladmark 1975:293-96). Briefly, this model states that sea level fluctuations along the Northwest Coast to 5000 B.P. resulted in reduced salmon productivity relative to the late Holocene, as river and lake beds (salmon spawning locations) would have been unstable during the period of sea level fluctuation. Fladmark (1975:293-96) argued that it was only with sea level stabilization and the resulting "climax productivity" of salmon, ca. 5000 B.P., that the ethnographic Northwest Coast cultural pattern began to develop.

There are two problems with this model. Clague's Lakelse Lake cores indicate that marine shorelines in the Kitimat-Kitsumkalum Valley dropped 200 metres in the 2000 year interval of the early Postglacial, and that shortly after 8000 B.P., the sea level in the Prince Rupert-Kitimat area was at its present level (Clague 1984:26).

Mathews' (1979) reconstruction of early Holocene sea levels is consistent with Clague's model. Mathews (1979:150) argued that sea levels, river and lake beds had stabilized by no later than 8000 B.P. Thus, we may envision salmon climax productivity at or shortly after this time.

Even if climax productivity did not occur until 5000 B.P., it is not clear that this was important. The size of the climax runs were not seriously affected by intensive fishing, even during the ethnographic period (see Kew 1976:2). It is entirely possible that "sub-climax" runs were still large enough to make salmon specialization profitable for the human procurer.

The relevant point here is that salmon probably existed in abundance on the Northwest Coast long before the advent of intensive procurement. Sea level stabilization and the attainment of salmon climax productivity probably had little to do with the evolution of the ethnographic north coast cultural pattern.

The Hypsithermal interval (Heusser 1960:184-86) succeeded the early Postglacial on the north coast of British Columbia at about 8000 B.P. and lasted until roughly 3500 B.P. This interval was marked by successional sub-divisions of forest cover. The first succession, lasting until about 6000 B.P., was marked by sitka spruce, alder and mountain hemlock, and was associated with ground cover dominated by sedge and fern. The later succession was marked by increased importance of western hemlock, which eventually predominated over sitka spruce.

Temperature and humidity fluctuations occurred throughout this 5000 year interval. Heusser (1960:185) states that at Prince Rupert, successions of peat types (two horizons of ligneous peat separated and underlain by sedge peat) indicate two discrete episodes of humidity increase, followed by decrease.

Miller and Anderson (1974:49-50) indicate that at Atlin, warm, wet conditions existed throughout the Hypsithermal. This is consistent with their shifting Arctic Front model. Taku was experiencing warm, dry conditions at this time. Again, this has ramifications for Kitselas Canyon. While relatively warm, dry conditions (although fluctuating)

72

existed at Prince Rupert during the Hypsithermal, it is possible that increased humidity and storminess prevailed at Kitselas Canyon. This implies that more extensive, luxuriant vegetation existed in the area throughout the Hypsithermal than in preceding and succeeding intervals.

It is unlikely that an open, semi-arid environment ever existed at Kitselas Canyon during the Holocene. If Miller and Anderson's model has even remote applicability to Kitselas Canyon, it is entirely possible that the forest cover of the late Hypsithermal was even more extensive than it is today.

The final climatic interval in Heusser's scheme is the late Postglacial. On the north coast, in the Prince Rupert area, this began about 3500 B.P., and is marked by cooler temperatures and generally higher precipitation (although again fluctuating) than at present. Heusser (1960:187) noted that these conditions were particularly conducive to glacier development. Western hemlock remained the dominant species on the coast, but sitka spruce appears to have declined, being replaced by mountain hemlock and lodgepole pine. On the ground, heath and Sphagnum became dominant, succeeding Lysichitum.

At Atlin, Miller and Anderson (1974:47-48) divided the period covered by the late Postglacial into three intervals. Their pollen cores indicate that the earliest interval (to 2500 B.P.) was marked by continuing wetness and decreasing temperatures. This is indicated by the appearance of alpine fir in the Atlin spruce forest. The middle interval to 750 B.P. was characterized by cooler and somewhat drier conditions than the preceding interval. The most recent interval embraces the "Little Ice Age" on the immediate coast (Taku), but Miller and Anderson (1974:47) state that at Atlin conditions were actually slightly warmer and drier than in the preceding phase.

At Kitselas Canyon, cool, wet conditions are likely to have existed during the late Postglacial because of the ameliorating effects of the maritime air mass, via the Skeena Valley access route. Late Postglacial climatic conditions at Kitselas Canyon were probably cooler than during the preceding Hypsithermal, and similar in general to climatic conditions that exist in the area today.

Summary

Kitselas Canyon was probably habitable by 8000 B.P. at the latest. At this time, postglacial temperatures were becoming warmer, and precipitation may have been increasing moderately. Rapid forest succession may be envisioned. In the ensuing 5000 years, warmer conditions may have existed (relative to the present). At no time however, should we envision truly xerothermic conditions at Kitselas Canyon. The ameliorating effects of the off-shore maritime air mass would have maintained moderate to high moisture levels throughout the Hypsithermal, and inland, storm tracks from the Arctic Front may have actually produced wetter conditions during the thermal maximum than at present. The last 3000 years have been characterized by cool and moderately moist conditions, similar to the present. Little vegetation change from the preceding phase is envisioned, except for the forest floor replacement of Lysichitum by heath and Sphagnum.

Dense coniferous forest conditions, similar to those of the present, may have developed at Kitselas Canyon shortly after 8000 B.P.. They were almost certainly in existance by 5000 B.P. Following Clague (1984), sea levels were stable, or nearly so, by 8000 B.P., with only minor oscillations after this time. River downcutting, as a response to these oscillations, would have been minimal. Gravel spawning beds for salmon would have stabilized by this time. Thus, we may envision salmon runs approaching present size by shortly after 8000 B.P. Throughout the Holocene, minor climatic oscillations may have resulted in the altitudinal raising or lowering of certain biotic communities, but in general, major environmental change in the last 8000 years is unlikely.

The initial condition of the model presented in Chapter 2 was one in which human access to important edible resources was restricted by environmental conditions. Kin-based corporate groups are most likely to form at primary locations of resource access. The natural environment of Kitselas Canyon satisfies the initial condition. An abundant, reliable, localized resource--salmon--could be procured at Kitselas Canyon. In fact, Kitselas Canyon is a critical procurement location on the Skeena River. Further, a variety of other resources were available in the area because of the unique location of the canyon. This contributed to the importance of the canyon as a primary location for resource control.

Chapter 4

KITSELAS CANYON: CULTURAL SETTING

Introduction

This chapter includes detailed ethnographic (Part 1) and prehistoric
(Part 2) information on the Kitselas and lower Skeena areas.  The
ethnographic summary presents a model of Kitselas life at the time of
European contact.  This represents the culmination of evolutionary trends
in prehistoric settlement, subsistence and social organization.  It is
demonstrated that the Kitselas were permanent residents of the canyon, who
controlled a defined territory along the Skeena River.  Their subsistence
was oriented strongly toward salmon.  The Kitselas were organized in ranked
corporate groups, based on ascribed status differences.  This model
constitutes a base of comparison for the prehistoric evidence from Kitselas
Canyon.

The prehistoric summary begins with an examination of the evidence
for early occupation of the north coast.  The remainder of this section
focusses on the lower Skeena localities of Prince Rupert Harbour, Kitselas
Canyon and Hagwilget Canyon.  The archaeology of these three areas is
presented in detail; there is, at present, no comprehensive discussion of
lower Skeena archaeology in the literature.  These data are used in
subsequent chapters to investigate change in prehistoric social
organization.  Existing models of prehistoric cultural change from Prince
Rupert Harbour (MacDonald 1969a) and Kitselas Canyon (Allaire 1979) are
critically examined.

Part 1

REGIONAL ETHNOGRAPHY

Cultural and Linguistic Affiliation

Kitselas Canyon is the traditional homeland of the Gitdsilasshoo
people (Emmons 1912:468) or Kitselas, "people of the canyon".  Although
visited on many occasions during the late 19th and early 20th centuries,
the Kitselas were never described in a detailed ethnography.  Brief
descriptions exist (Schoolcraft 1860; Dawson 1881; Dorsey 1897; Emmons
1912; Shotridge 1918), but these are generally incomplete and in some cases
unreliable.  For example, Schoolcraft (1860) published a Kitselas census,
but he never actually visited Kitselas Canyon.  Much of the information in

these reports relates to a period when the Kitselas villages were abandoned or in a state of decline.

Allaire, MacDonald and Inglis (1979), using early photographs and the fieldnotes of H.I. Smith, and Marius Barbeau and William Beynon, have meticulously compiled an ethnohistoric reconstruction of the Kitselas, focussing mainly on Gitlaxdzawk (the "Fortress"), one of the historic Kitselas villages. This report is of great value, not only because it describes each house structure at the site, but it also identifies the owner of each house, and where possible, provides the owner's phratric and clan affiliation.

Linguistically, the Kitselas speak a Tsimshian dialect more closely related to Coast Tsimshian than to Gitksan (Allaire et al. 1979:58). Duff (1965:18-19) refers to the Kitselas and the Kitsumkalum, who occupied the Kitsumkalum Valley north of Terrace, as the Canyon Tsimshian, and he too includes them linguistically with the Tsimshian tribes of the lower Skeena (see Figure 4.1). Allaire et al. (1979:58) suggest that this coastal rather than interior affiliation of the Kitselas was due to their closer proximity to the summer villages of the Coast Tsimshian on the Skeena below the canyon, than to the more distant Gitksan villages of the middle and upper Skeena.

Emmons (1912:468) states that the Kitselas were intermediary between the Coast Tsimshian and the Gitksan, but it is not clear whether Emmons is speaking of Kitselas regional group affiliation here, or their role in coast-interior trade relations.

Settlement Pattern and Yearly Round
**The General Coast Tsimshian Model**
Despite their ties to the coast, the Kitselas differed from most other Coast Tsimshian groups in some important respects. One difference was in settlement pattern. Prior to 1834, when the Hudson's Bay Company trading post was established at Port Simpson, the Coast Tsimshian local groups or tribes wintered in villages on the coast. Each tribe-- Ginakangeek, Gitando, Gispakloats, Gilutsau, Gitlan, Gitwilgiots, Gitsees, Ginadoiks, Gitzaklahth (Garfield 1939:175-76)--had its own winter village location in the Metlakatla Pass area of Prince Rupert Harbour (Boas

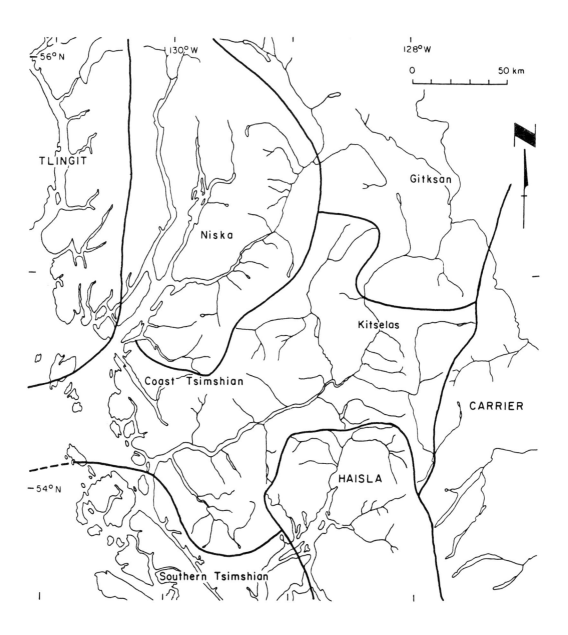

Figure 4.1   Tsimshian linguistic divisions (from Duff 1965).

1916:394; Garfield 1939:177; Drucker 1950:160, 1965:115). These were
permanent villages in the sense that they were maintained year after year,
and the dwellings were owned by "House" groups. They were only occupied
seasonally, however, from roughly November to March. Winter was primarily
a time for social and ceremonial activities among the Tsimshian.
Subsistence pursuits were minimal, but not altogether absent. There are
references to land and sea mammal hunting (Boas 1916:339; Garfield
1951:15-16; Drucker 1965:119), and Inglis (1977:2) states that shellfish
collecting and bird hunting were also practised.

The annual round of the Coast Tsimshian groups of Metlakatla can be
seen in terms of three major seasonal movements (see Figure 4.2). From
their winter villages, most local groups moved in March to the Nass estuary
for the eulachon fishery. Each winter village group had its own camping
location on the lower Nass River (Boas 1916:44; Garfield 1939:199, 270,
1950:13, 15), and some household groups maintained permanent dwellings at
these locations (Garfield 1939:277). Eulachon was a critical element in
the Tsimshian diet because the oil or grease rendered from the fish was an
important source of carbohydrates (Kuhnlein et al. 1982:155; Stewart
1975).

Grease was highly desired by most northern groups, and the Coast
Tsimshian and Niska in particular actively traded it. Garfield (1951:16)
states that these groups were the primary producers. The Niska traded
inland via the "grease trails" with the Gitksan and Carrier. The Coast
Tsimshian traded with the people of Kitkatla and with the Haida. The many
groups that congregated at the Nass undoubtedly resulted in some of the
largest, pre-contact aboriginal aggregations on the north coast.

While most Coast Tsimshian journeyed to the Nass in the spring, some
task-specific groups formed to pursue two other resources that were also
available at this time; herring and halibut. On the north coast, herring
spawn in early spring in great numbers in shallow water close to shore
(Carl 1964:22; Hart 1973:97), and halibut, after spawning in deep water in
late winter, move into shallow water offshore in the spring (Nolan
1977:321).

If the eulachon fishery ended early, some groups might proceed to the
offshore islands where they engaged briefly in sea mammal hunting

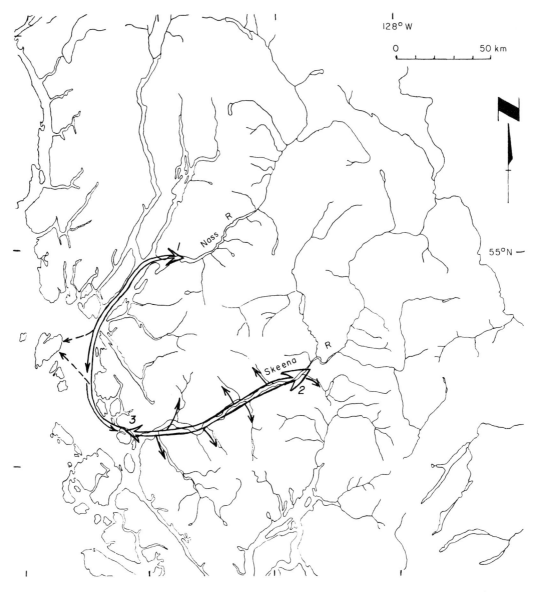

*1* late winter – early spring: Nass River eulachon fishery. Some task groups (broken arrows) engage in sea mammal hunting, herring and halibut fishing en route to and from Nass River.

*2* early summer: Skeena River fishing, hunting and gathering. Small arrows indicate migration to tribal territories.

*3* fall: return to winter village at Prince Rupert Harbour.

Figure 4.2  Schematic of Coast Tsimshian seasonal round.

80

and halibut fishing (Boas 1916:399; Drucker 1965:117-18). This practice
was usually ad hoc, and did not occur every year.

The salmon runs began in May or June, and this signalled the second
major phase of the Coast Tsimshian annual pattern of movement. The winter
village groups journeyed up the Skeena River to fish for salmon and collect
berries. There is some disagreement over the summer residence pattern.
Boas (1916:399) indicates that the winter village groups simply relocated
themselves to summer villages on the Skeena. However, Garfield (1939:277,
1951:16) states that the winter village groups did not stay together, and
even the large household groups fragmented into smaller family groups that
became the primary residential and productive units. It is likely that
both authors are correct. The Coast Tsimshian tribal groups had
traditional, contiguous territories along the Skeena (Inglis and MacDonald
1979:3). Each tribe derived its name from these territories. For example,
Ginadoiks means "people of the swift current" (Garfield 1939:176). These
territories were sub-divided into resource areas that were owned by the
various House groups. Inglis and MacDonald (1979:3) indicate that each
tribe had a major village location in its traditional summer territory,
usually at the confluence of the Skeena and a major tributary (see also
Allaire 1984:88). Most of the time, however, was spent in small camps of
simply constructed dwellings, smokehouses and drying racks, distributed
throughout the territory. Each House owned multiple camps, and from each
camp, one or two families engaged in subsistence activities. Men fished
and hunted in late summer and early fall. Women processed fish, and also
collected berries (Inglis and MacDonald 1979:7). A great deal of mobility
could be expected of these small family units at this time, as they moved
from one resource location to another.

In late October or early November, when the peak of the salmon runs
had passed, the third major seasonal movement occurred. The Coast
Tsimshian returned to their winter villages at Metlakatla.

## The Kitselas Model

This brief description of general Coast Tsimshian settlement and
annual round differs markedly from that of the Kitselas. The Kitselas
wintered in the canyon (Emmons 1912:468). They also spent their summers

there, collecting food resources, mainly salmon and berries. This resulted in a less mobile lifestyle than that of the Coast Tsimshian, in that there was no residential shift from summer fishing to winter village location. Allaire et al. (1979:70) state, "Despite their limited territories the Kitselas could depend on sufficient quantities of salmon going through the canyon each summer to live in their village throughout most of the year". The Kitselas followed "a way of life very similar to that on the coast except that the Kitselas were very much more sedentary" (Allaire et al. 1979:71).

There is some disagreement concerning Kitselas mobility in the spring. Allaire et al. (1979:71) state that the Kitselas joined the rest of the Tsimshian at the eulachon fishery on the Nass River, "going there on foot by the trail through the Kitsumkalum Valley". McNeary (1976:117) on the other hand, states, "the Canyon Tsimshian did not depend on the Niska for eulachon oil, as they had an alternative source in the Kitimat people of Douglas Channel".

It is not clear whether the Kitselas actually **fished** for eulachon (as implied by Allaire et al.), or **traded** for grease (as implied by McNeary). In the latter case, it is unlikely that a major spring residential move occurred. More likely, only a brief expedition involving a few Kitselas traders would have been mounted. If the Kitselas did fish for eulachon, it is unlikely that all Kitselas people moved to the Nass. The journey from Kitselas Canyon to the Nass, whether by land or by water, is much longer and more arduous than from Prince Rupert Harbour to the Nass. Likely, many people stayed home.

In any event, the Kitselas were much less mobile than the Coast Tsimshian of Prince Rupert Harbour, spending most, if not all, of the year at Kitselas Canyon.

The sedentary lifestyle of the Kitselas was based on an extreme dependence on salmon--perhaps more so than the other Coast Tsimshian groups. In part, this dependence was facilitated by the Kitselas' control of the canyon, a critical fishing location on the lower Skeena. Although other resources, especially land mammals and berries, were available in the vicinity of the canyon (see Tables 3.2, 3.3), the Kitselas had little or no direct access to the marine and foreshore resources that were used by other

Coast Tsimshian groups. Allaire et al. (1979:136-37) suggest that the
Kitselas may have traded for these resources. This is supported by the
presence of sea mammal bones and marine shell, recovered at Gitlaxdzawk.
In return, the Kitselas may have traded mountain goat wool or soapberries,
both of which are more abundant on the east side of the Coast Mountains
than on the west side.

Herring, cod, halibut, shellfish and sea mammals were all important
resources to the Coast Tsimshian, but not to the Kitselas. As Emmons
(1912:468) states, to compensate for the lack of these resources the
Kitselas "have always looked to the river with its wealth of salmon for
their chief support".

### Kitselas Villages and Territories

At the time of European contact, the Kitselas occupied two villages
in the canyon. One, Gitlaxdzawk (the "Fortress"), "people of the ravine"
(Allaire et al. 1970:65) or "people of the place where they steal canoe
bottom boards" (Emmons 1912:469) was situated on a rocky promontory near
the upper end of the canyon on the west side (see Figure 4.3, 4.4). At
present, this promontory is connected to the river shore, adjacent to the
CNR line. Prior to railway construction, the promontory may have been
separated from the shore by a narrow channel (Allaire et al. 1979:72). The
other village was Gitsaex, "people at the edge of the lake", located on the
east side of the river at the north end of the canyon (see Figure 4.3,
4.4). Allaire et al. (1979:66) state, "These two sites constituted a
single community, and were the only two occupied in historic times".

### Origins

The Kitselas, like many Coast Tsimshian tribes, claim Temlehem, a
mythical village on the upper Skeena, as their place of origin (Robinson
and Wright 1962). The myth states that after a famine or great flood at
Temlehem some families migrated downriver, and eventually settled on the
west side of the river just below Kitselas Canyon at Tsunyow, "landing
place" (Emmons 1912:469). Sometime later, these original settlers were
joined by new people, and according to Allaire et al. (1979:65), this
resulted in a move across the river to Gitaus, "people of the sand bar"

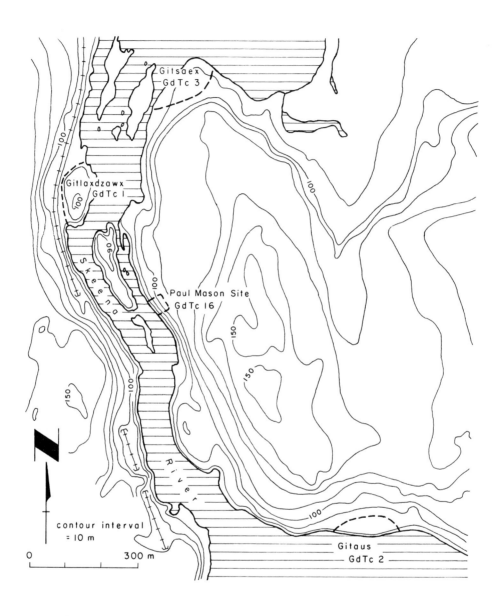

Figure 4.3  Kitselas Canyon archaeological sites.

84

(see Figure 4.3).

According to the myth, the Kitselas abandoned Gitaus when beavers mined the soil from under the village. This is interesting, given that the archaeological excavation of Gitaus in 1968 was prompted by the erosion of the site as a result of extensive river undercutting. In addition, there is an unstable slide area directly behind the site. These factors may have been important reasons for not maintaining a permanent village here.

Allaire et al. (1979:65) state that after leaving Gitaus, the Kitselas established their village at Gitlaxdzawk. Gitsaex was established soon after, when overcrowding at Gitlaxdzawk caused some people to move across the river.

The timing of the events described above is difficult to establish because they are based on oral history. When Emmons passed through the canyon in 1909, Gitlaxdzawk and Gitsaex were abandoned. Of Gitsaex, Emmons (1912:470) states:

> The decayed remains of other carvings and
> house-timbers half-buried in the moss and
> overgrown with brush confirm the statement
> of the natives that this was the largest and
> most important of the villages hereabouts.

In 1879, George Dawson visited Kitselas Canyon, and described Gitaus and Gitlaxdzawk as follows:

> Near the lower end of the canyon, on the right
> bank are perched a few Indian houses, with
> some rudely executed carved posts... At the
> upper end of the canyon, on the opposite or
> left bank, is a second and larger village with
> eight or ten houses, a few in good order, but
> most in various stages of dilapitation [sic]
> (1881:13).

Dawson apparently did not see Gitsaex, and the structures at Gitaus were probably associated with the white settlement that developed during the 1870's gold rush.

## Gitlaxdzawk

Gitlaxdzawk was first investigated in 1927 by H.I. Smith as part of a joint National Museums of Canada - Canadian National Railway reconstruction project. The site was not investigated from an archaeological perspective, however, until 1971 when mapping and test

85

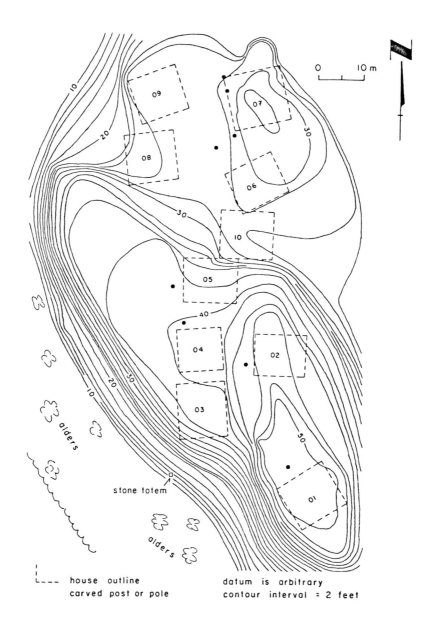

0      10 m

09

07

08

06

10

05

40

04      02

03

50

alders

stone totem

01

alders

⌐
└---   house outline      datum is arbitrary
    carved post or pole      contour interval = 2 feet

Figure 4.4   Gitlaxdzawk.

86

excavations were conducted by Allaire and MacDonald (1971).

The village area covered about 100 metres (north/south) by 50 metres. The implication that the site was fortified is reflected today by its location. It is separated from the river bank by a dry gulley, which may have been a river channel prior to railway construction. The site is surrounded by steep slopes and its access by river or by land is difficult at all times. The village was located on top of this promontory which consisted of three terraces.

The village does not appear to have been surrounded by a palisade wall. Rather than a wall, spiked logs were placed around the perimeter of the village, ready to roll down on attackers below (Allaire, MacDonald and Inglis 1979:70; MacDonald pers. comm. 1981).

Allaire and MacDonald (1971:49) described the residential pattern at Gitlaxdzawk as unusual for a Tsimshian village. Instead of the usual row of houses facing the water, the houses were placed irregularly and oriented in various directions (see Figure 4.4) as a result of the unusual site topography. The remains of ten house floors were cleared and mapped. The general construction of the houses is described by Allaire and MacDonald (1971:50):

> The type of the houses corresponds to that used
> by the Tsimshian for the same period on the
> coast. They are thirty feet square with two
> heavy roof beams (nearly two feet in diameter)
> placed halfway between the lateral walls and the
> centre of the house. The adzed planks which
> supported them were of the same width and about
> eight inches thick and nine to eleven feet high
> ...the upper plank of the lateral wall was
> joined to the short corner posts by either
> mortice and tenon or lap joints. The gable
> planks were also fitted into the corner posts
> by the same techniques. In one photograph
> the gable planks of one house are shown with
> a series of notches to hold smaller rafters.
> Similar notches held the transverse rafters
> on the upper plank of the lateral walls.
> The covering of the walls was probably made
> of vertical split planks fitted into a grooved
> sill at both ends of the house. The covering
> of the lateral walls must have consisted of
> horizontally laid planks.

Three houses at Gitlaxdzawk were unusual (Allaire and MacDonald 1971:50) (see Figure 4.4). House 2 was a traditional structure that was covered with modern sawn planks. House 3 was large and had a raised platform at the rear, and House 7 was also very large, had a dug out floor, and was built partly on piles over the cliff above the river (see Table 8.7 for house floor dimensions).

The dwelling structures at Gitlaxdzawk are examined in greater detail later in this study.

### Gitsaex

Gitsaex has not been described in detail in the literature. The site was surveyed and mapped in 1981 (MacDonald and Coupland 1982), and the following description is based on that investigation.

The site is situated on a flat bench or terrace, approximately five metres above the high water line of the Skeena River. It is bounded on the north side by a shallow bay and swampy marsh, and on the southwest side by two islands at the head of the canyon. The east and southeast portions of the site are bounded by slopes that rise steeply away from the site.

Surface features at Gitsaex include seventeen house floors (see Figure 4.5). These appear as flat, rectangular levelled areas, in most cases bounded by low earth ridges that were formed as a result of the levelling of the floors.

Post depressions helped to define the perimeters of the floors. In a few cases, pieces of the wall footings remained in place, precisely defining the location of the structural wall. The orientation of the floors is consistent with the ethnographic village pattern. There are two rows of floors, arranged parallel to each other and facing the river. There are eight floors in the front (west) and nine floors in the back (east) row. In addition, a cultural feature including five circular surface depressions was identified between floors 2 and 3. These were evidently post holes of free-standing columns.

The entire eastern portion of the site includes numerous and varied cultural features. There is a small area (12 metres by 12 metres) located east of floors 14 and 15 that is marked by a lithic scatter (mainly fire-cracked rock). There is also an earth ramp which may have functioned

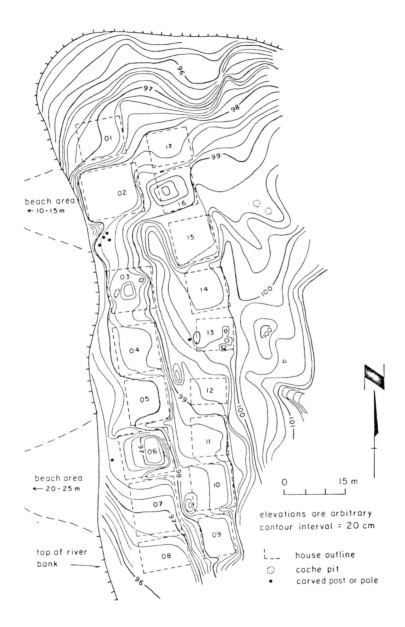

Figure 4.5  Gitsaex.

as a formal entrance to the site from the east. It is located east of floor 12. Six circular cache pits are located in this area. These may have been used for food storage. Three large, flat, unmarked stone slabs, likely grave markers, were recorded, and there is an historic Christian grave stone located east of floor 17.

No standing architecture remains at Gitsaex, although this condition has prevailed for only a short time. Emmons (1912:470) described standing house frames in 1909.

The most significant features identified from archaeological reconnaisance at the site were the seventeen levelled floors, thought to have been formerly associated with plank house superstructures. The average size of these floors was about 10 metres by 10 metres (individual floors are examined in greater detail later in this study) which is consistent with house floor size at Gitlaxdzawk. Post depressions along the edges of most floors at the front and back walls suggest the use of off-centred main beams as described by Allaire and MacDonald (1971) for Gitlaxdzawk and by Boas (1916:46-48) for the Coast Tsimshian village of Kitkatla. Pieces of wall sills at Gitsaex in association with floors 3 and 16 correspond to plank house construction techniques noted at Gitlaxdzawk (Allaire and MacDonald 1971:50).

In addition to the earth ramp, there are two likely access points to Gitsaex from the river. These are small beach areas (see Figure 4.5) where canoes could be landed at the north and south ends of a large back eddy that fronts the site. The north beach is directly in front of floor 2 and the adjacent small open area with the five post depressions. The south beach fronts floor 6.

Gitsaex was a large village occupied during the early historic and perhaps late prehistoric periods. The house floors, arranged in two rows, are spaced at roughly equal distance (see Chapter 8), and do not overlap. It is reasonable to infer from this that most if not all floors were used simultaneously during the peak occupation of the village. This was probably in the late 18th or early 19th century. Our Kitselas informant stated that after Gitsaex was abandoned as a village, it continued to function as a burial site. This is substantiated by the presence of a late 19th century Christian tombstone on site. In addition, a small cemetery with seven graves is located on the upper terrace east of Gitsaex.

**Territories**

There is some confusion concerning the territories held by the Kitselas (Figure 4.6). Allaire et al. (1979:70-71) simply state that Kitselas territory extended "some thirty miles along the Skeena", and was bounded above the canyon by Gitksan territory and below by the Coast Tsimshian. Inglis and MacDonald (1979:3) indicate that Gitlan territory included the area around the modern town of Terrace and the lower Zymoetz (Copper) River, and Gispakloats territory extended beyond this, virtually to the foot of the canyon. Inglis and MacDonald's map, based on the fieldnotes of Wallace and Beynon, does not indicate the extent of Kitselas territory, but it is implied that the Kitselas did not control the river below the canyon, or that their claim to this territory is disputed.

Emmons (1912:468) states that the Kitselas "held the canyon, claiming the river from Lorne Creek above to the little canyon below". Lorne Creek, a tributary of the Skeena is 40 km upriver from Kitselas Canyon. Little Canyon is at Terrace, 16 km below Kitselas Canyon. This conflicts with Wallace and Beynon's notes, especially concerning Gitlan and Gispakloats territories. The river between Terrace and Kitselas Canyon today is regularly fished by members of the Kitselas Band, but the situation may have been different in the early historic or prehistoric periods. Boas (1916:381) refers to a Gispakloats group who camped one summer "below the canyon at G'at-aus (Sandy Camp)", where they dried salmon and other provisions. It is not stated whether the Gispakloats actually owned the camp, or simply received permission from the Kitselas to use it one summer.

The upriver extent of Kitselas territory to Lorne Creek is not disputed. This area is important because it is substantially drier, less rugged and more open in forest coverage than the area around Kitselas Canyon. As stated in Chapter 3, this facilitated access to a variety of resources, both floral and faunal, that are either non-existent or not readily available near the coast.

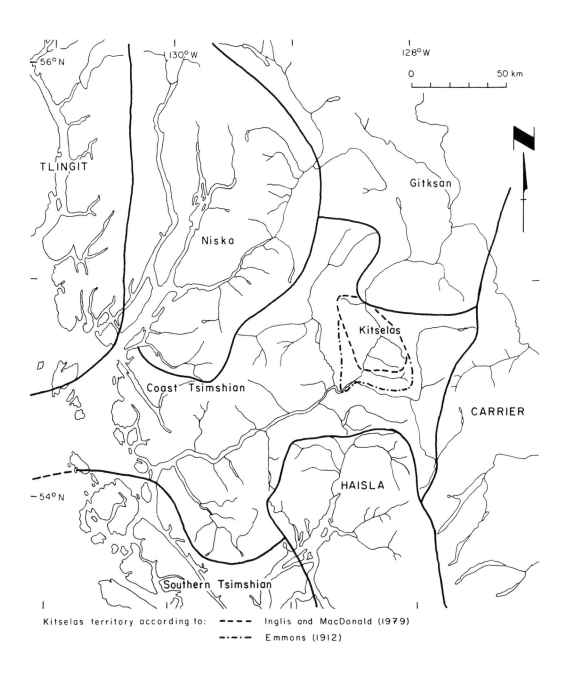

Figure 4.6  Kitselas territories of the Skeena Valley.

## Subsistence Technology and Material Culture

The subsistence technology and material culture of the Kitselas are poorly documented. The following review is based on information culled from ethnographies of the Tsimshian and Niska, and is thought to be generally applicable to the Kitselas.

### Fishing Technology

The Kitselas were river fishermen, and as such were likely to have used all river fishing techniques known to the Tsimshian. Prior to European contact, their principal food procurement technology included dip nets (Boas 1916:400; Drucker 1950:169, 239; Nolan 1977:135-36; Allaire et al. 1979:71), traps (Boas 1916:50; Drucker 1950:166-67; Nolan 1977:140-42; McNeary 1976:93-95;) and weirs (Drucker 1950:166-67; Nolan 1977:140-41; McNeary 1976:93).

According to Drucker (1950:166-67) and Nolan (1977:135-36), the dip net was the only netting technology used aboriginally by the Tsimshian. The Tsimshian dip net consisted of a hoop, manufactured by bending and lashing together two arms of a natural wooden fork. The net was attached to the hoop and the hoop was then attached to the end of a long pole (Boas 1916:400). The net itself was probably made of stinging nettle fibres or sinew (McNeary 1976:74). Duff (1952:63) states that dip-netting is most effective for sockeye, which swim close to the surface.

Allaire et al. (1979:71) suggest that dip-netting was the Kitselas' principal fishing technique. However, our informant stated that the use of dip nets was secondary to wooden traps or baskets. The Kitselas trap was similar to one described by Drucker (1950:166-67). Essentially, it was a large cylindrical basket, weighted in the bottom with rocks so that it was submerged below the surface. The trap could be used with or without a funnel entry. The funnel opened downstream, and fish caught therein would be forced into the trap. Most fishermen operated numerous traps of this type simultaneously in different locations.

Another trap that may have been used by the Kitselas is the type described by McNeary (1976:93-95) for the Niska:

> A fence was built part way out into the river
> on a frame of stakes driven into the river
> bed. This fence channelled the fish into the

> trap. Apparently the trap forced the salmon
> to ascend to the surface of the water where
> they met a barrier that was so constructed
> that as the fish tried to jump they were
> knocked backwards into a tray or bin above
> the water.

Morice (1893:89) described a similar trap used by the Carrier where rivers
were deep and swift.

It is not clear to what extent the Kitselas used weirs. Nolan
(1977:140-42) indicates that weirs were a very important Tsimshian fishing
technique, used in shallow spawning streams. Although these would have
been ineffective in the canyon where the river is deep, Kitselas territory
included a number of shallow spawning streams, including Kleanza Creek at
the foot of the canyon, and Chimdemash, Legate, Oliver and Lorne Creeks,
all above the canyon. They may also have fished Zymoetz River. Weirs may
have been constructed on any of these tributaries. The fish were probably
speared as they congregated below the weir. Nolan (1977:133) describes
single and double-headed salmon harpoons, and two-pronged leisters used by
the Coast Tsimshian. The Niska used a leister with two detachable toggle
heads, lashed together with root and barbed with bone (McNeary 1976:95).

Dip-netting is a mobile technology. It allows the fisherman to move
up and down the river and use more than one dip-net location. Traps and
weirs are fixed technologies, associated with permanent fishing sites. The
most productive of these locations often had processing stations located
nearby (McNeary 1976:95), so that the fish could not only be harvested in
large numbers, but they could also be efficiently processed for storage.

The Tsimshian preserved fish by means of smoking. The lower Skeena
climate is generally too wet to allow the wind drying techniques used in
other places such as the Fraser Canyon. Today, most smoking is done in
smokehouses. Formerly, low open fires and frame racks were used. Rotten
cottonwood (McNeary 1976:97) or alder (Drucker 1965:118) was used for
smoking salmon. Fish were generally processed by women. The fish was
cleaned and the head and tail were removed. The body of the fish was then
spread out and the flesh scored. The fish was smoked for a few hours until
firm, and then the flesh cut into strips to be fully smoked (McNeary
1976:97).

Fish were smoked for winter consumption. Coho salmon could sometimes

94

be caught into December (McNeary 1976:96). For the remainder of the winter the Tsimshian, and particularly the Kitselas, subsisted mainly on smoked salmon and dried berries.

## Storage

The Coast Tsimshian of Metlakatla stored their food inside their winter dwellings, in smokehouses, or occasionally in cabins constructed for storage (Garfield 1951:11). Within dwellings, food was stored in boxes which were sometimes kept in underground pits beneath the sleeping benches (Garfield 1951:10), or stacked high against the house walls to form partitions for individual family space (Drucker 1965:120). Garfield (1951:10-11) also states that "dried foods were stored on shelves suspended from the beams and rafters or hung in bundles from the beams". There is no mention of food storage in pits outside the winter dwellings. This is perhaps the most basic of storage techniques, but at Prince Rupert Harbour winter precipitation is heavy and usually in the form of rain, so it is likely that food stored in outdoor pits would quickly spoil. Among the Niska, however, McNeary (1976:90) states that "fish were stored in pits near each house". This was in addition to the use of boxes (McNeary 1976:80). MacDonald (1979:69, Figure 29) indicates that the Gitksan also made extensive use of food storage pits. The hillfort at Kitwanga has a number of food storage pits at the base of the hill. Some of these are over 200 metres from the residential area of the site. Although it is not documented, the Kitselas also stored food in pits. MacDonald (pers comm, July 1981) stated that food pits were lined with birch bark or skunk cabbage leaves. The pits were often located outside the immediate area of the village, perhaps as a deterrent to raiding. In part, the use of food storage pits by the "upriver" Tsimshian was facilitated by the fact that winter temperatures are usually at or below freezing, and precipitation is in the form of snow. Coho salmon and steelhead trout can both be taken late in the year, and so are particularly suited to this type of storage.

**Hunting and Trapping**

Allaire et al. (1979:71) state that the Kitselas hunted and trapped in the winter. Hunting and trapping was important for the Gitksan (Cove 1982:4-5) and for the upriver Niska (McNeary 1976:101). It is likely that the same was true for the Kitselas, at least relative to other Coast Tsimshian groups who had access to marine and foreshore resources. The area around Lorne Creek, at the upriver end of Kitselas territory, was probably one important hunting area. The sub-alpine and alpine zones were also important for hunting marmot and mountain goat.

McNeary (1976:101) states that land mammals were more frequently trapped than hunted by the Niska. The Niska used two types of traps; the deadfall and the snare. Both varied greatly in size, and were suitable for catching animals ranging in size from rabbits to bears (McNeary 1976:103).

Hunting equipment included the spear and the bow and arrow. McNeary (1976:102-03) states that mountain goats, highly prized for their meat and wool, were hunted with spears by the Niska.

The hunting season began in September (mountain goat) and generally continued through the winter, depending on snow conditions and the availability of the resource. Very little hunting and trapping were done during the summer when fishing was of primary importance.

**Plant Gathering**

Like hunting, plant foods supplemented the essentially fish oriented diet of the Kitselas. Spring through fall was the gathering season. Among the Niska, this was primarily women's work; men fished and hunted. In the spring, hemlock cambium was edible when the sap was running. Most edible greens were available from April through June. These included stonecrop, cow parsnip, lady fern and Kamchatka lily. The Niska roasted fern roots in earth ovens, and the Kitselas may have done the same, although no earth ovens were recorded during the survey of Kitselas Canyon.

Berries, including wild crabapple, were collected in late summer and early fall. These were probably more important to the Kitselas than greens because they could be preserved for winter consumption. Blueberries, huckleberries, soapberries and salal were all available in Kitselas territory. The Niska crushed these berries and spread them over skunk

96

cabbage leaves under which a low fire burned. When the mash dried, it was rolled up and stored for later consumption (McNeary 1976:109). Soapberries do not grow in the coastal environment, but they do grow in the upriver end of Kitselas territory, near Lorne Creek. They are considered "chief's food" among the Niska, who traded for them with the Gitksan (McNeary 1976:109).

Plants were not only important for food. Stinging nettle was spun into twine for nets and snares, and birch bark and skunk cabbage leaves were important for wrapping food. Birch bark was also used to make containers, and spruceroot was woven into baskets (McNeary 1976:75-76). Alder and cottonwood were used as fuel.

Finally, a discussion of the plant use habits of any Northwest Coast group would be incomplete without mention of the importance of cedar. Tributes to cedar have been made on numerous occasions elsewhere (H. Stewart 1984; Hebda and Mathewes 1984), so I will be brief here. The Kitselas used cedar to construct their dwellings, manufacture canoes, and make containers (boxes and baskets), rope, clothing, mats, personal adornment and monumental art. Boas' (1916:46) general ode is appropriate as well to the Kitselas: "It may be said that the salmon and cedar are the foundations of Northwest Coast culture".

Demography

Population estimates for the two historic Kitselas villages have been reviewed by Allaire et al. (1979:67-68) and Allaire (1978:28-29). There are four estimates pertaining to the late 19th century, before the complete abandonment of the villages. These range from 186 (Kane 1859: Appendix I) to 1000 (Emmons (1912:468). Allaire et al. (1979:68) favour the lower of these two estimates, arguing that at a time when European diseases were ravaging aboriginal populations in North America, an estimate of 1000 people at Kitselas Canyon seems inordinately high. In fact, all four estimates are neither useful nor reliable. Kane's and Schoolcraft's estimates were the only ones based on census data (taken in 1845). Kane reported 72 men, 49 women, 29 boys, 31 girls and 5 slaves. Apparently, there was some discrepancy over these numbers because Schoolcraft used the same data, and his figures were 82 men, 47 women, 29 boys, 31 girls and 5

slaves.  Adding to the confusion is the fact that the census was probably
not taken at Kitselas Canyon.  Allaire et al. (1979:66) state that the
first white men on the Skeena did not arrive at Kitselas Canyon before
1859.  The census was probably taken from Fort Simpson on the basis of
native estimates.  The inaccuracy of this data is further seen in the ratio
of adult males to females.  It approaches 2:1.  This discrepency is not
accounted for in any of the estimates, and I think it contributes to the
unreliability of the data.  In addition, the number of dwellings in the
census was estimated at twenty.  Allaire et al. (1979:67) state that this
gives an average of 100 people in ten houses per village (Gitlaxdzawk and
Gitsaex), or ten people per dwelling.  This is extremely low by most
Northwest Coast standards, where household size is usually estimated at 20
to 25 people (e.g., Donald and Mitchell 1975:333; McNeary 1976:128).  Fort
Simpson was established in 1834, and it is reasonable to assume that there
was a steady population decline from this time, as more and more families
moved to the coast.  Therefore, the 1845 census, which indicates many
unoccupied dwellings and others occupied by only small numbers of people,
probably reflects a depleted population at Kitselas Canyon.

In 1879, Dawson (1881:20) estimated the Kitselas population at 300 in
eight or nine houses.  He cautioned that these figures are "uncertain owing
to the number of people away at the coast and elsewhere, yet calling this
place their home".  Thus, the number could have been substantially higher
than 300, and in fact probably was, given that Dawson did not see Gitsaex
when he passed through the canyon.  Dawson's figure was used by Allaire and
MacDonald (1971:48) in their population estimate of Gitlaxdzawk.  This
estimate gives about 30 to 35 people per dwelling (not counting absentees),
which is higher than the usual estimate of 20 to 25 people.

It is unfortunate that no population estimate exists for Kitselas
Canyon prior to 1834.  We are left to speculate about what the size of this
population may have been.  If Dawson's estimate is brought in line with the
ethnographic model (20 to 25 people per dwelling), the Gitlaxdzawk
population may have been 200 to 250 people.  But given the statement by
Allaire et al. (1979:65) about overcrowding at the site, it is possible
that Dawson's estimate is close to being accurate.  A conservative estimate
would be 250 people.  Gitsaex was a much bigger village in terms of number

of house floors (17 compared to 10 at Gitlaxdzawk). Conservatively, the maximum Gitsaex population may have been 50% larger than at Gitlaxdzawk. This gives an estimate for Gitsaex of 375 people, making a total of 625 people for both villages.

## Social Organization

The social organization of the Kitselas is consistent with that of other Coast Tsimshian groups. The Coast Tsimshian are divided into four units, called phratries (Garfield 1939:173). They are Laxgibu (wolf), Laxskik (eagle), Ganhada (raven), and Gispawedwada (blackfish or killer whale). Phratries are sub-divided into clans, non-localized matrilineal descent groups that share properties and privileges (Garfield 1951:20). The localized segment of a clan--the people who functioned as a group--was a House or lineage (Garfield 1951:22). Theoretically, each phratry could be represented in each tribe or winter village group by a lineage. For example, Allaire et al. (1979:68, 111) state that at Gitlaxdzawk there were Eagle, Blackfish and Raven Houses. There were no Wolves at Gitlaxdzawk, but there may have been a Wolf House at Gitsaex (Allaire et al. 1979:68).

The lineage or House was the autonomous socioeconomic unit of Tsimshian life. Villages were local units consisting of various families, some related, some not (Barbeau 1917:403). They functioned as political units (with contiguous territories, a name etc.; Mitchell 1983b) although not with the same level of integration as Houses.

The House was a corporate unit that held title, in the sense of proprietory rights, to lands and resources (Garfield 1951:14).

The importance of House, power and property has been analyzed by Cove (1982). The analysis pertains to the Gitksan, but it has applicability to the Kitselas and Coast Tsimshian as well. Briefly, a House held title to a territory because it had merged its essence with that piece of land. A House's essence was its stock of supernatural powers acquired by ancestors of the House from supernatural beings (naxnox) (Cove 1982:7). Supernatural beings were identified with specific locations (spanaxnox). A person entering that space could acquire powers from the being, and in so doing could become a "real person" (semooget). Acquired powers became part of the House and were given life by it (Cove 1982:7). The locale (spanaxnox), and its resources, also became part of the House.

The complex of crests, names, myths and songs stood in relationship to a House, its powers and territories. In one way or another, they expressed the powers of the House. For example, crests stand for the form taken by a supernatural being when it was encountered (Halpin 1973:107). Typically depicted on poles, house posts and dancing blankets, crests publicly stated a House's stock of powers (Cove 1982:9). Carved poles were often complete statements of acquired powers. Placing a pole in the ground was a means of putting a House's powers into it, acting as a "deed" to a territory (Duff 1959:12; Cove 1982:9). Names also express power. For example, "real" names, a political extension of chieftainship, denote the ancestor who acquired powers from a supernatural being. These names were given to acknowledge that encounter and the subsequent transformation to real status. Myths and songs were historical statements about how, when and where powers were received. Through oral tradition, a House preserved and legitimized its powers and titles to territories (Cove 1982:11).

In a sense, the property of a House was not the territories that it used, but rather the complex of crests, names and oral traditions that expressed the exclusive rights of access (title) of a House to the territories. These expressions or evidence of title were formally presented at potlatches or feasts. Feasts provided a public forum for the host House to validate newly acquired or existing powers, their origins and associated rights in property (Cove 1982:12). Guests at feasts were witnesses to the host's claims. The giving of gifts to guests was in part payment for their witness, but also an endorsement of the successor to title and a demonstration of his or her worthiness.

The Kitselas conformed to Fried's (1967:109) definition of a ranked society. Within each House, the members were ranked according to primogeniture. Status differences were ascribed. Garfield (1939:177) states that this resulted in a virtual caste system among the Tsimshian. At the top were chiefs (semooget) and close members of their lineage who collectively constituted Tsimshian nobility. These people held ranking names and usually lived in the same dwelling. The name of the dwelling and the name of the chief were usually the same. The wealth of the House, in the form of slaves, accumulated food stores and manufactured goods, was controlled by the chief.

Chiefs held high ranking names, enjoyed prominent seats at potlatches, and had the right to distribute House-owned wealth. Chiefs made decisions about resource use, but their decisions were not binding; a chief could not deny another House member access to subsistence resources (Drucker 1939:58).

Next in rank to chiefs and nobles were common people (lekayiget). Garfield (1939:178) states that these people formed the bulk of Tsimshian population. They included people who assumed hereditary personal names, but not "real" names. While they were House members, and related to the chief, they were not in the direct ancestral line of the chief. They typically lived in separate dwellings, near that of the chief, and the senior or most important individual in the dwelling assumed the name of the dwelling. For example, at Gitlaxdzawk, the Eagle chief was Gitxan, but other Eagle dwellings included Nieskadek, Nieswitxo, Iyoos, and Tacoleplip (Allaire et al. 1979:68).

Commoners formed the bulk of the labour force in Tsimshian society. According to Garfield (1939:178), their lot in life was to "help their chief" because generally they were unable to acquire property to initiate a potlatch for themselves.

At the lower end of the social scale were slaves and their families. If there was a class distinction in Tsimshian society, it was between freemen (chiefs, nobles, commoners) and slaves. Slaves, typically captives of raids or wars, held no rights in property and had no status. They were often given as potlatch gifts. Early research on Northwest Coast slavery held that slaves were not functioning members of society (Drucker 1939; Codere 1950). Recent research, however, has stressed the economic importance of slaves in everyday life (Donald 1983:114; Ruyle 1973:610-11). Slaves provided cheap labour, and a House that owned slaves could increase production at low cost. Mitchell (1984:45) states that slaving was a "business", and predatory warfare for capturing slaves was a "business venture". Slaves were viewed as wealth, and through the potlatch, this wealth could be transformed into prestige (Mitchell 1984:45). It is conceivable that much of the warfare and raiding that was endemic historically on the Northwest Coast was aimed at acquiring slaves as a means of increasing social standing and productive efficiency.

## Summary

This ethnographic summary of the Kitselas has introduced three salient points. First, the Kitselas were permanent, year-round occupants of the canyon. Second, their subsistence was based on the intensive production of salmon. Third, the Kitselas were part of a ranked society, as defined by Fried (1967). Status differences were ascribed from birth, and there were only a limited number of positions of high status (_semooget_) within society. Although chiefs did not technically own resources - these were controlled by the corporate lineages - it is clear that chiefs had unequal access to resources (food, wealth, and prestige) through their central position in redistributive exchange.

In subsequent chapters, the prehistoric evidence from Kitselas Canyon will be compared to this model of the Kitselas to determine the nature of prehistoric social integration.

Chapter 4   Part 2

## REGIONAL CULTURE HISTORY

### Early Evidence

This section investigates the existing culture history of the lower
and middle Skeena Valley, and reviews models of prehistoric cultural change
that have been proposed for the area.  The earliest evidence of human
settlement in this area is ca. 5000 B.P.  Radiocarbon dates of this age
have been obtained from cultural components in two localities; Kitselas
Canyon (Paul Mason Site, GdTc 16) (Coupland 1984:61), and Prince Rupert
Harbour (Dodge Island, GbTo 18; Kitandach, GbTo 34; Ridley Island GbTn 19)
(MacDonald and Inglis 1981:43).  At Hagwilget Canyon (GhSv 2), Ames
(1979a:202) has inferred an initial date of occupation of 4500 to 5000
B.P., based on the radiocarbon date, 3430 $\pm$ 200 B.P. (GSC 746), obtained
from a test excavation by MacDonald (1969a:249).  This was not a basal
date, but Ames has suggested an initial occupation 1000 to 1500 years
earlier, based on rate of sedimentation.

It is significant that there is no dated occupation in excess of 5000
years in the region.  Elsewhere in northwestern British Columbia (and
Alaska and Yukon), there is evidence of human occupation 3000 to 5000 years
earlier than in the Skeena Valley.

Fladmark (1982a:109) suggested that the absence of early Holocene
prehistoric components at the mouth of the Skeena "probably reflects lower
sea levels... and the submergence of most inner coastal sites".  However,
this does not explain the absence of pre-5000 B.P. components at Kitselas
Canyon or at Hagwilget Canyon.  Moreover, it is not clear that sea levels
were lower in Prince Rupert Harbour during the early Holocene.  Elsewhere,
Fladmark (1975:152, 1983:72) suggested that prior to 5000 B.P. north coast
sea levels were actually higher than at present, and in Prince Rupert
Harbour, sea levels may have stood 40 metres higher than at present about
7500 B.P. (Fladmark 1975:151).  Following this argument, if early Holocene
sites exist in the area, they would be located above current sea levels.
It will be recalled from Chapter 3 that Clague's (1984:3) research in the
Kitimat/Prince Rupert Harbour area, the most recent study to date,
indicates only minor sea level fluctuations during the last 8000 years.

There has been no shortage of archaeological investigation in the

Prince Rupert Harbour region during the last 20 years. Yet after recording nearly 200 sites, eleven of which were excavated, and obtaining 121 radiocarbon dates from the area (see MacDonald and Inglis 1981:41), the earliest evidence for human settlement of the area is 5000 B.P.

Early settlement elsewhere in northwestern British Columbia is nonetheless important, and is reviewed here as a prelude to the discussion of the post-5000 B.P. settlement of the lower Skeena area.

### The Late Pleistocene: the Question of Origins

There is disagreement between the earliest **evidence** for human occupation of the northern Northwest Coast, and the earliest **possiblity** for man in the region. The earliest evidence, based on radiocarbon dated cultural components, is between 9000 and 8500 B.P. The earliest possibility, according to some (e.g. Fladmark 1975, 1979b) is at least 2000 to 3000 years earlier, and assumes the existence of pre-Clovis man in North America.

Charles Borden (1968a, 1969, 1975) argued that the antecedents of northern Northwest Coast culture were to be found in the late Pleistocene assemblages of south central Alaska and southwest Yukon. Borden thought that the early assemblage at the Healy Lake Site (see Cook 1969), stratigraphically earlier than a radiocarbon date of 11,090 $\pm$ 170 B.P., was similar to later assemblages recovered on the northern Northwest Coast. This early Alaskan assemblage was characterized by well-established microcore-and-blade and burin industries.

Borden (1975:12) included the Healy Lake assemblage and virtually all other late Pleistocene assemblages from the Yukon River drainage in his "Early Boreal Tradition". While recognizing local and regional specializations over this broad area, Borden (1975:12) generalized that:

> these northern late Pleistocene - early
> Holocene groups possessed a flexible culture,
> including subsistence techniques capable of
> being adapted to the efficient exploitation
> of a wide range of ecological niches, from
> steppe and tundra to lake and riverine
> environments. Further... when opportunity or
> need arose some of their interior utilization
> techniques were readily adaptable to the
> exploitation of coastal resources.

The presence of early microblade-bearing assemblages in central Alaska and southwest Yukon prompted Borden (1969:5) to argue that coastal settlement was from the interior via major river valleys. This model implies initial settlement of the northern coast no earlier than 10,000 B.P. because river valleys would not have been ice-free prior to this time. Current dates from archaeological sites on the north coast support this argument (see Chapter 1, and this chapter).

An alternative model to Borden's, presented by Fladmark (1975, 1979b), posits the coast as a migration corridor at a time of lowered sea levels during the late Pleistocene. Fladmark argues that settlement of northwestern British Columbia and southeastern Alaska was from the coast rather than the interior. This model, based entirely on paleoenvironmental evidence, hinges on the presence of a chain of ice-free refugia, a narrow migration corridor between the ice-front and salt water. To date, Fladmark's research has been aimed at demonstrating that suitable conditions existed for Pleistocene human migration along the coast. This has become a point of contention in recent years. In addition to the fact that there is no archaeological evidence to support the model, Mathews (1979:150) argues that at the time of the glacial climax (17000 to 13000 B.P.), the ice front was in contact with the open ocean over much of the distance between Cape Flattery and southeast Alaska. Mathews (1979:150) argues that the benthic fauna of the shore zone was eradicated at this time, and the food sources of inland refugia were meagre. There would also have been the difficulty of "leap-frogging" over broad stretches of barren ice from one refugia to the next.

At present, if the "coastal route" model is to be accepted, two lines of evidence must be forthcoming. First, there must be some consensus among Quaternary researchers that the environment of the Northwest Coast was habitable during the late Pleistocene. Secondly, the model requires clear archaeological evidence in the form of radiometrically dated components that pre-date the period of river valley deglaciation that opened migration corridors from the northern interior to the coast.

## The Early Holocene: Settlement and Subsistence

A variety of terms has been applied to the early Holocene culture of the northern Northwest Coast, including the "Early Boreal Tradition", the "Microblade Tradition" (Carlson 1979), and the "Early Coast Microblade Complex" (Fladmark 1975). Despite the variation in names, there is general agreement that the early occupants of the north coast looked to the sea for subsistence. Carlson (1979:224) states, "the culture of the early Microblade Tradition people was likely specialized in the areas of fishing and sea hunting". In reviewing the early Holocene culture from the Queen Charlotte Islands, Borden (1975:23) states, "the small size as well as the location of the sites suggests an early maritime estuarine adaptation by small transient groups".

This interpretation is in need of review. It is based on meagre evidence at best, and is directly at odds with the faunal data, where it exists.

The components in question are from a handful of sites on the Queen Charlotte Islands, the southeast coast of Alaska, and the central coast of British Columbia. The assemblages are typically small, and are characterized by microblades, a variety of unifacially retouched flakes, cobble cores and tools, rare abraders and rare notched or ground sinker stones. Some assemblages have poorly formed leaf-shaped bifaces and unifaces, but Fladmark (1975:238-41; 1982a:109) states that these are rare and do not occur in all assemblages. Organic artifacts (bone, antler, wood) were almost certainly part of this early coastal complex, but they were not preserved (Fladmark 1982a:109). Also important is the absence of shell in these early components.

On the Queen Charlotte Islands, early lithic assemblages were recovered from three sites, each located on raised beach or estuarine deposits: Kasta and Lawn Point (Fladmark 1971), and Skoglund's Landing (Fladmark (1970). Kasta and Lawn Point form the basis of the Moresby Tradition of the Queen Charlotte Islands sequence (Fladmark 1975, 1979a). Skoglund's Landing, which lacks radiocarbon dates and microblades, may also be a component of this tradition.

Farther north, early Holocene lithic assemblages, technologically comparable to the Moresby Tradition, have been recovered at Groundhog Bay 2

(Ackerman 1968; Ackerman, Hamilton and Stuckenrath 1979), and at the nearby Hidden Falls Site (Davis 1979). These latter two coastal sites, with radiocarbon dates of ca. 8500 B.P., have the oldest dated microblade-bearing assemblages on the north coast, and indicate that the Early Boreal Tradition had reached the coast by the early Holocene.

Moving south to the central coast, the early assemblages from Namu (Carlson 1978, 1979; Hester and Nelson 1978) are included by Fladmark (1982a:108) in the early coastal complex. The relevant assemblages here are from stratigraphic units IIa and IIb, for which radiocarbon dates range from 9700 to 5100 B.P. The presence of a faunal assemblage from zone IIb provided the first direct evidence of subsistence for an early coastal component. The assemblage includes elements of land mammals (deer, dog) sea mammals (seal, sea lion, sea otter, dolphin) and fish (salmon). Although analysis of this data was based only on raw counts of bones, Conover (1978:96) indicates that the coastal forest was the habitat most heavily exploited at this time.

In general, the evidence cited above provides no clear support for a marine specialist economy on the north coast during the early Holocene. Borden (1975:24) admits that "evidence for fishing is weak" at Kasta and Lawn Point, and "direct evidence for the taking of sea mammals has not yet been found".

Borden's interpretation of the Moresby Tradition, as a marine-estuarine adaptation, is based solely on the location of the Kasta and Lawn Point sites (on raised beaches). No bone harpoons or fish hooks were recovered. This may be a result of poor organic preservation, but this does not explain the paucity of abraders, which should be numerous if bone fishing and sea hunting tools were manufactured.

It is difficult to generalize about the economy of a cultural tradition on the basis of two small site components. A marine-estuarine focus may have existed at Kasta and Lawn Point (although this not clear), but other, potentially larger Moresby Tradition components may be located away from raised beaches, and may have little to do with a marine-estuarine adaptation. The early Holocene "sea hunting" hypothesis is biased because only coastal sites have been investigated. Moreover, at one coastal site, Namu, the faunal evidence suggests that land mammal hunting was an important aspect of the subsistence pattern until at least 5000 B.P. (Conover 1978:96).

Following Borden's model of the Early Boreal Tradition, the early emigrants to the north coast (ca. 10,000 B.P.) had a generalized economy that included hunting and fishing. Upon reaching the coast, adaptation to the new environment was made, specifically to marine resources. However, the land mammal hunting base continued to be important.

It will be seen shortly that land mammal hunting continued to be an important aspect of the early economy (5000-3500 B.P.) at Prince Rupert Harbour.

Prehistory of the Lower Skeena

The preceeding section briefly outlined the late Pleistocene and early Holocene cultural sequence in northwestern British Columbia and adjacent areas, leading up to the earliest known settlement of the lower Skeena Valley/Prince Rupert Harbour area. This sets the framework for investigating cultural developments in the lower Skeena area after 5000 B.P. This section critically examines the archaeology that has been conducted in the latter region (since the mid-1960's), and reviews the relevant existing data on which our study of social change is based. Three localities are considered here: Prince Rupert Harbour, Kitselas Canyon and Hagwilget Canyon.

**Prince Rupert Harbour**

The earliest and most intensive archaeological investigations along the lower Skeena were conducted at Prince Rupert Harbour. These included excavations in 1967 and 1968 at Garden Island (GbTo 23), Dodge Island (GbTo 18), Parizeau Point (GbTo 30), the Boardwalk Site (GbTo 31), Grassy Bay (GbTn 1), and Lucy Island (GbTp 1) (see Figure 4.7). The first archaeological excavation at Prince Rupert Harbour was actually conducted in 1954 by James Baldwin at the Co-op Site (GbTo 10), but was not reported until much later (Calvert 1968).

MacDonald's (1969a) original synthesis of culture history at Prince Rupert Harbour was a three-horizon scheme, in which he designated lower (4500 to 2500 B.P.), middle (2500 to 1500 B.P.), and upper (1500 to

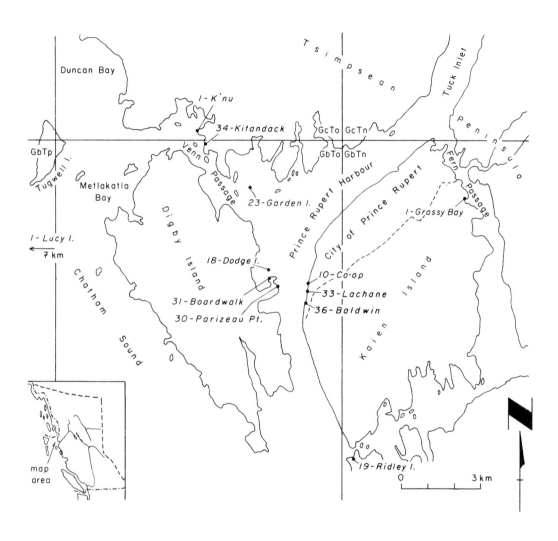

Figure 4.7   Prince Rupert Harbour sites.

historic period) horizons. Subsequent investigations led to an alteration
of the sequence. The term "period" was substituted for "horizon", and the
dates were extended (MacDonald and Inglis 1981). The revised sequence is:
Period III (5000 to 3500 B.P.), Period II (3500 to 1500 B.P.), and Period I
(1500 to historic period). The revision was based in part on post-1969
excavations at Boardwalk, Parizeau Point, Lachane (GbTo 33) (Inglis
1974:27-31), Kitandach (GbTo 34) (Inglis 1972:101-05), the Baldwin Site
(GbTo 36) (Inglis 1974:27-31), and K'nu (GcTo 1) (Inglis 1972:101-05). The
earliest radiocarbon dates from Dodge Island, Kitandach and Lachane
approach 5000 B.P., and the evidence for rapid shell midden accumulation,
which marks the beginning of Period II, was dated about 3500 B.P.

The basic theme of MacDonald's reconstruction--one of basic cultural
continuity with a net accretion of cultural elements through time--remained
unchanged. MacDonald (1969a:242-43) stated that all artifacts relating to
economic and manufacturing activities show continuity from the earliest to
latest periods. The differences among the periods are essentially based on
changes in the frequency of artifacts, rather than their presence or
absence. For example, the lithic industries, including chipped stone,
ground slate and pecked stone, all peak in frequency during early Period II
(ca. 3500 to 3000 B.P.) (MacDonald and Inglis 1981:45), but are present in
other periods. Basic tool forms are said to have overwhelming continuity
throughout the sequence (MacDonald 1969b:259). This is also true of the
cobble and flake tools (choppers, cores, cortex spalls) which are present
in abundance in each of the three periods.

Generally, the assemblage became more diverse through time, with new
tool forms (adzes, net sinkers, socketed bone points, bone scrapers, bark
shredders and mauls) gradually added. The only significant deletion was
bilaterally barbed bone harpoons in Period I.

A weakness of MacDonald's model is that, to date, quantitative
supporting evidence is generally lacking. Ames' (1976) study of the bone
tool assemblage from the Garden Island Site, occupied during the middle and
late periods, offers partial support. A factor analysis of the bone tools
from the site indicated little temporal varibility in bone tool form or
function (Ames 1976:63-92).

Despite the lack of quantitative analysis, MacDonald (1969a) effectively dispelled the old argument for a late Tsimshian migration to the coast. Many of the lithic and shell tools, thought by Smith and Drucker to be representative of developed Coast Tsimshian culture, are shown by MacDonald to be present from at least the middle period of occupation. These include ground slate daggers, stone clubs, ground slate pencils, mussel shell knives and zoomorphic art.

The addition of new artifact forms in the late period is argued to represent ongoing cultural change (MacDonald 1969b:259), not population displacement. These additions (splitting adzes, mauls, bark shredders, stone bowls, shell rattles, bone combs and pins) were clearly not the result of downriver migration, as Smith and Drucker believed, because none of these artifacts have been recorded in excavations upriver at Gitaus (Allaire 1978), the Paul Mason Site (Coupland 1984) or Hagwilget Canyon (Ames 1979a). Indeed, MacDonald (1969b:259) states that on the north coast there was never any great influx of new traits that might be suggestive of discontinuity. In MacDonald's view the only important addition to the late period was the classic art style, and this has been shown to have earlier antecedents (MacDonald 1983:101).

To date, most of the analysis of the Prince Rupert Harbour material has centred on the artifacts. Studies related to prehistoric settlement and subsistence have, unfortunately, been more cursory.

The most complete reported faunal analysis comes from the first site excavated at Prince Rupert Harbour, the Co-op Site (Calvert 1968). Recently, this site was re-designated as part of the Lachane Site (MacDonald and Inglis 1981:43). Calvert identified three stratigraphic zones at the site. The lower zone (I) comprised dark greasy soil and a small amount of mussel shell. This is consistent with the matrix of Period III components as described by MacDonald and Inglis (1981:42-45) from other Prince Rupert Harbour sites (Boardwalk, Dodge Island, Lachane). A radiocarbon date of 3040 ± 100 (Gak 1477) from Zone I is somewhat late for an early period date (but not overly so), and as it was the only sample dated from the site, it should not be given undue importance. Zone II comprised ash and humus, and was culturally sterile. This may represent abandonment of the site during Period II, because Zone III, a 1.5 metre deep shell deposit, includes splitting adzes and hafted mauls, which are diagnostic artifacts of the late period.

Although the faunal assemblage from Co-op was small, and collected by uncertain excavation techniques, two points are important. One was the obvious increase in the use of shell after Zone I. The other point is the apparent emphasis placed on land mammal hunting in the occupation represented by Zone I (as compared to Zone III). Whereas sitka deer was present in abundance in both zones, elements of mountain goat, wapiti, and smaller land mammals were restricted to Zone I. Stewart (1974:25) noted a similar predominance of land mammal elements from the lower levels (Period III) of the Boardwalk Site.

Sea mammal remains, recovered from both zones at Co-op, attest to a long-standing maritime adaptation. Fish bones, including salmon, were recovered, but not in great quantity. This low recovery is probably due to the excavation of one of the test pits without the use of screens.

Calvert (1968:96) concluded that in addition to sea mammal hunting, fishing, and some shellfish (blue mussel) collecting, land mammal hunting was an important economic pursuit to the early occupants at Co-op. Given a similar pattern at the Boardwalk Site (Stewart 1974), it is unlikely that the predominance of land mammal elements at Co-op was merely a factor of site function. A reasonable inference is that the Period III inhabitants of Prince Rupert Harbour had a generalized economy, in which both terrestrial and maritime fauna were of major importance, and shellfish was of minor importance.

This represents a continuation of the early Holocene subsistence pattern of the north coast.

The question of seasonality at Prince Rupert Harbour is more difficult to address. Wapiti elements in Period III components suggest winter occupation, which is consistent with the late prehistoric and ethnographic settlement pattern. The paucity of salmon elements may be due in large part to excavation technique. Alternatively, it is possible that salmon fishing was conducted upriver in summer and fall (as done ethnographically), which again implies winter use of Prince Rupert Harbour.

During the early period, only blue mussel (Mytilus californianus) was present in large amounts in the middens. At the onset of Period II, there was "rapid midden build-up" (MacDonald and Inglis 1981:45). In addition to blue mussel, cockle (<u>Clinnocardium nuttali</u>), butter clam (<u>Saxidomus</u> <u>gigantus</u>), horse clam (<u>Tresus capax</u>), and sea urchin (<u>Strongylocentrotus</u> <u>drobachiensis</u>) were all present in the middens in large amounts. This represents new and intensified use of foreshore habitats.

An important question is whether the increasing importance of shellfish was correlated with a decrease in the use of other resources. In other words, did this change in subsistence pattern merely represent a shift in preference, or an increase in resource diversity?

In her preliminary investigation, Stewart (1974:25) stated that sea mammal elements increased in frequency in the upper levels of the Boardwalk Site. Calvert's analysis revealed a similar trend at the Co-op Site. Thus, more intensive use of foreshore resources was associated with **increased** use of maritime resources at the onset of Period II. Land mammal bones no longer predominate in the shell deposit, as they did in the pre-shell zone, but land mammal elements continue to be present, albeit less frequent, in Period II components (Stewart 1974:25; Calvert 1968:96).

Changes in the artifact assemblage support the inference of continued land mammal hunting, at least during the early part of Period II. Chipped stone tools, including square-based lanceolate points and leaf-shaped bifaces, "peak in frequency in this period" (MacDonald and Inglis 1981:45). Ground slate points and "pencils" (see Appendix II) also occur in abundance. These tool forms are generally associated with land mammal hunting, and their increase in frequency during Period II suggests that land mammal hunting continued to be important at this time.

The increase in shellfish procurement is particularly interesting. The addition of clam and cockle to blue mussel indicates exploitation of inter-tidal resource habitats that were not previously important. MacDonald and Inglis (1981:45) have inferred a substantial population increase from this rapid midden accumulation. To the extent that increasing shellfish (and sea mammal) procurement **added** to, rather than **replaced** land mammal hunting, I believe there is justification in MacDonald's and Inglis' inference. It is not the increase in midden size per se, but rather the apparent increase in resource diversity, reflected in the middens that substantiates an inference of population growth during Period II.

The conditions of increasing shellfish exploitation and human population growth at Prince Rupert Harbour are consistent with the conditions described for the southern Northwest Coast (Croes and Hackenberger 1984) at roughly the same time, 4000 to 3000 B.P.  It will be recalled from Chapter 2 that Croes and Hackenberger argued that, in the absence of a storing economy, the limitation to population growth in this area was the winter resource base.  Shellfish was the most suitable resource for intensive exploitation throughout the winter.

The implication here is that the occupants of Prince Rupert Harbour had reached a point of maximum resource diversity and niche width (cf. Christenson 1980) by ca. 3500 B.P.

Turning to change in prehistoric social organization, the earliest evidence for the transition from egalitarian to ranked society occurred at ca. 2500 B.P.  Primarily, this is seen in the burial evidence recovered from Prince Rupert Harbour (Cybulski 1972, 1973, 1974, 1975, 1978, 1979).  Over 200 human burials were recovered during the course of excavations at Prince Rupert Harbour, and most of these date to the latter half of Period II (ca. 2500 B.P.) (MacDonald 1983:101-02).  Cybulski (1978) reported 12 modified human skull fragments, four altered long bones, and nine complete or partial skeletons with skull and/or long bone modification from this time range.  In all cases, the modification was post-mortem, and Cybulski (1978:27) speculated that the preponderence of skull modification may have had ritual significance.  Underlying this was the belief that the dead held great "power", an indication that only those few individuals in society who deigned to harness that power (chiefs, shamans?) would tamper with the remains of the dead.  Another possibility is that the modified human long bones reflect cannibalism, a practice recorded ethnographically for the Tsimshian (Garfield 1939:313-16).

Although these suggestions are tempting, they are also highly speculative.  Less speculative is the evidence for inter-group or intra-group hostilities beginning about 2500 B.P.  Cybulski (1979) and MacDonald and Inglis (1976:77) report mass interments with osteological evidence of healed forearm "parry" fractures, which may have been incurred in attempts to block striking blows, and evidence of blows to the head causing severe skull fractures.  MacDonald (1983:101) states that bone

114

clubs appear initially in the Prince Rupert Harbour middens at 2500 B.P., and a basalt dagger, which may date to this time was also recovered from a burial context. The earliest evidence for the use of elaborate stone clubs, which Duff (1963) called the "Skeena River club style", is 2000 B.P. MacDonald (1983:102) anticipates that further research may push this date back to 2500 B.P., based on a 2500 year old stone club from Blue Jackets Creek on the Queen Charlotte Islands (Severs 1974).

The presence of "war" clubs at Prince Rupert Harbour during later Period II, in addition to the osteological evidence, has lead MacDonald and Inglis (1976:76) to argue that inter-group hostilities were present at this time, in which raids for slaves or other property may have been conducted. Recently, Ferguson (1983) argued that warfare was an important factor in the complex system of redistributive exchange of the late prehistoric and historic Northwest Coast, and Donald (1983) and Mitchell (1984) have shown that slave labour was an important factor in intensified production and the improvement of social standing (see also Ruyle (1973)).

There is also evidence of long-distance trade for status goods during later Period II, seen in the presence of amber beads, copper ornaments and dentalium. These materials were probably items of personal adornment that symbolized the accumulation of wealth by some members of society. MacDonald and Inglis (1981:52) state specifically that ornamental items of copper, amber, dentalium and sea otter teeth, which appear initially about 2500 B.P. (MacDonald 1983:101), have been recovered from some Period II burials. They argue this to be a reflection of status differentiation in the community, although it is not clear whether the "status" burials are independent of age and sex.

Both lines of evidence--warfare and possible slavery, and differential status reflected in burials--are consistent with the postulate of ascribed status differences by 2500 B.P.

A third, possible line of evidence relates to changes in dwelling size. MacDonald and Inglis (1981:52) argued that there was an increase in dwelling size, associated with population growth, at Prince Rupert Harbour during Period II. They do not state specifically when this increase occurred, but in light of the above evidence for ascribed status differences, 2500 B.P. would seem to be a likely date. Social ranking and large, corporate households were integrally related during the ethnographic period.

There are, however, two problems with the "dwelling floor" argument. First, no complete dwelling floors are reported from Period III components, so it is not clear how MacDonald and Inglis base their claim for increased dwelling size during Period II.

Secondly, it is equally unclear whether the authors are referring to actual Period II dwelling floors or generalized living floors. Reference is made to large hearth features, floors of beach sand and gravel, post moulds and concentrations of fire-cracked rock (MacDonald and Inglis 1981:52), all of which may be related to habitation, but do not necessarily define the extent of the dwellings. There is no reference to surface outlines of dwellings, from which size could be accurately measured. Inglis (1972:102-03) reported housefloors, recognizable from surface contours at Kitandach and K'nu, but these are historic. No housefloors from Period II context have been described from Lachane or the Baldwin Site (Inglis 1974:27, 30). At Boardwalk, MacDonald and Inglis (1976:17) state that Period II housefloors were identified by black, humus-rich soil and gravel with little or no shell. This may simply represent activity areas in generalized living floors. Features typical of housefloors, including post moulds, slab-lined hearths and caches of boiling stones, indicate that housefloors were probably present within these living floor areas, but not necessarily that each living floor represented a discrete housefloor.

In the absence of housefloor depressions or a clear line of post moulds indicating a structure wall, it is often extremely difficult to delineate the boundaries of dwellings within generalized living floor horizons. Indeed, MacDonald (1969b:259) has cautioned that settlement pattern studies on the Northwest Coast have often been neglected in the past because "house structures and settlement information is extremely difficult to obtain from shell middens".

While it is tempting to accept MacDonald and Inglis' argument for larger dwellings during Period II, evidence of this increase awaits further research.

If ranked corporate groups evolved during the latter half of Period II at Prince Rupert Harbour, as suggested by the above evidence, what

116

developments in social organization occurred during the first half of Period II (3500 to 2500 B.P.)?  There is evidence to indicate the initiation of artistic expression at Prince Rupert Harbour at this time. This is seen in the presence of decorative personal effects including incised canine tooth pendants, inverted human figure bone pendants, and siltstone concretions modified with incised ribs, joint marks, vertebral columns, and other skeletal features (MacDonald 1983:101).

MacDonald emphasizes the importance of the anthropomorphic representation of this art, because it is the basis of later developments of the classic Northwest Coast style.  He states that as early as 3500 B.P., the inhabitants of the harbour area were "approaching a threshold where graphic symbols of **corporate identity** became meaningful" (MacDonald 1983:101; emphasis mine).  MacDonald argues not only that a system of graphic symbolism expressed in art and requiring shared cognitive modes and beliefs was developing, but that a cohesive group structure was also developing, whereby these symbols derived meaning.

Yet, MacDonald does not suggest evidence of ascribed status differences at Prince Rupert Harbour until at least 2500 B.P.  In other words, corporate identity may have preceded social ranking during early Period II.  As we shall see, it was during this period that egalitarian corporate groups evolved at Kitselas Canyon.

With the onset of Period I, MacDonald and Inglis (1981:52) state that the Northwest Coast pattern was "in full stride".  It is reasonable to refer to this period as "Developed Coast Tsimshian".  Analogous terminology is now used by some for the Gulf of Georgia, where the late prehistoric period, which has equivalent dates to Period I on the north coast, has been referred to as Developed Coast Salish (e.g. Ham 1982; Fladmark 1982a:115). Late prehistoric material remains from both areas are consistent with the regional ethnographic material cultures, and it is possible to associate the late prehistoric and ethnographic inhabitants of the respective areas.

Whereas the Marpole culture may have been the "climax" phase in Gulf of Georgia prehistory, in terms of the elaboration and diversity of the assemblage, Period I, the Developed Coast Tsimshian phase, marked the cultural climax on the north coast.  The pattern of gradually elaborating the assemblage, by adding new tool types and maintaining old ones, continued in this period. MacDonald (1969a; MacDonald and Inglis 1981) has shown that this pattern is consistent, at least in the Prince Rupert Harbour area, for the entire 5000 year prehistory of the region.

MacDonald and Inglis (1981:52) state that zoomorphic art flourished in this period, and the style is clearly linked with that of the ethnographic northern Northwest Coast. Zoomorphic labrets, mauls and adzes all apear about 1000 B.P. (MacDonald 1983:102). Zoomorphic designs on bone combs and pins also appear at this time, but MacDonald (1983:103) suggests that these may have greater antiquity, given the presence of similar items from Queen Charlotte Islands components dated between 2500 and 2000 B.P. (Severs: pers. comm. to MacDonald 1977). In fact, MacDonald (1983:103) concedes that many of the Period I elements from Prince Rupert Harbour with zoomorphic designs may have antecedents in late Period II components.

**Kitselas Canyon**

The excavations at Gitaus, at the lower end of Kitselas Canyon revealed a cultural sequence reflecting an estimated 2500 years of occupation, beginning at roughly 4000 B.P. (Allaire 1979:46-48). In Allaire's (1978) analysis of the cultural material (mainly stone tools) recovered from the site, three cultural components are identified. The earliest component, contained within the lower strata of the site (zone VI), is identified by Allaire (1979:46) as a component of the type of cultural pattern present on the coast at the time, defined as Period III at Prince Rupert Harbour. Radiocarbon dating of the initial occupation at Gitaus (3680 ± 130 B.P., GSC 1157; 3760 ± 140 B.P., GSC 1113; 4100 ± 310 B.P., GSC 1141) (Allaire 1978:286) supports a late Period III temporal association. This is a small assemblage of 46 retouched stone tools and 153 cobble spalls (Allaire 1979:29). Cobble and flake tools predominate in this assemblage (53.4 percent), with groundstone implements (25.7 percent) (mainly abraders), and chipped stone tools (19.0 percent) comprising the remainder of the assemblage (Allaire 1979:34).

The second or middle component at Gitaus is interpreted by Allaire (1979:47) as an indigenous complex, comprising the middle stratigraphic zones (V, III-lower, III-upper, II+III). Allaire (1979:47) calls this the "Skeena Complex". It is characterized by an increase in proportion and variety of unifacially and bifacially chipped stone tools. The Skeena Complex includes 401 retouched stone tools and 584 acute angle cortex spalls. Of the retouched tools, chipped stone comprises 40.2 percent of the zone V assemblage, increasing to 59.0 percent in zone III-upper. The diagnostic element of the Skeena Complex is the elongate lanceolate point form, including variants with convex, straight and concave bases, and occasionally with tapering or stemmed bases. Many of the chipped stone implements of the Skeena Complex were manufactured from a distinctive green chert (57.8 percent) (Allaire 1978:287). Groundstone tools (abraders) decline drastically in zone V to only 3.0 percent of the assemblage, increasing to 15.2 percent in zone III-upper. Cobble tools actually increase in zone V to 57.3 percent of the assemblage, but then decrease to 25.7 percent in zone III-upper. It should be noted that zone V includes gravel fill and probably represents a disturbed context (Allaire 1979:33).

Finally, the third and most recent component identified at Gitaus by Allaire comprises the upper stratigraphic zones (I, II). This is termed the "Kleanza Complex" (Allaire 1979:48), and it is characterized by an increase in the proportion of cobble tools (55.0 percent) and groundstone tools (25.3 percent). New elements include ground slate points with hexagonal cross section, labrets, slate mirrors, and a variety of shaped abraders, including ovoid, trapezoid and rectangular forms. Abraders (shaped and unshaped) now comprise 21.5 percent of the total assemblage, which Allaire (1979:45) suggests as an indication of a well-developed bone industry not preserved at the site. Chipped stone tools decrease in the Kleanza Complex to 19.7 percent, but lanceolate point forms are still present.

The dating of the Gitaus components is problematic. Although the initial occupation of the site is firmly established at around 4000 B.P., no radiocarbon dates were obtained for the subsequent duration of the sequence. Allaire (1979:46) argued that the Skeena Complex could be assigned a date of roughly 3400 B.P., based on a date of 3430 ± 200 B.P. (GSC 746) from Zone A of the Hagwilget Canyon site, GhSv 2 (MacDonald 1969a:249). This zone produced a chipped stone assemblage, including lanceolate points, similar to that of the Skeena Complex at Gitaus. In addition, the Skeena Complex is stratigraphically superior to the dates of

4000 B.P. from Zone VI. Allaire's dating of the Kleanza Complex (2500 to 1500 B.P.) is also based on certain trait similarities, shared in this case with the late time range of the middle period at Prince Rupert Harbour. Late period elements such as splitting adzes and hand mauls were not recovered. Recently, a charcoal sample from lower Zone I at Gitaus was submitted for radiocarbon dating. This yielded a date of 2390 ± 85 B.P. (NMC 1318), which supports Allaire's proposed initial date for the Kleanza Complex.

In his reconstruction of the prehistoric cultural developments at Gitaus, Allaire (1979:48-50) argued that a migration of people, presumably from farther upriver, is the best explanation to account for the introduction of the Skeena Complex. The Kleanza Complex was thought to be the result of coastal acculturation at the end of the Skeena Complex (Allaire 1979:49).

The interior migration argument for the Skeena Complex is based on the numerous similarities in artifact types between the Skeena Complex at Gitaus and the early materials recovered from GhSv 2 (Allaire 1979:46). These similarities include parallel-flaked lanceolate points, and a chipped stone tool kit including various bifaces (daggers, knives, picks), scrapers (keeled, thumbnail, flat, fan-shaped), perforators, gravers and notched and denticulated flakes. Allaire (1979:48) argued that the early occupants of Hagwilget Canyon and Kitselas Canyon were, in fact, the same population, who migrated from the former locality to the latter around 3600 to 3400 B.P. Allaire (1979:48) and Ames (1979a:208-10, 1979b:234-36) both regard the people of the Skeena Complex as an "interior" population, ethnically and culturally distinct from their coastal neighbours at Prince Rupert Harbour. Their contention is that a diversified, well-made chipped stone assemblage, which characterizes the Skeena Complex, is more typical of the interior than the coast.

Some similarities, however, do exist in stone tool forms between the Skeena Complex and the Period II assemblages at Prince Rupert Harbour. Of particular importance here is MacDonald and Inglis' (1981:45) statement that chipped stone tools "peaked in frequency" at Prince Rupert Harbour during Period II. This includes long, square-based lanceolate points and bifaces, leaf-shaped bifaces and scrapers, all similar in form and identical in manufacturing technique (Ames 1979a:208) to those of the Skeena Complex. In addition, it now appears that there was contemporaneity between the Skeena Complex and early Period II at Prince Rupert Harbour, given MacDonald's re-assignment of the beginning of the middle period to 3500 B.P.

To be sure, the coastal and upriver tool assemblages at this time are not identical. But does this mean that they necessarily represent two distinct populations?

This important question has direct relevence to the model of cultural change proposed in this study. I have argued (Chapter 2) that long-term economic changes led to the permanent settlement of critical resource localities such as Kitselas Canyon, and ultimately to the formation of egalitarian corporate groups. This model assumes evolutionary change within the same cultural group--not change as a result of population displacement.

Let us examine the evidence from Kitselas Canyon and Prince Rupert Harbour. The assemblage differences exist mainly in terms of the frequency of occurence of certain artifact types (especially chipped stone tool forms) rather than presence or absence. For example, projectile points and bifaces (19.0 percent) and formed unifaces (12.0 percent) occur more frequently in the Skeena Complex at Gitaus than at Prince Rupert Harbour during Period II. MacDonald and Inglis (1981:46) list lanceolate points, leaf-shaped bifaces and formed unifaces as present (but rare) at this time. They also list flaking detritus and cores, which suggests that these tools were manufactured at Prince Rupert Harbour (i.e., not acquired through interior trade). Moreover, both localities share high proportions of cobble tools (25 percent at Gitaus, Skeena Complex) and cortical spall tools.

Thus, the differences between early Period II assemblages from Prince Rupert Harbour and the Skeena Complex at Gitaus appear more quantitative than qualitative, and the presence of parallel-sided lanceolate points in both localities seems especially important. Lanceolate points have also been recorded from the Queen Charlotte Islands (Fladmark 1970) and southeastern Alaska (Keithan 1962).

Further, even the quantitative differences between the assemblages

121

from the two localities may be distorted because of differential factors of
preservation (shell versus non-shell contexts). Bone tools occur
frequently at Prince Rupert Harbour (see Ames 1976). No bone tools were
recovered from the Skeena Complex at Gitaus, but abraders (5.0 percent) are
present in the Skeena Complex (especially Zone III), which suggests that
bone tools were manufactured at this time, but not preserved.

There may be another reason for the paucity of chipped stone tools at
Prince Rupert Harbour, and in most prehistoric coastal assemblages.
Coastal archaeology in British Columbia has concentrated almost exclusively
on deep shell midden sites. Survey is often done from boats, and typically
only the coastline is investigated. This represents an extreme sampling
bias. If shell midden components primarily reflect shellfish harvesting,
then the absence of chipped stone tools from these contexts does not seem
surprising. Prehistoric land mammal hunting has been well-documented for
Prince Rupert Harbour, Namu and other coastal localities. Despite this
fact, the hinterland around these areas has been virtually ignored by
archaeological investigations. I suspect that the reasons for this are the
often impenetrable bush and the fact that sites away from the shoreline are
difficult to recognize. It may be that entirely different tool kits would
be found in these contexts, perhaps including high proportions of chipped
stone tools.

Turning to the interior of British Columbia, it is unclear which
prehistoric components pre-dating 3000 B.P. Allaire and Ames are referring
to as possible places of origin for the Skeena Complex. There are very few
sites with dates coeval with the Skeena Complex. Those that do exist--
Tezli (Donahue 1975, 1977), Punchaw Lake (Fladmark 1976)--have uncertain
relations to the Skeena Complex. For example, Fladmark (1976:28) recovered
six square-based lanceolate points from Punchaw Lake, but these are
described as small and poorly made, which is quite different from the
elongate, well-made Skeena Complex points. Moreover, the dating of the
Punchaw Lake Site is very uncertain; it is possible that any or all of
these points are no more than 500 years old.

More problematic is the apparent lack of consensus over what
constitutes a middle prehistoric (ca. 3500 B.P.) interior tool assemblage.

In his proposed prehistoric chronology of the north-central interior of British Columbia, Helmer (1977:95, 97) argued that the prehistoric period from 5000 to 2000 B.P. is characterized by fish-tail and leaf-shaped points, corner-notched points, and microblades. Only leaf-shaped points occur in abundance in the Skeena Complex at Gitaus (there is one fish-tail point); corner-notched points and microblades are not present.

Farther north in the southern Yukon and the Fisherman Lake area of the Northwest Territories, Taye Lake Phase sites (MacNeish 1964; Workman 1978) and Julian Complex sites (Fedirchuk 1970; Millar 1981; Morrison 1984) are the closest analogues to the Skeena Complex. Lanceolate points with square bases have been recovered from sites in both areas, but again these points are different in morphology from the Skeena Complex points. They tend to be quite wide in relation to their length and not truly parallel-sided (see Morrison 1984:45 for lanceolate points from the Julian Complex). Moreover, these northern assemblages also include notched points and burins, which are not found in the Skeena Complex.

Thus, while the Skeena Complex does share some elements with interior assemblages (emphasis on stone chipping, lanceolate points), there are many "interior" elements not present in the Skeena Complex (notched points, burins, microblades), and there are many "non-interior" elements included in the Skeena Complex (abraders, ground slate, ribbed stones).

Allaire (1979:47) concluded that the Skeena Complex was part of the Northern Archaic Tradition. This may ultimately prove correct, but the differences noted above are important. Perhaps more important is the most recent assessment of the validity of the Northern Archaic:

> ... traits often appear to be distributed
> in time and space essentially independent
> of one another. Patterns and associations
> can shift disconcertingly, so that maximal
> cultural syntheses often seem more arbitrary
> than elsewhere" (Morrison 1984:54).

It is difficult to accept the Skeena Complex as an aspect of the Northern Archaic Tradition when disagreement exists as to the nature or even the existence of the latter.

An alternative to the "population displacement" model proposed by Allaire and Ames is that the Skeena Complex represents a **seasonal** inland orientation toward riverine and forest exploitation within a larger annual settlement/subsistence system. At other times of the year, the same

123

population may have located near the mouth of the Skeena River (Prince Rupert Harbour) to exploit marine, terrestrial and foreshore resources, and perhaps to take advantage of the milder winter climate. This should not seem unusual. It was a pattern of settlement mobility practised by the historic Coast Tsimshian.

This alternative model is developed further in Chapter 7.

### Hagwilget Canyon

Hagwilget Canyon is located at the confluence of the Skeena and Bulkley Rivers near Hazelton B.C., roughly 100 km upriver from Kitselas Canyon.

The three cultural zones at GhSv 2 at Hagwilget Canyon cover a minimal time range from 3400 B.P. to the historic period. The earliest zone, A, is characterized by a predominance of chipped stone tools, including lanceolate points, leaf-shaped points and bifaces, preforms and formed unifaces. Chipped stone tools comprise roughly 50 percent of the Zone A assemblage, modified cobbles 23 percent, and groundstone implements including ground slate and abraders 16 percent. Allaire (1979:46) includes the assemblage from this zone in the Skeena Complex, and Ames (1979a:208) generally agrees, noting numerous similarities.

Cultural zone B probably reflects a period of decreased activity at GhSv 2. Two cores, an abrader, some rolled birch bark and scattered fire-cracked rock were recovered (Ames 1979a:207). Although radiocarbon dates are lacking for this zone, it appears to represent the middle and late prehistoric periods (roughly 3000 B.P. to the historic period). Ames (1979a:210) suggests sporadic use of the site as a fishing camp during this time.

Zone C, although undated, includes clay pipe fragments, gunflints and glass, and likely represents an historic Carrier occupation. Aboriginal implements include bone tools (18.7 percent of the assemblage) ground slate (12.5 percent), and cobble tools (6.3 percent). Chipped stone tools are not represented (Ames 1979a:212).

The single radiocarbon date (3430 ± 200 B.P., GSC 746) was assigned by Ames (1979a:208) to Zone A. This seems reasonable, based on the depth of the sample (1.7 metres). There is no apparent justification, however,

for Ames' (1979a:208) contention that this is a terminal date for Zone A.
There was no attempt to correlate the physical stratigraphy from
MacDonald's test unit to Ames' excavations, and it is not stated whether
MacDonald's sample was recovered at a depth that coincided with a change in
tool assemblage or stratigraphy that might reflect the end of Zone A.  At
best, it is only possible to assign the date to somewhere within Zone A.
It is further argued by Ames (1979a:208) that this date should be
considered in conjunction with the three dates from Zone VI at Gitaus, even
though those dates are 300 to 500 years earlier than the Hagwilget date.
This manipulation of radiocarbon dates appears to be aimed at an attempt to
establish contemporaneity between the end of Zone VI (beginning of the
Skeena Complex) at Gitaus and the end of Zone A at Hagwilget Canyon.  In
turn, this could be used to support a model of population migration from
Hagwilget Canyon to Kitselas Canyon about 3400 B.P.

If we accept the existing radiocarbon dates for Gitaus and GhSv 2 at
face value, it is equally plausible to argue that the Skeena Complex
existed contemporaneously at Kitselas Canyon and Hagwilget Canyon, some
time during the fourth millenium B.P.  Rather than inferring population
displacement on the basis of similar tool assemblages, it may be argued
that these assemblages simply represent similar seasonal adaptations to
similar environments.

Based on existing data, the Skeena Complex represents a
riverine-forest adaptation, emphasizing land mammal hunting and fishing,
centred on the Skeena River between Kitselas Canyon and Hagwilget Canyon.
Both components (Gitaus, GhSv 2) represent minimally summer-fall base camp
occupations.  This interpretation of seasonality is consistent with the
apparent emphasis on land mammal hunting and fishing, which are essentially
summer-fall activities.  At Gitaus, 58 faunal elements were assigned to
the Skeena Complex (Allaire 1978:297).  Of these, 41 were land mammal
elements, including marmot, fisher, beaver, caribou and black bear), and 16
were fish.  At GhSv 2, zone A, faunal material included an unspecified
amount of mammalian and fish remains.  This included a concentration of
mammal and fish bones in a storage pit at the bottom of zone A (Ames
1979a:203).

Of particular interest was the identification of sub-adult fisher

(<u>Martes pennanti</u>) elements at Gitaus, a strong indicator of late summer occupation (see H. Savage in Allaire 1978:157-58). Likewise, the presence of salmon bones in both components (Allaire 1978:297; Ames 1979a:206) is a further seasonal indicator of summer occupation. The interpretation of both components as base camps is based on the large and diversified tool assemblages recovered from each, and the presence of multiple hearth features in each component (Allaire 1979:37; Ames 1979a:213). Allaire (1979:37) states that numerous small post moulds in Zone III-lower at Gitaus indicate the use of drying racks. If so, this would be a further indication of site use during summer months. Alternatively, these post moulds may have been associated with crude summer dwellings. Either interpretation generally supports the summer base camp model.

The possibility of winter occupation of these sites at this time is less likely, but cannot be completely ruled out. There is no evidence of winter house pits at either site, or of large post moulds that might be associated with winter dwelling construction. This may reflect sampling error, although large post moulds were recorded in the upper zones at both sites. The Skeena Complex at Gitaus also lacks fire-cracked rock (which was abundant in the Kleanza Complex) and pit features. Again, the absence of these features does not deny the possibility of winter habitation.

### Summary

In this review of north coast prehistory, it has been argued that the early inhabitants of the area had a generalized economy, adapted to land and sea mammal hunting, and fishing. This generalized focus was maintained with the earliest settlement of Prince Rupert Harbour at 5000 B.P. (Period III), as seen at the Boardwalk and Co-op sites. By 3500 B.P. (Period II), shellfish procurement had become an important subsistence strategy, and sea mammal hunting was becoming increasingly important. In addition, the inhabitants of the coast were probably moving upriver seasonally, to hunt and fish for salmon. It is likely that maximum resource diversity and niche width were achieved on the lower Skeena at this time.

By 2500 B.P. (middle of Period II), there is evidence from the Boardwalk Site burials for social ranking at Prince Rupert Harbour.

At Kitselas Canyon, Allaire and Ames argued that the Skeena Complex

126

at Gitaus represented population displacement from the interior. Allaire (1979) further argued that the Kleanza Complex could be seen in terms of the "coastal acculturation" of the people of the Skeena Complex.

However, there is reason to doubt the "population displacement" argument for the Skeena Complex. Further, given the uncertain dating of the Kitselas Canyon and Hagwilget Canyon components, we cannot be sure that the Kleanza Complex and the Skeena Complex are contiguous. This casts doubt on the "acculturation" argument.

The following chapters (5 and 6) present and analyze new archaeological data from Kitselas Canyon. These data fill in the gaps in the existing chronological sequence, and provide the basis for a revised sequence. This sets the temporal framework for the investigation of change in social organization.

Chapter 5

## THE PAUL MASON SITE

### Introduction

This chapter presents archaeological data from the Paul Mason Site at Kitselas Canyon. The surface contours and sub-surface matrix of the site are described. Radiocarbon age estimates are given, and the lithic artifacts from the site are classified and described.

These data are used to expand the existing cultural sequence (see Chapter 7). They also provide the data base for the investigation of prehistoric social change (see Chapter 8).

### Site Description

The Paul Mason Site was named in honour of Paul Mason, a village elder of the Kitselas Band. There is no Tsimshian name for the site. Its existence was unknown to the members of the band until it was recorded during the course of archaeological survey in 1981 (Figure 5.1).

The site is situated in a heavily forested area on the upper terrace level on the east side of the canyon, 138 metres above sea level, and roughly 25 metres above the July (high) water level of the Skeena River. It is located at mid-canyon, and is sheltered from the main channel of the river by a small island directly in front of the site. At low water, this channel becomes dry, creating a long narrow back eddy. In late spring and early summer, water flowing on the near side of the island is notably less turbulent than in the main channel of the river.

The site measures roughly 175 metres long by 105 metres wide, oriented on a northwest by southeast axis.

The topography is rugged and uneven. Below the site, the canyon wall rises almost vertically from the river. A steep slope extends back from the canyon wall for a distance of 60 metres, with a vertical rise of 10 metres. At the base of the slope, near the north end, there is a deep gully or swale. This may be an ancient stream bed that was active at a time when the river was at this level. The slope ultimately yields to a relatively flat narrow terrace that extends the length of the site, and is 50 metres in width. Following Clague's (1984) model of glacial recession in the area, this terrace may have formed as a periglacial beach prior to

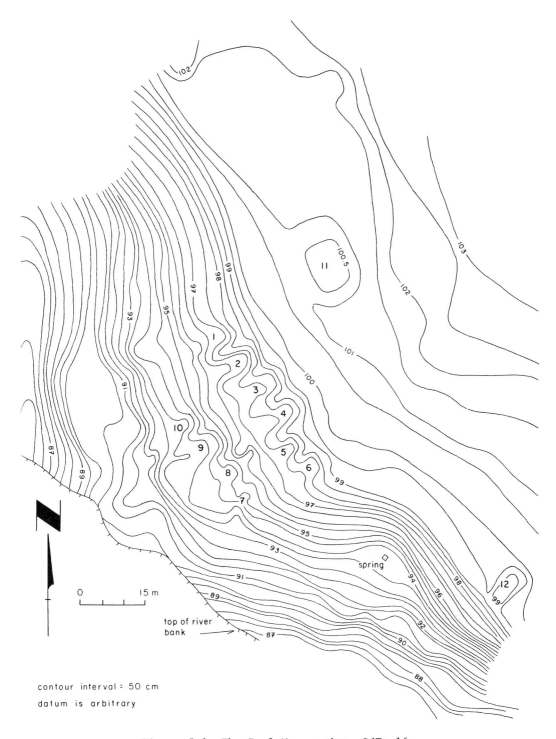

contour interval = 50 cm

datum is arbitrary

Figure 5.1  The Paul Mason site, GdTc 16.

129

8000 B.P. The site is rimmed by another steep slope extending back from the terrace. This slope extends in a curving arc from the north end of the site, along the eastern edge, and finally intersects the canyon wall at the southern end of the site.

The modern vegetation on the site is mixed. The slope rising from the canyon wall is characterized by mature growth of alder, hemlock, cottonwood, spruce and white birch. Generally, surface visibility is very good, although the upper terrace at the rear of the site includes a thick undergrowth of thimbleberry, ferns, devil's club, thistle and stinging nettles. A sparse growth of young alder, hemlock and white birch is also found here. The vegetation on this part of the site suggests disturbance of recent origin.

Cultural surface features at the Paul Mason Site include a series of prepared house floors, indicative of a small village occupation. These features are recognizable by their very distinct surface contours. In effect, the floors were "dug in" to the upper slope at the edge of the terrace to prepare a series of flat level surfaces. Earth-moving was deepest at the upslope end of the floors, while no excavation is apparent at the downslope end. The fill from these excavations was piled around the perimeter of the floors. Ten prepared floor features were identified (see Figure 5.1). Their orientation is generally consistent with the ethnographic village pattern for the Tsimshian area, and much of the Northwest Coast. Floors are oriented side by side, facing the river, each floor being separated from the next by a ridge of earth fill. The floors are arranged in two rows, one behind the other. The "back" row (floors highest on the slope and farthest from the river) includes six floors, and the "front" row (closest to the river) has four floors.

Other surface features at the Paul Mason Site include a small fresh water spring, lined at the surface with flat stone slabs. It measures about 1 x 1 metre, and is located on the slope, south of the prepared floor area (see Figure 5.1). A small area of the slope, about 5 x 5 metres, has been levelled around the spring. There are two other small levelled areas on the slope at the south end of the site, but it is unclear whether these were cultural or natural formations. Each measures about 5 x 5 metres· They may have been used as activity areas.

130

On the upper terrace level, two prepared floor features were identified. One (floor 11) is located about 20 metres northeast of the back row of floors (see Figure 5.1). This floor is larger than any other floor at the site. It is rectangular in shape and defined by a low earth ridge around the entire perimeter. The interior has been dug out to a depth of about 0.5 metres. The floor is oriented northwest/southeast and measures 12 x 10 metres.

The second floor (floor 12) is located at the extreme south end of the site, on the upper terrace level at the crest of the slope (see Figure 5.1). This floor is also defined by a low earth ridge around the entire perimeter. It is rectangular in shape, oriented northeast/southwest (facing the river), and the interior has been excavated to a depth of approximately 0.6 metres. This floor measures 8 x 5 metres. The location of this floor affords an excellent view downriver from the site.

Floors 11 and 12 are similar in that the earth ridges defining their perimeters are squared in relation to the floor--that is, little slumping or erosion of these ridges has occurred. By contrast, the earth ridges surrounding the floors on the lower slope are rounded as a result of erosion. The difference in extent of erosion suggests that the floors on the upper terrace are of more recent origin than the floors on the slope.

## Sampling Methodology

Binford (1964) and Struever (1971) were among the first archaeologists to emphasize the importance of devising a sampling strategy as a coherent and integrated part of an overall research design. The basic problem is to derive a sample that best reflects the population at large. They urged a strategy based on the principles of probability or random sampling as a means of satisfying the criteria of data adequacy and representativeness. This was primarily aimed at archaeological investigations of regional scope.

Sampling a deeply stratified site, however, often poses particular problems (see Brown 1975:155). One problem pertains to "site coverage". It is often logistically impossible to draw representative samples from the entire area of the site. Flannery (1976:68) cautions that it may even be unwise to try. To do so, usually involves the excavation of small randomly

131

placed units ("telephone booths"), and the data derived from these deep dark holes is usually uninformative, and can be misleading because of the lack of stratigraphic control.

Another problem is defining the extent of the population to be sampled. This can prove difficult if the population in question is a buried cultural horizon of unknown extent. How does one ensure that a representative sample is drawn? Typically, the population is arbitrarily defined because the archaeologist does not know the extent of the buried horizon.

If the site to be tested is deeply stratified, and only a few excavation blocks can be dug, it may be preferable to adopt a judgemental sampling strategy. Asch (1975:191) states that a non-probabilistic design is often useful "to investigate spatial structure" and "to select more representative, if biased, samples when only a few sampling units can be excavated".

The Paul Mason Site provided a good case for judgemental sampling. The primary aim of the research was to obtain archaeological data pertaining to prehistoric social organization. The presence of a series of prepared floor features, whose boundaries were well-defined, afforded the opportunity to collect archaeological data relating to the size and construction of dwellings, household size, and domestic organization.

Random sampling from a population of only 12 prepared floors would not likely increase the representativeness of the sample. Moreover, selective sampling would ensure the excavation of large, well-defined floors that did not have obstructions to excavation (such as large trees growing in the floor).

To determine the depth and spatial extent of the cultural deposit, soil cores were taken from around the site and five 1 x 1 metre test units were excavated. Three of these units were excavated within prepared floor areas on the slope (test units 1, 2, 3), one in a non-floor area of the slope (test unit 4), and one on the upper terrace (test unit 5) (see Figure 5.2). These tests revealed a deeply stratified cultural deposit on the slope, greater than 1.5 metres. By contrast, the cultural deposit on the upper terrace was thin and discontinuous.

It was decided that excavation should be concentrated on the slope.

132

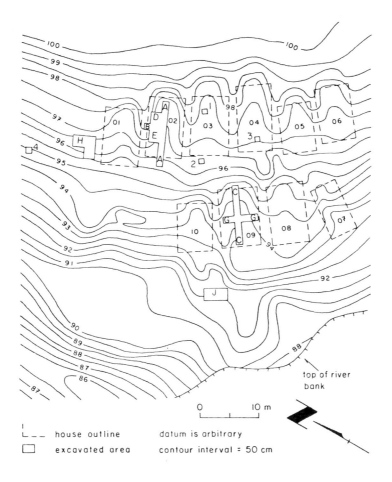

Figure 5.2   The Paul Mason site: house floors and excavations.

133

This decision was guided by two factors. First, the surface outlines of the ten house floor depressions on the slope indicated that this was the main residential area of the site. Secondly, the deepest cultural deposit was located here, which implies more intensive human activity, and perhaps a greater time range of occupation than the upper terrace. Thus excavation of the slope would yield data related to village life and domestic organization, and in addition, data related to earlier occupations of the site. This would allow for investigation of the evolution of village life at Kitselas Canyon in diachronic perspective.

Two prepared floors, 2 and 9 (see Figure 5.2) were selected for excavation. Both floors were excavated by means of a trench oriented along the long axis of the floor. In the excavation of floor 2, it was possible to extend units off the north side of the trench to reveal most of one side of the floor. In the excavation of floor 9, a crossing trench was excavated at roughly the mid-point of the floor. These were the major prepared floor excavations. The purpose of these excavations was two-fold. First, they were intended to provided data relating to domestic organization, including household size and internal household divisions. Secondly, they were intended to provide data related to dwelling construction technique.

Floor 12, the small floor on the upper terrace was also tested by means of a 3 x 1 metre transect.

A problem with the excavation of prepared floors, especially those that have undergone extensive earth-moving, is that the underlying cultural deposit has often been disturbed (see Wilmeth 1977; Fladmark 1982a:123). To control for disturbance, and to develop a reliable, complete cultural sequence for the site, it was necessary to conduct excavations away from areas of possible disturbance. Two areas (H and J), adjacent to the prepared floors were selected for excavation (Figure 5.2). Excavation H was located immediately north of the prepared floors. Excavation J was just west or "in front of" the prepared floors. These areas were selected for excavation because their proximity to the prepared floors indicated that they were probable midden areas, associated with the occupation of the floors. These excavations were expected to yield a relatively high frequency of artifacts from undisturbed cultural deposits.

The non-floor excavations were important for two reasons. First, they would yield an undisturbed stratigraphic record to control for disturbance that had taken place in the prepared floor areas. Second, they would provide data concerning spatial variability at the site.

Excavations were undertaken in block or trench areas, utilizing 1 x 1 metre units. All excavation was done by trowel, and all excavated material was screened through 6 mm mesh. Excavation followed natural soil layers whenever possible, and 10 cm levels within layers. A total of 64 square metres of the site was excavated.

## Stratigraphy at the Paul Mason Site

The range in depth of exacavations at the Paul Mason Site was from 0.60 to 2.13 metres. In the four main excavations, the cultural deposit was overlaid by the surface littermat. At the base of the littermat was a continuous discrete layer of charcoal and partially burned wood, 3 to 8 cm thick. A similar layer was encountered in most of the shovel tests conducted during the survey of the east side of the canyon. It probably represents a forest fire of the late 19th or early 20th century, as burning seems to have been intensive in some areas, and moderate to absent in other areas.

Underlying the littermat was a thin layer of humo-ferric podosol, representing post-occupational soil development at the site (see Figure 5.3). This horizon averaged 10 cm thick, and was encountered in each of the four main excavation areas. It was a light yellow-brown humus, typical of the non-cultural matrix in and around Kitselas Canyon (Valentine, Sprout, Baker and Lavkulich 1981:104).

The cultural deposit underlying the post-occupational horizon included two physical stratigraphic zones. The upper zone was a silty-sand matrix, dark brown in colour. It included intrusions of pure coarse sand, gravel, charcoal and ash. Fire-cracked rock was also abundant throughout the upper layers of this zone. The dark brown soil zone constituted most of the cultural deposit at the site, ranging in depth from 0.50 to 1.75 metres. It included numerous lenses and discontinuous layers. Most of the cultural material was recovered from this zone.

In the two house floor excavations this zone was "wedge-like" in

135

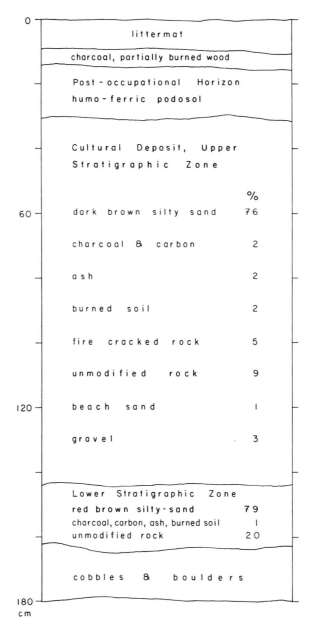

Percentages based on volume, derived from column samples
from Excavation H and Floor 2.
Proportions under 5% are estimates.

Figure 5.3   Schematic matrix profile of the Paul Mason site.

136

shape.  It was thickest near the west or downslope end of the floors, and
became progressively thinner toward the rear or upslope end (see Figure
5.4).  This was most apparent in Trench A of floor 2 (see Appendix I;
Figure I.1).  The wedge shape is a result of the levelling of the slope to
prepare the floors.  The most substantial amount of earth would have been
removed from the rear area of the floor, with little or no earth removed
from the front of the floor.  The fill resulting from this earth-moving was
then deposited around the perimeter of the floor forming ridges on either
side.  The cultural material, originally deposited in the lower levels of
the dark brown soil zone, may have been disturbed as a result of floor
preparation.  Disturbance was probably greatest toward the rear of the
floor.

The profile of Trench B of floor 2 (Appendix I; Figure I.2) shows
that in cross-section, the floor was probably formed in two levels.  A
lower level extended along the middle of the floor, and a raised bench
extended along either side.  This perspective is also shown in Figure 5.5,
a cross-sectional schematic of house floor transformation during the
construction, occupation and abandonment phases.  At the time of
construction, an earth ridge was formed as the central floor area was
levelled.  During occupation, debris probably accumulated on the ridge in
the narrow space between dwelling walls.  After abandonment, and the
collapse of the dwellings, this debris would have slumped down into the
central house floor areas.

Figures 5.6 and 5.7 are plan drawings taken at 70 cm below surface of
the excavated areas of floors 2 and 9, respectively.  These give some
indication of the internal organization of the dwellings.  Both dwellings
had two hearths, one located in the middle of the floor; the other near the
front or downslope end of the floor.  This suggests that the dwellings were
occupied by more than one family.  The positioning of one hearth near the
front of the dwelling may be related to a desire for heat in winter.

Lithic concentrations were located in the central areas of each
floor, identifying these areas as the main activity loci.  Figure 5.6 shows
that the lithic concentration in floor 2 stopped abruptly at the base of
the raised lateral bench on the north side.  This suggests use of the
benches as sleeping areas.

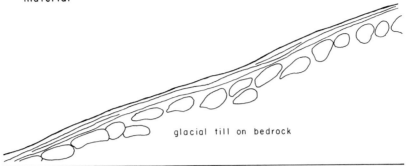

A - hill-slope prior to human occupation and deposition of cultural material

glacial till on bedrock

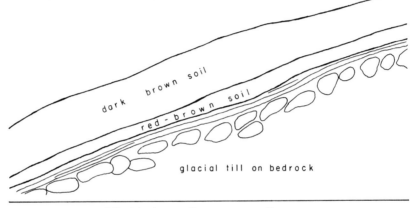

B - hill-slope after deposition of red-brown and dark brown soil zones, but prior to house floor preparation

dark brown soil

red-brown soil

glacial till on bedrock

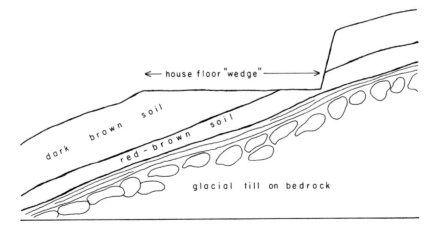

C - hill-slope modified by house floor preparation

← house floor "wedge" →

dark brown soil

red-brown soil

glacial till on bedrock

Figure 5.4  Schematic profile showing slope transformation during the occupation of the Paul Mason site.

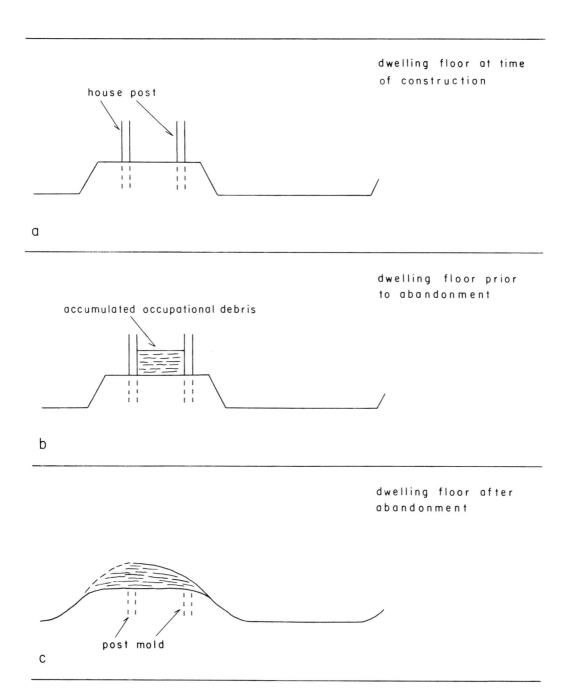

dwelling floor at time
of construction

house post

a

dwelling floor prior
to abandonment

accumulated occupational debris

b

dwelling floor after
abandonment

post mold

c

Figure 5.5  Cross-sectional schematic of house floor transformation.

139

contour interval = 50 cm

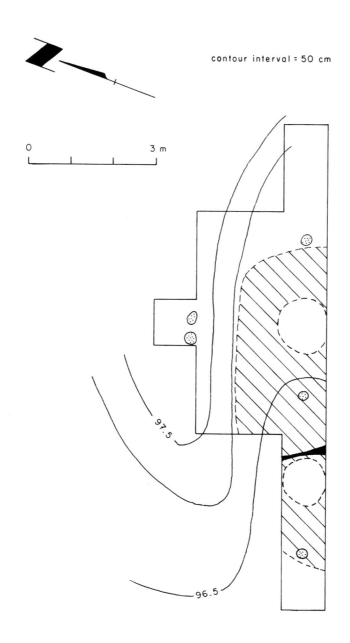

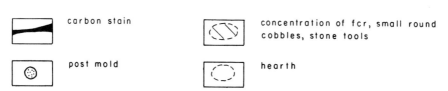

carbon stain

post mold

concentration of fcr, small round cobbles, stone tools

hearth

Figure 5.6  Plan of floor 2 (depth = 70 cm).

140

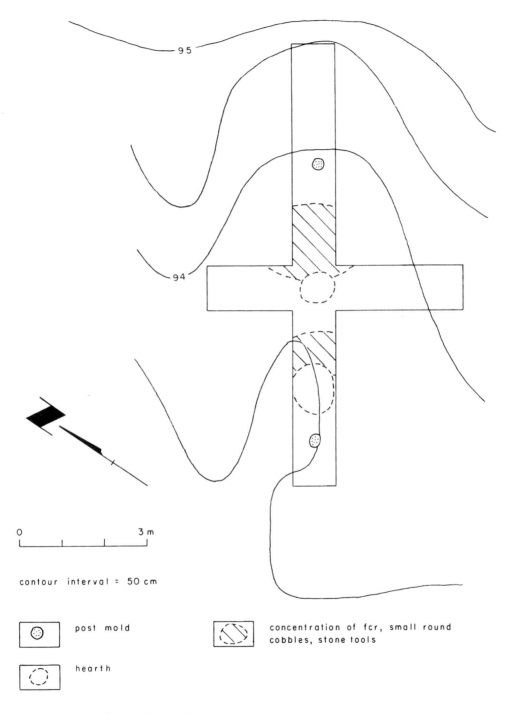

95

94

0          3 m

contour interval = 50 cm

post mold

hearth

concentration of fcr, small round
cobbles, stone tools

Figure 5.7  Plan of floor 9 (depth = 70 cm ).

141

Post moulds were located along the mid-line of both floors. This probably reflects the use of a central ridge pole in the construction of the dwellings. In addition, two large post moulds were identified near the crest of the ridge, flanking floor 2. These were probably external wall posts, although it is not known if they were used in conjunction with split planks.

The lower zone of the cultural deposit included a thin series of banded soil layers, oriented along a southwest slope, roughly following the general surface slope of this portion of the site. These layers were clearly different in colour and texture from the overlying dark brown zone. The colour range was from yellow-brown to red-brown, and the soil tended to be moister and stickier than the overlying zone. This zone ranged in thickness from 0.10 to 0.50 metres, and was encountered in the floor 2 excavation and Excavation H.

Underlying the cultural deposit in most units was a culturally sterile deposit of poorly sorted glacial till. This was a mixture of gravel-sized rocks and large boulders, most of which had been water-rounded. In some areas, most notably Excavation H, glacial till was not present. The cultural deposit rested directly on bedrock.

Detailed stratigraphic descriptions of the four main excavation areas, floor 12, and the test units are presented in Appendix I.

Soil samples were taken at 10 cm intervals, beginning at a depth of 0.30 metres below surface, and continuing to 1.70 metres below surface. Granulometric analysis of these samples indicates that the predominant soil grains in the cultural deposit are in the coarse to fine sand range (particle size 0.125 to 0.5 mm) (Figure 5.8). According to Shackley's (1975:53) four principle varieties of sand grains, the soils from the Paul Mason Site are "worn, rounded and glossy grains...this type of surface texture indicated the action of running water, and the characteristics are found on sand grains of marine or fluviatile deposits". Soil pH levels reveal strongly acidic soil, ranging from 4.6 to 4.9.

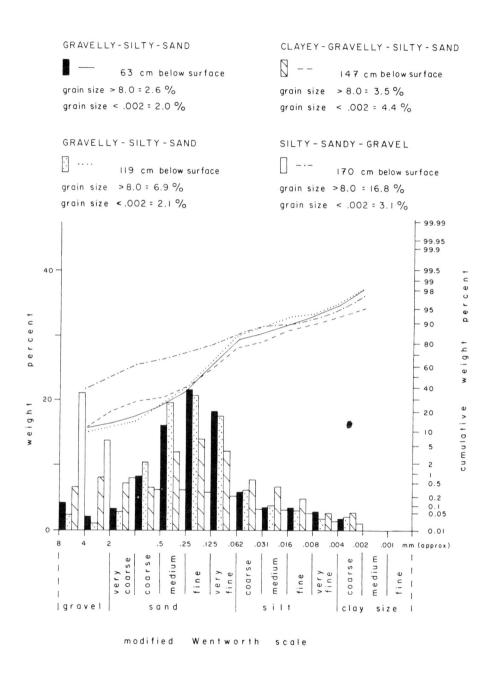

GRAVELLY-SILTY-SAND

■ ——————  63 cm below surface

grain size > 8.0 = 2.6 %

grain size < .002 = 2.0 %

CLAYEY-GRAVELLY-SILTY-SAND

▨ — —  147 cm below surface

grain size > 8.0 = 3.5 %

grain size < .002 = 4.4 %

GRAVELLY - SILTY - SAND

▢ · · · ·  119 cm below surface

grain size > 8.0 = 6.9 %

grain size < .002 = 2.1 %

SILTY - SANDY - GRAVEL

▢ — · —  170 cm below surface

grain size > 8.0 = 16.8 %

grain size < .002 = 3.1 %

Figure 5.8  Particle size of Paul Mason site soils.

143

<u>Dating</u>

There are 19 radiocarbon dates for the site (Table 5.1, Figure 5.9), ranging from 635 ± 100 B.P. to 5050 ± 140 B.P. A few of these estimates are problematic in terms of their stratigraphic position. This is not suprising, considering the amount of earth-moving that occurred during the occupation of the site. A few other dates seem quite recent, but again, there are plausible explanations for these. In general, however, these estimates present a coherent picture of the sequence of occupation of the site.

The earliest, 5050 ± 140 B.P. (SFU 259), was taken from the middle of the lower stratigraphic zone (red-brown zone) of Excavation H. A date of 4655 ± 130 (NMC 1293) from Excavation H marks the transition between the lower (red-brown) and upper (dark brown) zones. The date 4745 ± 195 (NMC 1292), is from the bottom of the dark brown zone in Trench G, unit 1. These estimates suggest that the time of transition from the red-brown zone to the dark brown zone was probably about 4700 B.P.

No radiocarbon sample was obtained from the lower stratigraphic zone in the excavation of floor 2 or Excavation J.

Of the remaining 16 dates, 13 fall into two major clusters. The earliest of these includes eight estimates ranging from 3780 ± 120 to 4395 ± 130 B.P. Using the single standard deviation values, these dates overlap between 4030 and 4185 B.P., and all eight are within a 365 year span (3900 to 4265 B.P.). Four of these samples were recovered from the excavation of floor 2; three from the excavation of floor 9; and one from Excavation H. Their stratigraphic positions are generally in good agreement. All but one were recovered from the middle or lower portions of the dark brown soil zone, with depths ranging from 0.9 to 1.4 metres below surface. The exception is the date 4395 ± 130 (NMC 1290). That sample was taken from the upper dark brown soil zone (Trench A, unit 5) at a depth of 0.6 metres below surface. The date seems too early for this depth. The sample comprised scattered pieces of charcoal from across the unit. Considering the amount of earth-moving that took place at the rear of the floor, it is possible that some, if not all, of this sample had been re-deposited during floor preparation.

Six of the above eight samples were recovered from depths of 0.9 to

1.4 metres below surface. This includes a date of 4280 ± 95; WSU 2923) taken from the hearth feature at the base of the upper dark brown layer in Excavation H, the ostensibly undisturbed cultural deposit. It will be recalled from Chapter 4 that the dates from the early component at Gitaus also clustered around 4000 B.P. This suggests a temporal overlap in the occupation of these sites.

The second cluster of radiocarbon estimates from the Paul Mason Site includes five dates ranging from 2750 ± 90 to 3230 ± 160 B.P. The samples were recovered from four different areas of the site; two from Excavation J, and one each from Excavation H, floor 9 and floor 5 (test unit 3). Each of these samples was recovered from the upper portion of the dark brown soil zone. Their range in depth below surface was from 0.45 to 0.9 metres. Using the single standard deviation values, these dates are within 230 years of each other, and three of the dates--3080 ± 85 (WSU 2921); 3130 ± 100 (SFU 132); 3230 ± 160 (SFU 133)--overlap between 3070 and 3165 B.P.

These dates appear to reflect a discrete occupation of the site. They are separated from the previous group of eight dates by 500 to 1000 years. The fact that two of the samples were recovered from prepared floor features, and all five were recovered from the upper portion of the dark brown soil zone suggests that these dates are associated with the occupation of the floors.

The three most recent dates were all taken from the top of the dark brown zone. The first two, 635 ± 100 (NMC 1291) and 890 ± 160 (SFU 135), were both taken from depths of 0.2 metres in floor 9 and floor 5, respectively. These dates seem inordinately late compared to the other dates for the site. Moreover, in the lithic assemblage from the Paul Mason Site (see following section), there are no artifact forms to indicate an intensive late prehistoric occupation of the site. One possible explanation for these dates is that the samples may have been contaminated by the surface layer of charcoal and partially burned wood. Both samples were recovered from just below this layer.

It is unlikely that the 1330 ± 90 (SFU 260) date was affected by contamination from surface charcoal. It was taken from the top of a cultural hearth feature, 0.3 metres below surface, sufficiently deep to reduce the possibility of contamination.

One possibility, which may be applicable to each of the three late dates, is that they represent periodic short-term re-use of the site. This possibility seems most likely for the 1330 ± 90 date. Because Kitselas Canyon is an important fishing location, in an area where fishing was critical to the late prehistoric aboriginal economy, it is not unlikely that the canyon was used intensively during the last 2000 years (although archaelological evidence of this has yet to be recovered). Thus, periodic re-use of a site that offered existing prepared floor features is a distinct possibility.

In summary, radiocarbon estimates from the Paul Mason Site indicate that the most intensive settlement of the site was from roughly 5000 to 2800 years ago, with numerous dates clustering at 4200 to 4000 B.P., and again at 3200 to 2800 B.P. Periodic short-term re-use of the site may have ensued throughout the late prehistoric period.

---

### Table 5.1
### Radiocarbon dates from the Paul Mason Site

| Laboratory No. | Date (uncorrected) | Unit | Layer | Depth (cm) |
|---|---|---|---|---|
| NMC 1291 | 635 ± 100 | C3 | C | 21 |
| SFU 135 | 890 ± 160 | TU3 | - | 26 |
| SFU 260 | 1330 ± 90 | C2 | E | 30 |
| WSU 2922 | 2750 ± 90 | J1 | E | 70 |
| WSU 2920 | 2840 ± 85 | J1 | D | 44 |
| WSU 2921 | 3080 ± 85 | H2 | D | 57 |
| SFU 132 | 3130 ± 100 | C4 | E | 78 |
| SFU 134 | 3230 ± 160 | TU3 | - | 65 |
| SFU 133 | 3780 ± 120 | C4 | F | 110 |
| SFU 255 | 4060 ± 120 | E2 | H | 95 |
| SFU 256 | 4130 ± 90 | A1 | H | 140 |
| SFU 257 | 4250 ± 100 | C8 | G | 114 |
| SFU 258 | 4270 ± 200 | C8 | F | 96 |
| WSU 2923 | 4280 ± 95 | H2 | D | 110 |
| SFU 261 | 4350 ± 320 | A7 | H | 98 |
| NMC 1290 | 4395 ± 130 | A5 | E | 58 |
| NMC 1293 | 4655 ± 130 | H3 | D | 103 |
| NMC 1292 | 4745 ± 195 | G1 | H/J | 102 |
| SFU 259 | 5050 ± 140 | H3 | G | 101 |

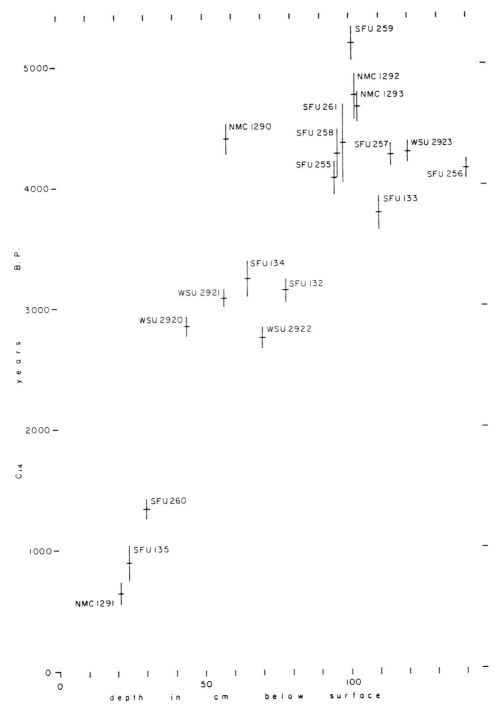

Figure 5.9 Radiocarbon dates from the Paul Mason site plotted against depth of sample.

## Artifact Descriptions

A total of 1194 artifacts was recovered during excavation at the Paul Mason Site. All are stone tools. Grinding and chipping were the principal means of stone tool manufacture. Extensive pecking was not in evidence. Chipping was most frequent on large, unformed cobbles and flakes. Formed, chipped bifaces and unifaces were also manufactured, but less frequently than the cobble-based implements.

Classification of stone tools was based on physical attributes, including size, shape, location and quality of retouch, edge angle, presence or absence of wear, and raw material.

With respect to size, some artifacts (cobble core tools, utilized flakes, spalls) were separated into large or small types on the basis of weight, length or a combination of the two (see Plate IV a-c).

Edge angle also refers to a bipartite quantitative division. Retouched, utilized edges were classified as "steep" if they exceeded $45^0$ (angles measured at 2 mm from the edge; see Pokotylo 1978:215) (Figure 5.10). "Acute" edge angles were less than $45^0$ (Figure 5.10). Implements with edge angles less than $45^0$ were probably used as knives or cutting tools, whereas edges greater than $45^0$ were best suited to skinning or hide-scraping, plant fibre shredding, and heavy wood or bone working (Semenov 1964; Wilmsen 1970; Gould 1971).

Two types of wear were distinguished: microflaking, in which edges were often undercut; and abrasive dulling, in which edges were smoothed and polished, often with parallel striations (Figure 5.11). Acute, polished edges with parallel striations are inferred as cutting edges. Steep edges with microflaking may reflect scraping, chopping, shredding or rasping activities.

Distinction was made with respect to quality of retouch. "Regular" retouch refers to numerous, small, evenly-spaced flake scars on the edge or face of the implement. "Irregular" retouch refers to a few large, unevenly-spaced flake scars, usually on the edge of the tool (Figure 5.12).

Classification was made independent of the component in which the artifacts were found, although this undoubtedly had an effect on the distribution of certain artifact types.

Three lithic categories--cobble and flake, ground stone, and chipped

148

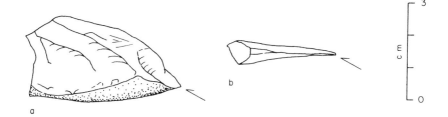

Figure 5.10   Implements with varying edge angles
a- implement with steep edge angle
b- implement with acute edge angle.

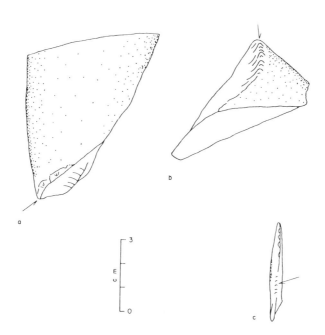

Figure 5.11   Implements showing different types of edge wear
a- battered, undercut edge
b, c- polished, smooth edge.

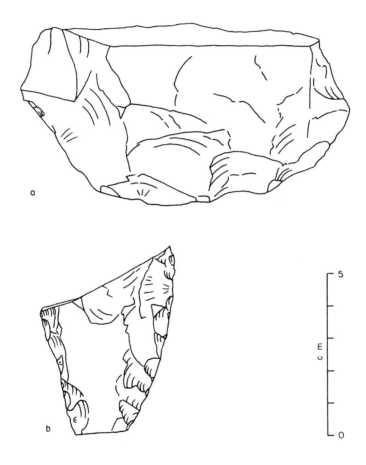

Figure 5.12   Implements with varying quality of edge retouch
a- implement with irregular edge retouch
b- implement with regular edge retouch.

150

stone--form the major classificatory divisions.  These are sub-divided into
19 artifact classes The artifact classes are divided into a number of
individual types (see Appendix II for artifact type descriptions).  Cobble
and flake tools are, by far, the most numerous in the assemblage; they are
described first, followed by groundstone tools, then chipped stone or
flaked tools.  Comparison to other established classifications, especially
Mitchell (1971), Matson (1976), Allaire (1978) and Lightfoot (1983), is
made where appropriate.

## Cobble and Flake Tools

Cobble implements and large, irregular flake tools based on cobble
cores consitute the largest portion of lithic artifacts recovered from the
Paul Mason Site (60.9 percent of all artifacts; N=718).  These are simply
manufactured implements, based on locally available lithic material
(primarily beach cobbles).  Classification of these implements on
morphological characteristics was often difficult. They generally show
evidence of only minimal reduction.  For example, core tools were formed,
in some cases, by the removal of only a few flakes.  In other cases, flake
tools were used with little or no edge retouch (although wear is present).

The question of tool function is also difficult to address, except in
a general sense.  Undoubtedly some implements served more than one purpose.
Although it is difficult to perceive such implements as "personal gear",
subject to curation, (Binford 1979, 1980), this does not mean that some
cobble tools could not have been extensively used.  For example, Ackerman
(1968:68) suggested a variety of uses for cobble implements from Groundhog
Bay 2, including tree bark removal and processing, chopping down saplings,
and girdling larger trees.

One of the best functional treatments of cobble and flake tools from
a Northwest Coast site is by Mitchell (1971).  He considered basic tool
attributes such as size and overall shape, edge angle, location and pattern
of wear, and raw material to determine probable function.  The kinds of
uses suggested by Mitchell (1971:102-08) for the various cobble and flake
tools from Montague Harbour include chopping, pulping and rasping for core
tools, and scraping or cutting for flake tools.  Core tools were generally
argued to be woodworking tools (see also Borden 1968; Ackerman 1968).

Ackerman (1968:68) has argued that choppers from level II at Groundhog Bay 2 were later functionally replaced by ground stone adzes. Although chopping tools were prolific at the Paul Mason Site, no ground adzes or celts were recovered.

### I-A Cobble Tools (N=360)

These implements, sub-divided into six types, are core tools, based on beach cobbles and pebbles. Most have received minimal reduction, and retain a large amount of original cortex.

The larger of these implements--cobble core tools, choppers, split cobble tools (Plate I, II, III) (see Appendix II)--were probably used as heavy woodworking tools (Borden 1968; Ackerman 1968). Most implements (N=330; 91.7 percent) have steep edge angles. Edge wear is invariably in the form of microflaking, with substantial undercutting suggesting heavy use.

These tools were based on locally available raw material, primarily argillite, sedimentary rock and basalt. Although reduction was unsystematic in terms of core preparation, there was a marked tendency for the sequential removal of flakes, beginning at one end or side of the cobble, using the cortex edge as a ready-made striking platform (Figure 5.13).

Cobble tools occur in great frequency at most north coast sites. The cobble tools from Gitaus (see Allaire 1978:135, 45, 294) are similar to those from the Paul Mason Site in reduction technique and raw material. Calvert (1968:39) reports only three "large unifacially flaked pebble tools" from the Co-op Site. Despite this paucity, Calvert (1968:39) states, "pebble tools are found in great numbers on the Prince Rupert beaches and have been excavated at all levels of Tsimshian sites". At Hagwilget Canyon, (GhSv 2) zone A, cobble tools were the most frequent tool type, comprising 23.0 percent of the assemblage. Lightfoot (1983:110-18) describes flaked cobbles from Component II at the Hidden Falls Site. Component II has radiocarbon dates in the 3200 B.P. range, which are consistent with the late cluster of dates at the Paul Mason Site. The cobble tools from Component II do not, however, compare favourably with the Paul Mason Site material. Angular fragments of rhyolite, andesite and tuff

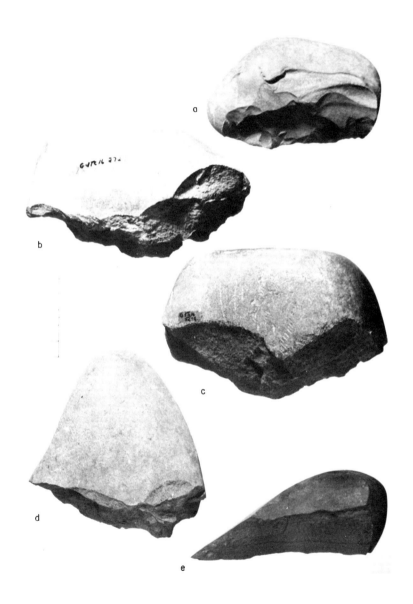

Plate I
a-d cobble core tools;  e pointed cobble implement

153

cm in

a

b

c

d

Plate II

a-d cobble choppers

154

Plate III

a-c split cobble tools;   d-f acute angle cobble tools

155

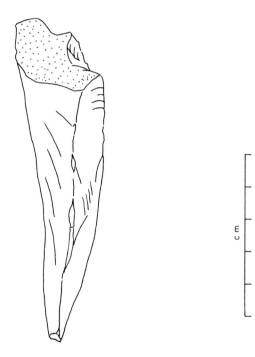

Figure 5.13   Modified cobble flake with platform cortex.

were used extensively at Hidden Falls; argillite and sedimentary rock were rarely used.

Cobble tools have considerable spatial and temporal range on the north coast. They occur less frequently in the Interior. Their high frequency at the Paul Mason Site in all levels (30.2 percent of the overall lithic assemblage) suggests a coastal affiliation.

### I-B Utilized Flakes (N=215)

This class includes flakes with evidence of wear, either in the form of abrasive dulling or micro-flaking (Plate IV). Although the distinction is often subtle and subjective, edge modification on these tools is argued to be the result of use, rather than retouch.

The implements are sub-divided into six types (see Appendix II) on the basis of extent and location of cortex, flake size and edge angle.

Included among these types are large and small utilized cortex spalls (Plate IV a-c; Figure 5.14). These implements have acute edge angles, and often have polished edges with parallel striations. Some Northwest Coast archaeologists (Hanson 1972; Allaire 1979) have argued that cortex spalls were used in the initial stages of fish processing.

Like cobble tools, the distribution of cortex spalls is widespread spatially and temporally on the Northwest Coast. At Gitaus and Prince Rupert Harbour, they occur in great frequency in all levels (Allaire 1978; MacDonald and Inglis 1981:46). They are reported from south coast sites, including Montague Harbour I (Mitchell 1971:102) and Glenrose (Matson 1976:133). They are also reported from numerous interior sites in British Columbia.

The vast majority of the utilized flakes, including cortex spalls, from the Paul Mason Site (178; 82.9 percent) have acute edge angles, which suggests that they were used as cutting tools.

A wide variety of raw materials were used, but sedimentary rock (N=59) and argillite (N=86) were the most common.

### I-C Retouched Cobble Flakes (N=52)

These large flake implements, based on river cobbles, are sub-divided into three types. Two pertain to retouched spalls (Plate V a-d). Following

157

Plate IV

a-b large utilized spalls;  c small spalls;  d-e acute angle utilized
flakes;  f-g steep angle utilized flakes

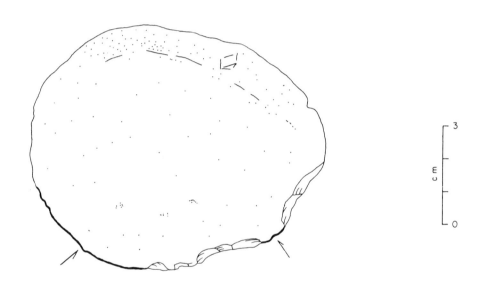

Figure 5.14  Utilized spall with smooth edge.

Plate V

a-b steep angle retouch spalls;  c-d acute angle retouch spalls;
e-h retouched cobble flakes;  i-j cortex-based cores

Matson (1976:135), these implements are sub-divided according to edge angle - steep or acute. It is likely that steep angle retouch cortex spalls were used as scraping tools. Acute angle retouched spalls were probably used as cutting implements. Allaire (1978:147) defines a class of retouched cortex spalls from Gitaus--*ecailles entieres a retouche corticale*--but they are not sub-divided by edge angle. The third type is large retouched flakes from unprepared cobble cores (Plate V e; Figure 5.13). These are consistent with *ecailles de galets* or *grande ecailles de galets* from Gitaus (Allaire 1978:145-51), and with "large utilized flakes" from Glenrose (Matson 1976:133).

These implements are generally larger and more simply manufactured than the retouched flakes of the chipped stone category.

The raw materials are sedimentary rock (N=24), argillite (N=21), basalt (N=4), slate (N=2), and sandstone (N=1).

## I-D  Cobble Cores  (N=42)

The implements in this class are cores based on river cobbles. There is no indication that these implements were used as tools, although that possibility cannot be totally discounted. The implements are sub-divided into three types based on extent of reduction and orientation of the core for flake removal (see Appendix II). Two types are consistent with the "unformed cores" and "cortex-backed cores" (Plate V i-j) defined by Matson (1976:131) at Glenrose. The third type includes minimally reduced cobbles (see Matson 1976:142). At Gitaus, Allaire (1978:151) identified only one type of cobble core - *nuclei informes*.

Raw materials include sedimentary rock (N=23), argillite (N=16), and basalt (N=3).

## I-E  Hammerstones  (N=59)

These are unformed cobbles, modified by battering or crushing, usually at one end. In four cases, a large flake or fragment was removed, as a result of hammering. The size of these implements ranged along a continuous gradient; there were no obvious break points for distinguishing types on the basis of size.

Locally available raw materials were used, including sedimentary rock

161

(N=43), argillite (N=14), and igneous rock (N=2).

## II  Groundstone Tools

Stone grinding was essentially a coastal industry, and one of
substantial antiquity.  In the Gulf of Alaska, Clark (1968) has documented
the existence of a ground slate industry as early as 6000 B.P.  Stone
grinding was not well developed in the interior.  Groundstone implements
constitute 15.5 percent (N=180) of the total lithic assemblage.

At the Paul Mason Site, there is evidence of a complete stone
grinding industry, including all stages of manufacture.  Stone saws were
recovered, as well as sawn and snapped fragments of metamorphic and
microcrystalline rock.  Shaped and unshaped abraders were recovered
throughout the deposit.  Formed groundstone implements, including
projectile points, drills, "pencils" and single-edged knives, were also
recovered, although these were rare.

The presence of numerous abraders and rare groundstone implements
indicates that something in addition to stone was ground at the site.  The
most probable candidates are bone, antler and wood, all organic materials
not likely to survive in the highly acidic, non-shell matrix.

The general groundstone classes are based on probable function (saws,
abraders, etc.), raw material (slate, green schist, sedimentary, etc), and
general morphological characteristics (form, location and extent of
grinding).

### II-A  Saws and Sawn Fragments  (N=14)

This class includes all implements related to stone sawing, one of
the initial steps in the manufacture of groundstone tools (Plate VI a-d).

Stone sawing has been described by Clark (1979:170) in the context of
the Ocean Bay sites where there is evidence of stone sawing and ground
slate manufacture at 6000 B.P.  Clark states that thin, often unretouched
boulder flakes were used as saws.  They were recognized by smooth,
longitudinally striated edges (Figure 5.15).  Tablets were typically sawn
one third to one half way through, "and then snapped through the remaining
septum" (Clark 1979:170).

At Gitaus, Allaire (1978:130, 132) identified two stone saws and ten

Plate VI

a-b stone saws;  c-d sawn fragments;  e-f finished ground slate;
h-i thin ground slate fragments

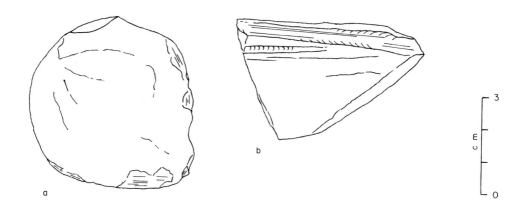

Figure 5.15 Saw and sawn fragment.

sawn fragments. Stone saws from the Paul Mason Site were manufactured from sedimentary rock, argillite and green schist.

## II-B Ornamental/Decorative Objects (N=14)

A variety of ornamental and decorative items were recovered from the Paul Mason Site (see Plate VII). These include five polished, spherical stones (Plate VII a-e), a slate disc bead (Plate VII f), polished fragments of mica and serpentine (Plate VII g-h), and a bird effigy (Plate VII j). One of the incised tablets is a ribbed stone (Plate VII k). In the Tsimshian area, ribbed stones were manufactured as early as 3500 B.P., and became common between 3000 and 2500 B.P.

In addition to formed ornaments and items of personal adornment, 19 small, unmodified fragments of ochre (red and yellow) and 9 small nodules of graphite were recovered. These materials were probably cut and ground, and used as pigments.

## II-C Pointed Groundstone Tools (N=22)

Ground, pointed tools from the Paul Mason Site are sub-divided into five types based primarily on form and raw material. One type--"ground slate points"--includes implements that were well-made (Plate VIII a-g). In general, however, other tools were poorly manufactured. Grinding was minimal and the implements appear unfinished. Often, poor quality raw material such as green schist or sedimentary rock was used, instead of high quality slate.

Groundstone points are common from most north coast sites. The finished or nearly finished slate points from the Paul Mason Site (N=7) closely resemble those from Prince Rupert Harbour (see MacDonald and Inglis 1981:46; Calvert 1968:36). They are typically thin and hexagonal in cross-section; the edges are bifacially bevelled (Figure 5.16). In contrast, ground slate points from the Hidden Falls Site (Lightfoot 1983:70) appear thicker and more lanceolate than the Paul Mason Site points. Many have stemmed or tapering bases, attributes not in evidence at the Paul Mason Site.

The ground schist points from the Paul Mason Site (Plate VIII k-m) (N=10) are interesting for two reasons. Allaire (1978:122) reports two

165

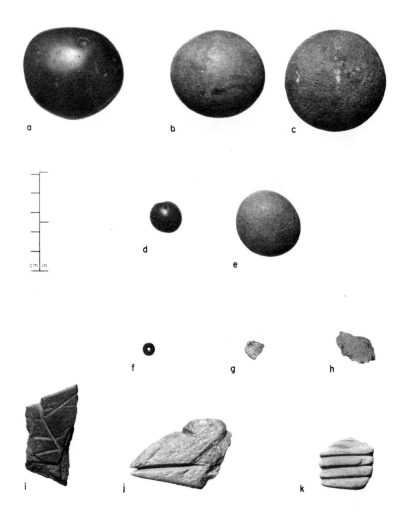

Plate VII

a-b spherical polished hematite;  c-e spherical stones;  f slate disc bead;
g mica fragment; h highly polished fragment;  i incised tablet;  j bird
effigy;  k ribbed stone

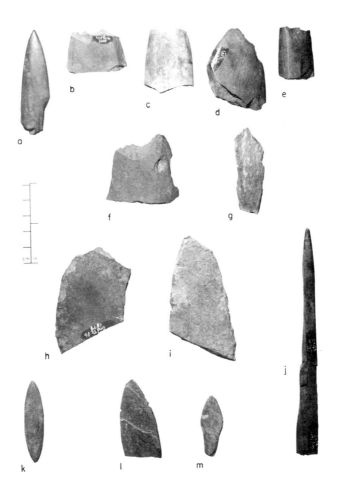

Plate VIII

a-g ground slate points;   h-i ground and chipped bifaces;   j groundstone
drill;   k-m pointed ground schist implements

167

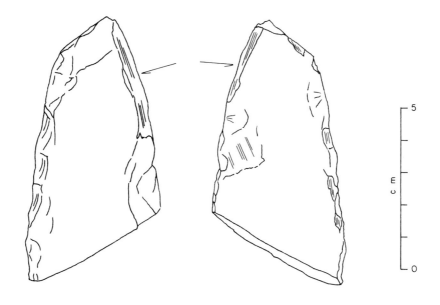

Figure 5.16   Implement with ground bifacially bevelled edge.

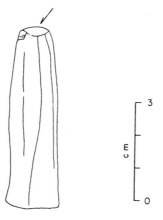

Figure 5.17   "Pencil" showing blunted end.

schist points from Gitaus, but otherwise schist is rarely used in the manufacture of ground stone points on the Northwest Coast. It is possible that schist was more readily available than slate at Kitselas Canyon, or that schist was simply preferred over slate by the inhabitants of the canyon because it was easier to grind. Secondly, the schist points at the Paul Mason Site have squared lateral edges, rather than sharp, bevelled edges. They do not resemble groundstone points from other Northwest Coast assemblages.

### II-D  Blunted Groundstone Implements  (N=20)

The implements in this class are long and flat or rod-like. They have been ground to form a rounded or blunted tip at one end. The grinding is continuous on to the proximal ends of the implements, so it is apparent that the blunt tips were formed in manufacture, not derived through use. These implements are subdivided into three types. Two types include long, thick, poorly manufactured implements (Plate IX g-q). The third type includes facetted "pencils" (Plate IX a-f; Figure 5.17), which are common in Period II components at Prince Rupert Harbour (MacDonald and Inglis 1981:45; Calvert 1968:36). These are finished rod-like implements. Drucker (1943:57), who first defined pencils, indicated that those from Prince Rupert Harbour had either pointed or blunt tips. All pencils from the Paul Mason Site (N=5) have blunt tips. They may have been used as stone awls.

Slate (N=7) and green schist (N=6) were the most commonly used raw materials. Sedimentary rock (N=5) and argillite (N=2) are also present.

### II-E  Miscellaneous Groundstone  (N=30)

A number of small fragments and broken or unfinished groundstone implements were recovered. They are grouped into seven types based on raw material, and on existing morphological characteristics, such as edge angle. Five probable fragments of thin slate cutting implements were recovered (Plate VI h-l). In other cases, miscellaneous grinding and/or wear was present, but functional classifications could not be made.

169

Plate IX

a-f pencils;  g-q other blunt groundstone implements

170

## II-F  Finished Ground Slate  (N=3)

These are tabular, rectangular pieces of well-made ground slate
implements.  Unlike the implements in the previous class these are large
fragments (almost complete) that give some indication of the general shape
of the implement.

One implement is trapezoidal, thin, and extensively ground on both
faces (Plate VI e).  One face is slightly concave in cross-section; the
other face is slightly convex.  Both lateral edges and one end are ground
flat (the other end is broken).  The implement may be a shaped slate
abrader.  Tabular, shaped slate abraders are reported from Component II at
Hidden Falls (Lightfoot 1983:52).

The other two fragments are smaller and less distinctive of overall
shape (Plate VI f-g).  Both resemble the implement described above in that
they have evidence of extensive bifacial grinding, and two edges
intersecting at right angles that are also ground flat.

## II-G  Unshaped Abraders  (N=43)

Flat abrasive stones are divided into two classes: unshaped and
shaped.  Unshaped abraders show no evidence of forming or shaping at the
edge.  The only shaping of these implements resulted from use, in the form
of abrasion on one or two surfaces.  They are subdivided into eight types
according to size, shape and location of abrasion (Plate X g-h).

As stated earlier, at the Paul Mason Site, abraders were probably
used to manufacture groundstone implements such as points and pencils, and
also to manufacture implements of bone, wood and antler.  In three cases,
pigment stains were visible, indicating that abraders were also used to
grind or crush these materials.

## II-H  Shaped Abraders  (N=34)

Shaped abraders have abrasion on one or both faces, and are
distinguished from unshaped abraders in that the edges are formed, usually
by squaring the edge to the abrading surface, and grinding the edge flat.
They are divided here into four types (Plate X a-f).

Shaped and unshaped abraders have wide spatial and temporal
distributions on the Northwest Coast.  They are present throughout the

Plate X

a-c trapezoidal abraders;   d-e edge rounded abraders;   f re-worked
unifacial abrader;   g-h unshaped abraders

Prince Rupert Harbour sequence, apparently with little change in frequency through time (see MacDonald and Inglis 1981:46). At Gitaus, abraders occur in highest proportions in the early and late complexes, but they are also present in the Skeena Complex. Shaped abraders are most abundant in the Kleanza Complex (see Allaire 1979:45, 1978:300), with ovoid, rectangular and trapezoidal forms present.

Farther south, Mitchell (1971:167) describes shaped and irregular abraders from Montague Harbour, where they occur throughout the sequence.

## II-I  Grinding Stones (N=5)

These implements have been used extensively as grinding tools; each has a concavity on one face. The surfaces of the abraders described above are flat to slightly convex. Two implements in this class are bar-shaped, and have a deep linear concavity extending the length of one face (Plate XI a-c). These implements may have been whetstones, used to sharpen the edges of bone or stone cutting implements.

The other three implements are flat discoid river cobbles of coarse crystalline material (Plate XI d-f). Each has a unifacial, shallow circular depression, with evidence of grinding and pecking. These may be milling stones. Matson (1976:155) reports a probable milling stone from the St Mungo Component of the Glenrose Site, and Mitchell (1971:125) describes two "round abrasive stones" with shallow depressions from Montague Harbour I that are similar to the Paul Mason Site implements.

Farther north, Allaire (1978:131) describes four possible milling stones (fragments a depressions) from the Kleanza Complex at Gitaus.

Raw materials include sedimentary rock (N=1), argillite (N=2), and sandstone (N=2).

## III  Chipped Stone Tools

Chipped stone tools from prepared cores were present at the Paul Mason Site, but like the groundstone tools, the technology was poorly developed. Chipped stone tools constitute 23.6 percent (N=281) of the total lithic assemblage.

Some features of the chipped stone tools that distinguish them from cobble and flake tools include the fact that chipped stone tools tend to be

173

Plate XI

grinding stones

174

small and well-formed (with the exception of retouched flakes). Many implements were manufactured from obsidian. Other lithic materials used rarely in the cobble and flake category include chert, chalcedony and vitreous basalt. Argillite and other sedimentary rock, which were used frequently in the manufacture of cobble and flake tools were also used in the manufacture of chipped stone tools.

The chipped stone category is divided into five classes: formed bifaces, formed unifaces, retouched flakes, chipped cores, and microblades.

The lack of development of good quality stone chipping at the Paul Mason Site is fairly typical of most recorded north coast sites. MacDonald (1969) and MacDonald and Inglis (1981) indicate that scrapers, chipped bifaces and chipped projectile points were present in the Prince Rupert Harbour components, but occurred infrequently, especially during the early and late prehistoric periods. The same is generally true of the Queen Charlotte Island sites (see Fladmark 1970, 1971; Severs 1974), and sites in the Tlingit area (de Laguna et al. 1964; Ackerman 1968, Lightfoot 1983). At many of these sites, stone chipping is limited to flakes, cores and angular fragments, with no formed implements present. In most cases, bone implements greatly outnumber chipped stone implements, and it seems likely that pointed bone tools or groundstone functionally replaced pointed chipped stone tools in many activities. As previously noted, there is strong circumstantial evidence in the presence of the varied and numerous abraders to indicate the presence of a developed bone tool industry at the Paul Mason Site. This may partially explain the paucity of formed bifaces and the virtual absence of chipped stone projectile points.

III-A  **Formed Bifaces**  (N=33)

These implements are sub-divided into six types, based on general form, extent of reduction and edge angle. They all show some evidence of being "formed" by bifacial flaking around the periphery of the implement.

Only one projectile point is included here. This is a small, probable dart point, manufactured from obsidian (Plate XII e). It was recovered from the lower dark brown soil zone.

The remainder of the implements show great variability in form and quality of manufacture. Many are irregular and thick, with a circular to

175

Plate XII

a-i chipped bifaces;  j biface edge fragment;  k-m unilateral "backed"
bifaces

oval outline. Of the regular or well-made implements, four are complete, leaf-shaped bifaces, manufactured from argillite and basalt (Plate XII b-c, f). They have regular bifacial flaking around the entire periphery.

Leaf-shaped bifaces are common from interior sites, less so from north coast sites. The regular, leaf-shaped bifaces from the Paul Mason Site are generally consistent in form, size and manufacturing technique with those from Prince Rupert Harbour (see MacDonald and Inglis 1981:48) and from Gitaus (Allaire 1979: Plate 4a, Plate 5a). They are distinct, however, from the lanceolate points from these two localities. The lanceolate points from Gitaus and Prince Rupert Harbour are long, narrow and parallel-sided, often with square bases. In contrast, leaf-shaped implements from these two areas, and from the Paul Mason Site, are not parallel-sided, and usually have round bases.

A variety of raw materials were used in biface manufacture. The most common were obsidian (N=8), argillite (N=9), sedimentary rock (N=5) and basalt (N=5).

### III-B  Formed Unifaces  (N=13)

Formed unifaces include implements with retouch covering most or all of one face, reflecting an attempt to shape the implement. They are divided here into three types including two types of steep angled formed unifaces (Plate XIII a-c, f), and perforating implements (Plate XIII d-e). Steep angled formed unifaces were initially defined by Sanger (1970:76), and later, by Pokotylo (1978:220). The retouched margins of these implements have edge angles greater than 45°, implying a scraping function. Three scraper re-sharpening flakes (see Frison 1968; Shafer 1971) were recovered (Plate XIII f; Figure 5.18). These are the dulled, retouched edges of steep angled formed unifaces. Each was made from obsidian, which suggests that formed obsidian implements were maintained and curated more than implements based on other types of raw materials.

Steep-angled formed unifaces of obsidian and chert occur frequently in all levels at Prince Rupert Harbour and Gitaus.

177

Plate XIII

a-c formed unifaces;  d-e perforators;  f scraper re-sharpening flake;
g denticulated retouch flake;  h-m regular steep retouch flakes;
n-p irregular steep retouched flakes;  q-s regular acute retouched flakes;
t-u irregular acute retouched flakes;  v-w regular bifacial retouched
flakes;  x-y irregualr bifacial retouch flakes

Figure 5.18    Scraper retouch flake.

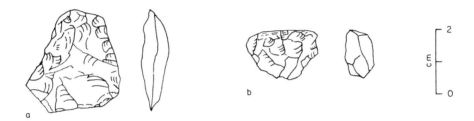

Figure 5.19    Pièces esquillées (a) and bipolar core (b).

Figure 5.20    Microblades and microcore rejuvenation flakes.

### III-C Retouched Flakes (N=77)

A variety of types of retouched flakes was recovered from the Paul Mason Site (Plate XIII g-y). This class is distinguished from "modified cobble flakes" primarily on the basis of size (smaller), absence of original cortex, and quality of retouch (better). They show no evidence of forming.

Retouched flakes are sub-divided into seven types based on edge angle, bifacial or unifacial retouch, and quality and nature of retouch. This breakdown follows Matson (1976).

There was a greater preference for steep unifacial retouch (N=49) (Plate XIII h-p) than for acute angle retouch (N=28) ((Plate XIII q-u), which suggests that the majority of these implements were used as scraping tools. Bifacial retouch was rare (N=6) (Plate XIII v-y). This is consistent with Gitaus, where Allaire (1978:114-16) reports 121 retouched flakes, of which only six were bifacially retouched.

Three denticulated retouched flakes were recovered (Plate XIII g). Denticulated retouched flakes are not reported from other lower Skeena sites. Farther south, Matson (1976:122) reports denticulated flakes from the Glenrose Site.

A wide variety of raw materials was used. The most common are obsidian (N=28), chert (N=18), argillite (N=10), and basalt (N=7). Only four of the chert flakes are green chert. This is in contrast to Gitaus where 57.8 percent of chipped stone tools (N=41) in the early Skeena Complex were manufactured from green chert (see Allaire 1978:287). That proportion decreased to 14.5 percent (N=7) in the Kleanza Complex. The high proportion of green chert in the Skeena Complex is associated with the increased manufacture of chipped stone tools in this component. It occurs rarely at the Paul Mason Site, where stone chipping was poorly developed. It also occurs infrequently in the early component at Gitaus (14.3 percent; N=3), where again cobble tools and groundstone tools predominate.

### III-D Chipped Cores and Pieces Esquillées (N=41)

Two stone flaking techniques are represented at the Paul Mason Site-- direct, freehand percussion, and bipolar flaking. Direct, freehand percussion was used for most tools in the chipped stone category, and all tools in the cobble and flake category. In this class, chipped cores were all reduced by freehand percussion (Plate XIV j-l). This technique was used on all raw materials represented at the site. This is consistent with most north coast sites (see Lightfoot 1983:98).

Bipolar flaking is represented in this artifact class in two types: bipolar cores (Plate XIV m-n) and pièces esquillées (Plate XIV a-i). In this technique, the implement is held against an anvil, and then struck with a hammerstone. Force is applied simultaneously to both ends. This technique tends to shatter the implement, and is less controlled than freehand percussion.

The distinction between bipolar cores and pièces esquillées made here follows that made recently by Hayden (1980:2-3), who states that pièces esquillées were tools usually produced on thin flakes (see Figure 5.19). This is contrary to MacDonald (1968), who introduced the term to North America. MacDonald (1968:85-89) argued that pièces esquillées from Debert were core tools, often thick in cross-section, with evidence of bipolar flaking. Both authors agree, however, that pièces esquillées are tools. Hayden (1980:3) also states that pièces esquillées lack primary flake removals (for micro-tool use), lack flake scars that extend the length of the tool, and often show evidence of the ventral flake scar of the original flake. In contrast, bipolar cores are true cores, sometimes thick, with no evidence of a ventral scar. They show evidence of primary flake removals extending the length of the core.

The bipolar technique is evident on a variety of raw materials at the Paul Mason Site, including obsidian (N=5), argillite (N=7), sedimentary rock (N=4), quartz crystal (N=3), basalt (N=2), and chert (N=1). This is in contrast to Hidden Falls II, where Lightfoot (1983:98) reports that the bipolar technique was used almost exclusively on chalcedony.

### III-E Microcores and Microblades (N=118)

Although no complete microcore was recovered from the Paul Mason Site, two definite fragments or rejuvenation flakes were recovered. One is made of obsidian (Plate XV a'; Figure 5.20d). It is a mid-section fragment of the fluted surface of the core. There are five parallel blade scars present, each 7 to 8 mm wide.

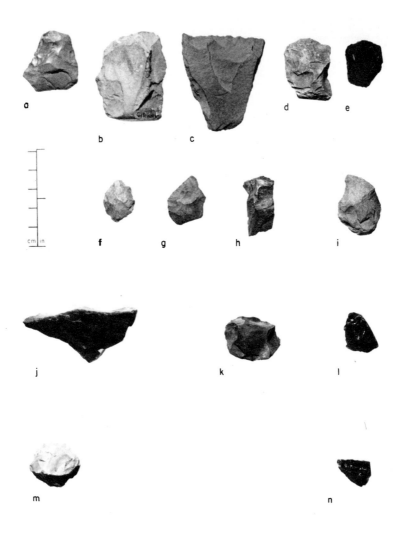

Plate XIV

a-i pìecès esquillées;   j-l chipped cores;   m-n bipolar cores

182

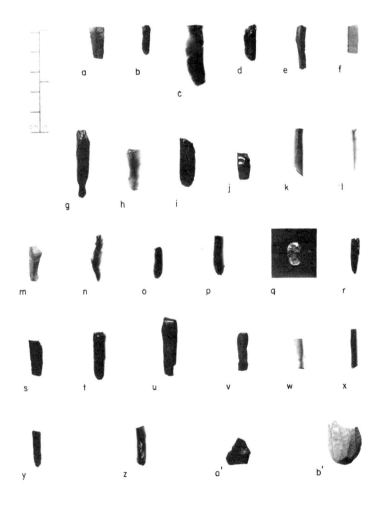

Plate XV

a-z microblades; a'-b' rejuvenation flakes

The other is chert (Plate XV b'; Figure 5.20c). It is a relatively thin flake from the fluted surface of the core. The flake appears to have been removed by a force applied to the base of the core, perhaps in an effort to rectify the platform striking angle. There are four parallel blade scars present on the flake.

Unfortunately, it is impossible to reconstruct the shape of the cores from the existing fragments. Matson (1976:126) states that the cylindrical microcore form is common along the coast, at least in the Gulf of Georgia region (see also Mitchell 1968), whereas the keeled form is more common in the interior.

A total of 116 microblades was recovered. These are blade implements, with length greater than or equal to two times the width (Plate XV a-z; Figure 5.20). They are either triangular or trapezoidal in cross-section. Edge retouch was present on only four microblades, but 57 had evidence of use, in the form of microflaking or polish. Where present, retouch and use wear were restricted to the lateral edges of the implement. This may be related to side hafting or direct use on some material. In either case, a cutting function is indicated. Two blades show evidence of nicking and tiny flake scars along one edge, while the other edge is rounded or polished, perhaps as a result of rubbing or abrasion in a haft. There is no evidence of end wear or retouch that might result from use as points.

Sixteen complete microblades were recovered. Undoubtedly many microblades were broken accidentally, before, during or after use. However, in light of the preponderance of lateral edge wear, it is also likely that many blades were purposely broken to create relatively short straight sections, that could be readily hafted.

Obsidian was used overwhelmingly in the manufacture of microblades (N=106; 91.4 percent). Chert (N=8) and quartz crystal (N=2) were also used. As stated previously, there is no local obsidian source in the Kitselas Canyon area. To determine the source of the obsidian, two microblades and three unretouched obsidian flakes were submitted for X-ray flourescence analysis by D. Godfrey-Smith of Simon Fraser University (Godfrey-Smith 1984). The results (Figure 5.21; Table 5.2) show that the microblades were made of obsidian from the Anahim area in the south-central

184

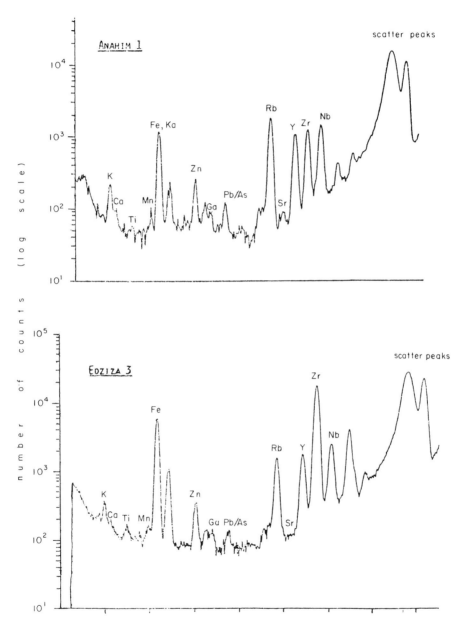

Figure 5.21  Element spectre for Anahim I and Mt Edziza III obsidian
source: Godfrey-Smith 1984.

185

## Table 5.2
## Element Peaks for Five Obsidian Samples from the Paul Mason Site

Obsidian Sample

| Element | 2872* | 7161 | 6941 | 8297 | 9493 |
|---------|-------|------|------|------|------|
| K | 0.77 | 6.84 | 5.72 | 0.99 | 0.85 |
| Ca | - | - | - | - | - |
| Ti | 0.22 | + | 0.29 | 0.26 | 0.21 |
| Mn | 0.06 | 2.30 | 2.59 | 0.17 | 0.03 |
| Fe | 33.93 | 108.92 | 102.51 | 33.61 | 34.13 |
| Zn | 1.62 | 15.60 | 16.18 | 1.74 | 1.77 |
| Ga | - | - | - | - | - |
| Pb/As | 0.33 | 7.32 | 4.73 | 0.59 | 0.59 |
| Rb | 9.45 | 179.80 | 183.70 | 9.30 | 9.07 |
| Sr | + | 4.05 | 3.46 | + | + |
| Y | 10.16 | 105.10 | 105.90 | 10.00 | 10.16 |
| Zr | 100.00 | 100.00 | 100.00 | 100.00 | 100.00 |
| Nb | 13.79 | 135.90 | 132.10 | 14.10 | 13.88 |

\* artifact number; 7161 and 6941 are microblades
- element below detectionlimits
+ element present, but cannot be extracted

source:  Godfrey-Smith 1984

interior of British Columbia.  The other three flakes of obsidian are from the Mt. Edziza flow.

Microblades have been recovered from a number of prehistoric components in the southern and central interior.  The best known of these are the components from the Lochnore-Nesikep locality in the Southern Plateau (Sanger 1970).  The dating of these components has come under considerable recent scrutiny (e.g. Stryd 1973).  According to Fladmark's (1982a:128) most recent synopsis, microblades in the southern and central Interior are not known to be present in quantity before ca. 6600 B.P., although a 7500 B.P. date exists for one microblade from the Drynoch Slide Site (Sanger 1968).  On the central coast at Namu, obsidian microblades are also present at ca. 6000 B.P., and one dates to ca. 7800 B.P. (Carlson 1979:220).  The obsidian source for most of these microblades is Anahim Peak (Carlson 1979:220).

Summary

This chapter has presented archaeolgical data from the Paul Mason Site, a prehistoric site in Kitselas Canyon to augment the existing data from Gitaus. The Paul Mason Site is deeply stratified, with two discrete soil zones. The surface contours reflect the placement of 10 dwelling floors on the slope, overlooking the canyon wall. This suggests a small village occupation during the later use of the site.

A suite of 19 radiocarbon estimates from the site cluster at three distinct time periods: 5000 to 4500 B.P., associated with the lower soil zone; 4300 to 3800 B.P., associated with the bottom of the upper soil zone; and 3200 to 2700 B.P. associated with the upper deposits including the dwelling floors.

The poor conditions for organic preservation at the site precluded recovery of non-lithic artifacts, although it is likely that a bone tool industry existed, based on the presence of numerous abraders. Lithic artifacts were divided into 19 classes. These are further sub-divided into 83 artifact types (see Appendix II). Cobble and flake tools, grouped into four classes, predominated at the site, accounting for 60.9 percent of all artifacts. These implements were typically large, and expediently manufactured from locally available raw material. The groundstone and chipped stone categories are not well represented. Groundstone tools, grouped into nine classes, constitute 15.5 percent of the assemblage. Shaped and unshaped abraders were most prevalent in this category, comprising 42.8 percent (N=77) of all groundstone tools. Hexagonal ground slate points and "pencils", similar to forms from Prince Rupert Harbour, were also recovered. The chipped stone category (23.6 percent of the assemblage) included bifaces, but lacked projectile points. Steep-edge scrapers were also rare, which suggests that land mammal hunting was not of critical importance to the occupants of the site. The presence of a microblade technology is interesting. This represents the first radiometrically dated context for microblades in the Skeena area (see Chapter 6).

In the next chapter, the lithic artifacts from the Paul Mason Site are analyzed in terms of their stratigraphic position to identify discrete cultural component.

Chapter 6

THE PREHISTORIC SEQUENCE AT THE PAUL MASON SITE

This chapter presents the analysis of the lithic data from the Paul
Mason Site. The objective is to delineate discrete cultural components to
facilitate the investigation of cultural change through time. The
radiocarbon dates for the site, presented in Chapter 5, indicate two
things. First, the early dates, ca. 5000 to 4500 B.P., are older than the
early dates from Gitaus by 500 to 1000 years. This suggests the presence
of a cultural component at the Paul Mason Site that pre-dates the initial
occupation at Gitaus. Secondly, the dates from the Paul Mason Site that
cluster in the 3000 B.P. time range are again suggestive of a discrete
component. This would be earlier than the Kleanza Complex, for which a
date of 2400 B.P. now exists, and later than the Skeena Complex, for which
a date of 3500 B.P. is projected (Allaire 1979; Ames 1979a).

Thus, it is likely that identification of cultural components at the
Paul Mason Site will add significantly to the development of the
prehistoric sequence at Kitselas Canyon.

The delineation of cultural components from the Paul Mason Site was
based on a multivariate analysis of artifact inter-assemblage variability
among the stratigraphic zones and layers from the site. Only the data from
the four major excavations (floor 2, floor 9, Excavation H, Excavation J)
were used in the analyses. The data from the excavation of floor 12
(Trench F) were not used because they comprise a total of only six
artifacts--a sample too small for analysis. Artifacts from the 1 x 1 test
units were not included because the samples were small, and the
stratigraphic position of the artifacts, in terms of soil layers or zones,
could not be accurately compared to the other excavations.

Multivariate quantitative analyses were used in this investigation
because these techniques consider interassemblage variability in terms of
all elements in the data set, not just certain "diagnostics".

Generally, the artifacts from each layer of each excavation were
treated as discrete assemblages in the analyses. There were, however, a
few exceptions. In some cases, two layers were combined and the artifacts
were treated as one assemblage. In other cases, inordinately thick layers
were sub-divided by incremental levels (each 10 cm thick), and the

artifacts for each layer-level were treated as separate assemblages.  The
rationale for these manipulations is explained in this chapter as they
occur.

The 19 artifact classes (see Chapter 5) used in the analyses include
five classes of cobble and flake implements, nine classes of groundstone
implements, and five classes of chipped stone implements.  They are
represented in the four major excavations by 1144 artifacts.

Artifact frequencies, converted to proportions, were used in the
analyses because of the great variability in tool frequency.  For example,
360 cobble core tools were recovered, versus four whetstones.  Binary
transformation of the data would have given equal weight to these two
classes, which was clearly not the case.  Moreover, change in frequency of
individual artifact classes through time would not have been detected using
binary data.

Q-mode analyses were used in this study (Stephenson 1953; Dumond
1974:253-54).  The analyses sought to classify stratigraphic units on the
basis of assemblage similarity.  Two quantitative data reduction techniques
were used: cluster analysis and multidimensional scaling.  These techniques
have received widespread application in archaeological research
(e.g., Hodson et al. 1966; Hodson 1970; Cowgill 1972; Johnson 1972; Matson
1974; Matson and True 1974; Drennan 1976; Wood 1978).

Cluster analysis is a sequential, agglomerative, hierarchical,
non-overlapping grouping technique  (Sneath and Sokal 1973:214).  Pairs of
entities, in this case lithic assemblages from layer-levels, are grouped at
incremental decreasing levels of similarity, based on a matrix of distance
coefficients, until one all-encompassing group is produced.  Unstandardized
city-block distance matrices were calculated in the analyses.  This
coefficient maximizes the distance between entities (Sneath and Sokal
1973).

Two types of clustering, unconstrained (Sneath and Sokal 1973:214)
and constrained (Adam 1976; Adam and West 1983:169), were employed in this
study.  Both types follow the same general grouping procedure described
above, except that unconstrained clustering groups **any** pair of
entities from within the data set at decreasing levels of similarity,
assuming no inherent order in the array of entities in the input data.  The

entire distance matrix is used in the formation of clusters, and it is theoretically possible for any entity to link with any other entity or cluster of entities if they have the lowest remaining distance coefficient.

Constrained clustering, as used here, only groups pairs of **neighbouring** entities as they are arrayed in the data set. The assumption is that there is an inherent linear order in the way in which the input data is arrayed. In effect, only the right diagonal margin of the distance matrix is used in forming linkages. Thus, in an ordered data set with three entities (A, B, C), A cannot link directly with C. The only possibilities are AB with C, or A with BC, even though AC may have the lowest of the three distance coefficients. In a constrained cluster analysis, the linear array of the entities in the input data is maintained in the output. The advantage of this is that constrained cluster analysis delineates "breaks" in the array. In the example given above, the break would be between A and B, or B and C, depending on the distance coefficient values for AB and BC. In an unconstrained cluster analysis, the input array could be re-ordered if the lowest distance coefficient is for AC. Thus, breaks in the input array would not be detected in the output. Constrained cluster analysis was used in this study because the objective was to delineate the "breaks" in a series of arrays of stratigraphic layer-level assemblages.

Elsewhere on the Northwest Coast, the constrained clustering technique should have applicability where sites form as a result of the sequential deposition of layers. Shell middens sites are an obvious example of this type of formation. Constrained clustering can be used as long as the order of the depositional sequence can be identified. If this order cannot be identified, or if there is no inherent order in the data (e.g., clustering of components from numerous sites), then unconstrained cluster analysis must be used.

The specific technique used for both the constrained and unconstrained analyses was the furthest neighbour (complete linkage) technique. This technique was readily applicable to both analyses. An evaluation of the numerous clustering techniques available (see Matson and True 1974:57) considered complete linkage to be a preferable technique since it does not concentrate or reduce the space between entities. This is because the criterion used to determine whether or not an entity should be added to a developing cluster is the distance between that entity and the farthest member of the cluster.

The HCLUS routine (Wood 1974) was used for unconstrained clustering. Constrained clustering was done by hand.

Multidimensional scaling (Torgerson 1958) reproduces, in a series of vectors or dimensions, the actual configuration represented by the matrix. Each dimension accounts for a certain percent of the total variance in the data set, and the dimensions are usually given in rank order beginning with the dimension that accounts for the highest percent of variance. Along any given dimension, an inverse relationship exists with respect to the distance between variables and the level of similarity. Thus, a small distance between variables indicates a high level of similarity. The objective of multidimensional scaling is to reduce the dimensionality of the original data set by constructing a small number of dimensions that account for most of the variability present in the input data.

The specific scaling technique used in this study was metric multidimensional scaling Torgerson 1958, 1965), or principal co-ordinates analysis (Gower 1971). In this technique, a matrix of the distances from the centroid of the configuration is calculated from the original (city-block) distance matrix. This is then factored, resulting in the production of a number of axes in rank order of importance, which are interpreted as representing dimensions of variation present in the original data set (Torgerson 1958:254-76; Matson and True 1974:64). The metric multidimensional scaling routine developed by Matson (1975) was used in the analyses.

Clustering and multidimensional scaling are generally regarded as complementary forms of analysis. Clustering links entities at incremental levels based on the total variance in the input data. Multidimensional scaling orders entities along individual dimensions of variance, and provides the proportion of the total distance contributed by each dimension.

Before proceeding with the analyses, a few qualifying statements should be made about the data. It will be recalled that two of the four

191

major excavations at the Paul Mason Site were in probable areas of disturbed cultural deposit. These were the excavations of floor 2 and floor 9. Layer D in both excavations was a "fill" layer, comprising a mixture of early and late material. Since this layer was formed at the time of dwelling construction, it is treated in the constrained cluster analysis as part of the linear array. However, as the layer contains an unknown amount of early material, it will likely appear as a unique entity in the constrained clustering results. The artifact totals for layer D are low in both excavations, so its inclusion should not greatly affect the overall configuration of the clusters. Since layer D is a fill layer, and technically not part of the linear array, it is probably best represented in the unconstrained cluster analysis.

Excavation J yielded a small number of artifacts, and the presence of a large hearth feature in the upper layer of this excavation indicates that this was a special activity area of the site, with low associated artifact density.

One of the major excavations (H) was in an area apparently undisturbed by earth-moving. The matrix was well-stratified, and the artifact density was high (N=338). It also produced four radiocarbon dates ranging from roughly 5000 to 3000 B.P., thus covering the period of intensive occupation of the site, as suggested by the suite of dates (see Table 5.1). Because of these factors, the data from Excavation H was analyzed first as the "secure" or "target" data set. The results of this analysis were then used as a basis for comparison to the data from the other excavations.

Only artifacts from buried cultural deposits were used in the analyses. Surface artifacts (layers A, B) were not used because they occurred rarely, and because the original provenience of these artifacts was unknown. In each analysis, layer C represents the post-occupational humus horizon.

**Lithic Analysis of Excavation H**

Table 6.1 presents the original data from Excavation H. The cell values include both raw frequencies and row proportions. The stratigraphic units are based on the original layer designations, and are arranged in

# Table 6.1
## Artifact frequencies and proportions for Excavation H stratigraphic units

| stratigraphic designation | cobble core tools | utilized cobble flakes | retouched cobble flakes | cobble cores | saws | ornamental/decorated | ground stone points | blunted ground stone tools | ground stone fragments | finished ground slate | unshaped abraders | shaped abraders | grinding stones | bifaces | formed unifaces | retouched flakes | cores/piece esquillees | microblades and cores | hammerstones | TOTALS |
|---|---|---|---|---|---|---|---|---|---|---|---|---|---|---|---|---|---|---|---|---|
| C (count / proportion) | 8 / .33 | 6 / .25 | 1 / .04 | 1 / .04 | | | | | | | 2 / .08 | 3 / .13 | | 1 / .04 | | | 1 / .04 | | 1 / .04 | 24 |
| D1 | 6 / .21 | 10 / .36 | 1 / .04 | | 1 / .04 | | | | 1 / .04 | | 2 / .07 | 2 / .07 | | 1 / .04 | 1 / .04 | 1 / .04 | 1 / .04 | 1 / .04 | | 28 |
| D2 | 9 / .26 | 6 / .17 | 2 / .06 | 2 / .06 | | | 1 / .03 | 2 / .06 | 1 / .03 | | 2 / .06 | 1 / .03 | | 2 / .06 | | 1 / .03 | 4 / .11 | 1 / .03 | 1 / .03 | 35 |
| D3 | 8 / .16 | 18 / .35 | | | 1 / .02 | 1 / .02 | 4 / .08 | 3 / .06 | 3 / .06 | | 2 / .04 | 1 / .02 | | 2 / .04 | 1 / .02 | 3 / .06 | | 2 / .04 | 2 / .04 | 51 |
| D4 | 13 / .29 | 10 / .22 | 2 / .04 | 1 / .02 | 3 / .07 | | | | 3 / .07 | | 2 / .04 | 3 / .07 | | 1 / .02 | | 5 / .11 | | 2 / .04 | | 45 |
| D5 | 3 / .18 | 2 / .12 | 1 / .06 | 2 / .12 | | | | | 1 / .06 | | 2 / .12 | | | | | 3 / .18 | 2 / .12 | | 1 / .06 | 17 |
| F | 16 / .43 | 4 / .11 | 2 / .05 | 3 / .08 | | | | 1 / .03 | 2 / .05 | | | | | | 1 / .03 | 4 / .11 | 1 / .03 | 1 / .03 | 2 / .05 | 37 |
| G | 10 / .13 | 2 / .03 | 1 / .01 | | 1 / .01 | | | | 2 / .03 | | | | | 1 / .01 | | 3 / .04 | 4 / .05 | 54 / .69 | | 78 |
| H | | 1 / .14 | | | | | | | | | | | | | | | | 6 / .86 | | 7 |
| | | | | | | | | | | | | | | | | | | | | 322 |

193

descending order from the surface. There are eleven discrete stratigraphic units, beginning with the humus zone, layer C. Layer C includes a large number of artifacts (24; 7.1 percent of the Excavation H assemblage). Layer D is the thick, homogeneous layer of dark brown soil that comprised most of the upper or dark brown soil zone of Excavation H. A radiocarbon date of 3080 ± 85 (WSU 2921) was obtained from near the top of the layer, and a date of 4280 ± 95 (WSU 2923) was obtained from the bottom of the layer. This suggests a long duration in the deposition of the layer, and it is possible that change in the artifact assemblage occurred during this time. For this reason, and because the layer was so thick, it was sub-divided into five levels, each 20 cm thick. Each layer-level (D1 to D5) was treated as a discrete entity in the analysis. This allows for the detection of possible assemblage variability within the layer. Layer F is the lower layer of the dark brown soil zone. Layers G and H represent the lower or red-brown soil zone.

Layer E was not included in the analysis. It contained only eight artifacts, a low number for quantitative analysis based on frequency data. One might ask why the material from Layer H was included when it contained only seven artifacts. The reason is that six of these artifacts were microblades. This suggests that microblades are more strongly represented in the lower stratigraphic zone than in the upper zone. The assemblage was therefore retained for analysis.

The unconstrained furthest neighbour cluster analysis produced a two-cluster solution (Figure 6.1). One of the clusters is further divided into two sub-clusters. The cluster configuration generally reflects stratigraphic position, even though the analysis was unconstrained. Cluster 1 comprises the assemblages of the dark brown soil zone. The assemblages from the upper 1.0 metre of the matrix (Layer C and layer-levels D1 to D4) are somewhat distinct from those comprising the bottom of the dark brown soil zone (D5, F). This distinction is probably not great enough to warrant separate cluster designations, so the two groupings are treated as sub-clusters; 1A (C, D1 to D4) and 1B (D5, F).

Cluster 2 includes layers G and H, from the lower or red-brown soil zone. It is clearly distinct from cluster 1, linking at a very high level.

The unconstrained cluster solution is in good agreement with the

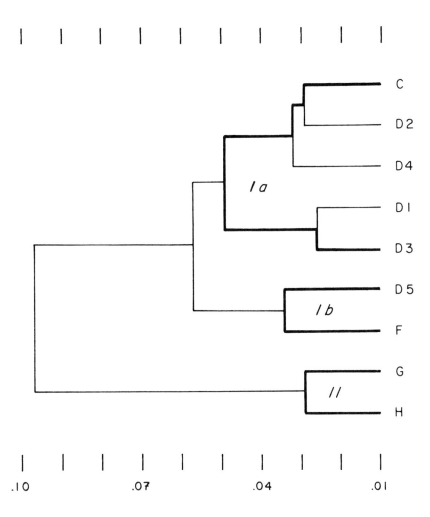

Figure 6.1  Unconstrained clustering of excavation H stratigraphic units.

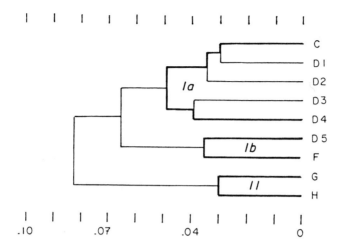

Figure 6.2  Constrained clustering of Excavation H stratigraphic units.

Table 6.2
Excavation H distance matrix

|     | C     | D1    | D2    | D3    | D4    | D5    | F     | G     | H   |
|-----|-------|-------|-------|-------|-------|-------|-------|-------|-----|
| C   | 0.0   |       |       |       |       |       |       |       |     |
| D1  | 0.030 | 0.0   |       |       |       |       |       |       |     |
| D2  | 0.031 | 0.035 | 0.0   |       |       |       |       |       |     |
| D3  | 0.048 | 0.026 | 0.039 | 0.0   |       |       |       |       |     |
| D4  | 0.031 | 0.026 | 0.034 | 0.038 | 0.0   |       |       |       |     |
| D5  | 0.048 | 0.052 | 0.035 | 0.056 | 0.045 | 0.0   |       |       |     |
| F   | 0.043 | 0.052 | 0.038 | 0.054 | 0.037 | 0.035 | 0.0   |       |     |
| G   | 0.082 | 0.071 | 0.072 | 0.075 | 0.074 | 0.076 | 0.075 | 0.0   |     |
| H   | 0.090 | 0.086 | 0.087 | 0.086 | 0.086 | 0.093 | 0.091 | 0.030 | 0.0 |

196

radiocarbon dates from Excavation H.  The date 3080 ± 85 came from
layer-level D2 (sub-cluster 1A).  The date 4280 ± 95 came from layer-level
D5 (sub-cluster 1B), and the date 5050 ± 140 (SFU 259) came from layer G
(cluster 2).  Cluster 2 is clearly distinct from cluster 1, indicating that
major assemblage changes occurred between roughly 5000 and 4200 B.P.
Sub-clusters 1A and 1B are not as clearly distinct, suggesting only minor
assemblage differences between the two groupings.

The constrained cluster analysis essentially duplicated the results
of the unconstrained analysis (Figure 6.2).  Cluster 1 includes all
layer-levels in the dark brown soil zone.  Layer-levels D5 and F join the
other members of Cluster 1 last, again suggesting separate sub-clusters.
Cluster 2 (G, H) is clearly distinct from cluster 1.

The unconstrained and constrained cluster solutions for Excavation H
both reflect assemblage change through time.  The most pronounced break is
between the assemblages of the red-brown and dark brown soil zones.
Cluster 2 is characterized by an extremely high proportion of microblades,
a minimum of groundstone tools and a low proportion of cobble tools in
relation to cluster 1 (Figure 6.3).  The assemblages of cluster 1 show a
major reduction in the proportion of microblades, and a concomitant
increase in the proportion of cobble implements, especially cobble core
tools.  There is also an apparent increase in the overall proportion and
variety of groundstone implements in cluster 1, but the main difference
between clusters 1 and 2 appears to be the difference in the frequency of
microblades.

There are two trends separating sub-clusters 1A and 1B.  One is the
frequency of cobble tool classes.  Sub-cluster 1B has a high proportion of
cobble core tools, and lower proportions of unmodified cobble flake tools,
retouched cobble flake tools and cobble cores.  In sub-cluster 1A, the
proportions of cobble core tools, retouched cobble flake tools and cobble
cores are all slightly reduced compared to 1B, but the proportion of
unmodified flake tools is greatly increased.  The other trend separating
the sub-clusters is the difference in the number of artifact classes
represented, especially groundstone implements.  In sub-cluster 1A, most
groundstone classes are present, albeit in low proportions.  Only finished
ground slate and grinding stones are absent, and these classes occurred

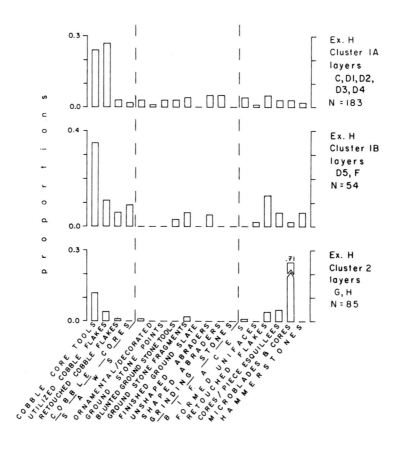

Figure 6.3  Artifact profiles for Excavation H clusters.

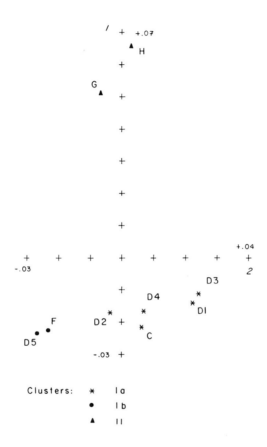

Figure 6.4  Multidimensional scaling of Excavation H stratigraphic units;
dimensions 1 x 2.

very infrequently at the site. In sub-cluster 1B, the groundstone industry is represented only by blunted rod-like implements, ground slate fragments and unshaped abraders. Saws, ornamental/decorated items, groundstone points, finished ground slate, shaped abraders and whetstones are all absent from sub-cluster 1B. Absent too are chipped stone bifaces, which are represented in sub-cluster 1A. In short, there is greater diversity in the assemblage of sub-cluster 1A than 1B.

The metric multidimensional scaling of Excavation H generated a four-dimension configuration that accounts for 93.73 percent of the total variance in the data set. Only the first two dimensions (Figure 6.4) could be interpreted. They account for 81.66 percent of the total variance.

Dimension 1 (63.57 percent of variance) separates cluster 1 (dark brown soil zone) from cluster 2 (red-brown zone). This reflects separation of those layers with high proportions of microblades and low proportions of cobble tools (lower) from layers with low proportions of microblades and high proportions of cobble tools (upper).

Dimension 2 accounts for 17.09 percent of variance. This dimension is difficult to interpret in isolation. Sub-clusters 1A and 1B are separated, but the cluster 2 assemblages are inter-mixed with sub-cluster 1A. This suggests some similarity between the latter two assemblage groupings, but the nature of the similarity could not be detected. However, when the two dimensions are considered together (see Washburn and Matson 1985), the cluster solutions are re-affirmed. A roughly U-shaped curve is formed. The overall configuration (Dimensions 1 and 2) separates cluster groupings according to their stratigraphic position, reflecting early, middle and late components.

In summary, the clustering and scaling analyses of the layer-level assemblages from Excavation H produced two major groupings, one of which sub-divides into two sub-groups. These groupings reflect assemblage variability through time, indicating three discrete temporal components, a pattern supported by the radiocarbon dates. The early component, represented by layers G and H, is characterized by a high proportion of microblades, low proportions of cobble tools and a virtual absence of groundstone. This component is dated from 5000 to roughly 4500 B.P.. The middle component (D5, F), has a radiocarbon date of 4280 B.P., and is characterized by a reduction in the proportion of microblades and an increase in the proportion of cobble tools. The late component (C, D1 to D4) is dated to ca. 3000 B.P. and is characterized by an increase in the number of tool classes represented, especially groundstone. There is a slight reduction in the proportion of cobble tools relative to the previous component.

The results of the analysis of inter-assemblage variability for Excavation H may now be used as a comparative base to determine whether similar results are obtained from the other three major excavations at the Paul Mason Site. The cluster groupings shown in Figure 6.3 are included as entities in the subsequent analyses.

## Lithic Analysis from the Floor 2 Excavation

The original data from the excavation of floor 2 are presented in Table 6.3. The cell values include raw frequencies and row proportions. The stratigraphic units are based on the original excavation layer designations. Layer D comprises the fill deposited around the perimeter of the floor. Layer E was the uppermost undisturbed layer of the dark brown zone. Layer H comprised the remainder of the dark brown soil zone. It included a series of thin discontinuous layers and lenses, with evidence of disturbance near the rear of the housefloor area. Layer H was about 80 cm thick, and was divided into four separate levels (H1 to H4), each 20 cm thick. Layers J and K represent the lower or red-brown soil zone.

The unconstrained furthest neighbour cluster analysis of the nine layer-level assemblages from floor 2 and the three cluster assemblages from Excavation H produced a three-cluster solution (Figure 6.5). Cluster 1 combined sub-cluster 1A from Excavation H with the "upper" assemblages from floor 2 (C, D, E, H1, H2). Cluster 2 included sub-cluster 1B from Excavation H and the remainder of the assemblages from floor 2 (H3, H4, J, K). A residual third cluster was formed by cluster 2 from Excavation H.

This solution basically divides the matrix of the floor 2 excavation into an upper and lower component.

The constrained furthest neighbour cluster analysis of the nine layer-level assemblages from floor 2 also produced a two-cluster solution, again dividing the floor 2 assemblages into upper and lower components

| stratigraphic designation | | cobble core tools | utilized cobble flakes | retouched cobble flakes | cobble cores | saws | ornamental/decorated | ground stone points | blunted ground stone tools | ground stone fragments | finished ground slate | unshaped abraders | shaped abraders | grinding stones | bifaces | formed unifaces | retouched flakes | cores/piece esquillees | microblades and cores | hammerstones | TOTALS |
|---|---|---|---|---|---|---|---|---|---|---|---|---|---|---|---|---|---|---|---|---|---|
| C | count | 4 | 3 | 4 | 1 | | 1 | 2 | | 1 | | 1 | 2 | | 2 | | 1 | | 3 | 4 | 29 |
|   | proportion | .14 | .10 | .14 | .03 | | .03 | .07 | | .03 | | .03 | .07 | | .07 | | .03 | | .10 | .14 | |
| D |  | 1 | 11 | 2 | | | 1 | 1 | | | | 1 | | 1 | 1 | 1 | 3 | 2 | | 2 | 27 |
|   |  | .04 | .41 | .07 | | | .04 | .04 | | | | .04 | | .04 | .04 | .04 | .11 | .07 | | .07 | |
| E |  | 55 | 29 | 8 | 7 | 2 | | 1 | 3 | 3 | | 7 | 8 | 1 | 8 | 3 | 10 | 6 | 8 | 17 | 176 |
|   |  | .31 | .16 | .05 | .04 | .01 | | .01 | .02 | .02 | | .04 | .05 | .01 | .05 | .02 | .06 | .03 | .05 | .10 | |
| H1 |  | 7 | 5 | 1 | 1 | 1 | | 1 | 1 | | | | 2 | 1 | 2 | | 2 | | | 1 | 25 |
|   |  | .28 | .20 | .04 | .04 | .04 | | .04 | .04 | | | | .08 | .04 | .08 | | .08 | | | .04 | |
| H2 |  | 23 | 11 | 1 | | 1 | 2 | 2 | 1 | 3 | 1 | 3 | | | 1 | 1 | 3 | 2 | 4 | 3 | 62 |
|   |  | .37 | .18 | .02 | | .02 | .03 | .03 | .02 | .05 | .02 | .05 | | | .02 | .02 | .05 | .03 | .06 | .05 | |
| H3 |  | 30 | 12 | 1 | 3 | | 2 | 1 | 1 | | | 2 | | | | | 2 | 3 | 1 | 2 | 60 |
|   |  | .50 | .20 | .02 | .05 | | .03 | .02 | .02 | | | .03 | | | | | .03 | .05 | .02 | .03 | |
| H4 |  | 11 | 1 | 1 | 1 | | 1 | | 1 | | | 1 | 2 | | | | 2 | | 1 | 2 | 24 |
|   |  | .46 | .04 | .04 | .04 | | .04 | | .04 | | | .04 | .08 | | | | .08 | | .04 | .08 | |
| J |  | 32 | 3 | 1 | 4 | | | | | | | | 1 | | | | 1 | 2 | 6 | 3 | 53 |
|   |  | .60 | .06 | .02 | .08 | | | | | | | | .02 | | | | .02 | .04 | .11 | .06 | |
| K |  | 19 | 6 | 2 | 2 | | 1 | 1 | | 1 | | | | | | | 4 | 1 | 10 | 3 | 50 |
|   |  | .38 | .12 | .04 | .04 | | .02 | .02 | | .02 | | | | | | | .08 | .02 | .20 | .06 | |
|  |  | | | | | | | | | | | | | | | | | | | | 506 |

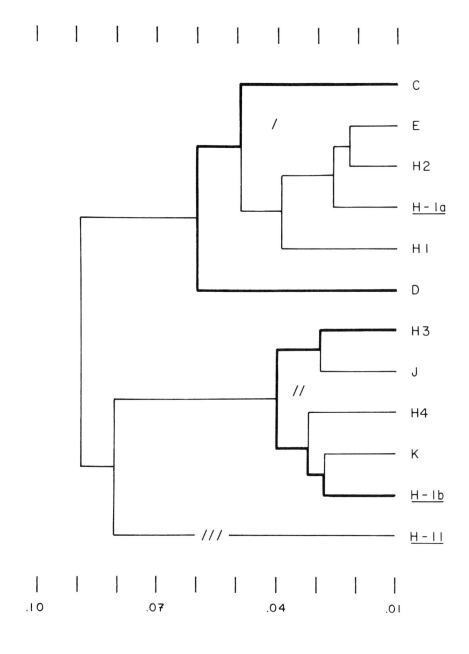

Figure 6.5   Unconstrained clustering of floor 2 stratigraphic units with
Excavation H̲ clusters.

(see Figure 6.6). This time, however, the break was between H1 and H2. The difference in the two clustering solutions is based on the different coefficient values of E/H2 and H2/H3 (see Table 6.4). In the unconstrained analysis, E and H2 link at .022 on the Y-axis, the lowest distance coefficient value in the matrix. When the analysis is constrained, E and H2 cannot link directly. In this study, the effort is to determine where the breaks occur in the matrix. The question is whether the clearest break is between H1 and H2, or H2 and H3. To address this question, we must consider only the distance coefficients for these assemblage pairs. The distance coefficient for H2/H3 is .023; for H1/H2, it is .038. The clearest break in the matrix is between H1 and H2.

This demonstrates the advantage of constrained clustering in an analysis such as this, where there is an inherent order in the input array. Constrained clustering detected the break between H1 and H2. Unconstrained clustering did not detect this break. In fact, it included H1 and H2 in the same cluster, and excluded H3, even though H2 and H3 were more similar than H1 and H2. From the perspective of this study, constrained clustering is the most suitable technique to search for patterning in the input data. It is hoped that future studies of deeply stratified, multi-component sites will consider this analytic technique.

Figure 6.7 shows the artifact profiles for the two clusters produced by the constrained analysis. The artifact profiles of the Excavation H clusters are also included. The essential differences in the floor 2 clusters are as follows. Cluster 2 has a higher proportion of cobble core tools (46 percent) than cluster 1 (26 percent), and the ratio of cobble core tools to utilized cobble flake tools in cluster 2 (3.53:1) is higher than cluster 1 (1.37:1).

Cluster 1 has more groundstone artifact classes represented (N=8) than cluster 2 (N=6). In addition, important differences exist between clusters 1 and 2 in the proportions of shaped abraders. In cluster 1, the proportion of shaped abraders is 5.0 percent (N=12). In cluster 2, the proportion of shaped abraders is 1.0 percent (N=3).

There is an increase in the proportion of formed bifaces in cluster 1 (5.0 percent, N=13) compared to cluster 2 (0.4 percent, N=1). The differences between clusters 1 and 2 are consistent with the differences

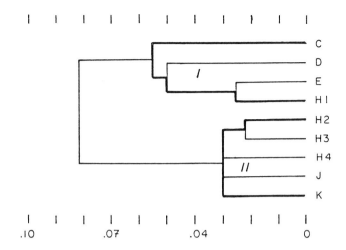

Figure 6.6  Constrained clustering of floor 2 stratigraphic units.

Table 6.4
Floor 2 distance matrix

|    | C     | D     | E     | H1    | H2    | H3    | H4    | J     | K   |
|----|-------|-------|-------|-------|-------|-------|-------|-------|-----|
| C  | 0.0   |       |       |       |       |       |       |       |     |
| D  | 0.056 | 0.0   |       |       |       |       |       |       |     |
| E  | 0.037 | 0.051 | 0.0   |       |       |       |       |       |     |
| H1 | 0.045 | 0.052 | 0.026 | 0.0   |       |       |       |       |     |
| H2 | 0.047 | 0.053 | 0.022 | 0.038 | 0.0   |       |       |       |     |
| H3 | 0.057 | 0.058 | 0.031 | 0.038 | 0.023 | 0.0   |       |       |     |
| H4 | 0.043 | 0.068 | 0.029 | 0.038 | 0.033 | 0.032 | 0.0   |       |     |
| J  | 0.058 | 0.082 | 0.042 | 0.055 | 0.041 | 0.028 | 0.032 | 0.0   |     |
| K  | 0.045 | 0.063 | 0.030 | 0.040 | 0.026 | 0.032 | 0.029 | 0.031 | 0.0 |

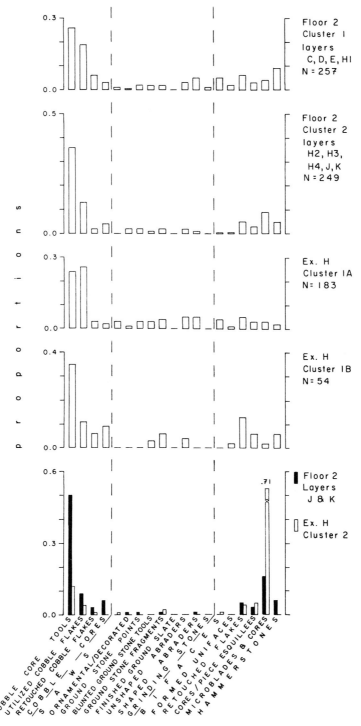

Figure 6.7  Artifact profiles for floor 2 clusters and Excavation H clusters.

between sub-clusters 1A and 1B from Excavation H.

There is an increase in the proportion of hammerstones in cluster 1 (floor 2) (9 percent, N=24) compared to cluster 2 (5 percent, N=13). In Excavation H, the proportion of hammerstones decreased in 1A (2.0 percent) compared to 1B (6.0 percent).

Hammerstones notwithstanding, there are clear similarities between the configurations of clusters 1 and 2 in floor 2, and sub-clusters 1A and 1B in Excavation H. In each case the assemblages of the upper dark brown soil zone cluster separately from the assemblages of the lower dark brown zone. These configurations appear to result from similar changes in artifact proportions.

There is one important difference, however, between the cluster configurations of Excavation H and floor 2. In Excavation H, the assemblages of the red-brown soil zone clustered separately from those of the dark brown zone. In floor 2, the assemblages of the red-brown zone (layers J and K) clustered **with** the assemblages of the lower dark brown zone. If the red-brown layers at the base of each excavation represent the same stratigraphic zone, then one might ask why the assemblages from this zone did not cluster together in the unconstrained analysis, or why J and K did not form a separate cluster in the constrained analysis?

One reason is the difference in proportions of cobble core tools in these assemblages. The combined J-K assemblage (see Figure 6.7) has 49 percent cobble core tools, while Excavation H-cluster 2 has only 12 percent cobble core tools. The high proportion of cobble core tools in J-K is consistent with the assemblages of the lower dark brown zone of floor 2.

There is also another reason. A total of 16 microblades was recovered from layers J and K (16 percent of the combined J-K assemblage). This constitutes 48.5 percent of all microblades recovered from the floor 2 excavation. By contrast, 60 microblades were recovered from the red-brown zone in Excavation H (71 percent of the cluster 2 assemblage) or 88.2 percent of all microblades in Excavation H.

Now, let us consider the possibility of disturbance in floor 2, as a result of the construction of the prepared floors. When the slope was levelled to prepare the floors, an unknown amount of underlying matrix was displaced, especially near the rear of the floor where the maximum amount of earth-moving took place. This accounts for the disturbance noted in layer H. This displacement would have brought some "early" material (layers J, K) to the surface. If microblades were an early phenomenon at the Paul Mason Site, as suggested by their distribution in undisturbed Excavation H, then in areas of suspected disturbance, such as floor 2, one might expect to find some microblades at the bottom of the matrix (undisturbed) and others near the top of the matrix (disturbed). In fact, this appears to have been the case in floor 2. Layer C contained three microblades, and eight microblades were recovered from layer E. Thus, 33.3 percent of microblades from floor 2 were recovered from the upper layers of the matrix, those layers formed **after** floor construction. If these were re-deposited microblades, they should be considered with the microblades recovered from J and K. Together, they comprise 27 microblades, or 81.8 percent of all microblades from the floor 2 excavation. This is very close to the proportion of microblades recovered from the red-brown zone in Excavation H (88.2 percent).

The effects of disturbance in the floor 2 excavation are also reflected in the layer D assemblage. Layer D comprised most of the fill deposited around the perimeter of the floor. It may be expected that layer D would include a mixture of "early" cultural material from disturbed deposits (fill), and "later" material, associated with the occupation of the floor. In the unconstrained cluster analysis, layer D was the last to link with cluster 1, indicating that it is the least similar or most unique member of the cluster. In the constrained cluster analysis, layer D again linked at a high level with layers E and H1. The matrix of distance coefficients for the floor 2 assemblages (Table 6.4) shows that layer D consistently produced the highest distance coefficients when paired with the other assemblages. This uniqueness may be due to the mixture of early and late cultural material contained within the layer.

In cases such as this, where there is a linear order to the matrix, but some disturbance has occurred, it may be best to use both constrained and unconstrained cluster analyses. The difference in the results may give some indication about the amount of disturbance that has occurred.

The metric multidimensional scaling of the layer-level assemblages of floor 2 and the cluster assemblages from Excavation H generated a five dimension configuration, accounting for 93.79 percent of the total variance in the data set. Only the first two dimensions are considered here (see Figure 6.8). They account for 38.25 percent and 30.95 percent of variance respectively, for a cumulative total of 69.2 percent of total variance.

Individually, the first two dimensions were difficult to interpret. Dimension 1 orders the assemblages very roughly on the basis of their position in the matrix. This may be a temporal vector. The assemblages from the red-brown zone, including layers J, K and Excavation H-cluster 2, all have negative values on Dimension 1. All assemblages from the dark brown soil zone have positive values on Dimension 1, and generally, the assemblages from the upper dark brown zone (D, E, H1 and Excavation H-sub-cluster 1A) have greater positive values than the assemblages from the lower dark brown zone. However, the order of layers J and K is reversed; E and H1 are reversed, and H2 and H3 are reversed. Layer C also appears to be out of place. Nonetheless, a comparison of the order of the assemblages in the matrix (C, D, E, H1...etc) to their order on this vector, by the calculation of a Spearman's rho rank-order correlation coefficient (Conover 1971:245-49), produced an r-value of 0.7, significant at the .018 level.

Dimension 2 is related to the proportion of cobble core tools in each assemblage. The ordering of the assemblages on Dimension 2 was compared to the rank-order of the assemblages in terms of the proportion of cobble core tools in each, again using Spearman's rho rank-order correlation coefficient. This produced an r-value of 0.97, significant at the .0001 level.

The best interpretation of the scaling analysis is provided by the combination of Dimensions 1 and 2 (Figure 6.8). This configuration separates the groupings obtained in the constrained cluster analysis. The entities comprising cluster 1 (C, D, E, H1) are in the upper left portion of the configuration with Excavation H-sub-cluster 1A. The entities comprising cluster 2 (H2, H3, H4, J, K) are in the middle-right portion of the configuration with Excavation H-sub-cluster 1B. The residual, Excavation H-cluster 2, is in the lower left portion of the configuration. The overall configuration is a wide parabolic curve, that seriates the cluster groupings from earliest to latest.

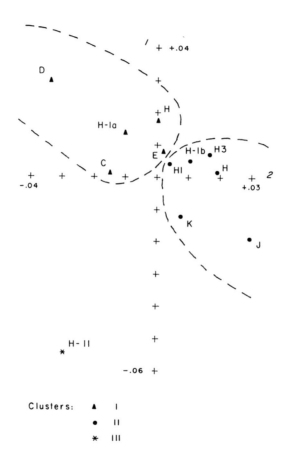

Figure 6.8   Multidimensional scaling for floor 2 and Excavation H clusters;
dimensions 1 x 2.

In this configuration, Excavation H-cluster 2 is isolated from the other assemblages. This is probably the result of the very high proportion of microblades in this assemblage. Following the general curve of the configuration, the J and K assemblages are most similar to Excavation H-cluster 2. This similarity was suggested previously in the discussion of the cluster analyses, given that: (1) almost 50 percent of the microblades recovered from floor 2 were in these layers, and (2) floor disturbance probably displaced some microblades from these layers. The main difference between Excavation H-cluster 2 and layers J and K is that in J and K cobble core tools have the highest proportional frequency and microblades have the second highest proportional frequency, whereas in Excavation H-cluster 2, this order is reversed. Moreover, the "red zone" assemblages are also similar in that most groundstone artifact classes are poorly represented or absent. Combining layers J and K (see Figure 6.7), a one to one comparison can be made of the red zone assemblages from Excavation H and floor 2. Treating the two assemblages as if they were independent, a comparison of the rank-order of the artifact classes in each assemblage, based on the proportion of each tool class in the assemblage, yielded a Spearman's rho rank-order correlation coefficient of 0.698, significant at the .002 level (note that in fact the two assemblages are not independent univariate populations. The use of the Spearman's coefficient here is simply intended as a demonstration of similarity). The result indicates that, indeed, the assemblages from the red-brown soil zone at the Paul Mason Site are similar, and probably represent the same cultural component.

The cluster 2 assemblages from the lower dark brown zone of floor 2 (H2, H3, H4) are closer on the curve to the cluster 1 assemblages (C, E, H1, but note that D is distinct) than to layers J and K. This pattern was not indicated by the cluster analyses, which only grouped "upper" and "lower" assemblages for floor 2. The scaling analysis suggests a somewhat more complex grouping of upper assemblages (upper dark brown soil zone), middle assemblages (lower dark brown soil zone) and lower assemblages (red-brown zone). Admittedly, this tri-partite division is not as clear as one might expect because of the effects of mixing.

## Lithic Analysis of Floor 9

The input data from the excavation of floor 9 are presented in Table
6.5. The cell values include raw frequencies and row proportions. The
stratigraphic units are based on the original layer designations.

Layer D comprised the fill deposited around the perimeter of the
floor, and was only represented in excavation units G1, G2 and G6. Layer E
was the uppermost undisturbed layer of the dark brown zone. Layer F was
the lower layer of the dark brown zone. Layer G was the thin, greasy black
layer. Layers H and J include all artifacts from the bottom of the
cultural deposit. They were combined because the distinction between them
was not always clear.

The furthest neighbour unconstrained cluster analysis of the six
layer assemblages of floor 9 and the three cluster groupings of Excavation
H produced a three cluster solution (Figure 6.9). All floor 9 assemblages
were in the first two clusters. Excavation H-cluster 2 was, again, a
residual and constitutes the third cluster. The configuration of clusters
1 and 2 cannot be interpreted in terms of breaks in the matrix. Cluster 1
includes the assemblages of layers E and F and Excavation H-sub-cluster
1A. However, in this analysis, Excavation H-sub-cluster 1B is also
included in cluster 1. This suggests that sub-cluster 1B is more similar
to sub-cluster 1A than to the assemblages of cluster 2 (C, D, G, HJ).

Cluster 2 includes assemblages from the upper portion of the matrix
(C, D) and from the bottom of the matrix (G, HJ). There is no "break" in
the matrix along stratigraphic lines, as was the case in the unconstrained
cluster analyses of Excavation H and floor 2.

The unconstrained cluster configuration for floor 9 probably reflects
the inadequacies of the small data set. Cluster 1 includes those
assemblages for which most artifact classes have a frequency of one or more
(although layer F has eight artifact classes not represented). The
assemblages of cluster 2 are generally small and have ten or more artifact
classes not represented (C=14 artifact classes not represented, D=10, G=14,
HJ=14).

The furthest neighbour constrained cluster analysis yielded more
satisfactory results in terms of detecting breaks in the matrix. A two
cluster configuration was produced (Figure 6.10). Cluster 1 included

## Table 6.5
## Artifact frequencies and proportions for floor 9 stratigraphic units

| stratigraphic designation | | cobble core tools | utilized cobble flakes | retouched cobble flakes | cobble cores | saws | ornamental/decorated | ground stone points | blunted ground stone tools | ground stone fragments | finished ground slate | unshaped abraders | shaped abraders | grinding stones | bifaces | formed unifaces | retouched flakes | cores/piece esquillees | microblades and cores | hammerstones | TOTALS |
|---|---|---|---|---|---|---|---|---|---|---|---|---|---|---|---|---|---|---|---|---|---|
| C | count<br>proportion | 1<br>.17 | 2<br>.33 | | | | | 1<br>.17 | 1<br>.17 | | | | | | | | | | 1<br>.17 | | | 6 |
| D | | 4<br>.19 | 7<br>.33 | 2<br>.10 | 1<br>.05 | | | | | | | | 1<br>.05 | | 1<br>.05 | | 1<br>.05 | 2<br>.10 | | 2<br>.10 | 21 |
| E | | 23<br>.23 | 25<br>.25 | 8<br>.08 | 4<br>.04 | 1<br>.01 | 2<br>.02 | 1<br>.01 | 5<br>.05 | 4<br>.04 | | 3<br>.03 | 1<br>.01 | | 3<br>.03 | | 8<br>.08 | 3<br>.03 | 3<br>.03 | 7<br>.07 | 101 |
| F | | 6<br>.24 | 6<br>.24 | 1<br>.04 | | | | 1<br>.04 | 2<br>.08 | | | | 1<br>.04 | 1<br>.04 | | 1<br>.04 | 3<br>.12 | 2<br>.08 | 1<br>.04 | | 25 |
| G | | 2<br>.17 | 6<br>.50 | | | | | 1<br>.08 | | | | 2<br>.17 | | | | | | | | 1<br>.08 | 12 |
| HJ | | 7<br>.44 | 5<br>.31 | | 1<br>.06 | | | 1<br>.06 | | | | | | | 1<br>.06 | | | | | 1<br>.06 | 16 |
| | | | | | | | | | | | | | | | | | | | | | 181 |

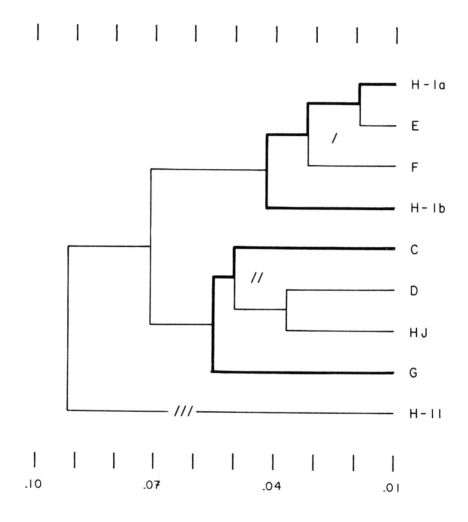

Figure 6.9  Unconstrained clustering of floor 9 stratigraphic units with
Excavation H̲ clusters.

layers C, D, E and F, representing the upper layers of the matrix. Once again, layer D is a "fill" layer, and as such is best represented by the unconstrained cluster analysis. Cluster 2 included layers G and HJ, the lower layers of the matrix. The artifact profiles for these clusters are shown, with the Excavation H profiles, in Figure 6.11. Both floor 9 clusters have high proportions of cobble core tools and utilized cobble flake tools. The main difference is that cluster 1 represents a more diversified assemblage. The only artifact class not represented is finished ground slate. In cluster 2, eleven artifact classes are not represented (retouched flake tools, saws, blunted rod-like implements, groundstone fragments, shaped abraders, whetstones, formed unifaces, retouched flakes, piece esquillees-cores and microblades).

In the floor 9 cluster analyses, there was no counterpart to Excavation H-cluster 2. The cluster 2 assemblages of floor 9 (G, HJ), which represent the lower portion of the matrix, did not include microblades. These assemblages were recovered from dark brown soil layers, not the red-brown soil seen in Excavation H and floor 2. Three microblades and one microcore fragment were recovered in the excavation of floor 9, but these were all from cluster 1 assemblages. The recovery of microblades in a similar context in floor 2 was argued to be the result of disturbance. This is also a likely explanation for the presence of the few microblades in the upper layers of floor 9. Disturbance, perhaps resulting from the levelling of other floors on the slope of the Paul Mason Site, may have displaced some microblades which were ultimately re-deposited in the upper layers of floor 9. There is, however, no evidence of an in situ "microblade-bearing" zone in the floor 9 excavation area.

The metric multidimensional scaling of the floor 9 data set concentrated only on the layer assemblages of floor 9. The Excavation H cluster assemblages were not included in this analysis because there was a substantial difference between the results of the constrained and unconstrained cluster analyses. The constrained analysis, which did not include the Excavation H cluster assemblages, reflected the break in the matrix. The unconstrained analysis, which included the Excavation H clusters, did not detect the break. Therefore, it was decided to scale only those assemblages used in the constrained cluster analysis.

215

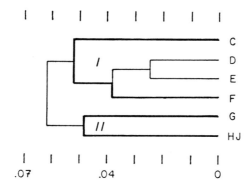

Figure 6.10   Constrained clustering of floor 9 stratigraphic units.

Table 6.6
Floor 9 distance matrix

|     | C     | D     | E     | F     | G     | HJ  |
|-----|-------|-------|-------|-------|-------|-----|
| C   | 0.0   |       |       |       |       |     |
| D   | 0.043 | 0.0   |       |       |       |     |
| E   | 0.052 | 0.027 | 0.0   |       |       |     |
| F   | 0.041 | 0.038 | 0.030 | 0.0   |       |     |
| G   | 0.053 | 0.044 | 0.049 | 0.062 | 0.0   |     |
| HJ  | 0.048 | 0.036 | 0.040 | 0.051 | 0.048 | 0.0 |

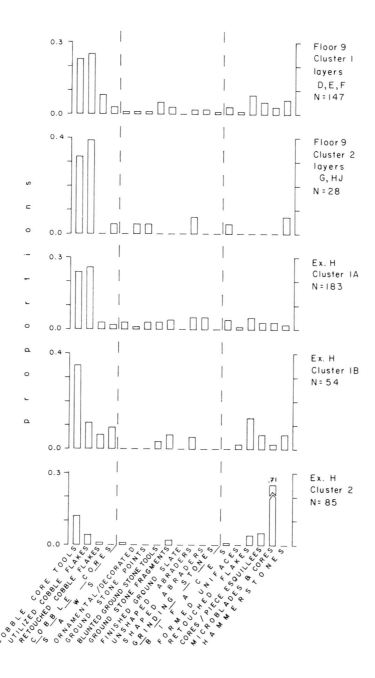

Figure 6.11  Artifact profiles for floor 9 and Excavation H clusters.

The scaling of the floor 9 assemblages generated a four dimension solution, accounting for 98.28 percent of the total variance in the data set. Only the first two dimensions are considered here (see Figure 6.12). They account for a cumulative total of 70.77 percent of the variance.

Dimension 1 accounts for 41.72 percent of the total variance. The ordering of the assemblages on this dimension is generally consistent with the configuration of the constrained cluster analysis. Cluster 2 assemblages (G, HJ) have positive values on Dimension 1, and cluster 1 assemblages have negative values. The ordering of the assemblages along the dimension appears to reflect the total combined proportions of ground and chipped stone tools in each assemblage. Layers G, H, D and C include mainly cobble tools, and have low proportions of other artifact classes. Layers E and F have higher proportions of groundstone and chipped stone classes. The assemblages were ordered in terms of combined ground and chipped stone tool proportions. This order was compared to the order of the assemblages on the dimension, using the Spearman's rho correlation coefficient. This produced an r-value of 0.771, significant at the .044 level.

Dimension 2 accounts for 29.05 percent of total variance. This dimension probably reflects the size and diversity of the assemblages. The assemblages from layers C and G have positive values on the dimension. Both assemblages are small, and numerous artifact classes are not represented. At the other end of the vector, the assemblage from layer E is the largest and most diversified, with 16 artifact classes represented. The order of the assemblages in terms of size (total number of artifacts) and diversity (total number of artifact classes) was compared to the order of the assemblages on the dimension. This yielded a Spearman's correlation coefficient of 0.829, significant at the .032 level.

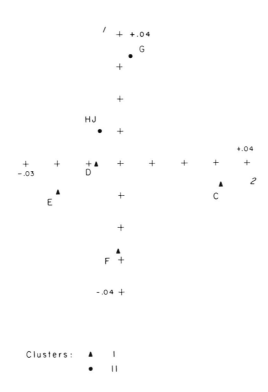

Figure 6.12  Multidimensional scaling of floor 9 stratigraphic units;
dimensions 1 x 2.

**Lithic Analysis of Excavation J**

The input data from Excavation J are presented in Table 6.7. The cell values include raw frequencies and row proportions. The stratigraphic units are based on the original excavation layer designations.

Layer D represents the large hearth feature at the top of the dark brown soil zone. Layer E is the dark brown matrix below the hearth. Layer F is the greasy black soil layer. Layers G and H were thin layers of dark brown to red-brown soil at the base of the matrix.

The furthest neighbour unconstrained cluster analysis of the six assemblages from Excavation J and the three cluster groupings from Excavation H resulted in a three cluster solution (Figure 6.13). Cluster 1 includes the assemblages from layers D, E and F, and Excavation H-sub-clusters 1A and 1B. Cluster 2 includes the assemblages from layers C, G and H. Excavation H-cluster 2 forms a residual third cluster.

Earlier, it was noted that Excavation J included a large hearth feature, and probably represented a special activity area at the site. It yielded a small sample of only 91 artifacts. This appears to have had an effect on the results of the cluster analyses. Clusters 1 and 2 are probably differentiated on the basis of sample size. The assemblages in cluster 1 are generally larger, and have more artifact classes represented than the cluster 2 assemblages. It is likely for this reason that the Excavation sub-clusters, 1A and 1B, were grouped in cluster 1.

Clusters 1 and 2 reflect a general separation of the upper (cluster 1) and lower (cluster 2) assemblages in the matrix. Layer C appears out of place, but this is probably due to the small sample size of C (6 artifacts). If layer C is not considered for the moment, the overall configuration of the unconstrained cluster analysis indicates a break in the matrix between F and G.

The constrained furthest neighbour cluster analysis of Excavation J resulted in a three cluster solution (Figure 6.14). Cluster 1 includes the assemblages of D, E and F. Cluster 2 includes the assemblages of G and H. Layer C is a residual. Once again, a break between F and G is indicated.

The artifact profiles for clusters 1 and 2 and the Excavation H clusters are shown in Figure 6.15. The assemblage from layer C is not

| stratigraphic designation | | cobble core tools | utilized cobble flakes | retouched cobble flakes | cobble cores | saws | ornamental/decorated | ground stone points | blunted ground stone tools | ground stone fragments | finished ground slate | unshaped abraders | shaped abraders | grinding stones | bifaces | formed unifaces | retouched flakes | cores/piece esquillees | microblades and cores | hammerstones | TOTALS |
|---|---|---|---|---|---|---|---|---|---|---|---|---|---|---|---|---|---|---|---|---|---|
| C | count<br>proportion | 4<br>.67 | 1<br>.17 | | | | | | | | | | | | | | | | | 1<br>.17 | 6 |
| D | | 4<br>.27 | 2<br>.13 | | 1<br>.07 | 2<br>.13 | | 1<br>.07 | | | | 1<br>.07 | | | | 1<br>.07 | 2<br>.13 | | 1<br>.07 | | 15 |
| E | | 15<br>.38 | 2<br>.05 | 3<br>.07 | 2<br>.05 | 1<br>.02 | 1<br>.02 | | | | | 3<br>.07 | 2<br>.05 | | 2<br>.05 | | 2<br>.05 | 3<br>.07 | 3<br>.07 | 1<br>.02 | 40 |
| F | | 4<br>.36 | 2<br>.18 | 1<br>.09 | | | | | | | 1<br>.09 | | | | | | 2<br>.18 | 1<br>.09 | | | 11 |
| G | | 6<br>.50 | 2<br>.17 | | 3<br>.25 | | | | | | | | | | | | | | 1<br>.08 | | 12 |
| H | | 4<br>.57 | | 1<br>.14 | 1<br>.14 | | | | | | | | | | | | | | 1<br>.14 | | 7 |
| | | | | | | | | | | | | | | | | | | | | | 91 |

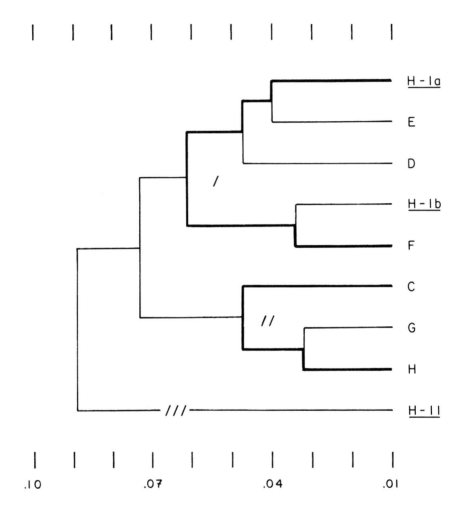

Figure 6.13   Unconstrained clustering of Excavation J with Excavation H̲
clusters.

included in the profiles because it does not appear to be clearly linked to constrained cluster 1.

Cluster 1 has most of the artifact classes represented (but not blunted rod-like implements, groundstone fragments or grinding stones), and appears most similar to Excavation H-sub-cluster 1A, although the proportion of utilized cobble flake tools is much smaller in Excavation J-cluster 1.

Cluster 2 is only represented by 19 artifacts, 10 of which are cobble core tools. A total of 14 artifact classes is not represented, making comparisons to Excavation H difficult, although the high proportion of cobble core tools does suggest some affinity with Excavation H-sub-cluster 1B. On the other hand, the presence of microblades (2) in these lower layers suggests some similarity to Excavation H-cluster 2. Moreover, numerous cobble core tools were also recovered from layers J and K in the floor 2 excavation. Thus, Excavation J-cluster 2 has some affinity to both cluster assemblages from Excavation H (1B, 2), but given the small size of the assemblage, more detailed comparisons cannot be made.

The metric multidimensional scaling of Excavation J produced a four dimension solution, accounting for 97.45 percent of the total variance in the data set. The first two dimensions are considered here (see Figure 6.16). They account for a combined total of 70.09 percent of the total variance.

Dimension 1 accounts for 45.57 percent of trace. The ordering of the assemblages on this dimension is in general agreement with the results of the cluster analyses. The assemblages from D, E and F each have positive values on the dimension. The assemblages from C, G and H each have negative values. The clearest break in the assemblages on this dimension is between F and G, as suggested in both cluster analyses. In general, the ordering of the assemblages on Dimension 1 is consistent with their stratigraphic position in the matrix. Only the assemblage from layer C is clearly out of place, and this is probably due to the small size of the assemblage.

Dimension 2, which accounts for 24.52 percent of variance in the data, could not be interpreted. The assemblages of D, E, G and H have positive values on this dimension, while F and C have negative values. The

223

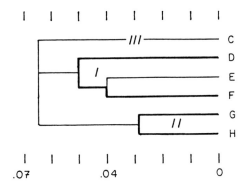

Figure 6.14  Constrained clustering of Excavation J stratigraphic units.

## Table 6.8
### Excavation J distance matrix

|   | C | D | E | F | G | H |
|---|------|------|------|------|------|------|
| C | 0.0 | | | | | |
| D | 0.063 | 0.0 | | | | |
| E | 0.058 | 0.045 | 0.0 | | | |
| F | 0.049 | 0.049 | 0.041 | 0.0 | | |
| G | 0.035 | 0.049 | 0.047 | 0.049 | 0.0 | |
| H | 0.045 | 0.063 | 0.045 | 0.057 | 0.029 | 0.0 |

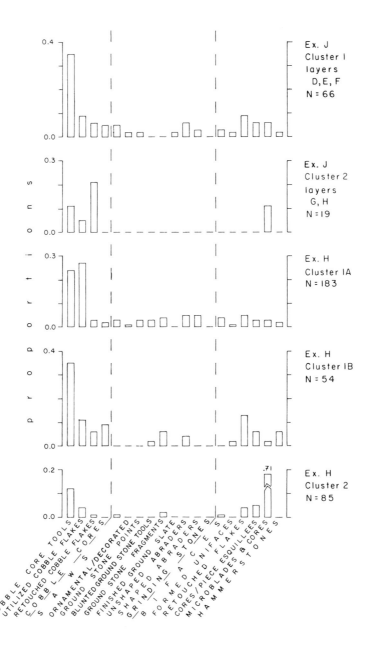

Figure 6.15  Artifact profiles of Excavation J and Excavation H clusters.

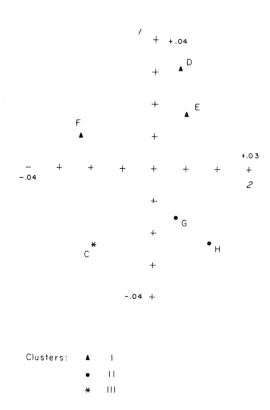

Clusters:  ▲  I
           ●  II
           *  III

Figure 6.16  Multidimensional scaling of Excavation J stratigraphic units;
dimensions 1 x 2.

226

only metric similarity between F and C is the proportion of utilized cobble flake tools, but D and G are similar to F and C in this regard, yet they are clearly distinct on the vector. It seems likely that Dimension 2 expresses some non-metric variable.

## Summary of the Paul Mason Site Lithic Analyses

In general, similar results were obtained in the clustering and multidimensional scaling analyses of the layer-level assemblages from the four main excavations at the Paul Mason Site. The data set from Excavation H was analyzed first as a "target" data set. The results of these analyses reflect assemblage variability and change through time. The assemblage clearly separated into early, middle and late cluster groupings. This is suggestive of three discrete cultural components, a pattern previously suggested by the radiocarbon dates. Further, there is good agreement between the cluster groupings and the dates. The early assemblages, represented by layers G and H, are characterized by high proportions of microblades and a near absence of groundstone implements. They were dated from ca. 5000 to 4500 B.P. These layers were combined with layers J and K from the red-brown zone of floor 2, which had similar artifact profiles. Together, these represent the early cultural component at the Paul Mason Site (see Figure 6.17).

The middle assemblages from Excavation H (F, D5) were characterized by reduction in the proportion of microblades, and increases in the proportions of cobble and some groundstone implements. These were combined with the lower dark brown zone assemblages from floor 2 (layers H2, H3, H4) and floor 9 (layers G, HJ). These assemblages, dated from ca. 4300 B.P. to 3800 B.P., represent the middle cultural component at the site (see Figure 6.17).

Finally, the upper assemblages (C, D1 to D4) were characterized by an increase in the number of tool classes, and generally in the size of the assemblages. These assemblages, dated to ca. 3000 B.P., represent the late cultural component at the Paul Mason Site. Layers C, D, E, and H1 from floor 2, D, E, and F from floor 9, and D, E, and F from Excavation J were shown to have similar artifact profiles to the upper layers of Excavation H, so they were added to this component (see Figure 6.17).

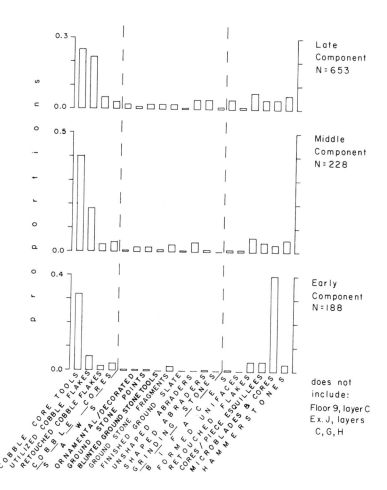

Figure 6.17   Artifact profiles for the three components of the Paul Mason
site.

The lower assemblage of Excavation J was problematic. It showed some affinity to both the middle and early component assemblages. Unfortunately, it yielded a very small artifact sample, and its position in the sequence is not clear at this time.

Assemblages of the upper component were recovered from floor 2, floor 9, Excavation J and Excavation H. This appears to have been the most intensive occupation of the site. These assemblages yielded the most artifacts, and had the most artifact classes represented, relative to assemblages from the earlier components. The increased proportion of abraders in this component indicates that bone, wood and antler implements were also more numerous at this time. In addition to the artifacts, a number of important features were associated with the upper component. The large hearth feature in layer D of Excavation J is included here. In the two housefloor excavations (floors 2, 9), it is clear that layers D (the ridge fill) and E were not formed prior to the levelling of the floors, and that they were associated with the use of the floors. Therefore, we may state that the prepared floor features on the slope also pertain to the upper component. In contrast, there was no evidence of house floor preparation in the middle or lower components.

In brief, three temporally discrete cultural components were identified at the Paul Mason Site. The early component (5000 to 4500 B.P.) is characterized by a limited assemblage emphasizing microblades and cobble implements. The middle component (4300 to 3800 B.P.) is characterized by a reduction in the manufacture of microblades, high proportions of cobble implements, and the introduction of some groundstone and chipped stone implements. Both the early and middle components lack evidence for permanent habitation or intensive processing of foodstuffs. The late component (3200 to 2700 B.P.) is characterized by a large diversified tool assemblage, probably including bone, wood and antler implements, and large prepared floor features oriented in a recognizable village alignment, and large, deep hearths within and outside the housefloor areas.

Chapter 7

## THE PREHISTORIC SEQUENCE AT KITSELAS CANYON

In order to investigate prehistoric cultural change at Kitselas
Canyon in diachronic perspective, this chapter integrates the cultural
components from the Paul Mason Site with those from Gitaus, as defined by
Allaire (1979).  This establishes a local sequence for Kitselas Canyon.
The sequence is divided into five prehistoric phases.

### The Bornite Phase

The Bornite Phase is named after Bornite Mountain, located east of
Kitselas Canyon.  It is represented by the early component at the Paul
Mason Site.  The date of 5050 ± 140 B.P. establishes this component as one
of the earliest in the entire Skeena Valley.  The diagnostic
characteristics of the Bornite Phase include a developed microcore and
blade industry, a variety of cobble core and flake tools, and the absence
of groundstone tools (see Figure 7.1).  Given the 5000 B.P. date, and the
microblades, the Bornite Phase is likely a late manifestation of the Early
Boreal Tradition.

The tool assemblage from this component suggests that the Paul Mason
Site probably functioned as a short term seasonal camp at this time.  It is
a limited assemblage.  Many artifact classes, including chipped bifaces,
projectile points, and formed unifaces are not represented (see Figure
7.1).  These implements would constitute personal gear (Binford 1979, 1980)
in a mobile hunter-gatherer settlement system.  Microblades and cobble core
and flake tools have the highest proportions in the artifact profile (see
Figure 7.1).  Following Binford's model, these represent expedient tools;
items that are manufactured to perform a task at hand, and generally
discarded after completion of the task without maintenance or curation.
Although microblades are present in this component in abundance, complete
microcores are absent.  Only two microcore rejuvenation flakes were
recovered.  If microcores were curated items, their absence at the Paul
Mason Site may be further evidence that the site was used as a short term
camp at this time.  The absence of other personal gear and permanent
habitation features supports this inference.

The lack of faunal material from this component precludes any

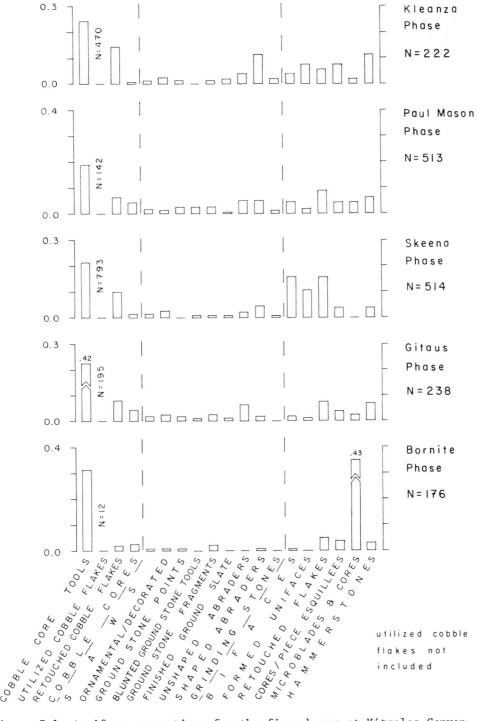

Figure 7.1  Artifact proportions for the five phases at Kitselas Canyon.

231

conclusive statement about season of occupation. A reasonable speculation would be mid to late summer. This would coincide with the maximum availability of salmon and berries. The presence of microblades with side edge use wear suggests that they were used as cutting tools, perhaps for processing fish. In an experimental study, Flenniken (1981:84) noted that hafted microliths were efficient fish processing tools. The acute angle utilized flakes may also have been used in the same capacity. The cobble core tools were probably crude woodworking tools, and these may have been used to make wooden traps or other fish harvesting or processing gear.

At present, it is unclear what relationship, if any, existed between the Bornite Phase and the contemporaneous early Period III components at Prince Rupert Harbour. The major problem here is that microblades have not been recovered at Prince Rupert Harbour. This may yet be a sampling problem, as microblades have been recovered from many other north coast sites. Alternatively, MacDonald and Inglis (1981:42) state that the excavated Period III components at Prince Rupert Harbour "are characterized by shallow midden accumulations and restricted site areas". These components may have been limited activity sites at which microblades were not used.

The obsidian used to manufacture the microblades at Kitselas Canyon was from the Anahim I source. This suggests possible interior trading relations for the people of the Bornite Phase. It will be recalled from Chapter 1 that microblades, unfortunately undated, were also recovered at GgSw 5, near Hagwilget.

At present, it is difficult to determine whether the cultural relations of the Bornite Phase lay to the coast or to the interior. In the end, it may be that, like the Old Cordilleran Culture to the south, there is no real cultural difference in the north between coast and interior prior to ca. 4500 B.P.

**The Gitaus Phase**

The Gitaus Phase is represented by assemblages at Gitaus (lower zone), for which the phase is named, and at the Paul Mason Site (lower dark brown zone). Radiocarbon dates from both assemblages range from roughly 4300 to 3600 B.P. Allaire (1979:45) argued that at Gitaus this assemblage

"does not seem to constitute an indigenous complex". It was identified by
Allaire (1979:45) "as a component of the type of cultural pattern prevalent
on the coast at the time". The radiocarbon dates place it within the late
time frame of Period III at Prince Rupert Harbour.

The coastal similarities include high proportions of cobble tools and
cortex spalls, and less frequently groundstone implements, including
abraders, rubbed slate points and stone saws. Leaf-shaped points also
occurred rarely (see Figure 7.1). Obsidian is present in small amounts in
both localities, but the source of this obsidian is Mt. Edziza, not
Anahim. This may be a further reflection of coastal relations for the
Gitaus Phase. The obsidian at Prince Rupert Harbour is also from
Mt. Edziza.

The major changes in the tool assemblage from the preceeding Bornite
Phase are the decline (if not absence) of microblades, and the presence of
a developed groundstone industry. Microblades were not recovered from the
early component at Gitaus, and their presence in the middle component at
the Paul Mason Site was argued to be a result of disturbance of the
red-brown zone related to house floor construction. Another important
change is the increase in proportion of the groundstone industry. This is
consistent with Prince Rupert Harbour. Abraders constitute 8.0 percent of
the Gitaus Phase assemblage. Only one abrader was present in the Bornite
Phase (see Figure 7.1).

Allaire (1979:46) interpreted the early component at Gitaus as a
seasonal camp, probably used for summer fishing. There is nothing from the
lower dark brown zone at the Paul Mason Site to suggest an alternative to
Allaire's interpretation. Remains of permanent winter dwellings were not
recovered. The paucity of chipped stone tools (projectile points, bifaces,
scrapers) suggests that land mammal hunting was of minor importance at this
time. The assemblages from both sites emphasize cobble and flake tools and
abraders. Considering the proximity of the two sites, it is likely that
the Gitaus and Paul Mason Site assemblages, each dating to ca. 4000 B.P.,
represent occupation of Kitselas Canyon by the same group of people.

Allaire (1979:46) concluded that these were "coastal peoples...
exploiting the lower Skeena Valley... as far east as Kitselas Canyon".
This seems reasonable, given the assemblage similarities between the

Kitselas Canyon components and the Prince Rupert Harbour components. Both localities appear to be part of the same settlement-subsistence system at this time, whereas this was not clear for the preceeding Bornite Phase. The evidence for the importance of summer fishing at Kitselas Canyon during the Gitaus Phase is seen in the abundance of cortex spalls and acute angle flakes (N=195) (see Figure 7.1), which may have functionally replaced microblades as fish processing implements; the remains of birch bark rolls (Allaire 1979:31), which may have been used as torches for night fisheries; and the carved fish effigy from Gitaus (Allaire 1979:30). In addition, the presence of groundstone tools, especially abraders, suggests the manufacture of bone implements such as fish hooks and leisters.

There is no evidence from Gitaus or the Paul Mason Site for the construction of permanent winter habitations. This may be further evidence for summer use of Kitselas Canyon. It also implies winter habitation elsewhere, most likely Prince Rupert Harbour, where the winter climate was milder, and marine and foreshore resources were seasonally available.

Given the coastal similarities, and the likelihood of only seasonal use of Kitselas Canyon, the Gitaus Phase represents the first evidence for the establishment of a coastal-lower Skeena settlement system.

**The Skeena Phase**

The Skeena Phase is represented at Gitaus by the Skeena Complex (Allaire 1979:46), but was not identified at the Paul Mason Site. Zone A at GhSv 2 at Hagwilget Canyon is also a Skeena Phase component. The Gitaus component was dated, on the basis of stratigraphic position and general assemblage similarity to GhSv 2 - Zone A, to between 3600 and 3200 B.P. This corresponds to the temporal hiatus between the lower and upper dark brown soil zones at the Paul Mason Site.

The Skeena Phase represents an important change in subsistence orientation at Kitselas Canyon. The tool assemblage shows substantial increases in the proportions of formed bifaces, including lanceolate points, unifaces, and retouched flakes, relative to the Gitaus Phase (see Figure 7.1). This suggests a greater emphasis on land mammal hunting at this time. Groundstone implements, are also present, but in lower proportions relative to the Gitaus Phase. One exception, however, is shaped abraders which increase in proportion from 2.0 percent in the Gitaus Phase to 5.0 percent in the Skeena Phase (see Figure 7.1).

Allaire (1979:47) states that the Skeena Complex represents an adaptation toward "riverine and forest efficiency". This much seems clear, given the location and environmental setting of Kitselas Canyon. Does this reflect population displacement during the Skeena Phase? Allaire (1979:49) favoured the displacement model, stating that "the people of the Skeena Complex... appear to be newcomers in the canyon, and perhaps the lower Skeena".

I argued in Chapter 4 that coastal affiliation for the Skeena Phase was also plausible. This would be consistent with the lower Skeena settlement system model introduced above. Under this model, prehistoric cultural change is explained as an **in situ** development.

The strength of Allaire's argument was some general similarities between the Skeena Complex and other interior assemblages. They share well-made chipped stone tools, and have in common some specific types including lanceolate points.

In reviewing Allaire's argument, I noted some points of contention. First, the similarities between the Skeena Complex and interior assemblages are, in many cases, obscure. There is only one fish-tail point in the Skeena Complex and the lanceolate points are more similar in form and manufacturing technique to those from Prince Rupert Harbour than from interior sites. Certain diagnostic interior tool types, such as corner-notched points, are not represented in the Skeena Complex. The lowest undisturbed zone of the Skeena Complex at Gitaus is Zone III-lower. Here, the proportion of groundstone tools is again low, but most tool forms, including ground slate points are present. This is atypical of most contemporaneous interior assemblages.

The differences between the Skeena Complex and the early Period II assemblages from Prince Rupert Harbour are essentially quantitative, not qualitative, and this may relate to differing site locations and seasons of occupation. For example, there is good evidence that the Skeena Complex represents summer-fall use of Kitselas Canyon (see Chapter 4); there is no clear indication of winter occupation of the canyon at this time. The possibility that wintering occurred at Prince Rupert Harbour is consistent with the earlier Gitaus Phase settlement pattern, and with the Coast Tsimshian ethnographic model (see also Chapter 4).

Let us consider the differences in the early Period II coastal assemblages versus the Skeena Phase assemblages in terms of seasonal adaptations to differing resource bases (coastal versus riverine-forest). Chipped projectile points, bifaces and unifaces are represented in higher proportions at Kitselas Canyon than at Prince Rupert Harbour, where MacDonald and Inglis (1981:46) state that they occur rarely. This implies greater emphasis on land mammal hunting and processing at Kitselas Canyon than at Prince Rupert Harbour. But this would not be unexpected if seasonal occupation of the canyon was during the summer.

The absence of bone implements in the Skeena Complex is undoubtedly a factor of artifact preservation. Shaped abraders, which could have been used in the manufacture of bone tools, are present in the Skeena Complex. Exotic items including obsidian and unfacetted pigments are present in the assemblages of both areas, as are more diagnostic items, such as ribbed stone pendants.

Thus, there are many similarities between the Skeena Phase and the early Period II coastal assemblages that are consistent with the model of a lower Skeena settlement system, in which winters were spent at or near the coast and summers were spent upriver. The assemblage differences, I believe, are best accounted for in terms of seasonal exploitation of differing resource bases.

Cultural change at this time may be explained in terms of **in situ** developments related to increasing resource diversity and niche width within a single settlement system, rather than population displacement.

By the end of the Skeena Phase (ca. 3200 B.P.) it is likely that people living along the lower Skeena had achieved maximum resource diversity and niche width (cf. Christenson 1980). At Prince Rupert Harbour, the major resources, in addition to plant food, included sea mammals, salt-water fish, shellfish and land mammals. Prior to this time, shellfish procurement was limited. After this time, the relative importance of land mammal hunting declined. At Kitselas Canyon, the major resources were land mammals and fish (including salmon). Land mammal hunting was not as important prior to or after the Skeena Phase as during it.

## The Paul Mason Phase

The Paul Mason Phase is represented at the Paul Mason Site, but was
not identified at Gitaus. The dating of the component, as stated earlier,
is 3200 to 2700 B.P.

There are important differences in the artifact assemblages at
Kitselas Canyon between the Skeena Phase and the Paul Mason Phase. These
include a reduction in the proportion of chipped stone tools (bifaces and
formed unifaces), and increases in the proportions of groundstone and
cobble and flake tools (see Figure 7.1). The high proportions of unshaped
(5.0 percent) and shaped (5.0 percent) abraders in the Paul Mason Phase
suggests that the manufacture of bone tools continued to be important.

The most important change in the Paul Mason Phase is the presence of
the prepared house floors at the Paul Mason Site. This marks the first
evidence of permanent residential structures at Kitselas Canyon, and the
first indication of a winter village in the canyon.

The reduction in the proportion of the chipped stone industry
(especially projectile points, bifaces and unifaces) in the Paul Mason
Phase probably reflects a decline in the economic importance of land
mammals at this time. A similar economic trend occurred at Prince Rupert
Harbour some time after the onset of Period II (perhaps about 3000 B.P.).

The overall indication is that after 3000 B.P., there was a reduction
in food niche width along the entire lower Skeena. At Prince Rupert
Harbour, the decline in the economic importance of land mammals was
associated with an increase in the importance of inter-tidal resources
(MacDonald and Inglis 1981:45). The economic base began to shift from one
of resource diversity to one that placed increasing emphasis on maritime
(sea mammals, salt water fish) and especially foreshore resources.

At Kitselas Canyon, the faunal evidence is far less complete than at
Prince Rupert Harbour. The limited analysis that was completed (see
Appendix III) concentrated only on bone material from upper component
hearth features. The results of this analysis are far from conclusive.
However, fish bone was identified in much greater proportion than non-fish
bone, and in the non-identifiable fraction, it was thought that most

fragments were fish bone (L. Roberts 1984). This evidence corroborates the artifact trends noted between the Skeena Phase and the Paul Mason Phase, and reflects a similar trend to that seen at Prince Rupert Harbour at this time. There was a reduction in the procurement of land mammals, reflected in the decline of the Skeena Phase about 3200 B.P. Increasing economic importance was placed on aquatic resources, specifically fish, as indicated by the faunal evidence and by the change in the tool assemblage in the Paul Mason Phase to increasing use of bone and groundstone implements.

These economic changes are generally consistent with Christenson's model (Christenson 1980). Following the achievement of maximum resource diversity and food niche width by the end of the Skeena Phase, there was a reduction in niche width in the Paul Mason Phase. Christenson (1980:35-36) argued that this reduction usually results from the intensification of one or a few related resources with high potential yield. At Prince Rupert Harbour, intensification of shellfish, beginning about 3500 B.P., is indicated by the increase of shell in the middens. This trend was predicted elsewhere on the Northwest Coast by Croes and Hackenberger (1984) as a means of solving the over-wintering problem in a non-storing economy. Later in Period II, the introduction of perforated and notched pebble net sinkers and unilaterally barbed harpoons with line guards may reflect increased procurement of fish and sea mammals. At Kitselas Canyon, reduction in niche width was probably the result of intensification of fish procurement, particularly salmon.

The shift to more intensive salmon procurement was associated with the establishment of a permanent village at the Paul Mason Site. The partially subterranean house floors and the multiple in-floor hearths suggest winter occupation of the village. This marks a significant departure from the lower Skeena settlement system described thus far. Prior to the Paul Mason Phase, human use of Kitselas Canyon was probably restricted to summer and fall. A short-term fishing camp was indicated for the Bornite Phase, while the Gitaus and Skeena Phases may have been represented by a larger summer base camps. During the Gitaus and Skeena Phases, winter settlement was probably at or near Prince Rupert Harbour, where shellfish were available.

The presence of a winter village at Kitselas Canyon during the Paul

Mason Phase suggests that a small group of people, perhaps those who already regularly used Kitselas Canyon in summer, were no longer returning to Prince Rupert Harbour for the winter.

Why would such a decision be made? One reason pertains to travel costs. It may have been decided that the distance between Kitselas Canyon and Prince Rupert Harbour was too great to make back and forth travel worthwhile. But this cannot be the only reason. It begs the question: why was this decision not made earlier?

A more important reason concerns the reduction of the food niche width. As the procurement of salmon intensified along the lower Skeena, the importance of Kitselas Canyon as a primary fishing location increased. If formalized territorial or resource ownership was absent at this time (as might be expected of egalitarian hunter-gatherers) control of this location may have been possible only through its permanent settlement. Control of the canyon may not have been possible from a winter village base at Prince Rupert Harbour. Indeed, MacIlwraith (1948(1):131-32) states that control of resources and territories by Bella Coola groups tended to decrease with distance from the winter village. Once a reliable technology for preservation and storage of salmon was developed, winter settlement of Kitselas Canyon would have been permitted. It is important to recall here that Kitselas Canyon is located about 90 km upriver from Prince Rupert Harbour. Salmon migrating this distance would lose some of their oil content. The area is also drier than Prince Rupert (see Table 3.1). Both factors combine to make Kitselas Canyon an ideal location for preserving salmon, as well as procuring it.

In this sense, the "travel cost" decision may have favoured permanent residence at Kitselas Canyon, rather than an annual commute to and from Prince Rupert Harbour.

**The Kleanza Phase**

The Kleanza Phase is represented at Gitaus by the Kleanza Complex. It was not identified at the Paul Mason Site. A single radiocarbon date of 2390 ± 85 B.P. has been obtained for this phase. This date is minimally 200 years later than the latest date for the Paul Mason Phase, and it is within Allaire's (1979:48) postulated time frame for the Kleanza Complex of

2500 to 1500 B.P.

There are assemblage similarities between the Paul Mason Phase and the Kleanza Phase, but there are sufficient differences to warrant assignment as separate cultures. The similarities include continuing low proportions of chipped stone tools, high proportions of groundstone and cobble implements (see Figure 7.1), and widespread litters of fire-cracked rock. Allaire (1979:48) argued that the fire-cracked rock and the presence of a large post outline in the river bank profile at Gitaus were suggestive of permanent house construction. If so, this would be another similarity to the Paul Mason Phase.

These general similarities in the artifact assemblages and cultural features between the Paul Mason Phase and the Kleanza Phase suggest little or no change at the level of subsistence and settlement. Cobble, bone and groundstone tools continue to dominate the artifact assemblage in the Kleanza Phase.

The addition of new artifact types in the Kleanza Phase, including net sinkers, indicates that intensive fish exploitation continued to be important.

The main difference between the Paul Mason Phase and the Kleanza Phase is the addition of new artifact forms in the Kleanza Phase related to personal adornment and status. These include T-shaped labrets, slate mirrors, and slate knives or daggers.

Allaire (1979:49-50) stated that these new forms all had coastal correlates in the Middle Horizon (late Period II) at Prince Rupert Harbour. He argued that their introduction at Gitaus reflected an advanced stage of coastal acculturation of the people of the canyon.

In the model presented here, the people of the canyon were "coastal" people from as early as 4300 B.P.--that is, people who had established a settlement system along the lower Skeena from Prince Rupert Harbour to Kitselas Canyon. By ca. 3200 B.P., a group of these people had established permanent settlement at Kitselas Canyon. But undoubtedly, these people maintained contact through exchange, inter-marriage and kinship affiliation with their coastal neighbours. This contact continued into the historic period (see Allaire 1984:91).

Rather than reflecting acculturation, an alternative explanation is that the new artifact forms at Kitselas Canyon and Prince Rupert Harbour reflect similar changes developing within the same general cultural system about 2500 B.P.

On the coast, these new artifact forms, and others including zoomorphic bark shredders, decorated and undecorated stone and bone clubs, kerfed boxes, beads, bracelets, nephrite adzes, amber, copper and dentalium have all been linked by MacDonald (1983) and MacDonald and Inglis (1981, 1975) to the emergence of social ranking. MacDonald (1983:102) states:

> the emphasis on weaponry noted at this time coincides with the brief appearance of status grave goods that may be related to increased differentiation of rank. The development of ranked social status may also explain the concentration of materials imported over considerable distances, such as copper, obsidian, jet, amber and dentalium.

If Kitselas Canyon and Prince Rupert Harbour were incorporated in the same general cultural system, then we must assume that social ranking was also present at Kitselas Canyon during the Kleanza Phase.

It is true that many of the new artifact forms from Period II at Prince Rupert Harbour are not represented in the Kleanza Phase. This may be accounted for, at least in part, by the fact that far more extensive excavation of Period II components has been conducted at Prince Rupert Harbour than at Kitselas Canyon, and also by the fact that many of the new artifact forms at Prince Rupert Harbour were manufactured from bone or wood, which would not have been preserved at Kitselas Canyon. Groundstone adzes are present for the first time at Kitselas Canyon in the Kleanza Phase, which suggests that fine wood-working was being done.


**Historic Period**

There is a gap in the cultural sequence from the end of the Kleanza Phase (ca. 2000 to 1500 B.P.) to the beginning of the Historic Period. Filling in this gap is an important research objective for future work.

The Historic Period represents the culmination of the evolution of aboriginal culture in the Tsimshian area. A detailed ethnographic description of the Kitselas was given in Chapter 4. To recap the salient points here, the Kitselas were part of Tsimshian ranked society. They had lineage chiefs, whose status was ascribed, and whose titles and prerogatives were passed on through matrilineal descent. Status differences were rigidly observed--from nobility to commoner to slave.

The Kitselas were permanent occupants of the canyon at the time of contact, residing in two villages--Gitlaxdzawk and Gitsaex. The combined population of these villages may have exceeded 600 people. Their economy was based on the intensive production of salmon, and supplemented by a variety of other coastal and interior resources indigenous to the Kitselas Canyon vicinity.

This model of ethnographic Kitselas culture constitutes the comparative base for our study of the evolution of prehistoric social organization in the area.

## Summary

The known prehistoric cultural sequence from Kitselas Canyon covers a period from 5000 B.P. to some time between 2000 and 1500 B.P. Five local phases have been identified from the two excavated sites, Gitaus and the Paul Mason Site. These phases are summarized in the following table.

Table 7.1
**The Prehistoric Cultural Sequence at Kitselas Canyon**

| Culture | Dates (B.P.) | Sites | Site Function |
|---|---|---|---|
| Historic | 250 to present | Gitlaxdzawk Gitsaex | permanent village |
| Kleanza Phase | 2500 to 1500 | Gitaus* | permanent village |
| Paul Mason Phase | 3200 to 2700 | PMS** | permanent village |
| Skeena Phase | 3600 to 3200 | Gitaus* | summer-fall base camp (?) |
| Gitaus Phase | 4300 to 3600 | Gitaus*, PMS | summer-fall base camp (?) |
| Bornite Phase | 5000 to 4300 | PMS | summer fishing camp (?) |

\* source: Allaire 1979
\*\* PMS: Paul Mason Site

Chapter 8

## PREHISTORIC SOCIAL ORGANIZATION AT KITSELAS CANYON

The establishment of a prehistoric cultural sequence at Kitselas Canyon, covering the period from 5000 to approximately 2000 B.P., provides the temporal framework for an investigation of prehistoric cultural change. This chapter investigates evidence related to the proposition that egalitarian corporate groups evolved at Kitselas Canyon during the Paul Mason Phase.

The local phases identified in the previous chapter are examined in terms of a series of selected variables that reflect social change. These are residential permanency, storage, population aggregation, household variability, and material indicators of wealth or prestige. The variables are defined, and their relation to the study of social change is explicated. Change in the state of each variable is determined by investigation and comparison of the cultural phases.

## Residential Permanency

### Definitions and Distinctions

Residential permanency, sedentism and mobility have received much attention from archaeologists in recent years (e.g., Flannery 1972; Harris 1978; Kelly 1983; Eder 1984; Rafferty 1985). These terms have often been used in reference to different concepts however, and have at times been poorly distinguished.

Some have contrasted sedentism and mobility (e.g., Kelly 1983), and have considered these two concepts as opposite ends of a continuum. Others such as Eder (1984:844) and Rafferty (1985:4) consider sedentism to be a threshold property. Rafferty (1985:4) states that "sedentary settlement systems are those in which at least part of the population remains at the same location throughout the entire year". If this threshold is not met, the population is considered mobile. This definition actually allows for considerable mobility within an erstwhile sedentary system, as long as the residence location is permanent and is inhabited year round by at least a few people. This approaches the concept of "logistical mobility" (Binford 1980; Hitchcock 1982; Kelly 1983), in which small groups range out from a base location for subsistence procurement purposes, while dependants stay at home (Hitchcock 1982:258). Thus, sedentary groups may be logistically mobile, as long as the residential base is permanent.

Clearly, the distinctions between residential permanency, sedentism and mobility are subtle, and can vary depending on the definitions used. In this study, concern is with the extent to which the basic socioeconomic unit functions as a permanent co-residential group. Therefore, the definition of residential permanency that I adopt is consistent with Rafferty's: the permanent or year-round use of a residence location by at least some members of the primary socioeconomic unit.

## Residential Permanency on the Northwest Coast

Residential permanency on the Northwest Coast is an elusive concept. At contact, most Northwest Coast groups practised some residential mobility as part of the economic life cycle. Mitchell (1983:97) states, "the people moved around a lot... they did so as a means of acquiring various resources from various places during the year". Most Northwest Coast groups maintained permanent villages with large permanent dwellings. Generally, each individual returned to the same dwelling in the same village year after year. In most cases, however, the dwellings were not permanently used. These villages were usually, but not always, occupied most intensively in winter. At other times of the year, residential mobility occurred, and the dwellings were vacated. This often involved an entire household moving en masse from one location to another. An example of this kind of mobility is seen in the late winter movement of Coast Tsimshian groups from the Prince Rupert Harbour area to the lower Nass River for the eulachon fishery.

Burley (1983:165) refers to this pattern of settlement as "semi-sedentary", and Matson (1983:126) states that for most Northwest Coast groups much of the year was spent at the winter village site, and that substantially less mobility took place among these groups than among egalitarian foragers (see also Kelly 1983:280-81).

## Residential Permanency and Social Organization

Residential permanency promotes the formation of permanent social groups larger than the nuclear family--that is, groups that do not seasonally disband and re-form later, often with new or different members. This is simply a factor of people living and working together on a more permanent basis. Social groups that form within sedentary communities are more likely to be enduring than groups that form within mobile foraging populations because group size and composition will be less subject to change.

High residential mobility may inhibit the formation of permanent social groups larger than the nuclear family. Among foraging populations, variance in the size and composition of the co-residential group will be continually adjusted to the specific resources exploited (see Smith 1981:42). For example, the size and composition of Cree hunting parties varies depending on whether caribou (large hunting party) or moose (small hunting party) are being exploited (Rogers 1972:111). Among the Great Basin Shoshone, large groups formed for rabbit drives, whereas small family groups foraged independently at other times of the year (Steward 1955:109).

Among mobile foraging societies the maximum effective social unit is the band, whose size rarely exceeds 30 to 40 individuals (Martin 1973). Band-size groupings are typically of short annual duration, however, with the nuclear family being the primary socioeconomic unit. Size and composition of the band may fluctuate from year to year.

In societies with greater residential permanency, the maximum social unit is the village, which on the Northwest Coast often consisted of several hundred people. Further, villages stay together for much greater duration than the foraging band, and as a result the unit as a whole is less subject to fluctuation. Thus, the primary socioeconomic unit of the sedentary village has the potential, at least, to be larger than the nuclear family. Residential permanency favours the formation of large enduring social groups of rigid or fixed membership more so than a mobile lifestyle. It does so simply by creating a situation in which face-to-face contact occurs among larger groups of people for longer durations.

## Residential Permanency at Kitselas Canyon

At Kitselas Canyon, the duration of annual residence appears to have increased through time, reaching the threshold of permanency during the Paul Mason Phase.

Initial settlement, during the Bornite Phase, was interpreted as a short-term or temporary camp. This was based on the small site size, the limited assemblage comprising expedient tools, and the absence of features such as housepits, fire-cracked rock, and postmoulds that might indicate more permanent habitation.

With the onset of the Gitaus Phase, technological change occurred at Kitselas Canyon that suggests greater use of the canyon and longer annual duration of residence. This includes a decline in the production of microblades and the introduction of new groundstone and chipped stone artifact forms. Some of the new artifact forms include items of personal gear (shaped abraders, groundstone points, leaf-shaped bifaces). Although their proportions were low, their presence suggests that settlement of the canyon at this time was in the form of a seasonal base camp, rather than a temporary camp.

During the Skeena Phase, the settlement of Kitselas Canyon was probably more intensive, in terms of the variety of resources exploited, than in the Bornite and Gitaus Phases. This is evident in the increase in the proportion of artifact forms associated with land mammal hunting in the Skeena Complex. It is not clear, however, if this reflects a change in duration of residence at the canyon at this time. The changes in the tool assemblage may have been related more to an increase in resource diversity, compared to the Gitaus Phase, than to longer duration of residence. Permanent house features were not identified for the Skeena Phase, nor was there an indication of intensive processing of foodstuffs for over-wintering (i.e., no fire-cracked rock or large hearths). Fishing, in addition to land mammal hunting, continued to be an important economic pursuit at this time, and coupled with the seasonal indicator of sub-adult fisher (Martes pennanti) elements, a summer base camp occupation is inferred.

The Paul Mason Phase represents substantial change in residential permanency at Kitselas Canyon. For the first time, permanent residential structures are represented in the prepared house floors at the Paul Mason Site. These floors reflect, minimally, residence at Kitselas Canyon during the winter. Prior to this time, there is evidence only for summer occupation at Kitselas Canyon.

A number of features attests to the use of these floors during the winter months. Their construction on the slope of the site appears to have been a conscious choice because abundant flat ground was available on the terrace directly behind the slope. By digging the floors into the slope, a semi-subterranean structure was created, which would be well-suited to the conservation of heat. The exposure of the open or down slope side of the dwellings was southwest (see Figure 5.2) which would have provided maximum protection against winter winds, and maximum exposure to the sun's heat. Both excavated house floors had two hearths, suggestive of multiple family occupation. In each case, one hearth was centrally located, and the other was located near the front or downslope side of the floor. The placement of these hearths suggests that they functioned to provide household heat in addition to cooking food.

The argument for residential permanency at Kitselas Canyon during the Paul Mason Phase is further supported when it is considered that the resource importance of the canyon is greatest during the summer when the salmon are running. The presence of salmon bones and a tool assemblage oriented toward fishing reflect continued use of the canyon during the summer months.

The change in human occupation of Kitselas Canyon during the Paul Mason Phase is the addition of a winter village. Intensive occupation of extended duration now existed for at least two periods of the year, summer and winter. This reflects residence by most of the population at Kitselas Canyon for a minimum of 8 or 9 months of the year. Logistical mobility may have been practised during the spring (eulachon fishing or trading for grease) and fall (hunting), but this was probably done by small groups. It is likely that the village was used throughout the year by at least some individuals, thus complying with our definition of residential permanency.

During the Kleanza Phase, there is no indication of change in the pattern of residence established in the Paul Mason Phase. Although house floor features were not identified for the Kleanza Phase, the presence of a litter of fire-cracked rock and the single large post mould probably reflect continued winter residence at Kitselas Canyon.

The pattern of residential permanency continued into the historic period, when the villages of Gitsaex and Gitlaxdzawk were occupied on a year-round basis.

In summary, two periods of residential change are inferred for the prehistoric sequence at Kitselas Canyon. The earliest change occurred after 4500 B.P. Although the data are incomplete, a probable shift from a temporary camp (the Bornite Phase) to a summer base camp occupation (the Gitaus Phase) is suggested, associated with the emergence of the lower Skeena settlement system. The next period of change occurred during the Paul Mason Phase about 3200 B.P. This was the establishment of a permanent winter village at the Paul Mason Site. Given continued intensive summer use of the canyon, this change marks the development of residential permanency at Kitselas Canyon.

## Storage

Testart (1982:523) states that food storage--the practice of putting up resources for future consumption--lies "at the intersection of four conditions". These are abundance and seasonality of resources, and efficient food-getting and food-storing techniques. Where these conditions are present, an economy in which storage provides the bulk of food during the season of scarcity is likely to develop.

### Storage and Social Change

The importance of storage as a necessary condition for cultural change is widely acknowledged by prehistorians. It has been linked to the adoption of sedentary life (Flannery 1972; Harris 1978; Testart 1982), to the origins of agriculture (Flannery 1969, 1973; Reed 1977a, 1977b; Redman 1977; Hassan 1977), and ultimately to the evolution of social stratification (Testart 1982). However, the practice of storage is rather ubiquitous. Although it is strongly associated with the above transformations, it does not necessarily cause them to occur, and it may be practised by groups who do not fit the above conditions. For example, the Inuit practise storage, as do many Athapaskan groups, who are neither sedentary, agricultural or socially stratified.  In general, food storage is an over-wintering strategy (Binford 1980:15) important to groups living in temperate environments whether their economies are based on extraction or production.

Storage is important to the process of social change as a prerequisite or necessary condition.  Stored commodities may come to be regarded as wealth or as an avenue to wealth, and differences in the commodities stored, or in the amounts stored, may serve to differentiate individuals in the community in terms of status.

## Storage: Practical and Social

In egalitarian societies, stored food is usually subject to the same system of reciprocal sharing that prevails for non-stored goods.  If one person's supplies are exhausted and another has something left, he will be expected to share out what remains (see Ingold 1982:532).

At this point, it is important to recognize two types of storage. Storage can serve the dual purpose of meeting future subsistence needs (over-wintering) and providing a base of wealth or potential wealth.  In this regard, Ingold (1982:532) distinguishes "practical storage" from "social storage".  Practical storage is the setting aside of food stocks for the future, and is a function of the scheduling of resource extraction and consumption.  Social storage refers to "the convergence of rights to specific resources... upon a specific interest... governed by the perception of scarcity of those resources conceived as property or wealth" (Ingold 1982:532).  In practical storage, a group stores only what it needs, or perceives to need, to meet the requirements of subsistence. Excess or surplus stores, as they exist, are expected to be shared out as the need arises, not transformed into wealth.  In social storage, there is a conscious desire to store beyond subsistence needs, and to transform the surplus into wealth.

Both egalitarian and ranked societies may practise practical storage. Only ranked societies, who are concerned with the accumulation of wealth, may practise social storage.

### Storage Practices at Kitselas Canyon

At Kitselas Canyon, cache pits provide evidence of abundant storage.
On the east side of the canyon, 375 cache pits were recorded (see
Figure 8.1) during a complete surface survey of the area. The pits were
measured for rim diameter and depth (see Table 8.1, 8.3), and shovel tested
to determine function. No fire-cracked rock was recovered from the shovel
tests, thus eliminating the possiblity that these features were earth
ovens. It is assumed that these were primarily food storage facilities,
although at times other commodities may have been stored.

The problem lies in dating these facilities. Food caching may be
coeval with the earliest known human settlement of Kitselas Canyon, and may
have continued unabated throughout the cultural sequence. In the absence
of radiocarbon dates, the assignment of cache pits to cultural phases
cannot be done with certainty.

The pattern of distribution of many of these facilities in relation
to village locations, however, suggests an association between pits and
villages. In the following analysis, cache pits within a 250 metre radius
of the two village locations on the east side of the canyon--the Paul Mason
Site and Gitsaex--are assigned to the respective sites. By using these two
sites in the analysis, we may compare differences in storage practices
between a site where social ranking was known to exist (Gitsaex) and a site
of unknown social complexity.

The distance of 250 metres was used because it is a relatively short
walking distance (maximum return distance is 500 metres), and because the
250 metre radii boundaries for Gitsaex and the Paul Mason Site do not
overlap. At the Kitwanga hillfort, the maximum distance between food
storage facilities and the residential area of the site was about 250
metres (MacDonald 1979:68).

Gitaus is not included in this analysis for two reasons. First, the
early twentieth century settlement of White Town Kitselas was located
adjacent to Gitaus, and may have been responsible for disturbing cache pits
in the immediate area. At any rate, very few cache pits were recorded in
close proximity to Gitaus. Second, as no house floors were recorded at
Gitaus, it is not clear where the main residential area of the site was, or
if indeed there was only one such area. Therefore, there was no way of

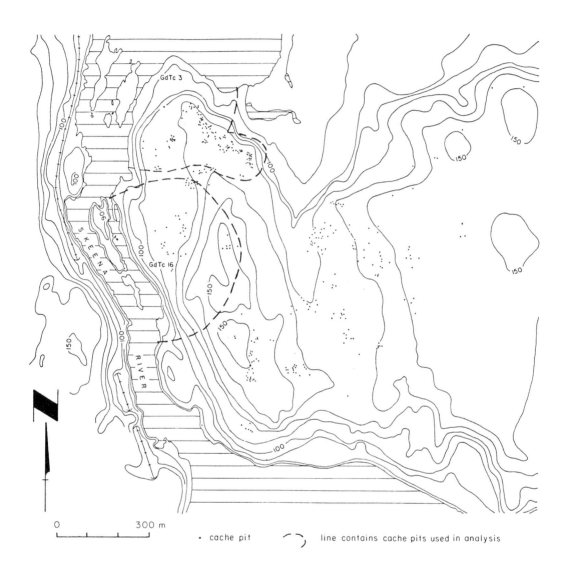

Figure 8.1  Cache pits on the east side of Kitselas Canyon.

knowing what locus to use in drawing a 250 metre radius.

The densest cluster of cache pits is located on a ridge overlooking the Gitsaex village site (see Figure 8.1). These cache pits were probably used by the inhabitants of Gitsaex, given their proximity to the village. There are 75 cache pits within the 250 metre radius. However, the cache pits extend east along the ridge in an unbroken cluster for a short distance beyond the 250 metre boundary. It is likely that these cache pits were also used by the inhabitants of Gitsaex. They are therefore included in the sample, bringing the total number of cache pits in close proximity to Gitsaex to 128 (Figure 8.1; Table 8.1). By comparison, 39 cache pits lie within a 250 metre radius of the Paul Mason Site (Figure 8.1; Table 8.3). Assuming that the two villages were occupied for roughly equal lengths of time, the difference in the number of cache pits may reflect relatively greater importance for storage in the historic period (Gitsaex) compared to the prehistoric period during the Paul Mason Phase. In turn, this may be related to a distinction between social storage and practical storage.

Before testing this proposition, a few caveats should be duly noted. First, cache pits are only one of many types of storage facilities that may have been used at Kitselas Canyon. A variety of above ground facilities may have been used, especially in the historic period when kerfed boxes are known to have existed in the Tsimshian area (MacDonald and Inglis 1981:45). Second, some cache pits may have filled with sediment or refuse and may no longer be recognizable as surface features. This is especially relevant for the prehistoric period, where the cache pits are theoretically much older than the historic period. Some cache pits may have been re-used through time. Finally, on the east side of the canyon, 208 cache pits lie outside the designated radii of Gitsaex and the Paul Mason Site. The association of these cache pits with specific habitation sites is unknown.

Given these factors, it must be emphasized that a simple comparison of the number of cache pits in close proximity to a given site provides only an approximation of the extent of storage practised by the inhabitants of the site. It is hoped that in future studies, this type of analysis can be applied with better control of ownership and duration of use of storage facilities.

## Estimating Storage Capacities

Was cache pit storage practised more intensively at Gitsaex than at the Paul Mason Site? In order to address this question an estimate of "per capita cache pit storage capacity" must be made. This is done by dividing the total cache pit storage capacity for each site by the site population estimate. The following formula is used:

$$\frac{(\pi \times CP\ radius^2 \times CP\ depth \times 1.5)}{site\ population\ estimate}$$

The numerator of the formula provides a means of estimating total cache pit storage capacity for each site. The cache pits are treated as cylinders. Although bowl-shaped at present, it is assumed that at the time of use, these facilities had relatively straight sides and flat bottoms. The bowl-shaped contour is probably a result of erosion. The volume of a cylinder is $\pi r^2 h$, where h is the height or depth of the cylinder. This value is multiplied here by a constant of 1.5, based on the following rationale. Originally, the cache pits were deeper than at present; erosion has partially filled each pit. Of the cache pits recorded on survey, mean depth of the basin was 28.6 cm. Shovel-testing of these pits revealed a mixture of dark brown soil and humus in the bottom, 10 to 15 cm thick, overlying sterile forest soil. This suggests that the original volume of the cache pits was roughly 50 percent greater than at present; hence multiplication of the present volume estimates by 1.5. Individual cache pit volumes are then summed to arrive at an estimate of total cache pit storage capacity for each site.

The denominator provides a means of controlling for differences in village size. This can prove difficult, however, because site population estimates can vary considerably depending on the model used. Most models estimate population size on the basis of the size and number of dwellings at the site, arguing that a correlation exists between dwelling size and household size (see Naroll 1962; LeBlanc 1971; Kramer 1979). Other studies have used total camp space as a means of estimating site population (see Wiessner 1974).

In a study of sedentary aboriginal Californian villages, Cook and Heizer (1968) obtained a strong correlation between dwelling size and household size, but their results indicate a logarithmic relationship; as household size increased, mean floor space per person also increased.

For Gitsaex, the most appropriate way to estimate village population is to make use of the ethnographic data. Coast Tsimshian winter dwellings at Kitkatla averaged about 10 x 10 metres, or 100 m$^2$ (Boas 1916:46-48). Emmons (1912:469) estimated one house structure at Gitsaex to be 36 feet (10.98 metres) by 36 feet (1296 square feet) or 120.53 m$^2$, which is within range of Boas' estimate. Therefore, I will use 100 m$^2$ as the average Kitselas dwelling size. As a household population average for Gitsaex, I will use the figure, 25. This is the number used by Donald and Mitchell (1975:333) based on Tolmie's (1963:304, 306, 307) estimates for the Kwakiutl at Fort McLaughlin and the same figure is used by McNeary (1976:128) for traditional Niska household size. When average dwelling size (100 m$^2$) is divided by average household size (25), the amount of house floor space per person is 4 m$^2$. This figure can then be applied to each of the 17 house floors at Gitsaex to arrive at household population estimates, the sum of which is the village estimate.

The ethnographic model may have dubious applicability to the Paul Mason Site, whose house floors are dated to 3000 B.P. In estimating village population during the Paul Mason Phase, the regression model developed by Cook and Heizer (1968) is used because their model considers differences in household size as a factor affecting the amount of house floor space per person. At the Paul Mason Site, house floor space ranged from 45.76 m$^2$ to 72.6 m$^2$. Within this range, the amount of house floor space per person may vary, and this could have an effect on the overall village population estimate.

The metric measurements of the cache pits in close proximity to Gitsaex are presented in Table 8.1. Measurements of 120 cache pits were taken; 8 cache pits were identified but not measured, either because of disturbance (road construction, gravel quarrying) or because they were located in inpenetrable bush. The estimated total volume capacity of the 120 cache pits, for which measurements were taken, is 106.47 m$^3$. The mean volume of these cache pits is 0.89 m$^3$. Applying the mean to the 8 unmeasured cache pits, a total volume of 113.59 m$^3$ is obtained for all 128 cache pits used in the Gitsaex sample.

## Table 8.1
## Cache Pit Measurements for Gitsaex*

| Diameter (metres) | Depth (metres) | Volume (metres³) | Diameter | Depth | Volume |
|---|---|---|---|---|---|
| 0.3 | 0.3 | 0.60 | 1.7 | 0.25 | 0.85 |
| 2.2 | 0.50 | 2.85 | 1.1 | 0.25 | 0.36 |
| 1.0 | 0.27 | 0.32 | 1.3 | 0.30 | 0.60 |
| 0.8 | 0.25 | 0.19 | 1.1 | 0.28 | 0.40 |
| 1.3 | 0.25 | 0.50 | 1.5 | 0.35 | 0.93 |
| 1.5 | 0.35 | 0.93 | 1.1 | 0.17 | 0.24 |
| 1.8 | 0.37 | 1.41 | 1.3 | 0.18 | 0.36 |
| 1.5 | 0.29 | 0.77 | 1.3 | 0.34 | 0.68 |
| 1.0 | 0.31 | 0.37 | 1.1 | 0.31 | 0.44 |
| 1.1 | 0.22 | 0.31 | 0.9 | 0.25 | 0.24 |
| 1.1 | 0.26 | 0.37 | 1.2 | 0.33 | 0.56 |
| 1.0 | 0.25 | 0.29 | 1.8 | 0.45 | 1.72 |
| 1.2 | 0.3 | 0.51 | 1.2 | 0.43 | 0.73 |
| 1.5 | 0.32 | 0.85 | 1.5 | 0.45 | 1.19 |
| 2.0 | 0.55 | 2.59 | 1.7 | 0.48 | 1.63 |
| 1.0 | 0.25 | 0.29 | 1.3 | 0.27 | 0.54 |
| 1.4 | 0.20 | 0.46 | 1.2 | 0.28 | 0.48 |
| 1.1 | 0.28 | 0.40 | 1.1 | 0.27 | 0.38 |
| 1.7 | 0.44 | 1.50 | 1.5 | 0.35 | 0.93 |
| 1.4 | 0.35 | 0.81 | 1.2 | 0.30 | 0.51 |
| 1.4 | 0.21 | 0.48 | 1.3 | 0.20 | 0.40 |
| 1.2 | 0.30 | 0.51 | 1.7 | 0.38 | 1.29 |
| 1.0 | 0.21 | 0.25 | 1.4 | 0.34 | 0.79 |
| 0.6 | 0.35 | 0.15 | 0.9 | 0.21 | 0.20 |
| 1.3 | 0.28 | 0.56 | 1.2 | 0.25 | 0.48 |
| 1.2 | 0.31 | 0.53 | 1.3 | 0.30 | 0.60 |
| 1.3 | 0.28 | 0.56 | 1.0 | 0.13 | 0.15 |
| 1.4 | 0.21 | 0.48 | 1.4 | 0.20 | 0.46 |
| 0.7 | 0.30 | 0.17 | 1.7 | 0.42 | 1.43 |
| 1.8 | 0.43 | 1.64 | 1.3 | 0.33 | 0.66 |
| 1.6 | 0.25 | 0.75 | 1.5 | 0.32 | 0.85 |
| 1.5 | 0.22 | 0.58 | 1.8 | 0.20 | 0.76 |
| 1.2 | 0.28 | 0.48 | 1.3 | 0.23 | 0.46 |
| 1.5 | 0.39 | 1.03 | 1.1 | 0.23 | 0.33 |
| 1.2 | 0.19 | 0.32 | 1.4 | 0.32 | 0.74 |
| 2.2 | 0.40 | 2.28 | 1.3 | 0.40 | 0.80 |
| 2.2 | 0.62 | 3.53 | 2.2 | 0.90 | 5.13 |
| 0.8 | 0.15 | 0.11 | 1.0 | 0.20 | 0.24 |
| 0.9 | 0.19 | 0.18 | 1.3 | 0.19 | 0.38 |
| 1.2 | 0.30 | 0.51 | 1.4 | 0.28 | 0.65 |
| 1.7 | 0.30 | 1.02 | 1.3 | 0.27 | 0.54 |
| 2.2 | 0.30 | 1.71 | 1.7 | 0.32 | 1.09 |
| 1.6 | 0.24 | 0.72 | 1.4 | 0.30 | 0.53 |
| 1.0 | 0.23 | 0.27 | 1.2 | 0.25 | 0.42 |

Table 8.1 (continued)

| Diameter | Depth | Volume | Diameter | Depth | Volume |
|----------|-------|--------|----------|-------|--------|
| 1.2 | 0.22 | 0.37 | 1.2 | 0.30 | 0.51 |
| 1.2 | 0.30 | 0.51 | - | unmeasured | - |
| - | - | - | - | - | - |
| 1.3 | 0.31 | 0.62 | - | - | - |
| - | - | - | - | - | - |
| 1.7 | 0.32 | 1.09 | 2.1 | 0.34 | 1.77 |
| 1.9 | 0.30 | 1.28 | 1.8 | 0.32 | 1.22 |
| 1.5 | 0.30 | 0.80 | 1.7 | 0.29 | 0.99 |
| - | - | - | 2.6 | 0.41 | 3.27 |
| 1.3 | 0.25 | 0.50 | 1.4 | 0.22 | 0.51 |
| 1.4 | 0.30 | 0.69 | 1.5 | 0.18 | 0.48 |
| 1.8 | 0.22 | 0.84 | 1.4 | 0.25 | 0.58 |
| 1.8 | 0.25 | 0.95 | 1.0 | 0.25 | 0.29 |
| 1.5 | 0.33 | 0.87 | 1.5 | 0.22 | 0.58 |
| 1.6 | 0.30 | 0.90 | 1.4 | 0.34 | 0.79 |
| 0.9 | 0.18 | 0.17 | 2.8 | 0.54 | 4.99 |
| - | - | - | 2.1 | 0.38 | 1.97 |
| 2.1 | 0.48 | 2.50 | 2.1 | 0.45 | 2.34 |
| 1.7 | 0.41 | 1.40 | 1.7 | 0.53 | 1.80 |
| 1.7 | 0.50 | 1.70 | 1.6 | 0.30 | 0.90 |

| cases | mean | median | range | quartiles | volume |
|-------|------|--------|-------|-----------|--------|
| 120 | 0.89 | 0.58 | 0.11-5.13 | 0.40-0.93 | 106.47 |

The metric measurements of house floor area at Gitsaex are presented in Table 8.2. The area of each floor was divided by the constant, $4m^2$, to produce individual household population estimates. The sum of these estimates produces a maximum village population estimate for Gitsaex of 426.59.

Dividing the total cache pit storage capacity in the Gitsaex sample by the village population estimate produces a per capita cache pit storage capacity of 0.266 $m^3$.

The metric measurements of the cache pits in close proximity to the Paul Mason Site are presented in Table 8.3. All 39 cache pits were measured. The estimated total volume capacity of these cache pits is 38.05 $m^3$.

House floor areas at the Paul Mason Site are presented in Table 8.4. Unlike Gitsaex, no external housepost depressions or wall sills were evident on the ground surface to mark the perimeters of the floors. The

Table 8.2
House floor measurements and household estimates for Gitsaex

| Dimensions (metres) | Area (metres$^2$) | Household estimate* |
|---|---|---|
| 10.8 x  9.4 | 101.52 | 25.38 |
| 12.3 x 12.0 | 147.60 | 36.90 |
| 10.6 x 10.2 | 108.12 | 27.03 |
| 10.0 x 11.6 | 116.00 | 29.00 |
|  9.5 x 10.4 | 98.80 | 24.70 |
| 13.1 x 10.8 | 141.48 | 32.67 |
| 10.9 x 13.6 | 148.24 | 37.06 |
| 11.3 x  7.7 | 87.01 | 21.75 |
|  8.0 x  9.9 | 79.20 | 19.80 |
| 10.0 x 11.2 | 112.00 | 28.00 |
|  8.9 x  9.6 | 85.44 | 21.36 |
|  8.7 x  6.1 | 53.07 | 13.27 |
|  9.1 x  7.7 | 70.07 | 17.52 |
|  9.5 x 10.0 | 95.00 | 23.75 |
| 10.2 x 10.4 | 106.80 | 26.52 |
|  8.7 x  9.6 | 83.52 | 20.88 |
| 10.0 x  8.4 | 84.00 | 21.00 |
| totals | 1706.35 | 426.59 |
| | | mean 25.1 |

\* based on 4 m$^2$ floor space per person

dimensions of the 10 floors were estimated in the following way.  The rear of each floor was taken as the point at which the levelled ground broke sharply upslope.  The front of the floor was taken as the point at which the earth ridges on either side of the floor dissipated and the levelled ground began to slope downhill.  The distance between these two points was taken as the floor length.  The width of the floors was taken as the distance from the top of one ridge slope (i.e., edge of the earth bench) across the levelled floor to the top of the opposite ridge slope, measured at the mid-point of the length of the floors.

The Cook and Heizer (1968:92-93) model for determining dwelling space per person is based on the regression formula,

$$y = a + bx$$

where **y** is the amount of dwelling space per person, **a** is a constant value of 1.485, **b** is the slope 0.0549, and **x** is the dwelling area in square metres.  Dwelling space per person was calculated for each of the 10 house floors at the Paul Mason Site (see Table 8.4).  Each floor area was then

257

Table 8.3
Cache Pit Measurements for the Paul Mason Site

| Diameter (metres) | Depth (metres) | Volume (metres$^3$) | Diameter | Depth | Volume |
|---|---|---|---|---|---|
| 2.0 | 0.26 | 1.23 | 1.5 | 0.28 | 0.74 |
| 1.5 | 0.20 | 0.53 | 1.2 | 0.18 | 0.31 |
| 2.4 | 0.35 | 2.38 | 2.1 | 0.50 | 2.60 |
| 1.2 | 0.18 | 0.31 | 1.2 | 0.20 | 0.34 |
| 1.1 | 0.27 | 0.38 | 1.2 | 0.42 | 0.71 |
| 1.8 | 0.28 | 1.07 | 1.8 | 0.30 | 1.15 |
| 2.1 | 0.28 | 1.45 | 1.0 | 0.20 | 0.24 |
| 1.1 | 0.21 | 0.30 | 1.3 | 0.27 | 0.54 |
| 1.5 | 0.32 | 0.85 | 1.1 | 0.29 | 0.41 |
| 2.0 | 0.41 | 1.93 | 1.6 | 0.21 | 0.63 |
| 1.3 | 0.30 | 0.60 | 0.8 | 0.25 | 0.19 |
| 2.2 | 0.50 | 2.85 | 1.5 | 0.32 | 0.85 |
| 1.7 | 0.45 | 1.53 | 1.8 | 0.45 | 1.71 |
| 1.2 | 0.33 | 0.56 | 2.0 | 0.50 | 2.36 |
| 1.5 | 0.35 | 0.93 | 1.2 | 0.25 | 0.42 |
| 2.2 | 0.37 | 2.11 | 0.7 | 0.38 | 0.22 |
| 1.3 | 0.38 | 0.76 | 1.3 | 0.24 | 0.34 |
| 1.5 | 0.44 | 1.17 | 1.1 | 0.24 | 0.34 |
| 1.5 | 0.33 | 0.87 | 1.4 | 0.32 | 0.74 |
| 1.7 | 0.37 | 1.26 | | | |

| cases | mean | median | range | quartiles | volume |
|---|---|---|---|---|---|
| 39 | 0.95 | 0.75 | 0.19-2.85 | 0.41-1.26 | 38.05 |

divided by its respective y-value to arrive at a household population
estimate. The sum of these estimates is the village population estimate,
which is 125.14.

When the total cache pit storage capacity for the Paul Mason Site
(38.05 m$^3$) is divided by the population estimate (125.1), a per capita
storage capacity of 0.304 m$^3$ is obtained.

The per capita cache pit storage capacity for the Paul Mason Site is
actually slightly greater than for Gitsaex. One might argue that these
values are not readily comparable because the population estimates for the
two sites were based on different models. However, the individual
estimates of the amount of floor area per person for the Paul Mason Site,
using the Cook and Heizer model, are very close to the 4 m$^2$ per person used
in estimating household population size at Gitsaex (see Table 8.4). If the
value of 4 m$^2$ per person is applied to the Paul Mason Site house floors

Table 8.4
House floor measurements and household estimates for the Paul Mason site

| Dimensions (metres) | Area (metres$^2$) | Dwelling space per person* (metres$^2$) | Household estimate* | Household estimate** |
|---|---|---|---|---|
| 7.0 x 10.1 | 70.7 | 5.73 | 12.34 | 17.68 |
| 6.5 x 10.2 | 66.3 | 5.12 | 12.95 | 16.58 |
| 6.8 x 10.1 | 68.68 | 5.26 | 13.06 | 17.17 |
| 6.6 x 11.0 | 72.6 | 5.47 | 13.27 | 18.15 |
| 6.4 x  8.0 | 51.2 | 4.30 | 11.91 | 12.80 |
| 6.2 x  8.8 | 54.56 | 4.48 | 12.18 | 13.64 |
| 5.2 x  8.8 | 45.76 | 4.00 | 11.44 | 11.44 |
| 6.4 x 10.2 | 65.28 | 5.07 | 12.88 | 16.32 |
| 7.0 x 10.0 | 70.0 | 5.33 | 13.13 | 17.50 |
| 6.5 x  8.0 | 52.0 | 4.34 | 11.98 | 13.00 |
| totals | 617.08 | | 125.14 | 154.28 |
| | | | mean 12.5 | mean 15.4 |

\* based on Cook and Heizer (1968)
\*\* based on 4 m$^2$ dwelling space per person

(see Table 8.4), the household population estimates are slightly greater in all but two cases than those arrived at using the Cook and Heizer model, and the village population estimate is 154.28. This produces a per capita cache pit storage value of 0.247 m$^3$. Now, the per capita cache pit storage capacity is greater for Gitsaex than for the Paul Mason Site, but again the difference is very small.

The results of this analysis indicate minimal difference in the emphasis placed on cache pit storage between the two sites. Recalling that the residents of Gitsaex were members of a ranked society that practised social storage, two possibilities exist. One is that the occupants of the Paul Mason Site were also members of a ranked society that practised social storage. In this case, the similarities between the two sites in per capita cache pit storage capacity would be reflective of similar socio-political organization. The other possibility is that cache pits were used by the occupants of both sites primarily for practical storage to meet over-wintering household subsistence requirements. In this case, the similarities in per capita cache pit storage capacity would be reflective of similar subsistence needs by two temporally distinct groups who were permanent residents of Kitselas Canyon. Both possibilities assume that the sites were occupied for approximately equal durations.

Of these two scenarios, the latter seems to me most plausible. It implies that surplus was not stored in cache pits. At Gitsaex, surplus food may have been stored in other containers, such as kerfed boxes. The box and its contents (social storage) would have been considered part of the House's wealth, and as such would have been controlled by the House chief, to be redistributed at feasts or traded for other items of wealth. As this represents the House's potential wealth, it would be important to guard it carefully, and perhaps to keep it separate from practical storage. The importance of the use of boxes in social storage by the Tsimshian has been underscored recently by Allaire (1984:86) who states that "Tsimshian oral traditions are explicit about the fact that a food without a proper container is ideologically no better than an empty container" (see Boas 1916:67, 292). Such storage may have been done within dwellings where the chief could exercise strict control.

It is possible, of course, that the same scenario applied to the villagers of the Paul Mason Site. I think this is unlikely, however, because there is no evidence at this time of items related to status or wealth. It is highly unlikely that social storage was practised if surplus was not subsequently converted into wealth. Moreover, there is no evidence from the Paul Mason Phase of woodworking tools such as adzes, which would be expected if bent box containers were being manufactured.

This brief analysis of storage practices at Kitselas Canyon raises more questions than it answers. For example, to what extent was storage practised prior to the Paul Mason Phase? What storage facilities in addition to cache pits were used prehistorically and historically at Kitselas Canyon?

The original question sought to compare storage practices between the Paul Mason Site and Gitsaex as a reflection of level of social integration. The estimates of per capita cache pit storage capacities for the two sites are virtually identical. This may reflect similar levels of social integration. Alternatively, it may reflect the use of cache pits for only practical storage related to over-wintering. In this event, differences between the two sites in per capita cache pit storage would not be expected and there would be no basis for inferring ascribed status inequalities during the Paul Mason Phase. Were the two sites different in terms of surplus storage? Unfortunately, very little direct evidence bears upon this question. MacDonald (1983:117) states that kerfed boxes appeared in the Tsimshian area no earlier than 2500 B.P. According to this date, these containers could have been used historically at Gitsaex, but not during the Paul Mason Phase.

At present, no final conclusions can be made concerning developments in storage practices at Kitselas Canyon. Nevertheless, on the basis of the foregoing analysis, the following model is presented for future testing.

Practical storage may have been practised by the earliest occupants of Kitselas Canyon. These people probably came to the canyon on a seasonal basis to extract specific resources. Some of these resources may have been processed and stored in cache pits until the people left the canyon, at which time the stored resources may have been transported to the next base camp location. This type of storage-related activity is typical of "collectors" (Binford 1980) who extract, process and store resources in one location and then transport those resources to another location. At Kitselas Canyon, this type of storage may have been conducted through the Skeena Phase.

With the onset of the Paul Mason Phase, and the first clear evidence of winter residence in the canyon, it is likely that practical storage became more intensive, as a result of increased residential permanency.

Although the volume of stored resources probably increased in the Paul Mason Phase, the type of storage continued to be "practical". There is no direct evidence of social storage at the Paul Mason Site. More important, items reflecting wealth or prestige that would imply social storage and conversion of surplus to wealth are lacking.

Little can be said of storage practices at Gitaus during the Kleanza Phase. At Prince Rupert Harbour, numerous changes were occuring at this time (ca. 2500 B.P.) that indicate the emergence of social ranking. If the Kleanza Phase was part of a cultural system that included Prince Rupert Harbour, then we may expect that social ranking was also emerging at Kitselas Canyon at this time. In turn, this would imply social storage.

Population Aggregation and Village Formation

**Northwest Coast Population Aggregates**

A population aggregate is an integrated group that shares a common geographical area or domain. In a recent study, Mitchell (1983b:97) defined three types of population aggregates for the Northwest Coast: camps, villages, and village aggregations. They essentially represent incremental levels of population aggregation and integration. Camps correspond to Houses, the basic or autonomous socioeconomic unit of the Northwest Coast. Seasonal camp settlements included one or more nuclear families whose collective corporate identity was the House.

Villages were aggregations of households. While recognizing the basic socioeconomic autonomy of the House, Mitchell (1983b:98) argued that for much of the Northwest Coast (except perhaps Coast Salish) the winter village may have been "the significant autonomous political unit". As evidence of this, Mitchell notes that winter villages were permanent locations with permanent dwellings, and each winter village group bore a name.

Although winter villages cross-cut kinship groups, it does appear that, among the Tsimshian, a definite sense of unity and integration existed among all village members. Resource locations were owned by individual Houses, but the territories of Houses within a Tsimshian village were contiguous, so that winter village group or tribal boundaries could be identified (see Inglis and MacDonald 1979:3). For example, all House territories among the Gitzaklalth were distributed along the Eckstall River and its tributaries. Moreover, Coast Tsimshian village groups may have been permanent units for much of the year, with separate winter (Prince Rupert Harbour) and summer (lower Skeena River) locations (Boas 1916). On occasion, co-operative labour and ceremonial efforts were undertaken on the village level.

Village aggregations occurred when two or more village groups came together at a particular location. These are described in some detail by Mitchell (1983b). Often, these groups assembled where and when particular resources were available. The political unity of these large groupings was probably not great, although the Nuu-chah-nulth-aht (Nootka) "confederacies" may have been an exception. According to Drucker

(1951:220-21), these were units for war and ceremonials, and within these groupings a feeling of solidarity existed.

The lower Nass eulachon fishery is an example of multi-village aggregation among the Tsimshian. These large annual gatherings lasted two months or more, and were the focal point of a well-developed trade network. The Niska regularly traded grease to the Gitksan, and some Coast Tsimshian village groups traded with the Southern Tsimshian and the Haida (Garfield 1950:16).

## Village Solidarity on the Northwest Coast

The rise of villages on the Northwest Coast marks a threshold change in the organization of population aggregates. Egalitarian foragers, organized in bands, have no counterpart for this level of integration. The largest Northwest Coast villages integrated hundreds of people in a single political unit. For example, McNeary (1976:52) states that the Niska village of Angidaa had a population in excess of 400 at the time of European contact.

Some have suggested that Northwest Coast villages were "accidental" units (Barbeau 1917:403). De Laguna (1983:71) states that the internal ties of Tlingit winter villages are only those of propinquity and frequent intercourse. However, Mitchell's remarks indicate that a greater sense of solidarity existed among the members of most Northwest Coast villages than either Barbeau or de Laguna recognized.

An example from Coast Tsimshian oral tradition illustrates this point. The Coast Tsimshian held a great potlatch to honour the Water Beings (Boas 1916:272-77). Contributions to this potlatch were made by all Coast Tsimshian people. In an analysis of this event, Allaire (1984) clearly indicates that the contributing units were the winter village groups, not the individual Houses. This implies that lineages within villages pooled their efforts to produce the necessary commodities for the feast, and according to the myth, this pooled labour effort lasted two years (Allaire 1984:84). Here, we are told that Tsimshian villages could not only organize as a single producing unit, but they could maintain this organization, apparently without centralized authority, for an extended period of time (two years).

263

There are other examples of Northwest Coast villages acting as integrated units. Fortified villages such as the Kitwanga tawdzep (MacDonald 1979), Gitlaxdzawk (Allaire et al. 1979), and those sites in the Johnstone Strait (Mitchell 1969) probably involved considerable organization of labour at the village level to construct and maintain fortification features. A similar level of labour involvement may be imagined for trench embankments in the Gulf of Georgia area.

Village members not only lived together for much of the year, they even migrated together. For example, oral tradition has it that the Kitsumkalum were originally Tlingits who migrated from Tongass, en masse, perhaps as recently as the early 18th century (Boas 1890:35).

These few examples demonstrate that Northwest Coast villages were more than just "accidental" units of propinquity. Although they lacked centralized authority, villages were capable of integrating large numbers of people for production, ceremony, and defense, often for periods of extended duration.

Elsewhere, Ames and Marshall (1981) and Matson (1983) have linked the rise of villages in northwestern North America to subsistence intensification, demographic change and the evolution of social ranking.

## Population Aggregation and Village Formation at Kitselas Canyon

For the early period of settlement at Kitselas Canyon (Bornite, Gitaus, and Skeena Phases), the evidence bearing on the size of population aggregates is fragmentary. There is no evidence of formal village organization. These early settlers were mobile hunter-gatherers, occupying the canyon on a seasonal basis. We may anticipate band-size groupings of 30 to 40 people, based on Martin's model of hunter-gatherer group size (Martin 1973). Unfortunately, there is no way to test this estimate archaeologically at Kitselas Canyon. There are no house floors from this period from which household population estimates could be derived (using Cook and Heizer's model for example). It is possible that two or more bands gathered seasonally to share the resource base of the canyon. Alternatively, as band-size groupings only reside as a unit during a portion of the year, groupings of less than 30 to 40 people may have resided at Kitselas Canyon at any one time during this early period of settlement. This latter possibility is especially relevant for the Bornite Phase. It was argued that the small, limited assemblage of this phase was representative of a short term limited activity site. Moreover, camp size during the Bornite Phase was probably very small. Taken together, this may reflect a population aggregate smaller than band-size at this time; perhaps on the order of 10 to 15 people.

The Gitaus and Skeena Phases were represented by larger assemblages and larger camp size. The Gitaus Phase was represented at both the Paul Mason Site and Gitaus. The Skeena Phase, only at Gitaus, included a large and diversified assemblage, which suggests that a variety of resources were exploited. Both assemblages suggest base camp occupations with more inhabitants than during the Bornite Phase.

The aligned house floors of the Paul Mason Phase represent the first evidence of population integration at the formal village level. Following Mitchell (1983b), I suggest that the establishment of a village at this time allowed for the integration of a substantially larger population than in the preceeding phases.

The house floors provide the basis for an accurate estimate of population aggregate size at Kitselas Canyon at this time. The estimate of village population, using Cook and Heizer's model was 125 (see Table 8.4). This figure may be too high, given that all ten house floors may not have been occupied simultaneously. At the time of maximum village size, it is possible that one or two houses stood unoccupied. A village estimate of 100 to 110 people might be more realistic.

Even with this conservative estimate, the population aggregate for the Paul Mason Phase was likely much larger than for the preceeding phases.

Household size during the Paul Mason Phase, based on Cook and Heizer's model, ranged from 11.91 to 13.27 (see Table 8.4). Mean household size was 12.51, which probably represents two nuclear family groups. This is supported by the archaeological evidence from the two house floor excavations. Two hearths were recorded in each excavation in the upper dark brown zone along the mid-line of the floor. The hearths may correspond to two separate family groups.

Perhaps more important than the mere presence of winter dwelling floors at the Paul Mason Site is their alignment in a formalized village layout. The floors are consistent in shape, and all face in the same direction, southwest towards the river.

The consistent spacing between the floors is further evidence of formalized village alignment. Between-floor spacing is an important concept, because it is a relative reflection of the amount of planning invested in the layout of the village. Generally, house floors spaced at regular intervals reflect considerable planning, whereas randomly spaced floors oriented in varying directions reflect an absence of village planning. Where village planning is evident, it is reasonable to assume greater social interaction among village members because planning and layout of the village is an activity in which all village members must participate.

The excavation of floor 2 exposed an earth bench along the north edge of the floor. This was incorporated within the earth ridge. The house wall was located at the top of the ridge slope, where two large post moulds indicate the presence of mid-wall support posts. From this, it was inferred that the width of the dwellings was the distance from the top of one ridge slope to the top of the next one. The spacing between dwellings was therefore represented by the flat or slightly rounded ridge tops (see Figure 5.5) The between-floor space measurements for the Paul Mason Site are presented in Table 8.5 (see also Figure 8.2), where they are compared to similar measurements from Gitsaex. Between-floor spacing at Gitlaxdzawk was not used in this comparison because its unusual location on a rocky promontory placed spatial constraints on the alignment of dwellings within the village. The spacing between floors 2 and 3 at Gitsaex was also not used. This space, 12.75 metres wide, was the small open area that probably functioned as a formal entrance to the village from the river. The other house floors at Gitsaex were aligned side by side, with no further evidence of special activity areas between dwellings.

The mean space between dwellings at Gitsaex (2.33 metres) was two times greater than at the Paul Mason Site (1.17 metres) (see Table 8.5). More importantly, the coefficient of variation is substantially lower for the Paul Mason Site (0.176) than for Gitsaex (0.62).

266

## Table 8.5
## Dwelling Spacing for Paul Mason Site and Gitsaex

| Paul Mason Site | | Gitsaex | |
|---|---|---|---|
| Dwellings | Spacing (metres) | Dwellings | Spacing (metres) |
| 1-2 | 0.84 | 1-2 | 2.60 |
| 2-3 | 1.20 | 3-4 | 3.43 |
| 3-4 | 1.22 | 4-5 | 1.43 |
| 4-5 | 1.10 | 5-6 | 1.80 |
| 5-6 | 0.95 | 6-7 | 1.02 |
| 7-8 | 1.53 | 7-8 | 1.33 |
| 8-9 | 1.38 | 9-10 | 1.41 |
| 9-10 | 1.17 | 10-11 | 1.62 |
| | | 11-12 | 2.90 |
| | | 12-13 | 6.92 |
| | | 13-14 | 2.00 |
| | | 14-15 | 2.35 |
| | | 15-16 | 2.62 |
| | | 16-17 | 1.21 |
| mean | 1.17 | | 2.33 |
| std dev | 0.206 | | 1.44 |
| CV | 0.176 | | 0.62 |

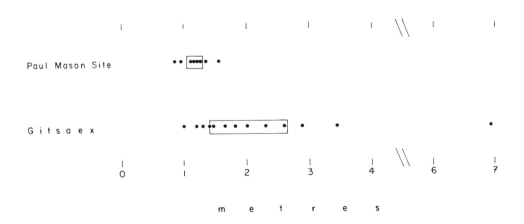

Figure 8.2 "Box and dot" plot of between-floor spacing for the Paul Mason Site and Gitsaex.

The coefficient of variation (standard deviation divided by the mean) is a measure of relative homogeneity within a data set, in this case, the space between dwellings in a village. The coefficient of variation approaches zero as the homogeneity of the data set increases (Blalock 1979:84). There was no physical restriction on the amount of space that could have existed between dwellings at the Paul Mason Site. The regularity in dwelling spacing and the alignment of dwellings in two rows appears to have been the result of an overall village plan, one in which all households participated. In turn, this may be seen as an expression of the solidarity of the village group as a social unit.

Another indicator of village planning is the orientation of the house floors in two rows (see Figure 5.2). Numerous bedrock outcroppings are located directly in front of the front row of floors. The two-row effect was achieved because the floors in the back row were systematically aligned along the upper slope, and the floors in the front row were systematically aligned at the base of the slope. Had the floors been placed irregularly or in the middle of the slope, the two-row effect could not have been achieved. This suggests that either all ten dwellings were constructed at the same time according to some plan, or that a specific plan existed for the addition of dwellings after the initial phase of construction.

The similarities in alignment among dwellings at the Paul Mason Site and late Northwest Coast villages are striking. On the Northwest Coast, the residential structures of permanent villages were generally aligned in rows. Multi-row plans were common. Houses were roughly equally-spaced, and oriented in the same direction, usually facing water. In fact, the alignment of dwellings at the Paul Mason Site, in terms of between-floor spacing, was more formalized than at Gitsaex. This implies that village members during the Paul Mason Phase were a highly integrated social unit.

Village planning during the Paul Mason Phase is also evident in the presence of special activity areas outside the nuclear residential area. For example, the sub-cluster 1A layer-levels of Excavation H probably represent a midden or trash-dumping area. This area was located immediately north of the house floors. The volume of lithic artifacts (number of artifacts per cubic metre) was higher in the sub-cluster 1A layer-levels than in the upper dark brown zone of either house floor

268

excavation or Excavation J (see Table 8.6), indicating a higher rate of discard in this area of the site.

Table 8.6
Artifact Density for Component IV

| Excavation | Stratigraphic Units | Number of Artifacts | Excavation in cu. m. | Artifacts per cu. m. |
|---|---|---|---|---|
| H | C - D4 | 183 | 11 | 16.64 |
| PFF2 | C - H1 | 257 | 22 | 11.69 |
| PFF9 | D - F | 145 | 15 | 9.67 |
| J | D - F | 66 | 8 | 8.25 |

Excavation J, immediately west or in front of the front row of floors included the large hearth feature in the upper dark brown zone. These layers yielded a low volume of artifacts compared to the other excavations. This part of the site was probably a special activity area used for cooking and food processing.

Little can be said of the population aggregate for the Kleanza Phase. Allaire (1979:45, 48) argued that the diversified tool assemblage of the Kleanza Complex, and the extensive litter of fire-cracked rock represented an intensive, village occupation of the canyon. Thus, we may expect that the population aggregate at this time was no smaller than during the Paul Mason Phase, and may even have been larger.

The population estimate for Gitsaex, based on the ethnographic household model, was 426.59. However, this does not represent the full historic population at Kitselas Canyon because Gitlaxdzawk was occupied at the same time as Gitsaex.

The Gitlaxdzawk population was estimated using the same model as for Gitsaex (see Table 8.7). The house floor areas are based on the dimensions given by Allaire et al (1979:69, 76-101) for each of the 10 houses recorded at the site. The population estimate is 266.51.

When added to the Gitsaex estimate, the total historic Kitselas Canyon population estimate is 693.1. Again, this figure may be too high if it is assumed that not all 27 historic house floors were simultaneously occupied. If, for example, four dwellings stood unoccupied at one time, the estimate would be closer to 600. It should be noted, however, that Rosa Herring, a native Kitselas woman who was an informant to Barbeau,

Table 8.7
House Floor Measurements and Household Estimates for Gitlaxdzawk

| Dimensions (metres) | Area (metres$^2$) | Household Estimate |
|---|---|---|
| 9.0 x  9.0 | 81.00 | 20.25 |
| 9.1 x  8.2 | 74.62 | 18.66 |
| 12.2 x 12.2 | 148.84 | 37.21 |
| 8.8 x  9.1 | 80.08 | 20.02 |
| 10.6 x  9.1 | 96.46 | 24.12 |
| 10.6 x 10.6 | 112.36 | 28.09 |
| 13.7 x 13.7 | 187.69 | 46.92 |
| 9.1 x  9.1 | 82.81 | 20.70 |
| 9.1 x  9.1 | 82.81 | 20.70 |
| 10.2 x 11.7 | 119.34 | 29.84 |
| Totals | 1066.01 | 266.51 |
|  |  | mean 26.6 |

stated that all 10 dwellings at Gitlaxdzawk were occupied simultaneously; she could name the heads of each household (see Allaire et al. 1979:68), 109). Given the stories of over-crowding at Gitlaxdzawk, it seems likely that the population estimate cited above is roughly accurate.

The differences in population aggregate size between the Paul Mason Site and the historic sites are significant at both the household and village levels. At the village level, the combined estimate for Gitsaex and Gitlaxdzawk (693) is 5.5 times greater than for the Paul Mason Site (125). Following Mitchell's (1983b:98) model, this substantial difference in size at the village level may reflect a more complex level of social integration during the historic period than in the Paul Mason Phase. The prehistoric and historic villages at Kitselas Canyon had essentially the same site location and resource structure, so it is reasonable to argue that a greater than five-fold increase in the size of the village population aggregate was correlated with greater social complexity during the historic period.

Also important was the difference in household size between the prehistoric and historic period. At Gitlaxdzawk, mean household size was estimated at 26.6 (see Table 8.7), and at Gitsaex mean household size was estimated at 25.1 (see Table 8.2). By contrast, at the Paul Mason Site, mean household size using Cook and Heizer's (1968) model was estimated at

12.5 (see Table 8.4). The average historic household was twice as large as the average prehistoric household during the Paul Mason Phase. The difference was probably the equivalent of two family groups per household. This doubling of size suggests that historic households were more efficient at complex simultaneous labour tasks related to production, and were better suited to surplus production than prehistoric households during the Paul Mason Phase.

It seems inconceivable that a system of ascribed internal household ranking (see Fried 1967:109), consistent with the ethnographic Kitselas model, could have existed at the Paul Mason Site, where households comprised only two families. More likely, relations within the Paul Mason Phase households were based on equality and reciprocity, rather than ascribed status inequalities. The "fireside group" of the Huron (see Chapter 2) is probably a close analogue to the Paul Mason Phase households.

In the following section, it is shown that there is little evidence for ascribed status differences **among** the Paul Mason Phase households.

Household Variability

This section focuses specifically on the Paul Mason Phase house floors and the historic house floors from Gitsaex and Gitlaxdzawk. Can differences in level of social integration be identified for these two periods, based on variability in dwelling size and construction?

**Dwellings, Households and Status**

There has been much interest recently in the study of household variability from both an ethnoarchaeological perspective (Kramer 1979, 1982; Watson 1978, 1979; Jacobs 1979; Hayden and Cannon 1982; Horne 1982; Wilk 1983), and a purely archaeological perspective (Bawden 1982; Wilk and Rathje 1982; Reid and Whittlesey 1982; Lightfoot and Feinman 1982). Much of this research has focused on two basic relationships:

1) dwelling size and household size,
2) household size and household wealth or status.

Netting (1982:641) summarized these relationships as follows: "it is a reasonable inference that pronounced differences in a representative sample of house floor areas would reflect some variation along a scale of average number of household residents and resources available to the household group".

The direct relationship between dwelling size and household size was demonstrated by Cook and Heizer (1965, 1968) in their study of aboriginal California village groups. In an ethnoarchaeological study in Iran, Kramer (1979:153) demonstrated strong correlations between dwelling size and household size and between dwelling size and household wealth. Her correlations were substantially stronger for land-owning households than for landless households, which suggests that wealthy (landed) households, with resources at their disposal, are more likely to increase the size of their living space as new household members are added, either by building new dwellings or adding on to existing ones. Landless people, typically lacking in wealth, are less likely to renovate in response to an increase in household size.

Some researchers have argued that factors other than household size and wealth may affect dwelling size. These arguments have been summarized by Wilk (1983:101). Residential mobility has been suggested as one such factor (see Kelley 1982). Mobile households will tend to have smaller dwellings than sedentary households, other things being equal. However, this relationship is misleading. Mobile households are also likely to be smaller than sedentary households, so it is not clear whether mobility or household size is the factor affecting dwelling size.

The duration of residence in a single locale has been suggested as another factor that may affect dwelling size (see Jacobs 1979). The argument here is that the earliest settlers at a site may have the largest and most elaborate dwellings. These may also be the wealthiest settlers, however, if their permanence in a single locale is an indication of their productive success. For example, among the Kekchi Maya, long-standing members of the community tended to be the wealthiest and highest ranked (Wilk 1983:110). Rather than duration of residence, it is likely that household wealth was the factor that really affected dwelling size in this case.

At this point, it is well to ask why households should increase in size in the first place. The answer, as suggested in Chapter 2, is probably related to a fundamental change in the transmission of rights of

Chapter 9

SUMMARY AND CONCLUSIONS

**Deviation Amplification and Corporate Groups: A Summary of the Model**

In this study of prehistoric cultural change, I have argued that the complex, ranked societies of the Northwest Coast evolved as part of a deviation amplifying system--a process of concentrating resources, including food, wealth and prestige, in the hands of fewer and fewer individuals. Further, egalitarian corporate groups were an important stage in this evolutionary process--a precursor of ranked corporate groups.

These two arguments are not unrelated. The existence of egalitarian corporate groups is an important piece of evidence that supports the deviation amplifying model. Egalitarian corporate groups represent a stage of development in which resources are controlled collectively by a small, unified group. This stage is intermediate between foraging bands, who generally do not recognize ownership of resources, and ranked societies, in which resources are controlled by a limited number of elite members. The existence of egalitarian corporate groups at Kitselas Canyon suggests, therefore, that ranking evolved as a means of concentrating resources, rather than as a mechanism for their distribution.

This is in contrast to the deviation counteracting model, in which it is argued that social ranking functioned as an equilibrating mechanism to speed information flow (Ames 1981, 1983), organize labour more efficiently in the face of demographic stress (Burley 1979), and balance fluctuating resources (Suttles 1960; Vayda 1961; Piddocke 1965).

The point is, simply, if egalitarian groups were capable of controlling resources and intensifying production, then what functional need did ranking serve? Rather than balancing resources, I suggest that the ranked corporate lineages of the lower Skeena evolved as a means of defining more precisely who had access to and control of productive resource locations. Ranking undoubtedly resulted in a more efficiently organized labour force, but I think this was related to competitive social production, rather than practical production.

At Kitselas Canyon, membership in egalitarian corporate groups was probably defined on the basis of residence. Although the demographic make-up of the group cannot be specified, it is likely that people who co-resided permanently in the same dwelling or same village would be members of the same corporate group because they constituted a stable and enduring social group. Households as corporate units were probably responsible for domestic activities and day-to-day production, although, again, empirical evidence for this is lacking. On a larger scale, the village was also a corporate unit, responsible for defense and control of the canyon. This does not mean that all sedentary villages functioned as corporate groups, or that all enduring social groups were corporate. It is important too that the members of the group collectively controlled resources, and worked co-operatively in the production of these resources. Permanent residence assured the group continued access to the resource, while denying access to outsiders. Complex simultaneous production is a good example of how corporate group members perform a series of related tasks that collectively benefit the group as a whole.

Membership in ranked corporate groups is defined on the basis of kinship. Among the historic Kitselas, ranked corporate groups were commensurate with lineage or "House" groups. Rather than group ownership of all resource locations, as was the case for the egalitarian corporate groups of the Paul Mason Phase, ownership of specific locations was vested in individual Houses, with unequal access to resources among House members. At the same time, the village maintained a corporate identity for defense, without centralized authority, as seen at Gitlaxdzawk.

Wilk and Rathje (1982:627) suggest that the shift in transmission of rights of access to resources from village to House results in a more precise definition of resource control. This shift becomes important as more and more extractive locations come under corporate control. Whereas village membership is simply defined--one is either born into the village, or admitted into the village later in life by mutual consent of the members--kinship affiliation may be more complex. There may be numerous lines of descent within a single kinship group, some with only tenuous association to the group. It is at this point that hereditary leadership may emerge, so that inheritence is reckoned through the most central line of descent within the kinship group, thus ensuring continued household ownership of critical resource locations from one generation to the next.

Thus, we see the pattern of deviation amplification. In order to ensure access to resources, the control of these resources becomes more rigidly defined and more restricted, ultimately resting with a limited number of elite members of society.

The shift to ranked corporate groups, as a process of amplification, is associated with even more intensive complex simultaneous production. This places the emerging chief is in a position to encourage "social" production, in addition to "practical" production, to finance his own political activities. Increased production may result in a more efficiently organized labour force than that of the egalitarian corporate groups. Hierarchical re-organization of labour is likely, and this reinforces the ranked structure of the corporate group. The important point here is that ranking evolves in association with social production, not practical production.

## Kitselas Canyon: An Ideal Setting for the Emergence of Corporate Groups

This study has focussed on Kitselas Canyon because it is an ideal location for the formation of corporate groups. Kitselas Canyon is the first major constriction of the Skeena River. An important fishing location, it is located far enough downriver that the salmon runs through the canyon are abundant and reliable. Most of the salmon (except chum) that spawn in the Skeena system run through Kitselas Canyon (see Chapter 3).

Although seasonal, salmon may be wind dried or smoked in wetter climates, and then stored for later consumption. Through preservation and storage, a resource that is only available in the river for a short period of time may become a dietary staple throughout the year.

These criteria of localized resource abundance, reliability and preservability are critical to the development of corporate groups because they allow the formation of large, permanent social groups, and promote resource intensification.

The physical setting of Kitselas Canyon, in an area of rugged terrain, just east of the Coast Mountains, also contributed to the formation of corporate groups. As stated in Chapter 3, Kitselas Canyon is situated roughly on the ecotonal boundary between coast and interior. The climate is transitional between these two zones, and the faunal and floral resources of both zones are present within close proximity of the canyon. Also, the abrupt change in altitudinal zonation, including valley bottom, mid-slopes/sub-alpine, and alpine zones, concentrates resources from each zone within the vicinity of the canyon. Thus, in addition to the critical resource--salmon--the occupants of Kitselas Canyon had access to a variety of other resources that occurred throughout the year, either in or near the canyon.

This richness and concentration of resources allowed a sedentary lifestyle, making control of the canyon possible.

## Models of Cultural Change

MacDonald (1969a) was the first to suggest that the ethnographic Tsimshian cultural pattern was the result of long-term _in situ_ developments along the lower Skeena. He argued that the cultural sequence from Prince Rupert Harbour, covering the last 5000 years, reflected steady, gradual change. This was contrary to the Smith/Drucker model of population displacement, in which the Tsimshian were seen as late arrivals to the coast from upriver. Arguing for a prehistoric cultural co-tradition, MacDonald suggested that the Tsimshian pattern evolved as a result of interaction with other Northwest Coast groups (Haida and Tlingit). He did not state, however, why this interaction should lead to social inequality.

The population displacement model was resurrected by Allaire (1979), in an attempt to explain prehistoric cultural change at Kitselas Canyon. Allaire argued that the Skeena Complex was the result of a migration by an "interior" group into Kitselas Canyon, displacing the earlier "coastal" group. The Kleanza Complex was interpreted by Allaire as marking a return to a "coastal" way of life, through a process of acculturation.

Like MacDonald, I have argued against the population displacement model; in this case, population displacement, followed by acculturation. I have suggested that prehistoric cultural change at Kitselas Canyon was the result of _in situ_ economic and social developments along the lower Skeena, including Prince Rupert Harbour.

At the core of this model is the contention that the Skeena Complex was not representative of an interior-based culture, ethnically distinct from Prince Rupert Harbour, but rather was part of the same lower Skeena settlement system. In Chapter 4, I noted certain problems with Allaire's interpretation of the Skeena Complex. His designation of the Skeena Complex as "interior-based" assumes that a discrete northern interior culture existed at this time. Recent research (e.g., Morrison 1984) suggests that this assumption is tenuous at best. The archaeology of north-central British Columbia is poorly known at present, and does not represent a sound base for comparison.

Further, artifact types diagnostic of the Skeena Complex, such as parallel-sided lanceolate points, were also recovered from contemporaneous deposits at Prince Rupert Harbour. The differences between the Skeena Complex and early Period II assemblages at Prince Rupert Harbour are quantitative, not qualitative.

While I agree with Allaire (1979:47) that the people of the Skeena Complex "show a type of adaptation definitely oriented toward a riverine and forest efficiency", I do not take this as evidence of interior origins for these people. It is well known that historic coastal people moved inland seasonally to procure resources, and it is reasonable to expect that the "inland" seasonal tool kit of these people would be distinct from the "coastal" seasonal tool kit.

Allaire's interpretation of the Skeena Complex reflects a larger problem in Northwest Coast archaeology. To date, most coastal archaeologists have restricted their investigations to shell middens. There has been little study, indeed little awareness, of inland sites used by coastal people. The extreme focus on shell middens, while suited to the reconstruction of coastal culture history, represents a sampling bias in settlement-subsistence studies. Northwest Coast archaeologists must begin to recognize the likelihood that prehistoric groups used inland sites seasonally. Future archaeological research designs must take this into account, if we are to understand the full range of variability of prehistoric Northwest Coast culture.

In short, I disagree with Allaire's interpretation of cultural change at Kitselas Canyon, as resulting from population displacement followed by coastal acculturation. I suggest that cultural change along the lower Skeena, including Kitselas Canyon and Prince Rupert Harbour, during the last 4300 years resulted from in situ developments within a single settlement system.

## The Cultural Sequence at Kitselas Canyon

In order to investigate these developments in chronological perspective, a revised prehistoric sequence was formulated for Kitselas Canyon. A partial sequence was already in existence, based on the Gitaus excavations (Allaire 1978, 1979). This sequence was poorly dated, however, and it was not known whether the components were temporally contiguous, or if earlier or later prehistoric components existed elsewhere in the canyon.

The Paul Mason Site was excavated to refine the sequence and provide more information about the prehistoric occupation of the canyon. Quantitative multivariate analyses of the stone tool assemblages from stratigraphic layer-levels revealed three discrete cultural components at the site. These components were compared to those from Gitaus. This resulted in the formulation of a five phase prehistoric sequence for Kitselas Canyon, ranging from 5000 B.P. to ca. 2000 B.P.

The earliest phase, the Bornite Phase, is characterized by high proportions of obsidian microblades and cobble core tools. It was argued that this phase reflects short-term seasonal use of Kitselas Canyon by a small group, probably for summer fishing.

The Gitaus Phase is characterized by larger site size, and a more diversified tool assemblage than the Bornite Phase. A summer base camp occupation was suggested, with fishing as the primary economic activity.

The Skeena Phase, characterized by a developed chipped stone assemblage, reflects a greater emphasis on land mammal hunting than in the early phases. Fishing continued to be important. A summer base camp occupation is again indicated.

The production of chipped stone tools declined in the Paul Mason Phase, relative to the Skeena Phase. This probably reflects decreased emphasis on land mammal hunting. The contention that fishing became the primary economic activity at this time is supported by the existing faunal data (see Appendix III), the evidence of decreasing procurement of other resources (land mammals), and the apparent emphasis on the manufacture of bone tools (fish hooks, leisters) reflected in the high proportion of abraders. The first clear evidence of winter habitation at Kitselas Canyon

294

is seen in the Paul Mason Phase. This phase also marks the first evidence of a formalized village plan, with multiple house floors arranged in two rows and equally spaced.

The pattern of permanent residence and intensive fishing probably continued during the Kleanza Phase, although this is not as clearly supported by house floor and faunal evidence as in the Paul Mason Phase. The Kleanza Phase artifact assemblage is essentially similar to that of the Paul Mason Phase. The most important difference is the addition of new artifact types--labrets and slate mirrors--possibly related to status differentiation. The suggestion that social ranking may have emerged at Kitselas Canyon at this time (ca. 2500 B.P.) is supported by coeval evidence for the emergence of ranked society at Prince Rupert Harbour.

## The Evolution of Corporate Groups at Kitselas Canyon:
## A Consideration of the Evidence

I have argued that corporate groups evolved at Kitselas Canyon during the Paul Mason Phase. This was probably related to economic changes that occurred during the early phases of the sequence. These early changes are consistent with Christenson's model of expanding resource diversity and niche width, leading up to intensification (Christenson 1980). The limited assemblage of the Bornite Phase suggests low resource diversity and niche width, an interpretation that is consistent with the demographic and economic conditions that existed at Prince Rupert Harbour at this time (early Period III).

During the Gitaus and Skeena Phases, steady growth in resource diversity and niche width is reflected in the increasingly diversified tool assemblages. This culminated during the time of the Skeena Phase, when there is evidence for land mammal hunting, sea mammal hunting, riverine and sea fishing, and shellfish collecting from Kitselas Canyon and Prince Rupert Harbour. This diversity did not exist for the phases preceeding or following the Skeena Phase. Christenson argued that once resource diversity and niche width reach a maximum point, intensification of one or a few related resources will likely occur. This appears to hold for Kitselas Canyon during the Paul Mason Phase, and it represents the "initial kick" in the deviation amplifying model toward the formation of corporate

295

groups.

The evidence for the early phases at Kitselas Canyon reflects increasing resource diversity, based on seasonal mobility. There is no evidence for permanent occupation of Kitselas Canyon prior to the Paul Mason Phase; only summer residence was indicated through the Skeena Phase. This evidence is consistent with the model of egalitarian bands, in which the nuclear family is the primary socio-economic unit, and corporate organization is absent.

During the Paul Mason Phase, a change in settlement pattern occurred at Kitselas Canyon that reflects the formation of corporate groups. The first evidence of large, permanent dwelling floors is seen at this time. The analysis of household size (Chapter 8) suggested that these were multi-family dwellings, each housing two or three nuclear families (10-15 people). Thus, each household could provide a labour group of four to six adults (males and females). This is consistent with the corporate households of the ethnographic period, albeit on a smaller scale.

The essential difference between the corporate households of the Paul Mason Phase and those of the historic period is related to internal social organization. Members of historic households (20-25 on average) were ranked in relation to each other. It is difficult to conceive of social ranking existing within the Paul Mason Phase households when they only consisted of two families. Egalitarian social organization is suggested. Further evidence of egalitarianism was demonstrated in Chapter 8. The analysis of variability in house floor size revealed substantially less homogeneity in the historic period than during the Paul Mason Phase. This reflects less emphasis on status differentiation prehistorically. The absence of status-related goods, and the complete lack of artifacts of high quality manufacture that might suggest specialized production of sumptuary goods further supports the argument for egalitarianism during the Paul Mason Phase.

Thus, there is independent evidence for corporateness and egalitarian social organization during the Paul Mason Phase. I do not suggest that some social differentiation did not exist at this time. No society is completely egalitarian. As stated in Chapter 2, status differences in egalitarian societies are based on skill and achievement. This seems most likely for the Paul Mason Phase. There is no evidence at this time for social ranking of the type seen historically.

While corporate groups can be identified for the Paul Mason Phase, there is no direct evidence bearing on their function. It is logical to infer, however, that the rise of corporate groups at this time was associated with salmon intensification. The large, permanent households provided a permanent, dependable labour group for intensive salmon production.

It is not clear, however, whether these households "owned" resource locations, as did historic Houses. It may be the case that the canyon fishery was controlled collectively by the village, while each household had "preferred" fishing locations. This introduces a second level of corporateness; the village as a corporate group. The analysis of between-floor spacing and alignment of dwellings in Chapter 8 revealed a more organized village plan during the Paul Mason Phase than during the historic period. From this it may be inferred that the Paul Mason Phase village had a stronger corporate identity, a logical conclusion since defense of the canyon against possible outside attack was important to the livelihood of all occupants. Mitchell (1983b) argued that historic Northwest Coast villages were more than just units of propinquity, sharing a common name and often contiguous resource territories. However, the analysis of village plan in this study reflects greater organization and cohesiveness for the Paul Mason village than for Gitsaex.

It may be possible to identify here a gradual shift in corporate focus through time from village to household. As households increased in size leading up to the historic period, they may have taken on greater corporate identity, while the corporateness of the village decreased (although it did not completely disappear). This reasoning is consistent with Wilk and Rathje's (1982) argument concerning the shift in control of resources from village to household. This argument is, of course, speculative at present, and requires more empirical support. It remains an intriguing question for future archaeological research.

The data from the Kleanza Phase are not as complete as one would like. Dwelling outlines and evidence of village layouts are lacking. It is reasonable to infer that corporate organization continued in this phase from the preceeding one, although there is no direct evidence for this. The important change reflected in the archaeological data is the addition of new elements in the Kleanza Phase related to status differences (labrets, slate mirrors, zoomorphic carvings). Although not overwhelming, these data are evidence of greater status differentiation than in the Paul Mason Phase. That this change reflects the development of ranked society is supported by evidence for the emergence of social ranking elsewhere on the Northwest Coast at this time (ca. 2500 B.P.). I interpret this evidence from the Kleanza Phase as reflecting the evolution of ranked corporate groups at Kitselas Canyon.

Does the archaeological evidence from Kitselas Canyon support the deviation amplifying model? Did cultural change at Kitselas Canyon place increasing restrictions on access to resources, thereby amplifying the environmental conditions? I think that the evidence of egalitarian corporate groups during the Paul Mason Phase supports the model. A three-stage process of amplification is suggested. The initial stage includes the Bornite, Gitaus and Skeena Phases. An egalitarian band level of social organization is indicated based on the evidence of low population and high resource diversity and residential mobility. Although ownership of resource locations cannot be categorically denied for any of the early phases, such control is inconsistent with existing models of band societies (e.g., Fried 1967:61). During the Paul Mason Phase egalitarian corporate groups evolved, marking the second stage of amplification. As sedentary corporate groups, these people controlled resources at Kitselas Canyon simply by being there year-round. As an egalitarian group, there was, by definition, equal access among group members to the resources of the canyon. The third stage of amplification probably occurred during the Kleanza Phase, and was certainly in effect by the historic period. It is marked by the evolution of ranked corporate groups. By definition, access to resources is not free and equal within these groups. Resources (especially wealth and prestige) are controlled by elites. The evidence for deviation amplification at Kitselas Canyon is the evolution of egalitarian corporate groups, and the subsequent transition to ranked corporate groups.

In conclusion, the people of the Paul Mason Phase practised

sedentism, resource intensification, and they controlled an important resource location for their own use. They did this in the absence of social ranking. If egalitarian corporate groups were capable of intensification and resource control, then the evolution of social ranking on the Northwest Coast cannot be explained as a deviation counteracting adaptation to subsistence related stress. Rather, Northwest Coast ranked societies amplified stress by placing control of resources in the hands of fewer and fewer individuals. Social ranking functioned to concentrate food, wealth and prestige among an emerging elite, rather than redistributing equally to all members of society.

**Egalitarian Corporate Groups: Beyond the Skeena**

Does the egalitarian corporate group model have applicability outside Kitselas Canyon? Two areas of the Northwest Coast where this investigation may lead are the Gulf of Georgia-Fraser River delta area, and the lower Fraser Canyon near Yale.

In the Gulf of Georgia, egalitarian corporate groups may have existed at the time of the Locarno Beach-Marpole interface. Burley (1980:73) has argued that the people of the Locarno Beach Phase were mobile, generalized hunter-gatherers. This is similar to the Skeena Phase at Kitselas Canyon. In general, Locarno Beach sites are not well situated for intensive salmon procurement (Mitchell 1971:57-58). Mitchell (1971:52) and Burley (1980:70) have both noted a shift in site location to the mouth of the Fraser at the beginning of the Marpole Phase. These sites were better situated for salmon procurement than the Locarno Beach sites in the gulf. If the shift in site location at the onset of the Marpole Phase reflects salmon intensification and control of prime fishing locations, then it is likely that corporate groups had emerged. But were these early corporate groups ranked? The answer to this lies in whether the shift in site location was associated with the manufacture of high-status goods. If high status goods and large multi-family plank dwellings, consistent with historic dwellings, came later in the Marpole Phase, then we may have a case for egalitarian corporate groups.

My purpose here is not to review the archaeological evidence for late Locarno Beach and early Marpole, but rather to suggest that future studies

299

might focus on this period with the model of egalitarian corporate groups in mind. Mitchell (1971:52-57) suggested that temporal variability existed in the Locarno Beach Phase, especially between Locarno Beach I and Locarno Beach II, and in the Marpole Phase. It is conceivable that re-examination of late Locarno Beach and early Marpole components might reveal a distinct intermediate phase. This could account for the apparent temporal overlap between the end of the Locarno Beach Phase and the beginning of the Marpole Phase (see Borden 1970:101). The critical question is whether evidence for salmon intensification and resource control predates the earliest evidence for social ranking.

In the Fraser Canyon, egalitarian corporate groups may have evolved some time between the late Eayem Phase (ca. 3500 B.P.) and the early Baldwin Phase (ca. 3000 B.P.). This would be roughly coeval with the emergence of egalitarian corporate groups at Kitselas Canyon. Burley (1980:73) notes that thin slate knives were common in the Baldwin Phase. To the extent that slate knives are thought to be efficient tools for processing salmon in large numbers (see Burley 1980:71), this may represent evidence for complex simultaneous production. Although Borden (1968c:14) stated that a "cultural efflorescence" was attained in the Baldwin Phase, including new evidence for personal decoration and artistic tradition in sculpture, I know of no serious proposal for social ranking at this time. Nonetheless, Burley (1979:138-39) suggests that the people of the Baldwin Phase were salmon specialists.

The Katz Site (DiRj 1), near Hope, is a strong candidate for the investigation of egalitarian corporate groups in this area. Zone B of this site has early Baldwin Phase dates of ca. 2500 B.P. (Hanson 1973:66). The overlying zone A lacks radiocarbon estimates, but may date to the middle or late Baldwin Phase. This zone contains a series of circular housepits, organized in two rows, facing the river. The pits appear to be of roughly equal size, and equal spacing (see Hanson 1973:62 - site contour map). The general layout of the village is remarkably similar to the Paul Mason Site. The Katz Site is located just below Fraser Canyon, a critical salmon fishing location. Numerous ground slate knives were recovered from zone A, attesting to the importance of fishing. It is possible that the late occupants of the Katz Site controlled this section of the Fraser River for the purpose of intensive salmon fishing. This may represent the formation of egalitarian corporate groups.

One way to test this proposition for the lower Fraser Canyon would be to correlate prime fishing locations with village locations. If egalitarian corporate groups did evolve during the Baldwin Phase, we might expect evidence for a shift in site location, similar to the Marpole Phase, focussing on critical areas for resource control.

## Conclusion

It may be argued that this study has been "long" on hypothesis and "short" on proof. Admittedly, the archaeological evidence from Kitselas Canyon has not been overwhelming. The lack of organic preservation, affecting both tools and faunal remains, is particularly unfortunate. I do think, however, that the existing evidence from Kitselas Canyon supports the model of cultural change developed here.

The essential contribution of this study has been the development of an alternative model for the evolution of cultural complexity. I think this model "works" for Kitselas Canyon, and it may have applicability elsewhere on the Northwest Coast.

Our understanding of prehistoric culture is only improved through the development and testing of new models. Archaeologists on the Northwest Coast may not yet have the final answer for the evolution of cultural complexity. Indeed, there may be no final answer. At the very least, however, we are now in a position to say something more than "a miracle occurred".

REFERENCES

Acheson, S.
    1977  Test excavations at GgSw5, Kitsegukla/Skeena Crossing.
          Unpublished report submitted to Heritage Conservation Branch,
          Victoria.

Ackerman, R.
    1968  The archaeology of the Glacier Bay region, southeastern Alaska.
          Washington State University, Laboratory of Archaeology, Report of
          Investigation 44, Pullman.

Ackerman, R., T. Hamilton, and R. Stuckenrath
    1979  Early culture complexes on the northern Northwest Coast.
          Canadian Journal of Archaeology 3:195-209.

Adam, D.
    1976  CABFAC/USGS, a FORTRAN program for Q-mode factor analysis of
          stratigraphically ordered samples.  US Geological Survey Open
          File Report 76-216.

Adam, D., and G. West
    1983  Temperature and precipitation estimates through the last glacial
          cycle from Clear Lake, California, pollen data.  Science
          219:168-70.

Adams, J.
    1973  The Gitksan potlatch: population flux, resource ownership and
          reciprocity.  Holt, Rinehart and Winston, Toronto.

Allaire, L.
    1978  L'archaeologie des Kitselas d'apres le site stratifie de Gitaus
          (GdTc2) sur la riviere Skeena en Colombie Britannique.  National
          Museum of Man, Archaeological Survey of Canada, Mercury Series
          No. 72.  Ottawa.

    1979  The cultural sequence at Gitaus: a case of prehistoric
          acculturation.  In Skeena River prehistory, edited by R. Inglis
          and G. MacDonald, pp 18-52.  National Museum of Man,
          Archaeological Survey of Canada, Mercury Series No. 87.  Ottawa.

    1984  A native mental map of Coast Tsimshian villages.  In The
          Tsimshian: Images of the past, views for the present, edited by
          M. Sequin, pp 82-98.  UBC Press, Vancouver.

Allaire, L. and G. MacDonald
    1971  Mapping and excavations at the Fortress of the Kitselas Canyon,
          B.C.: preliminary report.  Canadian Archaeological Association
          Bulletin 3:49-55.

302

Allaire, L. G. MacDonald, and R. Inglis
   1979  Gitlaxdzawk: ethnohistory and archaeology. In <u>Skeena River</u>
         <u>prehistory</u>, edited by R. Inglis and G. MacDonald, pp 53-166.
         National Museum of Man, Archaeological Survey of Canada, Mercury
         Series No. 87. Ottawa.

Ames, K.
   1971  Preliminary report of excavations at GhSv2, Hagwilget British
         Columbia. Unpublished report submitted to the National Museums
         of Canada, Ottawa.

   1973  Archaeological survey of the middle Skeena River valley.
         Unpublished report submitted to the National Museums of Canada,
         Ottawa.

   1976  The bone tool assemblage from the Garden Island Site, Prince
         Rupert Harbour, British Columbia: an analysis of assemblage
         variation through time. Unpublished PhD dissertation.
         Dept. of Anthropology, Washington State University.

   1979a Report of excavations at GhSv2, Hagwilget Canyon. In <u>Skeena</u>
         <u>River prehistory</u>, edited by R. Inglis and G. MacDonald,
         pp 181-218. National Museum of Man, Archaeological Survey of
         Canada, Mercury Series No. 87. Ottawa.

   1979b Stable and resilient systems along the Skeena River: the
         Gitksan/Carrier boundary. In <u>Skeena River prehistory</u>, edited by
         R. Inglis and G. MacDonald, pp 219-243. National Museum of Man,
         Archaeological Survey of Canada, Mercury Series No. 87. Ottawa.

   1981  The evolution of social ranking on the Northwest Coast of North
         America. <u>American Antiquity</u> 46:789-805.

   1983  Towards a general model of the evolution of ranking among
         foragers. In <u>The evolution of maritime cultures on the</u>
         <u>northeast and northwest coasts of North America</u>, edited by
         R. Nash, pp 173-84. Publication No. 11, Dept. of Archaeology,
         Simon Fraser University, Burnaby.

Ames, K., and A. Marshall
   1981  Villages, demography and subsistence intensification on the
         southern Columbia Plateau. <u>North American Archaeologist</u> 2:25-52.

Anderson, D.
   1968  A stoneage campsite at the gateway to America. <u>Scientific</u>
         <u>American</u> 218:24-33.

   1970  Akmak, an early archaeological assemblage from Onion Portage,
         northwest Alaska. <u>Acta Arctica</u> 16, Copenhagen.

Aro, K., and M. Shepard
    1967  Pacific salmon in Canada. <u>Spawning populations of North Pacific</u>
          <u>salmon</u>. International North Pacific Fisheries Commission,
          Vancouver.

Asch, D.
    1975  On sample size problems and the uses of non-probabilistic
          sampling. In <u>Sampling in archaeology</u>, edited by J. Mueller,
          pp 170-91. University of Arizona Press, Tucson.

Atmospheric Environment Service
    1982  <u>Temperature and Precipitation: 1941-1970, British Columbia</u>.
          Environment Canada, Ottawa.

British Columbia Lands Service
    1969  <u>The Prince Rupert-Smithers bulletin area</u>. Dept. of Lands and
          Forests, Victoria.

Barbeau, M.
    1917  Growth and federation in the Tsimshian phratries. <u>Proceedings of</u>
          <u>the 19th International Congress of Americanists</u>, pp 402-08.
          Washington.

    1950  Totem poles: volumes I and II. <u>Anthropological Series No. 30,</u>
          <u>Bulletin No. 119</u>. National Museums of Canada, Ottawa.

Bawden, G.
    1982  Community organization reflected by the household: a study of
          pre-Columbian social dynamics. <u>Journal of Field Archaeology</u>
          9:165-81.

Binford, L.
    1964  A consideration of archaeological research design. <u>American</u>
          <u>Antiquity</u> 29:425-41.

    1979  Organization and formation processes: looking at curated
          technologies. <u>Journal of Anthropological Research</u> 35:255-73.

    1980  Willow smoke and dog's tails: hunter-gatherer settlement systems
          and archaeological site formation. <u>American Antiquity</u> 45:4-20.

Bishop, C.
    1983  Limiting access to limited goods: the origins of stratification
          in interior British Columbia. In <u>The development of political</u>
          <u>organization in native North America</u>, edited by E. Tooker,
          pp 148-61. American Ethnological Society, Washington.

Blalock, H.
    1979  <u>Social statistics</u>. (second revised edition). McGraw-Hill, New
          York.

Boas, F.
  1890  The Indians of B.C.: Tlingit, Haida, Tsimshian, Kotomaqa. <u>Report
        of the British Association for the Advancement of Science 1889,
        fifth report of the northwestern tribes of Canada</u>, pp 797-893.
        London.

  1916  Tsimshian mythology. <u>31st annual report of the Bureau of
        American Ethnology 1909-1910</u>. pp 27-1037. Smithsonian
        Institution, Washington.

  1921  Ethnology of the Kwakiutl. <u>35th annual report of the Bureau of
        American Ethnology 1913-1914</u>, pp 41-1581. Smithsonian
        Institution, Washington.

  1935  <u>Kwakiutl culture as reflected in mythology</u>. American Folklore
        Society, Memoir 28. Washington.

Borden, C.
  1952  Results of archaeological investigations in central British
        Columbia. <u>Anthropology in British Columbia</u> 3:31-43.

  1962  West coast crossties with Alaska. In <u>Prehistoric cultural
        relations between the arctic and temperate zones of North
        America</u>, edited by J. Campbell, pp 9-19. Arctic Institute of
        America, Technical Paper No. 11. Calgary.

  1968a New evidence of early cultural relations between Eurasia and
        western North America. <u>Proceedings, VIII<sup>th</sup> Congress of
        Anthropological and Ethnological Sciences</u> 3:331-37. Tokyo and
        Kyoto.

  1968b A late Pleistocene pebble tool industry of southwestern British
        Columbia. In <u>Early man in western North America</u>, edited by
        C. Irwin-Williams, pp 55-69. Eastern New Mexico University
        Contributions in Anthropology No. 1.

  1968c Prehistory of the lower mainland. In <u>Lower Fraser Valley:
        Evolution of a cultural landscape</u>. B.C. Geographical Series
        No. 9, edited by A. Siemens, pp 9-26. UBC Press, Vancouver.

  1969  Early population movements from Asia into western North America.
        <u>Syesis</u> 2:1-13.

  1970  Culture history of the Fraser-delta region: an outline. <u>BC
        Studies</u> 6-7:95-112.

  1975  <u>Origins and development of early Northwest Coast culture to about
        3000 B.C.</u> National Museum of Man, Archaeological Survey of
        Canada, Mercury Series No. 45. Ottawa.

  1979  Peopling and early cultures of the Pacific northwest. <u>Science</u>
        203:963-71.

Brown, J.
    1975    Deep-site excavation strategy as a sampling problem.    In
            Sampling in archaeology, edited by J. Mueller, pp 155-69.
            University of Arizona Press, Tucson.

Bryson, R., W. Barreis, and W. Wendland
    1970    The character of late glacial and post-glacial climatic changes.
            In Pleistocene and recent environments of the central Great
            Plains, edited by W. Dort and J. Jones, pp 53-74.    University of
            Kansas, Lawrence.

Burley, D.
    1979    Specialization and the evolution of complex society in the Gulf
            of Georgia region.    Canadian Journal of Archaeology 3:131-43.

    1980    Marpole: anthropological reconstructions of a prehistoric
            Northwest Coast culture type. Publication No. 8, Dept. of
            Archaeology, Simon Fraser University, Burnaby.

    1983    Cultural complexity and evolution in the development of coastal
            adaptations among the Micmac and Coast Salish.    In The evolution
            of maritime cultures on the Northeast and Northwest Coasts of
            America,    edited by R. Nash, pp 157-72.    Publication No. 11,
            Dept. of Archaeology, Simon Fraser University, Burnaby.

Calvert, G.
    1968    The Co-op Site: a prehistoric midden site on the northern
            Northwest Coast.    Unpublished report, Laboratory of Archaeology,
            University of British Columbia, Vancouver.

Carl, G.
    1964    Some common marine fishes of British Columbia.    British Columbia
            Provincial Museum Handbook No. 2.    Victoria.

Carl, G., W. Clemens, and C. Lindsey
    1967    The fresh-water fishes of British Columbia.    British Columbia
            Provincial Museum Handbook No. 5.    Victoria.

Carlson, R.
    1979    The early period on the central coast of British Columbia.
            Canadian Journal of Archaeology 3:211-28.

    1983    The far west.    In    Early man in the New World, edited by R.
            Shutler, pp 73-96.    Sage Publications, Beverly Hills.

    1984    Prehistoric trade in British Columbia: obsidian.    Paper presented
            at the B.C. Studies Conference, University of British Columbia,
            Vancouver.

Chapman. M.
  1982 Archaeological investigations at the O'connor Site, Port Hardy.
       In Papers on central coast archaeology, edited by P. Hobler,
       pp 65-132. Publication No. 10, Dept. of Archaeology, Simon
       Fraser University, Burnaby.

Christenson, A.
  1980 Change in the human niche in response to population growth. In
       Modeling change in prehistoric subsistence economies, edited by
       T. Earle and A. Christenson, pp 31-72. Academic Press, New York.

Clague, J.
  1984 De-glaciation of the Prince Rupert-Kitimat area, British
       Columbia. Unpublished report, Geological Survey of Canada.
       Vancouver.

Clague, J., J. Armstrong, and W. Mathews
  1980 Advance of the late Wisconsin Cordilleran ice in southern British
       Columbia since 22,000 BP. Quaternary Research 13:322-26.

Clague, J., J. Harper, R. Hebda, and D. Howes
  1982 Late Quaternary sea levels and crustal movements, coastal British
       Columbia. Canadian Journal of Earth Sciences 19:597-618.

Clark, D.
  1968 Ocean Bay: an early north Pacific maritime culture. National
       Museum of Man, Archaeological Survey of Canada, Mercury Series
       No. 86. Ottawa.

  1972 Archaeology of the Batza Tena obsidian source, west-central
       Alaska. Anthropological Papers of the University of Alaska
       15(2):1-22.

Clark, G.
  1979 Archaeological testing of the Coffman Cove Site, southeastern
       Alaska. Paper presented at the 32nd annual Northwest
       Anthropological Conference, Eugene.

Connelly, J.
  1979 Hopi social organization. In Handbook of North American
       Indians, vol. 9, edited by A. Ortiz, pp 539-53, Smithsonian
       Institution, Washington.

Codere, H.
  1950 Fighting with property: a study of Kwakiutl potlatching and
       warfare, 1792-1930. University of Washington Press, Seattle.

Conover, K.
  1978 Matrix analysis. In Bella Bella prehistory, edited by J. Hester
       and S. Nelson, pp 67-100. Publication No. 5, Dept. of
       Archaeology, Simon Fraser University, Burnaby.

Conover, W.
    1971    Practical nonparametric statistics.   J. Wiley and Sons, Toronto.

Cook, J.
    1969    The early prehistory of Healy Lake, Alaska.   Unpublished PhD
            dissertation, University of Wisconsin.

Cook, S., and R. Heizer
    1965    The quantitative approach to the relation between population and
            settlement size.   Contributions of the University of California
            Archaeological Research Facility 14:17-40.

    1968    Relationships among houses, settlement areas, and population in
            aboriginal California.   In Settlement archaeology, edited by
            K.C. Chang, pp 79-116.   Stanford University, Palo Alto.

Coupe, R., C. Ray, A. Comeau, M. Ketcheson and R. Annas
    1982    A guide to some common plants of the Skeena area.   Information
            Services Branch, B.C. Ministry of Forests, Victoria.

Coupland, G.
    1984    A report of archaeological investigations in 1982 at Kitselas
            Canyon, Skeena River, British Columbia.   Unpublished report
            submitted to the Heritage Conservation Branch, Victoria.

Cove, J.
    1982    The Gitksan traditional concept of land ownership.
            Anthropologica 24:3-17.

Cowan, J., and C. Guiguet
    1964    The mammals of British Columbia.   British Columbia Provincial
            Museum Handbook No. 11.   Victoria.

Cowgill, G.
    1972    Models, methods and techniques for seriation.   In Models in
            archaeology, edited by D. Clarke, pp 381-424.   Methuen, London.

Croes, D., and S. Hackenberger
    1984    Economic modeling of anadromous fish utilization in the Hoko
            River region.   Paper presented at the 49th annual SAA Conference,
            Portland.

Cybulski, J.
    1972    Analysis of skeletal remains from the Prince Rupert Harbour area
            of British Columbia.   Canadian Archaeological Association
            Bulletin 4:87-90.

    1973    British Columbia skeletal remains.   Canadian Archaeological
            Association Bulletin 5:126-27.

    1974    Tooth wear and material culture: pre-contact patterns in the
            Tsimshian area, British Columbia.   Syesis 7:31-35.

1975 Skeletal Variability in British Columbia coastal populations: a
descriptive and comparative assessment of cranial morphology.
National Museum of Man, Archaeological Survey of Canada, Mercury
Series No.30.  Ottawa.

1978 Modified human bones and skulls from Prince Rupert Harbour, B.C.
Canadian Journal of Archaeology 2:15-32.

1979 Conventional and unconventional burial positions at Prince Rupert
Harbour, British Columbia.  Paper presented at the 12th annual
CAA Conference, Vancouver.

Davis, S.
1979 Hidden Falls: a stratified site in southeastern Alaska.  Paper
presented at the 32nd annual Northwest Anthropological
Conference, Eugene.

Dawson, G.
1881 Report of an exploration from Port Simpson on the Pacific coast,
to Edmonton on the Saskatchewan.  Geological Survey of Canada,
Report of Progress 1879-1880.  Ottawa.

Dixon, E.
1973 The Gallagher flint station, an early man site on the north
slope, arctic Alaska.  In The Bering Land Bridge and its role
for the history of holarctic floras and faunas in the late
Cenozoic, pp 132-37.  Khabarovsk, Soviet Far East.

Donahue, P.
1975 Concerning Athapaskan prehistory in British Columbia.  Western
Canadian Journal of Anthropology 5:21-63.

1977 4500 years of cultural continuity on the central Interior Plateau
of British Columbia.  Unpublished PhD dissertation, Dept. of
Anthropology, University of Wisconsin.

Donald, L.
1983 Was Nuu-chah-nulth-aht (Nootka) society based on slave labour?
In The development of political organization in native North
America, edited by E. Tooker, pp 108-19.  The American
Ethnological Society, Washington.

Donald, L., and D. Mitchell
1975 Some correlates of local group rank among the Southern Kwakiutl.
Ethnology 14:325-46.

Donnan, C., and M. Moseley
1968 The utilization of flakes for cleaning fish. American Antiquity
33:502-03.

Dorsey, G.
  1897  The geography of the Tsimshian Indians.  The American Antiquarian
        19:276-82.

Drennan, R.
  1976  A refinement of chronological seriation using nonmetric
        multidimensional scaling.  American Antiquity 41:290-302.

Drucker, C.
  1977  To inherit the land: descent and decision in northern Luzon.
        Ethnology 16:1-20.

Drucker, P.
  1939  Rank, wealth and kinship in Northwest Coast society.  American
        Anthropologist 41:55-64.

  1943  Archaeological survey on the northern Northwest Coast.  Bureau of
        American Ethnology Bulletin 133, pp 17-32.  Smithsonian
        Institution, Washington.

  1950  Culture element distributions: XXVI, Northwest Coast.  University
        of California Publications in Anthropological Records 9:157-294.

  1951  The northern and central Nootkan tribes.  Bureau of American
        Ethnology Bulletin 144.  Smithsonian Institution, Washington.

  1965  Cultures of the north Pacific coast.  Harper and Row, New York.

Drucker, P., and R. Heizer
  1967  To make my name good: a re-examination of the Southern Kwakiutl
        potlatch.  University of California Press, Berkeley.

Duff, W.
  1952  The Upper Stalo Indians of the Fraser River of British Columbia.
        Anthropology in British Columbia, Memoir No. 1.  British Columbia
        Provincial Museum, Victoria.

  1959  Histories, territories and laws of the Kitwancool.  Anthropology
        in British Columbia, Memoir No. 4.  British Columbia Provincial
        Museum, Victoria.

  1963  Stone clubs from the Skeena River area.  Provincial Museum Annual
        Report for 1962 pp 2-12.  British Columbia Provincial Museum,
        Victoria.

  1965  The Indian history of British Columbia.  volume 1: the impact of
        the white man.  Anthropology in British Columbia, Memoir No. 5.
        British Columbia Provincial Museum, Victoria.

Duff, W., and M. Kew
  1957  Anthony Island: a home of the Haidas.  Report of the Provincial
        Museum, pp 37-64.  British Columbia Provincial Museum, Victoria.

Duffell, S., and J. Souther
    1964    Geology of the Terrace map area, British Columbia (1031E1/2).
            Geological Survey of Canada, Memoir 329.  Ottawa.

Dumond, D.
    1974    Some uses of R-mode analysis in archaeology.  American Antiquity
            39:253-70.

Dyson-Hudson, R., and E. Smith
    1978    Human territoriality: an ecological assessment.  American
            Anthropologist 80:21-41.

Earle, T.
    1977    A reappraisal of redistribution: complex Hawaiian chiefdoms.  In
            Exchange systems in prehistory.  edited by T. Earle and
            J. Ericson, pp 213-29.  Academic Press, New York.

Eder, J.
    1984    The impact of subsistence change on mobility and settlement
            pattern in a tropical forest foraging economy.  American
            Anthropologist 86:837-53.

Emmons, G.
    1912    The Kitselas of British Columbia.  American Anthropologist
            14:467-71.

Farley, A.
    1979    Atlas of British Columbia.  UBC Press, Vancouver.

Fedirchuk, G.
    1970    Recent archaeological investigations at Fisherman Lake: the
            Julian Site.  In Early man and environments in northwest North
            America,  edited by R. Smith and J. Smith, pp 105-16.  University
            of Calgary, Calgary.

Fenton, W.
    1978    Northern Iroquoian culture patterns.  In Handbook of North
            American Indians, vol. 15, edited by B. Trigger, pp 296-321.
            Smithsonian Institution, Washington.

Ferguson, B.
    1983    Warfare and redistributive exchange on the Northwest Coast.  In
            The development of political organization in native North
            America, edited by E. Tooker, pp 133-47.  The American
            Ethnological Society, Washington.

Fladmark, K.
    1970    Preliminary report on the archaeology of the Queen Charlotte
            Islands.  B.C. Studies 6-7:18-45.

1971    Early microblade industries on the Queen Charlotte Islands,
        British Columbia.  Paper presented at the 4th annual CAA
        Conference, Calgary.

1975    A paleoecological model for Northwest Coast prehistory.  National
        Museum of Man, Archaeological Survey of Canada, Mercury Series
        No. 43.  Ottawa.

1976    Punchaw village: a preliminary report.  The archaeology of a
        prehistoric settlement.  In Current research reports, edited by
        R. Carlson, pp 19-32.  Publication No. 3, Dept. of Archaeology,
        Simon Fraser University, Burnaby.

1979a   The early prehistory of the Queen Charlotte Islands.  Archaeology
        32:38-45.

1979b   Routes: alternate migration corridors for early man in North
        America.  American Antiquity 44:55-69.

1982a   An introduction to the prehistory of British Columbia.  Canadian
        Journal of Archaeology 6:95-156.

1982b   Glass and ice: a report on the archaeology of the Mt. Edziza and
        Spectrum Ranges, northwestern British Columbia.  Unpublished
        report submitted to the Heritage Conservation Branch, Victoria.

1983    Times and places: environmental correlates of mid-to-late
        Wisconsinan human population expansion in North America.  In
        Early man in the New World, edited by R. Shutler, pp 13-41.  Sage
        Publications, Beverly Hills.

Flannery, K.
1968    Archaeological systems theory and early Mesoamerica.  In
        Anthropological archaeology in the americas, edited by
        B. Meggars, pp 67-87, Anthropological Society of Washington,
        Washington.

1969    Origins and ecological effects of early domestication in Iran and
        the Near East.  In The domestication and exploitation of plants
        and animals, edited by P. Ucko and G. Dimbleby, pp 73-100.
        Aldine, Chicago.

1972    The origins of the village as a settlement type in Mesoamerica
        and the Near East: a comparative study.  In Man, settlement and
        urbanism, edited by P. Ucko, R. Tringham and G. Dimbleby,
        pp 23-53, Duckworth, London.

1973    The origins of agriculture.  Annual review of anthropology
        2:271-310.

1976    The early Mesoamerican village, Academic Press, New York.

Flenniken, J.
   1981   Replicative systems analysis: a model applied to the vein quartz
          artifacts from the Hoko River site. Washington State University
          Laboratory of Anthropology, Report of Investigations No. 59,
          Seattle.

Forester, R.
   1968   The sockeye salmon. Fisheries Research Board of Canada Bulletin
          162. Ottawa.

Fried, M.
   1967   The evolution of political society. Random House, New York.

Frison, G.
   1968   A functional analysis of certain chipped stone tools. American
          Antiquity 33:149-55.

Garfield, V.
   1939   Tsimshian clan and society. University of Washington
          Publications in Anthropology No. 7. University of Washington.
          Seattle.

   1951   The Tsimshian and their neighbours. In The Tsimshian Indians
          and their arts, edited by V. Garfield and P. Wingert, pp 3-70.
          Douglas and McIntyre, Vancouver.

Geertz, C.
   1963   Agricultural involution. University of California Press,
          Berkeley.

Godfrey, E.
   1966   The birds of Canada. National Museums of Canada, Bulletin  203,
          Biological Series No. 73. Ottawa.

Godfrey-Smith, D.
   1984   Obsidian x-ray flourescence analysis of five samples from the
          Paul Mason Site. Unpublished report on file, Laboratory of
          Archaeology, Univeristy of British Columbia.

Goodenough, W.
   1959   Property, kin and community on Truk. Yale University
          Publications in Anthropology, No. 46. New Haven.

Goody, J.
   1972   The evolution of the family. In Household and family in past
          time, edited by P. Laslett and R. Wall, pp 103-24. Cambridge
          University Press, Cambridge.

Gould, R.
   1971   The archaeologist as ethnographer: a case study from the Western
          Desert of Australia. World Archaeology 3:143-77.

1978  Tolowa. In <u>Handbook of North American Indians, vol. 8</u>, edited by R.F. Heizer, pp 128-36, Smithsonian Institution, Washington.

Gower, J.
1971  Statistical methods of comparing different multivariate analyses of the same data. In <u>Mathematics in the archaeological and historical sciences</u>, edited by F. Hodson, D. Kendall, and P. Tautu, pp 138-49. Edinburgh University Press, Edinburgh.

Guiguet, C.
1961  The birds of British Columbia (No. 4) upland game birds. <u>British Columbia Provincial Museum Handbook No. 10</u>. Victoria.

1968  The birds of British Columbia (No. 6) waterfowl. <u>British Columbia Provincial Museum Handbook No. 15.</u> Victoria.

Hadleigh-West, F.
1967  The Donnelly Ridge Site and the definition of an early core and blade complex in central Alaska. <u>American Antiquity</u> 32:360-82.

Halpin, M.
1973  The Tsimshian crest system. Unpublished PhD dissertation, Dept. of Anthropology, University of British Columbia.

Ham, L.
1982  Seasonality of shell midden layers and subsistence activities at the Crescent Beach Site (DgRr1). Unpublished PhD dissertation, Dept. of Anthropology, University of British Columbia.

Hanson, G.
1973  The Katz Site: a prehistoric pithouse settlement in the lower Fraser Valley, British Columbia. Unpublished MA thesis, Dept. of Anthropology, University of British Columbia.

Harris, D.
1978  Settling down: an evolutionary model for the transformation of mobile bands into sedentary communities. In <u>The evolution of social systems</u>, edited by J. Friedman and M. Rowlands, pp 402-17. University of Pittsburgh Press, Pittsburgh.

Hart, J.
1973  Pacific fishes of Canada. <u>Fisheries Research Board of Canada Bulletin 180</u>. Ottawa.

Hassan, F.
1977  The dynamics of agricultural origins in Palestine: a theoretical model. In <u>Origins of agriculture</u>, edited by C. Reed, pp 589-609. Mouton, Paris.

Hayden, B.
1980  Confusion in the bipolar world: bashed pebbles and splintered pieces. <u>Lithic Technology</u> 9:2-7.

Hayden, B., and A. Cannon
    1982  The corporate group as an archaeological unit.  Journal of
          Anthropological Archaeology 1:132-58.

Hebda, R., and R. Mathewes
    1984  Holocene history of cedar and native Indian cultures of the North
          American Pacific coast.  Science 225:711-13.

Heidenreich, C.
    1978  Huron.  In Handbook of North American Indians, vol. 15, edited
          by B. Trigger, pp 368-88.  Smithsonian Institution, Washington.

Helmer, J.
    1977  Points, people and prehistory: a preliminary synthesis of culture
          history in north central British Columbia.  In Prehistory of the
          North American subarctic: the Athapaskan question, edited by
          J. Helmer, S. Vandyke and F. Kense,  pp 90-96.  University of
          Calgary, Calgary.

Hester, J., and S. Nelson (eds.)
    1978  Studies in Bella Bella prehistory, Publication No. 5, Dept. of
          Archaeology, Simon Fraser University, Burnaby.

Heusser, C.
    1954  Additional pollen profiles from southeast Alaska. American
          Journal of Science 252:106-08.

    1960  Late Pleistocene environments of north Pacific North America.
          American Geographical Society Publication No. 35.  Washington.

    1965  A Pleistocene phytogeographical sketch of the Pacific northwest
          and Alaska.  In The Quaternary of the United States  edited by
          H. Wright and D. Frey, pp 469-83.  Princeton University Press,
          Princeton.

Hitchcock, R.
    1982  Patterns of sedentism among the Basarwa of eastern Botswana.  In
          Politics and history in band societies,  edited by E. Leacock and
          R. Lee, pp 223-67.  Cambridge University Press, New York.

Hobler, P.
    1978  The relationship of archaeological sites to sea levels on Moresby
          Island, Queen Charlotte Islands.  Canadian Journal of Archaeology
          2:1-14.

Hodson, F.
    1970  Cluster analysis and archaeology: some new developments and
          applications.  World Archaeology 1:299-320.

Hodson, F., P. Sneath, and J. Doran
    1966  Some experiments in the numerical analysis of archaeological
          data.  Biometrika 53:311-24.

Holland, S.
   1964  Landforms of British Columbia: a physiographic outline. British
         Columbia Dept. of Mines and Petroleum Resources, Bulletin
         No. 48. Victoria.

Honigmann, J.
   1959  The world of man. Harper and Row, New York.

Horne, L.
   1982  The household in space. American Behavioural Scientist
         25:677-86.

Idler, D., and W. Clemens
   1959  The energy expenditures of Fraser River sockeye during the
         spawning migration. International Pacific Salmon Fisheries
         Commission Progress Report No. 6. New Westminster.

Inglis, R.
   1972  Staff research. In Archaeological Survey of Canada Annual
         Review 1972, edited by G. MacDonald, pp 19-22. National Museum
         of Man, Archaeological Survey of Canada, Mercury Series No. 10.
         Ottawa.

   1974  Contract research. In Archaeological Survey of Canada Annual
         Review 1973 edited by G. MacDonald, pp 27-30. National Museum
         of Man, Archaeological Survey of Canada, Mercury Series
         No. 21. Ottawa.

   1977  The Coast Tsimshian seasonal subsistence pattern: the
         ethnographic and archaeological record. Paper presented at the
         30th Northwest Anthropological Conference, Victoria.

Inglis, R., and G. MacDonald
   1979  Introduction. In Skeena River prehistory, edited by R. Inglis
         and G. MacDonald, pp 1-17. National Museum of Man,
         Archaeological Survey of Canada, Mercury Series No. 87. Ottawa.

Ingold, T.
   1982  Comments - reply to Ruyle. Current Anthropology 23:531.

Jacobs, L.
   1979  Tell-i-nun: archaeological implications of a village in
         transition. In Ethnoarchaeology, edited by C. Kramer,  pp
         175-92. Columbia University Press, New York.

Johnson, L.
   1972  Introduction to imaginary models for archaeological scaling and
         clustering. In Models in archaeology, edited by D. Clarke,
         pp 309-79. Methuen, London.

Jorgenson, J.
   1980  Western Indians. Freeman Press, San Francisco.

Kane, P.
   1859  Wanderings of an artist among the Indians of North America.
         Logographic Press, London.

Keithahn, E.
   1962  Stone artifacts of southeastern Alaska.  American Antiquity
         28:66-77.

Kelley, K.
   1982  Ethnoarchaeology of the Black Hat Navajos: historical and
         ahistorical determinants of site features.  Journal of
         Anthropological Research 38:45-74.

Kelly, R.
   1983  Hunter-gatherer mobility strategies.  Journal of Anthropological
         Research 39:277-306.

Kennard, E.
   1979  Hopi economy and subsistence.  In Handbook of North American
         Indians, vol. 9, edited by A. Ortiz, pp 554-63, Smithsonian
         Institution, Washington.

Kennedy, D., and R. Bouchard
   1978  Fraser River Lillooet: an ethnographic summary.  In Reports of
         the Lillooet archaeological project: No. 1, introduction and
         setting, edited by A. Stryd and S. Lawhead, pp 22-55.  National
         Museum of Man, Archaeological Survey of Canada, Mercury Series
         No. 73.  Ottawa.

Kew, M.
   1976  Salmon abundance, technology and human populations on the Fraser
         River watershed.  Paper presented at the 29th Northwest
         Anthropological Conference, Simon Fraser University, Burnaby.

Krajina, V.
   1973  Biogeoclimatic zones of British Columbia.  (map at scale 30
         miles/inch).  British Columbia Ecological Reserves Committee,
         Victoria.

   1976  Biogeoclimatic zones of British Columbia.  Van Dusen Botanical
         Gardens, Vancouver.

Kramer, C.
   1979  An archaeological view of a contemporary Kurdish
         village: domestic architecture, household size and wealth.  In
         Ethnoarchaeology, edited by C. Kramer, pp 139-63.  Columbia
         University Press, New York.

   1982  Village ethnoarchaeology: rural Iran in archaeological
         perspective.  Academic Press, New York.

Kuhnlein, H., A. Chan, J. Thompson and S. Nakai
   1982  Ooligan grease: a nutritious fat used by native people of coastal
         British Columbia. Journal of Ethnobiology 2:154-61.

Laguna, F. de.
   1934  The archaeology of Cook Inlet, Alaska. University of
         Pennsylvania Museum Press, Philadelphia.

   1956  Chugash prehistory: the archaeology of Prince William Sound,
         Alaska. University of Washington Publications in Anthropology,
         No. 13. Seattle.

   1972  Under Mount St. Elias. Smithsonian Institution, Washington.

   1983  Aboriginal Tlingit sociopolitical organization. In The
         development of political organization in native North America,
         edited by E. Tooker, pp 71-85. American Ethnological
         Society, Washington.

Laguna, F. de., F. Riddell, D. McGeein, K. Lane, J. Freed,and C. Osborne
   1964  Archaeology of the Yakutat Bay area, Alaska. Bureau of American
         Ethnology Bulletin 192. Smithsonian Institution, Washington.

Larsen, H.
   1968  Trail Creek. Acta Arctica 15, Copenhagen.

LeBlanc, S.
   1971  An addition to Naroll's suggested floor area and settlement
         population relationship. American Antiquity 36:210-11.

Leubbers, R.
   1978  Excavations: stratigraphy and artifacts. In Studies in Bella
         Bella prehistory, edited by J. Hester and S. Nelson, pp 11-66.
         Publication No. 5, Dept. of Archaeology, Simon Fraser University,
         Burnaby.

Lightfoot, K., and G. Feinman
   1982  Social differentiation and leadership development in early
         pithouse villages in the Mogollon region of the American
         southwest. American Antiquity 47:64-86.

Lightfoot, Ricky Ray
   1983  Component 2 at the Hidden Falls archaeological site, southeastern
         Alaska. Unpublished MA thesis. Dept. of Anthropology,
         Washington State University.

MacDonald, G.
   1968  Debert: a Paleo-Indian site in central Nova Scotia.
         Anthropological Papers No. 16. National Museums of Canada,
         Ottawa.

1969a Preliminary culture sequence from the Coast Tsimshian area,
British Columbia.  Northwest Anthropological Research Notes
3:240-54.

1969b Comments.  Northwest Anthropological Research Notes 3:259-60.

1973 Haida burial practices: three archaeological examples.  National
Museum of Man, Archaeological Survey of Canada, Mercury Series
No. 9.  Ottawa.

1979 Kitwanga Fort National Historic Site, Skeena River British
Columbia:  historical research and analysis of structural
remains.  Parks Canada Manuscript No. 341.  Calgary.

1983 Prehistoric art of the northern Northwest Coast.  In Indian art
traditions of the Northwest Coast, edited by R. Carlson, pp
99-120. Simon Fraser University, Burnaby.

MacDonald, G., and G. Coupland
1982 Ethnohistorical and archaeological investigations at Kitselas
Canyon.  Unpublished report submitted to Parks Canada.  Calgary.

MacDonald, G., and R. Inglis
1976 The Dig: an archaeological reconstruction of a west coast
village.  National Museum of Man, Ottawa.

1981 An overview of the North Coast Prehistory Project.  B.C. Studies
48:37-63.

MacDonald, J.
1982 Archaeological and ethnographic survey of Kitsumkalum Indian
Reserve No. 2.  Unpublished report, Dept. of Anthropology,
University of British Columbia.

1984 Trying to make a life: the historical political economy of
Kitsumkalum.  Unpublished PhD dissertation, Dept. of
Anthropology, University of British Columbia.

MacIlwraith, J.
1948 The Bella Coola Indians.  (2 volumes).  University of Toronto
Press, Toronto.

McNeary, S.
1976 Where fire came down from: social and economic life of the
Niska. Unpublished PhD dissertation, Dept. of Anthropology, Bryn
Mawr College.

MacNeish, R.
1960 The Callison Site in the light of archaeological survey of
southwest Yukon.  National Museum of Canada Bulletin 162.
Contributions to Anthropology 1957.  pp 1-51.  National Museum of
Canada, Ottawa.

1964    Investigations in southwest Yukon.  <u>Papers of the R.S. Peabody</u>
<u>Foundation for Archaeology</u> 6:199-488.  Andover.


Martin, J.
    1973    On the estimation of the sizes of local groups in a hunting and
            gathering environment.  <u>American Anthropologist</u> 75:1448-68.

Maruyama, M.
    1963    The second cybernetics: deviation-amplifying mutual causal
            processes.  <u>American Scientist</u> 51:164-79.

Mathews, W.
    1979    Late Quaternary environmental history affecting human habitation
            of the Pacific northwest.  <u>Canadian Journal of Archaeology</u>
            3:145-56.

Matson, R.G.
    1974    Clustering and scaling of Gulf of Georgia sites.  <u>Syesis</u>
            7:101-14.

    1975    Metric multidimensional scaling computer programme.  Department
            of Anthropology and Sociology, University of British Columbia.

    1976    <u>The Glenrose Cannery Site</u>.  National Museum of Man,
            Archaeological Survey of Canada, Mercury Series No. 52.  Ottawa.

    1981    Prehistoric subsistence patterns in the Fraser delta: the
            evidence from the Glenrose Cannery Site.  <u>B.C. Studies</u> 48:64-85.

    1983    Intensification and the development of cultural complexity: the
            northwest versus the northeast coast.  In <u>The evolution of</u>
            <u>maritime cultures on the Northeast and Northwest Coasts of</u>
            <u>America</u>, edited by R. Nash, pp 125-48.  Publication No. 11,
            Dept. of Archaeology, Simon Fraser University, Burnaby.

Matson, R.G., and D. True
    1974    Site relationships at Quebrada Tarapaca, Chile: a comparison of
            clustering and scaling techniques.  <u>American Antiquity</u> 39:51-75.

Meares, J.
    1790    <u>Voyages made in the years 1788-89</u>.  Logographic Press, London.

Millar, J.
    1981    Interaction between the MacKenzie and Yukon basins during the
            Holocene.  In <u>Networks of the past: Regional Interaction in</u>
            <u>archaeology</u>, edited by P. Francis, F. Kense and P. Duke, pp
            259-94.  University of Calgary, Calgary.

Miller, M., and J. Anderson
  1974  Out-of-phase Holocene climatic trends in the maritime and
        continental sectors of the Alaska-Canada Boundary Range.  In
        Quaternary environments: proceedings of a symposium, edited
        by W. Mahaney, pp 33-58.  York University Press, Toronto.

Milne, D.
  1955  The Skeena River salmon fishery with special reference to sockeye
        salmon.  Journal of the Fisheries Research Board of Canada
        12:451-85.

Mitchell, D.
  1968  Microblades: a long-standing Gulf of Georgia tradition.  American
        Antiquity 33:11-15.

  1969  Site surveys in the Johnstone Straits region.  Northwest
        Anthropological Research Notes 3:193-216

  1971  Archaeology of the Gulf of Georgia, a natural region and its
        cultural types.  Syesis 4 (Supplement 1).  Victoria.

  1983a Tribes and chiefdoms of the Northwest Coast: the Tsimshian case.
        In  The evolution of maritime cultures on the Northeast and
        Northwest Coasts of America, edited by R. Nash,
        pp 55-64.Publication No. 11, Dept. of Archaeology, Simon Fraser
        University, Burnaby.

  1983b Seasonal settlements, village aggregations, and political
        autonomy on the central Northwest Coast.  In  The development of
        political organization in native North America, edited by
        E. Tooker, pp 97-107.  The American Ethnological Society,
        Washington.

  1984  Predatory warfare, social status, and the north Pacific slave
        trade.  Ethnology 23:39-48.

Morice, A.
  1893  Notes archaeological, industrial and sociological on the Western
        Denes.  Transactions of the Canadian Institute 4:1-221.

Morlan, R.
  1967  The preceramic period of Hokkaido: an outline.  Arctic
        Anthropology 4:167-220.

Morrison, D.
  1984  A re-assessment of the Julian Complex, Fisherman Lake, Northwest
        Territories.  Canadian Journal of Archaeology 8:29-56.

Murdock, P.
  1949  Social structure.  The Free Press, New York.

Nadel, S.
  1951  Foundations of social anthropology.  The Free Press, New York.

Naroll, R.
  1962  Floor area and settlement population.  American Antiquity
        27:587-89.

Netting, R.
  1982  Some home truths on household size and wealth.  American
        Behavioural Scientist 25:641-62.

Nolan, R.
  1977  The utilization of fish resources by the Coast Tsimshian.
        Unpublished MA thesis, Dept. of Anthropology, Trent University.

Orans, M.
  1975  Domesticating the functional dragon: an analysis of Piddocke's
        potlatch.  American Anthropologist 77:312-29.

Oswalt, W.
  1976  An anthropological analysis of food-getting technology.  Wiley
        and Sons, New York.

Pasternack, B., C. Ember, and M. Ember
  1976  On the conditions favouring extended family households.  Journal
        of Anthropological Research 32:109-24.

Piddocke, S.
  1965  The potlatch system of the Southern Kwakiutl: a new perspective.
        Southwestern Journal of Anthropology 21:244-64.

Pokotylo, D.
  1978  Lithic technology and settlement patterns in Upper Hat Creek
        Valley, B.C.  Unpublished PhD dissertation, Dept. of Anthropology
        and Sociology, University of British Columbia.

Rafferty, J.
  1985  The archaeological record on sedentariness: recognition,
        development and implications.  In Advances in archaeological
        method and theory, volume 8, edited by M. Schiffer, pp 113-56.
        Academic Press, New York.

Redman, C.
  1977  Man, domestication and culture in southwestern Asia.  In Origins
        of agriculture, edited by C. Reed, pp 523-41.  Mouton, Paris.

Redman, C., E. Curtin, N. Versaggi, and J. Wanser
  1978  Social archaeology: the future of the past.  In Social
        archaeology: beyond subsistence and dating, edited by C. Redman,
        M. Berman, E. Curtin, W. Langhorne, N. Versaggi, and J. Wanser,
        pp 1-17.  Academic Press, New York.

Reed, C.

1977a A model for the origin of agriculture in the Near East. In
Origins of agriculture, edited by C. Reed, pp 543-67. Mouton,
Paris.

1977b Origins of agriculture: discussion and some conclusions. In
Origins of agriculture, edited by C. Reed, pp 879-953. Mouton,
Paris.

Reid, J., and S. Whittlesey
1982 Households at Grasshopper Pueblo. American Behavioural Scientist
25:687-703.

Richardson, A.
1982 The control of productive resources on the Northwest Coast of
North America. In Resource managers: North American and
Australian hunter-gatherers, edited by N. Williams and E.
Hunn, pp 93-112. AAAS Selected Symposium 67.

Roberts, L.
1984 Faunal analysis of the Paul Mason Site. Unpublished report on
file, Laboratory of Archaeology, University of British Columbia.

Rogers, E.
1972 The Mistassini Cree. In Hunters and gatherers today, edited by
M. Bichieri, pp 90-137. Holt, Rinehart and Winston, New York.

Robinson, W., and W. Wright
1962 Men of Medeek. Northern Sentinal Press, Kitimat.

Rosman, A., and P. Rubel
1971 Feasting with mine enemy: rank and exchange among Northwest Coast
societies, Columbia University Press, New York.

Ruyle, E.
1973 Slavery, surplus and stratification on the Northwest Coast: the
ethnoenergetics of an incipient stratification system. Current
Anthropology 14:603-31.

Sahlins, M.
1963 Poor man, rich man, big man, chief: political types in Melanesia
and Polynesia. Comparative Studies in Society and History
5:285-303.

Sanger, D.
1968 Prepared core and blade traditions in the Pacific Northwest.
Arctic Anthropology 5:92-120.

1970 The archaeology of the Lochnore-Nesikep locality, British
Columbia. Syesis 3 (Supplement 1). Victoria.

Schalk, R.
  1977  The structure of an anadromous fish resource. In <u>For theory building in archaeology</u>, edited by L. Binford, pp 207-49. Academic Press, New York.

Schoolcraft, H.
  1860  <u>Information respecting the history, conditions and prospects of the Indian tribes of the United States. Volume 5.</u>  Philadelphia.

Scott, W., and E. Crossman
  1973  <u>Freshwater fishes of Canada.</u>  Fisheries Research Board of Canada, Bulletin 184. Ottawa.

Semenov, S.
  1964  <u>Prehistoric technology.</u>  Adams and Dart, Bath.

Service, E.
  1962  <u>Primitive social organization.</u>  Random House, New York.

Severs, P.
  1974  Archaeological investigations at Blue Jackets Creek, FlUa4, Queen Charlotte Islands, British Columbia. <u>Canadian Archaeological Association Bulletin</u> 6:163-205.

Shackley, M.
  1975  <u>Archaeological sediments: a survey of analytical methods.</u> Butterworths, London.

Shafer, H.
  1970  Notes on uniface retouch technology. <u>American Antiquity</u> 35:480-87.

Shotridge, L.
  1918  A visit to the Tsimshian Indians. <u>Museum Journal of Pennsylvania</u> 10:117-48.

Simonsen, B.
  1973  <u>Archaeological investigations in the Hecate Strait-Milbanke Sound area.</u>  National Museum of Man, Archaeological Survey of Canada, Mercury Series No. 13. Ottawa.

Smith, E.A.
  1981  The application of optimal foraging theory to the analysis of hunter-gatherer group size. In <u>Hunter-gatherer foraging strategies</u>, edited by B. Winterhalder and E.A. Smith, pp 36-65. University of Chicago Press, Chicago.

Smith, H.
  1909  Archaeological remains on the coast of northern British Columbia and southern Alaska. <u>American Anthropologist</u> 11:595-600.

1927    A prehistoric earthwork in the Haida Indian area. _American Anthropologist_ 29:109-11.

1930    A list of archaeological sites near Prince Rupert, British Columbia. Report on file, National Museum of Man, Archaeological Survey of Canada, archives, Ottawa.

Smith, J.
1970    Preliminary report on archaeological investigation in northern British Columbia. In _Early man and environments in northwest North America_, edited by R. Smith and J. Smith, pp 87-104. University of Calgary Press, Calgary.

1971    The Ice Mountain microblade and core industry, Cassiar District, northern British Columbia, Canada. _Arctic and Alpine Research_ 3:199-213.

1974    The northeast Asian - northwest American microblade tradition (NANAMT). _Journal of Field Archaeology_ 1:347-64.

Sneath, P., and R. Sokal
1973    _Numerical taxonomy_. Freeman Press, San Francisco.

Sneed, P.
1971    Of salmon and men: an investigation of ecological determinants and aboriginal man in the Canadian Plateau. In _Aboriginal man and environments on the Plateau of northwest North America_, edited by A. Stryd and R. Smith, pp 229-242. University of Calgary Press, Calgary.

Spencer, H.
1885    _The principles of sociology_. (volume 1) (third edition). Appleton, New York.

Stephenson, W.
1953    _The study of behaviour: Q-technique and its methodology_. University of Chicago Press, Chicago.

Steward, J.
1955    _Theory of culture change_. University of Illinois Press, Urbana.

Stewart, F.
1974    Staff research. In _Archaeological Survey of Canada annual review 1973_, edited by G. MacDonald, pp 24-29. National Museum of Man, Archaeological Survey of Canada, Mercury Series No. 21. Ottawa.

1975    The seasonal availability of fish species used by the Coast Tsimshian of northern British Columbia. _Syesis_ 8:375-87.

Stewart, H.
   1973  Artifacts of the Northwest Coast Indians.  Hancock House
         Publishers, Saanichton.

   1984  Cedar.  UBC Press, Vancouver.

Struever, S.
   1971  Comments on archaeological data requirements and research
         strategy.  American Antiquity 36:9-19.

Stryd, A.
   1973  The later prehistory of the Lillooet area, British Columbia.
         Unpublished PhD dissertation, Dept. of Archaeology, University
         of Calgary.

Suttles, W.
   1951  Economic life of the Coast Salish of Haro and Rosario Straits.
         Unpublished PhD dissertation, Dept. of Anthropology, University
         of Washington.

   1960  Affinal ties, subsistence and prestige among the Coast Salish.
         American Anthropologist 62:296-305.

   1962  Variation in habitat and culture on the Northwest Coast.  Akten
         des 34 Internationalen Amerikanistenkongresses Wien 1960, pp
         533-537.  F. Berger, Vienna.

   1968  Coping with abundance: subsistence on the Northwest Coast.  In
         Man the hunter, edited by R. Lee and I. DeVore, pp 56-68.
         Aldine, Chicago.

   1973  Comments on Ruyle.  Current Anthropology 14:622-23.

Testart, A.
   1982  The significance of food-storage among hunter-gatherers:
         residence patterns, population densities and social
         inequalities.  Current Anthropology 23:523-37.

Titiev, M
   1944  Old Oraibi: A case study of the Hopi Indians of Third Mesa.
         Papers of the Peabody Museum of American Archaeology and
         Ethnology 22 (1).  Harvard University, Cambridge.

Tolmie, W.
   1963  The journals of William Fraser Tolmie: physician and fur trader.
         Vancouver.

Torgerson, W.
   1958  Theory and method of scaling.  J. Wiley and Sons, New York.

1965    Multidimensional scaling of similarity. <u>Psychometrika</u> 30:379-93.

Trigger, B.
    1969    <u>Huron: farmers of the north</u>.  Holt, Rinehart and Winston, New
            York.

Turner, N.
    1978    <u>Food plants of British Columbia Indians. Part 1: coastal peoples;
            Part 2: interior peoples</u>.  Handbook No. 36, British Columbia
            Provincial Museum, Victoria.

Valentine, K., P. Sprout, T. Baker, and L. Lavkulich
    1981    <u>The soil landscapes of British Columbia</u>.  British Columbia
            Ministry of the Environment, Victoria.

Vayda, A.
    1961    A re-examination of Northwest Coast economic systems.
            <u>Transactions of the New York Academy of Sciences</u> 23:618-24.

Walker, D.
    1979    Petroglyphs on the middle Skeena River.  In <u>Skeena River
            prehistory</u>, edited by R. Inglis and G. MacDonald, pp 167-80.
            National Museum of Man, Archaeological Survey of Canada, Mercury
            Series No. 87.  Ottawa.

Washburn, D., and R.G. Matson
    1985    Use of multidimensional scaling to display sensitivity of
            symmetry analysis of patterned design to spatial and
            chronological change: examples from Anasazi prehistory.  In
            <u>Decoding prehistoric ceramics</u>, edited by B. Nelson, pp
            75-101.  Southern Illinois University Press, Carbondale.

Watson, P.J.
    1978    Architectural differentiation in some Near Eastern communities,
            prehistoric and contemporary.  In <u>Social archaeology: beyond
            subsistence and dating</u>, edited by C. Redman <u>et al</u>, pp 131-58.
            Academic Press, New York.

    1979    Archaeological ethnography in western Iran.  <u>Viking Fund
            Publications in Anthropology 57</u>.  University of Arizona Press,
            Tucson.

Weber, M.
    1947    <u>The theory of social and economic organization</u>.  Oxford
            University Press, New York.

Weinburg, D.
    1965    Models of southern Kwakiutl social organization.  <u>General Systems</u>
            10:169-81.

Wiessner, P.
    1974  A functional estimator of population from floor area.  American
          Antiquity 39:343-50.

Wilk, R.
    1983  Little house in the jungle: the causes of variation in house size
          among modern Kekchi Maya.  Journal of Anthropological
          Archaeology 2:99-116.

Wilk, R., and W. Rathje
    1982  Household archaeology.  American Behavioural Scientist 25:617-39.

Willey, G., and J. Sabloff
    1974  A history of American archaeology.  Freeman Press, San Francisco.

Wilmeth, R.
    1977  Pithouse construction and the disturbance of stratified sites.
          Canadian Journal of Archaeology 1:135-40.

Wilmsen, E.
    1970  Lithic analysis and cultural inference.  University of Arizona
          Anthropological Papers No. 16.  Tucson.

Wood, J.
    1974  A computer program for hierarchical cluster analysis.  Newsletter
          of Computer Archaeology 9:1-9.

    1978  Optimal location in settlement space: a model for describing
          location strategies.  American Antiquity 43:258-70.

Wood, J., and R.G. Matson
    1973  Two models of sociocultural systems and their implications for
          the archaeological study of change.  In The explanation of
          culture change, edited by C. Renfrew, pp 673-683.  Duckworth,
          London.

Workman, W.
    1974  First dated traces of early Holocene man in the southwest Yukon
          Territory, Canada.  Arctic Anthropology 11:94-103.

Workman, W.
    1978  Prehistory of the Ashihik-Kluane area, southwest Yukon
          Territory.  National Museum of Man, Archaeological Survey of
          Canada, Mercury Series No. 74.  Ottawa.

Wright, H., and G. Johnson
    1975  Population, exchange and early state formation in southwestern
          Iran.  American Anthropologist 77:267-89.

Appendix I

EXCAVATIONS

This appendix provides detailed descriptions of the excavations
conducted at the Paul Mason Site. This includes the four major excavations
(floor 2, floor 9, Excavation H, and Excavation J) presented in Chapters 5
and 6, and the smaller excavations (Trench F and the test units). Features
recorded during excavation are described, and layer descriptions are given
for each excavation.

Floor 2

The excavation of floor 2 included two trenches and two 2 x 2 metre
units. Trench A was 11 metres long by 1 metre wide, and was oriented along
the long axis of the floor. Trench B was 3 metres long by 1 metre wide,
and extended north at right angles from Trench A. Excavation areas D and E
were 2 x 2 metre units extending of the north side of Trench A. Excavation
D extended off the east side of Trench B, and Excavation E extended off the
west side of Trench B (see Figure 5.2).

Trench A was intended to provide a stratigraphic profile of the
length of the floor (Figure I.1); Trench B, a cross-sectional profile of
the floor (Figure I.2). Excavations D and E were subsequently opened to
expose most of one half of the floor.

In general, the sequence of deposition conformed to the description
given in Chapter 5. Glacial till, comprising poorly sorted cobbles and
gravel, was at the base of the entire excavation area. It was encountered
at a depth of 60 cm in unit A10, and became progressively deeper westward.
In unit A11, it was encountered at a depth of 1.95 metres.

Overlying this was a thin series of layers (J, K) of red-brown sand
and silt. This was the red-brown zone. It ranged from 15 to 30 cm thick.

This was followed by deposition of the dark brown soil zone (layers
E, H). This zone was thickest (1.75 metres) at the west end of the trench
(unit A11), and became progressively thinner toward the rear of the floor
(unit A10). Layer D is a thick layer of loose fill, covering the raised
bench. Figure I.3 shows that the fill deposit becomes thicker towards the
front of the floor. This likely resulted from slumping or downslope
erosion following abandonment of the house.

329

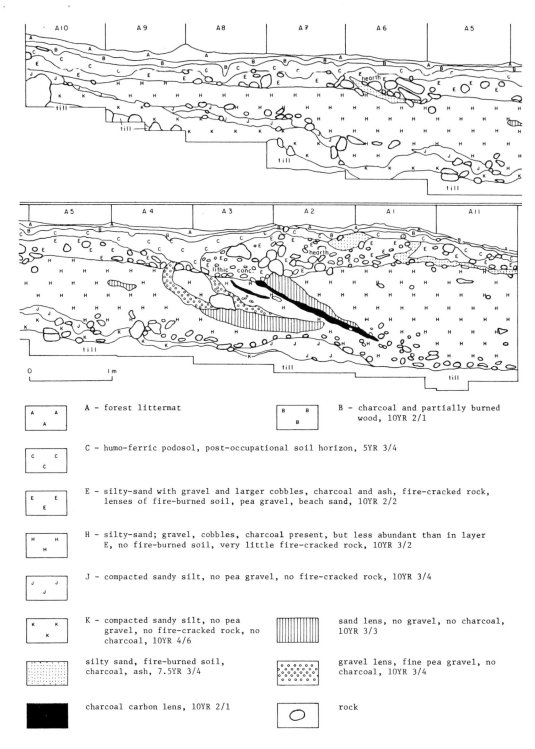

A - forest littermat

B - charcoal and partially burned wood, 10YR 2/1

C - humo-ferric podosol, post-occupational soil horizon, 5YR 3/4

E - silty-sand with gravel and larger cobbles, charcoal and ash, fire-cracked rock, lenses of fire-burned soil, pea gravel, beach sand, 10YR 2/2

H - silty-sand; gravel, cobbles, charcoal present, but less abundant than in layer E, no fire-burned soil, very little fire-cracked rock, 10YR 3/2

J - compacted sandy silt, no pea gravel, no fire-cracked rock, 10YR 3/4

K - compacted sandy silt, no pea gravel, no fire-cracked rock, no charcoal, 10YR 4/6

sand lens, no gravel, no charcoal, 10YR 3/3

silty sand, fire-burned soil, charcoal, ash, 7.5YR 3/4

gravel lens, fine pea gravel, no charcoal, 10YR 3/4

charcoal carbon lens, 10YR 2/1

rock

Figure I.1  Profile of Trench A: south wall.

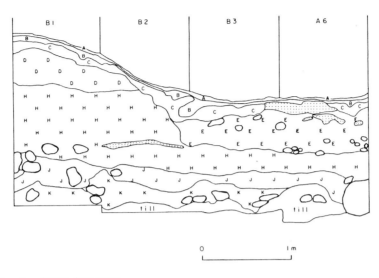

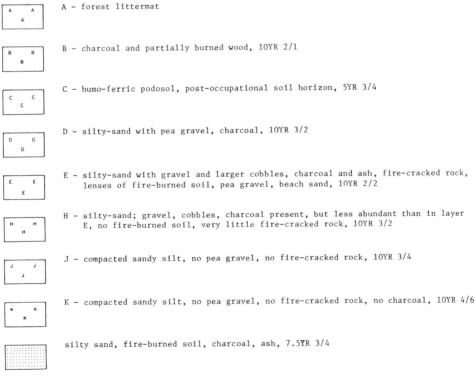

A — forest littermat

B — charcoal and partially burned wood, 10YR 2/1

C — humo-ferric podosol, post-occupational soil horizon, 5YR 3/4

D — silty-sand with pea gravel, charcoal, 10YR 3/2

E — silty-sand with gravel and larger cobbles, charcoal and ash, fire-cracked rock, lenses of fire-burned soil, pea gravel, beach sand, 10YR 2/2

H — silty-sand; gravel, cobbles, charcoal present, but less abundant than in layer E, no fire-burned soil, very little fire-cracked rock, 10YR 3/2

J — compacted sandy silt, no pea gravel, no fire-cracked rock, 10YR 3/4

K — compacted sandy silt, no pea gravel, no fire-cracked rock, no charcoal, 10YR 4/6

silty sand, fire-burned soil, charcoal, ash, 7.5YR 3/4

rock

Figure I.2  Profile of Trench B: east wall.

331

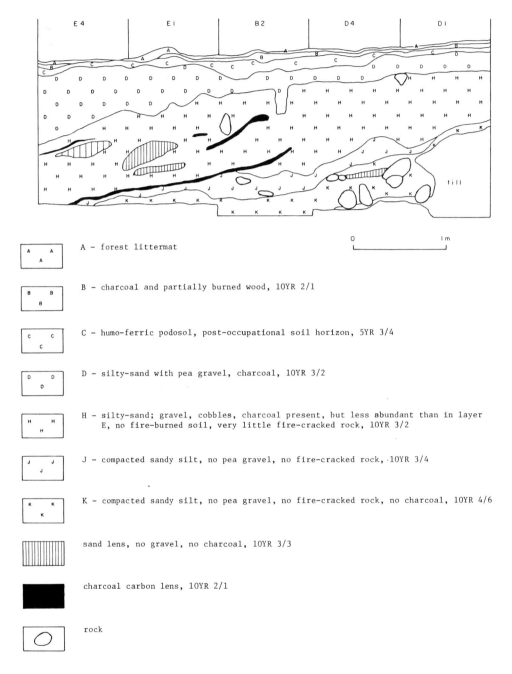

A – forest littermat

B – charcoal and partially burned wood, 10YR 2/1

C – humo-ferric podosol, post-occupational soil horizon, 5YR 3/4

D – silty-sand with pea gravel, charcoal, 10YR 3/2

H – silty-sand; gravel, cobbles, charcoal present, but less abundant than in layer E, no fire-burned soil, very little fire-cracked rock, 10YR 3/2

J – compacted sandy silt, no pea gravel, no fire-cracked rock, ·10YR 3/4

K – compacted sandy silt, no pea gravel, no fire-cracked rock, no charcoal, 10YR 4/6

sand lens, no gravel, no charcoal, 10YR 3/3

charcoal carbon lens, 10YR 2/1

rock

Figure I.3   Profile of Excavation E units 1, 4, Excavation B unit 2,
Excavation D units 1, 4: north wall.

The excavation also encountered two widespread lithic concentration features.  One was near the top of the dark brown soil zone, beginning 0.3 metres below surface (see Figure 5.6). It covered most of the front half of the floor area, including the west half of Trench A (units A11 through A6), and the south half of Trench B (B2, B3) and Excavation E (E2, E3).  It stopped abruptly at the base of the raised bench.  The second lithic feature was located below the first, near the base of the dark brown soil zone. It was equally widespread, although not as densely concentrated, covering the west half of Trench A and most of Excavation E.  Both concentrations included stone tools, debitage and scattered charcoal. The upper concentration contained a high proportion of fire-cracked rock (almost 50 percent of the rock), and two hearth features, one in the middle of the prepared floor area, and the other 3 metres west, in the front of the floor area.  Four post moulds, ranging from 0.12 to 0.20 metres deep were discerned within or at the edge of the prepared floor area, at the base of the upper rock concentration (see Figure 5.6).  The lower lithic feature contained very little fire-cracked rock.  Most of the rocks in this feature were fist-sized cobbles.

The upper concentration ranged up to 0.40 metres in depth, and may actually have comprised a series of layers of concentrated rock, although no discrete hiatus was noted.  The lower feature ranged from 0.20 to 0.50 metres thick, and the two features were separated by up to 0.30 metres of dark brown soil.

Floor 9

Floor 9 was excavated in a manner similar to that of floor 2.  Trench C was 10 metres long by 1 metre wide, and was oriented along the long axis of the floor.  Trench G crossed Trench C at right angles at the mid-point of the floor, extending 2 metres north of Trench C and 3 metres south of Trench C (Figure 5.2).

The sequence of deposition as revealed by these excavations is as follows (see Figure I.4, I.5).  The bottom of the deposit was culturally sterile, and comprised poorly sorted, rounded cobbles and gravel.  It was encountered at depths ranging from 0.8 metres (unit C4) to 1.6 metres (unit C8).  At the east and west ends of Trench C, and at the south end of Trench

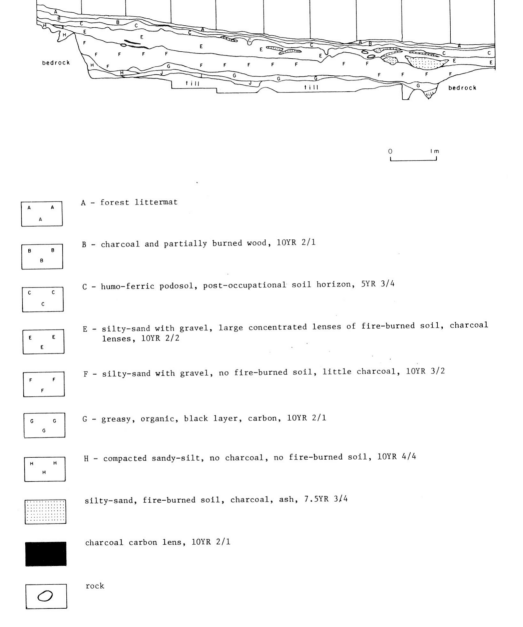

A - forest littermat

B - charcoal and partially burned wood, 10YR 2/1

C - humo-ferric podosol, post-occupational soil horizon, 5YR 3/4

E - silty-sand with gravel, large concentrated lenses of fire-burned soil, charcoal lenses, 10YR 2/2

F - silty-sand with gravel, no fire-burned soil, little charcoal, 10YR 3/2

G - greasy, organic, black layer, carbon, 10YR 2/1

H - compacted sandy-silt, no charcoal, no fire-burned soil, 10YR 4/4

silty-sand, fire-burned soil, charcoal, ash, 7.5YR 3/4

charcoal carbon lens, 10YR 2/1

rock

**Figure I.4 Profile of Trench C: south wall.**

334

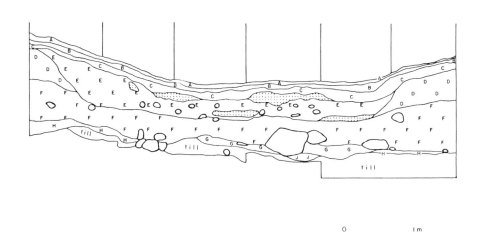

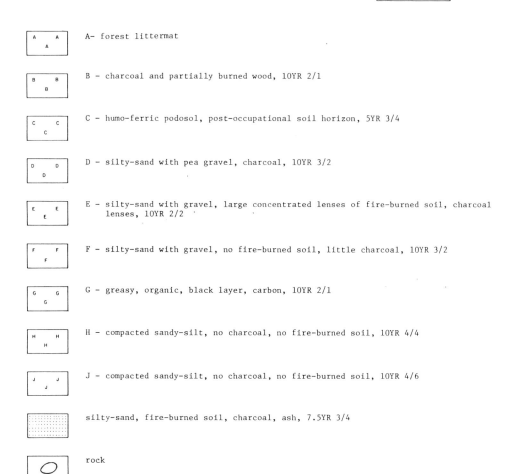

A- forest littermat

B - charcoal and partially burned wood, 10YR 2/1

C - humo-ferric podosol, post-occupational soil horizon, 5YR 3/4

D - silty-sand with pea gravel, charcoal, 10YR 3/2

E - silty-sand with gravel, large concentrated lenses of fire-burned soil, charcoal lenses, 10YR 2/2

F - silty-sand with gravel, no fire-burned soil, little charcoal, 10YR 3/2

G - greasy, organic, black layer, carbon, 10YR 2/1

H - compacted sandy-silt, no charcoal, no fire-burned soil, 10YR 4/4

J - compacted sandy-silt, no charcoal, no fire-burned soil, 10YR 4/6

silty-sand, fire-burned soil, charcoal, ash, 7.5YR 3/4

rock

Figure I.5  Profile of Trench G: east wall.

335

G, intrusions of bedrock cut through the glacial till.  In units C1 and C10
bedrock was encountered at less than one metre below the surface, and was
directly overlaid by cultural deposit, without interceding till.  In units
C4 and C8 bedrock was encountered at 1.8 to 2.0 metres below the surface,
and was overlaid by hard-packed till.

The till in Trenches C and G was overlaid by thin layers of alluvium
(H, J), 10 to 15 cm thick.  Overlying these layers was a thin layer (5 to
12 cm thick) of soil characterized by a greasy texture and black colour
(layer G).  This layer sloped gently southwest, roughly following the
surface contour of this portion of the site.  Layer G extended unbroken
from unit C9 to C3, and was also encountered in units G3 and G5.

There are two possible explanations for the unique appearance of this
layer.  It may represent an area of intensive cultural activity such as the
processing or burning of organic material.  However, there was no
specialized tool kit or noticeable increase in the amount of charcoal
associated with this layer that might support such a model.

Alternatively, it may represent the leaching of soil nutrients from
the overlying cultural deposit.  Heavy leaching is a characteristic of
coniferous forest soils.  In the other excavations, leached nutrients would
tend to move downslope.  Floor 9 is situated in a bedrock trough, however,
which would tend to trap leached soil nutrients.  It is noteworthy that the
greasy black layer was only encountered within the bedrock trough (not in
units C1, C10, G1, G5).

Overlying this layer was a thick zone (up to 1.0 metre thick) of dark
brown silty sand, identical to that seen in the excavation of floor 2
(layers E, F).  The matrix at the base of this zone (F) was slightly
lighter in colour than at the top (E).  However, this colour change was
more of a gradual transition than a sharp break, and was not apparent in
each excavation unit.  The upper layer (E) of this zone (0.20 to 0.30
metres thick) was characterized by much burned soil, charcoal, ash and
fire-cracked rock.  This included two hearth features, oriented along the
centre axis of the floor. One, near the front of the floor (units C2, C3)
was a large, deep, bowl-shaped hearth (1.4 metres in diameter; 0.85 metres
deep).  The other hearth, in the mid-floor area (unit C5) was smaller and
shallower.  Two post moulds were discerned in Trench C, at the base of the

336

burned soil layer (see Figure 5.7).

A layer of light brown humus (layer C) covered the cultural deposit, as in floor 2.

## Excavation H

Excavation H was an "L-shaped" block, dug in three adjoining 2 x 2 metre units. One unit was excavated in 1982; the other two in 1983. One of the latter units was reduced in size to 2 x 1.5 metres shortly after excavation had begun. A 50 cm baulk was maintained between this unit and the one excavated in 1982 to prevent backfill from collapsing in to the new unit. Due to time constraints in the 1983 field season, the lower 0.40 metres of the two units excavated that year were reduced in size to 2 x 1 · metres and 1.5 x 1 metres, respectively. All three units were excavated to bedrock, a maximum depth of 2.1 metres.

The chronological sequence of deposition in Excavation H is as follows (see Figure I.6). Lying directly on bedrock, was a thin discontinuous layer (H) of yellow-brown silty sand, gravel and larger fragmented sections of bedrock. It was very compact. Culturally modified lithic material was present, but minimal, and included tools and detritus of obsidian. This layer ranged in thickness from 3 to 10 cm.

Beginning at a depth of 1.4 metres below the surface, and continuing to a depth of just over 2.0 metres, was a layer (G) of red-brown, fine sandy soil, similar in colour and texture to the red-brown zone at the base of the floor 2 excavation. The layer included scattered gravel and small scattered flecks of charcoal. It also contained culturally modified lithic material, including obsidian microblades. This layer and the one below it constitute the lower stratigraphic zone of the excavation.

The upper stratigraphic zone of the cultural deposit comprised mainly dark brown sandy soil. Three discrete layers were identified. The lowest of these (F) was exposed at a depth of 1.35 metres below the surface, and continued to a maximum depth of 1.57 metres. It comprised mainly dark brown sandy soil, with some gravel and charcoal.

The next layer (E) was thin (12 to 17 cm thick), and medium to dark brown. It was first encountered at a depth of 1.05 metres. It was slightly lighter in colour and drier in texture than the rest of the matrix

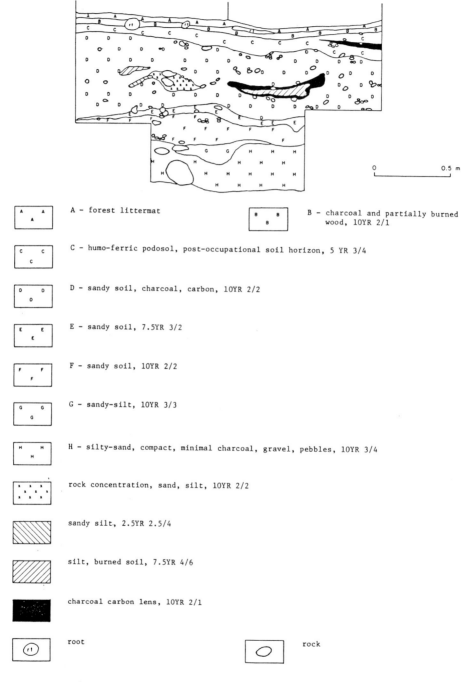

A — forest littermat          B — charcoal and partially burned wood, 10YR 2/1

C — humo-ferric podosol, post-occupational soil horizon, 5 YR 3/4

D — sandy soil, charcoal, carbon, 10YR 2/2

E — sandy soil, 7.5YR 3/2

F — sandy soil, 10YR 2/2

G — sandy-silt, 10YR 3/3

H — silty-sand, compact, minimal charcoal, gravel, pebbles, 10YR 3/4

rock concentration, sand, silt, 10YR 2/2

sandy silt, 2.5YR 2.5/4

silt, burned soil, 7.5YR 4/6

charcoal carbon lens, 10YR 2/1

root          rock

Figure I.6  Profile of Excavation H: east wall.

338

of the upper zone. Unmodified pebbles and small cobbles were present in some abundance in this layer. Culturally modified lithic material however, was virtually absent. The layer probably represents humic development during a time in which the site was abandoned or only sporadically used.

This was followed by deposition of the remainder of the upper zone, essentially one thick layer (D) of dark brown soil. It was first encountered at a depth of 0.26 metres, and continued to a depth of just over 1.3 metres. The texture of the soil in this layer was more compact, greasier and moister than the underlying humic layer. The clastic components of the layer were also more varied. Although fine-grained sand comprised most of the layer, other components included scattered and occasionally concentrated patches of charcoal, patches of pure coarse sand, gravel and ash, and dense lithic concentrations especially near the top of the layer. These included stone tools, detritus and fire-cracked rock.

A large hearth feature was encountered at the bottom of the layer. This feature included abundant and large fragments of burned wood (over 2.0 kg), but lacked the burned soil noted in hearth features in the other excavations. The presence of scorched soil in the other hearth features may be related to the relative intensity of use of hearths within house floors compared to those outside house floors. Hearths within house floors would likely be subject to repeated use, which could ultimately result in a thick layer of scorched soil.

The post-occupational soil horizon included a 10 to 12 cm thick layer (C) of light brown humus, covered by forest littermat (A) that included the thin layer of charcoal and partly burned wood (B).


## Excavation J

Excavation J was a 4 x 2 metre trench oriented north/south, and located immediately west of the west row of prepared floors. It was situated in a shallow bedrock trough. Prominent outcroppings of bedrock flank either side of the trench, so that deposits accumulated in the trough. The ground surface of the excavation area slopes slightly from south to north. The maximum depth of excavation was 1.58 metres. The entire trench was excavated to bedrock (see Figure I.7).

The first layer of deposit, resting on bedrock, was a thin, compact

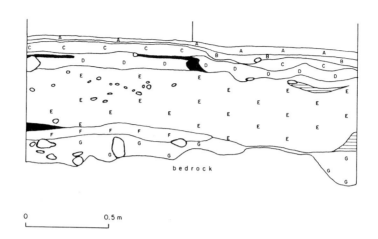

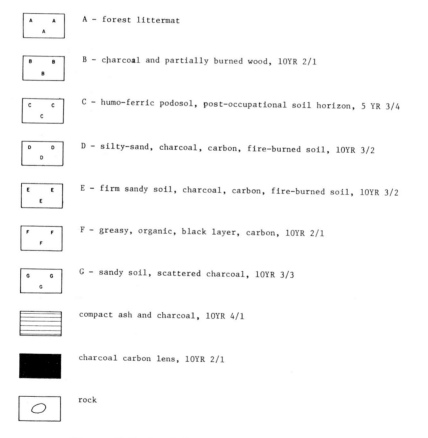

A – forest littermat

B – charcoal and partially burned wood, 10YR 2/1

C – humo-ferric podosol, post-occupational soil horizon, 5 YR 3/4

D – silty-sand, charcoal, carbon, fire-burned soil, 10YR 3/2

E – firm sandy soil, charcoal, carbon, fire-burned soil, 10YR 3/2

F – greasy, organic, black layer, carbon, 10YR 2/1

G – sandy soil, scattered charcoal, 10YR 3/3

compact ash and charcoal, 10YR 4/1

charcoal carbon lens, 10YR 2/1

rock

Figure I.7  Profile of Excavation J: east wall.

layer (H) of yellow-brown silty sand and large, angular fragments of bedrock.

Overlying this was another thin, compact layer (G) of moist, dark brown sandy soil with large water-rounded cobbles and angular bedrock fragments. Cultural material, including stone tools, detritus, and charcoal was also present.

The next layer (F) was a thin greasy black soil, identical to that seen in the excavation of floor 9. It was encountered in Excavation J at a depth of 0.95 metres and continued to a depth of 1.1 metres below the surface. Again, it is noteworthy that this layer formed near the base of the cultural deposit in a bedrock trough, lying directly on thin layers of compact soil and large angular bedrock fragments. This suggests that the colour and texture of the layer is a result of trapped leached soil nutrients.

A thick layer (E) of dark brown sandy soil comprised the upper portion of the cultural deposit in Excavation J. It began at 0.30 metres below the surface, and continued to a depth of just over 1.0 metres. The layer also included abundant charcoal and carbon staining, pea gravel and large patches of burned soil. Deep pockets of solid pea gravel and sand were encountered. Most of these materials were located in the upper 40 to 50 cm of the layer, designated as layer D, and are associated with a long narrow hearth that extended through the length of the excavation. There was only a small amount of fire-cracked rock (57 kg) associated with this feature.

The post-occupational deposit in Excavation J included a thin layer of humus (C) and the charcoal and partially burned wood layer (B) at the base of the littermat (A).


Prepared Floor Feature 12

Trench F was a 3 x 1 metre trench located in floor 12 on the upper terace area of the site, away from the cluster of house floors on the slope. The excavation extended from the middle of the floor through the southeast wall into the low ridge of earth that surrounded the floor.

The deposition of sediment at the bottom of Trench F, probably the result of alluvial or glaciofluvial action, may represent an ancient beach terrace. The physical appearance of the deposit indicated that sediments were well-sorted according to size. The base of the deposit comprised sorted gravels and cobbles, that continued to a depth of over 3.0 metres (zone F). Bedrock was not encountered in the excavation, and despite the eagerness of the excavators to continue digging, excavation was stopped at a depth of 3.0 metres, as a safety precaution. All lithic material in the bottom of the deposit had been rounded by water action. Overlying the gravel zone was a series of thin banded layers (E) of fine sands and silt. Within the prepared floor, where earth-moving had taken place, this zone was 30 cm thick, and comprised one homogeneous layer of grey-brown silty sand. At the perimeter of the floor, this zone comprised banded layers, and was 1.2 metres thick.

Cultural material was recovered from a thin layer (D) of dark brown soil that overlay the banded sand and silt zone.

The cultural deposit in Trench F was covered by a thin discontinuous layer of forest podosol. There was no indication of the layer of charcoal and partially burned wood seen in the other excavations at the Paul Mason Site. There are two possible reasons for its absence. First, the fire that produced this layer may not have been active in this area of the site. This seems unlikely because the burning appears to have been widespread throughout Kitselas Canyon. A more likely explanation is that the preparation of the floor may have post-dated the fire, in which case the charcoal would have been removed as part of the earth-moving process.

## Test Units

Five 1 x 1 metre test units were excavated at the Paul Mason Site. Test unit 1 was located in the middle of floor 3. Test unit 2 was five metres west of the first unit, near the "front" of the same floor. Test unit 3 was near the west end or "front" of floor 5. Test unit 4, a non-house floor test, was 10 metres north of Excavation H. Test unit 5 was located on the upper terrace level of the site, 10 metres northeast of floor 12.

A detailed description of physical stratigraphy as revealed by these units is not presented here. The purpose of these excavations was to test the depth and nature of the cultural deposit. Generally, test units 1 to 4 were characterized by thick layers of dark brown soil, similar to the dark brown zones seen in the major excavations. Test units 1 to 3 were each excavated to a depth of 1.5 metres. They did not reach sterile deposit. Test unit 4 was excavated to bedrock at 1.2 metres. Test unit 5 was excavated to a depth of 0.80 metres, the last 40 cm of which was sterile gravel.

The charcoal and partially burned wood layer was encountered near the surface of test unit 5, indicating that the fire responsible for this layer had burned in this area of the site (including floor 12). The fact that the layer was encountered in test unit 5, but not Trench F supports the inference that preparation of floor 12 must have occurred after the fire.

## Appendix II

## ARTIFACT TYPE DESCRIPTIONS

The 19 lithic artifact classes are sub-divided into 74 discrete types. These types are described in detail in this appendix. Artifact types from the cobble and flake tool category are described first, followed by groundstone and chipped stone types. In cases where artifact types are represented by only a few implements, it was possible to provide brief descriptions for individual implements. For types represented by more than a few implements, a tabular summary description is provided, with metric measurements including the range of highest and lowest values, arithmetic mean and medianas measures of central tendency, and standard deviation and inter-quartile range as measures of dispersion. Only complete measurements were taken. For example, if a tools was broken at one end, length and width were not taken because these measurements would have been incomplete. All lengths, widths and thicknesses are given in millimetres; weights in grams. Table II.1, at the end of the appendix, shows the distribution of each artifact type among the three components of the Paul Mason Site.

### Cobble and Flake Tools

#### Cobble Tools

**Steep Angle Cobble Core Tools**  (N=166) (Plate I a-d)

These implements have the highest frequency of occurence of any tool type at the site. Cobble core tools, previously defined by Mitchell (1971:106-07) at Montague Harbour, are beach cobbles with some evidence for use (polish or microflaking) along one or more edges where flake scars intersect with the cortex.

As implied by the name, these implements probably served alternately as tools and cores. Reduction of the cobbles tended to be more random than systematic. Flake scars appear at various locations around the surface of the cobble, rather than localized on one end or side. The flaking angle, formed by the intersection of an existing scar with the cortex, is steep, ranging from 45° to 90°. The implication is that the leading edge of the cortex was used as a ready-made platform for further reduction. Flake scars range up to 6 cm in length, indicating the removal of large, usable, flakes.

The utilized edges of the core tools are typically rounded with tiny
nicks and flake scars often undercutting both intersecting surfaces.
Mitchell (1971:106) has suggested that cobble core tools with similar wear
from Montague Harbour were used for chopping, pulping and rasping.    A
variety of raw materials were used, including basalt (N=8) and even slate
(N=2), but argillite (N=60) and sedimentary rock (N=96) were most common.

|  | cases | mean | median | range | std dev | quartiles |
|---|---|---|---|---|---|---|
| weight | 166 | 544.8 | 429.4 | 26.2-3471.9 | 475.2 | 26.7-629.7 |
| length | 166 | 98.9 | 95.4 | 50.4-191.1 | 24.7 | 83.6-110.7 |
| width | 166 | 78.5 | 78.9 | 29.5-153.4 | 20.3 | 65.1-90.6 |
| thickness | 166 | 48.0 | 47.7 | 13.0-99.8 | 16.6 | 37.4-58.2 |

**Acute Angle Cobble Core Tools**  (N=29) (Plate III d-f)

These tools are distinguished from those described above on the basis
of the edge angle formed by the intersection of the modified and cortical
surfaces. In this case, edge angles are acute (less than 45°), although in
no sense could these be described as sharp or knife-like.    Reduction of
these tools tended to be localized on one end of the cobble.  Microflaking
is invariably present on the edge formed by the cortex and the flaked
surface.  Worn edges are generally uneven and rough, with undercutting
present.  Polish and striations parallel to the edge were not evident.  The
acute edge angles and the nature of the wear indicate that, in addition to
chopping, these implements may have been scraping planes, making them
functionally similar to artifacts described by Matson (1976:145) from the
Glenrose Site.

Raw materials include sedimentary rock (N=19), argillite (N=9), and
basalt (N=1).

|  | cases | mean | median | range | std dev | quartiles |
|---|---|---|---|---|---|---|
| weight | 29 | 384.3 | 341.8 | 73.3-1585.0 | 283.4 | 196.1-490.0 |
| length | 29 | 96.7 | 96.0 | 60.6-166.5 | 21.1 | 84.9-107.3 |
| width | 29 | 75.6 | 76.8 | 42.3-127.2 | 17.6 | 65.2-85.2 |
| thickness | 29 | 38.5 | 37.9 | 17.3-79.0 | 12.3 | 30.3-47.6 |

**Cobble Choppers** (N=107) (Plate II a-d)

These cobble tools have steep edge angles formed by the removal of a limited number of flakes. The basic difference between these implements and cobble core tools is the apparent emphasis here for tool use. These implements have step-flaking along an extremely battered and undercut edge. Reduction tends to be localized on one end or side of the tool. These implements conform in size and shape to Allaire's (1978:135) cobble tool class "A"; _galets entiers a tranchant fendu_.

Eight implements have pecked or battered surfaces on the opposed or unmodified end of the tool, indicating alternate use as a hammerstone. In addition, two implements have unusual wear patterns. Both have smooth, even and polished edges between the cortex and flaked surface, the result of some form of grinding or abrasion. The direction of striations could not be detected under 10 power magnification. One also shows evidence of grinding and polishing on high ridges between flake scars.

Raw materials include sedimentary rock (N=57), argillite (N=40), basalt (N=8), igneous rock (N=1), and green schist (N=1).

|  | cases | mean | median | range | std dev | quartiles |
|---|---|---|---|---|---|---|
| weight | 107 | 430.6 | 352.8 | 49.5-1480.8 | 275.6 | 227.5-653.2 |
| length | 107 | 99.1 | 99.4 | 58.8-159.8 | 22.6 | 81.9-112.1 |
| width | 107 | 76.0 | 75.8 | 37.0-129.1 | 18.7 | 61.8-88.4 |
| thickness | 107 | 42.3 | 40.5 | 15.5-83.8 | 13.5 | 33.4-52.0 |

**Split Cobble Tools** (N=37) (Plate III a-c)

Split cobble tools, previously defined by Mitchell (1971:104), include "a range of crude cutting and chopping implements, all of which show coarse retouch on their cutting edges". These are river cobble fragments, with cortex completely covering one face. They are distinct from cortex spalls in that they constitute substantial portions of the cobbles with a greater thickness to length ratio than the average spall (Mitchell 1971:104).

Mitchell's suggestion that these implements served a chopping function is substantiated here by the nature of the wear patterns present on most tools. Edges are typically thick, heavily battered and undercut. Four implements, however, have smooth edges with high polish. This type of wear may have formed as a result of cutting or scraping activities. Alternatively, the polish may have formed from some form of abrasive use.

One implement has a small amount of unifacial grinding, indicating alternate use as an abrader.

Raw materials include sedimentary rock (N=18), argillite (N=12), slate (N=5), basalt (N=1), and green schist (N=1).

|  | cases | mean | median | range | std dev | quartiles |
|---|---|---|---|---|---|---|
| weight | 36 | 322.6 | 219.2 | 95.2-940.5 | 254.6 | 143.5-419.4 |
| length | 36 | 103.1 | 100.3 | 62.6-179.8 | 23.3 | 89.7-112.8 |
| width | 37 | 79.3 | 75.0 | 41.3-143.0 | 22.0 | 64.7-86.4 |
| thickness | 37 | 28.6 | 26.6 | 18.1-47.4 | 8.2 | 21.6-33.6 |

**Pebble Core Tools** (N=20)

Pebble core tools are distinguished from cobble core tools on the basis of size. Pebble core tools weigh less than 100 grams. Some overlap in weight and size exists (i.e. some cobble core tools weigh less than 100 grams), but this is essentially a factor of extensive reduction of a few cobble core tools. Pebble core tools have had only a few flakes removed. Their small size suggests that it is unlikely that they were used as choppers. Rather, most have been modified to form scraping planes, with edge angles of 45° to 60°. In two cases, the angle formed by the intersection of the modified and cortical surfaces is less than 45°, possibly indicating a cutting function.

Raw materials include sedimentary rock (N=11), and argillite (N=9).

|  | cases | mean | median | range | std dev | quartiles |
|---|---|---|---|---|---|---|
| weight | 20 | 36.6 | 32.0 | 8.1-87.8 | 21.6 | 18.5-52.3 |
| length | 20 | 48.0 | 46.9 | 28.6-66.2 | 9.1 | 43.1-52.3 |
| width | 20 | 37.3 | 37.2 | 22.9-53.2 | 7.2 | 32.2-43.5 |
| thickness | 20 | 14.6 | 12.0 | 7.4-30.2 | 6.7 | 10.1-18.4 |

**Pointed Cobble Tool** (N=1) (Plate I e)

This is a long, narrow, facetted cobble fragment, with cortex on one face. The cortical surface is rounded at one end, but narrows to a thick unretouched point at the opposite end. The formation of the point appears fortuitous. There is no retouch near the point, but the end was used.

Some polish is visible on the point, and on two flaked edges extending back from the point. This is the only cobble-based implement recovered from the site that appears to have functioned, however crudely, as a piercing or perforating tool. The raw material is sedimentary rock.

## Utilized Flakes

### Large Utilized Spalls (N=72) (Plate IV a-b)

These are cortex-backed flakes, manufactured by striking an unprepared surface of a cobble at an oblique angle. The result, usually, is a thin, elliptical or circular flake, plano-convex in cross-section, with sharp acute edges.

Utilized cortex spalls are quite common in most north coast sites, and are extremely abundant at Gitaus. Allaire (1978:133) recorded 1450 complete or broken spalls at that site. Most of these have acute edge angles, and Allaire (1979:31) argues that their primary use may have been as cutting implements for processing fish (see also Hanson 1972; Donnan and Moseley 1968).

Cortex spalls from the Paul Mason Site are consistent with those described from Gitaus. They have acute, slightly convex edges, typically smoothed and polished through use. They were probably used as cutting implements.

Raw materials include argillite (N=34), sedimentary rock (N=24), basalt (N=9), igneous rock (N=3), green schist (N=1), and slate (N=1).

|           | cases | mean | median | range | std dev | quartiles |
|-----------|-------|------|--------|------------|---------|-----------|
| weight    | 72 | 73.5 | 49.1 | 11.4-256.8 | 57.9 | 31.9-99.6 |
| length    | 72 | 75.5 | 69.5 | 38.5-132.8 | 19.1 | 63.4-86.5 |
| width     | 72 | 55.4 | 53.5 | 29.3-91.3 | 15.4 | 43.1-66.7 |
| thickness | 72 | 14.2 | 13.4 | 6.4-31.1 | 5.2 | 10.2-18.4 |

### Small Utilized Spalls (N=20) (Plate IV c)

These are utilized spalls that weigh less than 20 grams, and are less than 50 mm in length. Whether removed from large cobble cores or smaller pebble cores, they are complete flakes, not broken or retouched. All implements are thin with extremely acute edge angles of less than 20°. They undoubtedly functioned as cutting tools. Utilized edges are smooth, and highly polished.

One implement is elliptical in shape and has extensive polish around the complete circumference of the flake (Plate IV c). In addition, wear and polish cover the entire ventral surface of the flake. It is apparent that this implement was used extensively and repeatedly as a cutting tool.

Raw materials include argillite (N=8), sedimentary rock (N=7), basalt (N=3), and slate (N=1).

|  | cases | mean | median | range | std dev | quartiles |
|---|---|---|---|---|---|---|
| weight | 20 | 9.3 | 8.8 | 2.8-17.9 | 4.1 | 5.9-11.6 |
| length | 20 | 41.9 | 43.1 | 29.4-49.0 | 5.4 | 39.9-45.8 |
| width | 20 | 30.4 | 30.9 | 19.5-39.9 | 6.0 | 25.0-34.8 |
| thickness | 20 | 6.8 | 6.3 | 3.7-10.5 | 2.2 | 5.0-9.0 |

**Large Acute Angle Utilized Flakes** (N=45) (Plate IV d-e)

Large acute angle utilized flakes are those in excess of 10.0 grams. The distinction between large and small utilized flakes follows that made by Matson (1976:133) and Allaire (1978:147-49). Whereas all acute angle utilized flakes are assumed to have been used as cutting tools, it seems likely that functional differences related to size may have existed. For example, flakes in excess of 10 grams typically have thick unmodified edges opposite the cutting edge. They probably functioned as heavy-duty cutting tools.

Raw materials include argillite (N=20), sedimentary rock (N=19), green schist (N=5), and basalt (N=1).

|  | cases | mean | median | range | std dev | quartiles |
|---|---|---|---|---|---|---|
| weight | 45 | 39.3 | 31.2 | 10.0-118.1 | 24.4 | 20.1-55.5 |
| length | 45 | 64.4 | 60.6 | 41.5-114.6 | 16.2 | 51.2-74.9 |
| width | 45 | 44.8 | 44.9 | 24.9-70.9 | 11.2 | 35.7-52.6 |
| thickness | 45 | 12.9 | 13.0 | 6.8-22.4 | 3.8 | 9.8-15.0 |

**Small Acute Angle Utilized Flakes** (N=41)

Small acute angle utilized flakes weigh less than 10.0 grams, and 31 of these weigh less than 4.0 grams. It is likely that these flakes were used as fine cutting implements, (e.g., scoring salmon flesh), and this is further suggested by the fact that the most common raw material is obsidian

(N=18).  Flenniken (1981:77) has arrived at a similar conclusion based on his experiments with microliths at Hoko River.

Given the small size of these implements, it is likely that many were secured in a haft for use.  It certainly seems unlikely that flakes weighing less than 1.0 gram were hand-held during use.

Other raw materials used include slate (N=6), argillite (N=5), basalt (N=5), quartz (N=4), and chert (N=3).

|  | cases | mean | median | range | std dev | quartiles |
|---|---|---|---|---|---|---|
| weight | 41 | 2.9 | 1.9 | 0.1-9.4 | 2.8 | 0.7-4.7 |
| length | 41 | 25.6 | 24.8 | 9.3-46.8 | 11.7 | 13.6-34.8 |
| width | 41 | 18.0 | 16.7 | 4.7-38.7 | 8.1 | 11.8-22.8 |
| thickness | 41 | 4.7 | 4.3 | 1.0-11.3 | 2.4 | 2.8-6.5 |

**Large Steep Angle Utilized Flakes**  (N=32) (Plate IV f-g)

These implements have edge angles greater than 45°, and weight in excess of 10.0 grams.  They were probably used as large, unretouched scraping tools.  Generally, the utilized edges of these tools have been undercut through use, with irregular microflaking present.

Three implements show evidence of polish, in addition to microflaking along the scraping edge, and in two cases, polish is present on the high ridges of the dorsal surface of the flake.  It is possible that this wear resulted from extensive use as hide scraping or tanning tools.  Generally, water-smoothed cortex is present along part of the margin of the flake, and the utilized edge is formed by the intersection of the cortex and flaked surface.

Raw materials include argillite (N=21), sedimentary rock (N=9), slate (N=1), and green schist (N=1).

|  | cases | mean | median | range | std dev | quartiles |
|---|---|---|---|---|---|---|
| weight | 32 | 68.0 | 42.9 | 11.2-347.4 | 84.1 | 27.2-53.7 |
| length | 32 | 66.6 | 61.6 | 33.2-107.8 | 19.0 | 53.2-76.5 |
| width | 32 | 46.2 | 43.0 | 17.9-101.0 | 19.5 | 33.7-54.5 |
| thickness | 32 | 17.0 | 15.6 | 8.6-36.8 | 7.0 | 12.8-20.3 |

**Small Steep Angle Utilized Flakes**  (N=5)

These flakes, weighing less than 10 grams, also have microflaking and undercutting along the utilized edge.  They probably functioned as small, unretouched scrapers.

Raw materials include obsidian (N=2), basalt (N=1), slate (N=1), and quartz (N=1).

|  | cases | mean | median | range | std dev | quartiles |
|---|---|---|---|---|---|---|
| weight | 5 | 2.8 | 3.7 | 0.6-5.0 | 2.0 | 0.7-4.5 |
| length | 5 | 22.1 | 21.3 | 11.7-31.3 | 8.4 | 14.1-30.5 |
| width | 5 | 17.5 | 17.9 | 7.7-29.0 | 9.3 | 8.3-26.5 |
| thickness | 5 | 5.3 | 3.8 | 2.7-10.8 | 3.2 | 3.2-8.1 |

## Retouched Cobble Flakes

**Steep Angle Retouched Spalls**  (N=11) (Plate V a-b)

These are cortex-backed spalls with steeply retouched edges.  All are based on river cobbles of argillite (N=4), sedimentary rock (N=6) and basalt (N=1).  Ten spalls have been unifacially retouched along the ventral surface of the flake.  One roughly circular-shaped spall has bifacial edge retouch, and large flake scars on the ventral surface, perhaps indicating thinning (Plate V a).  Two other implements have alternate unifacial retouch; one section of the edge is retouched on the ventral side, the other section of the edge is retouched on the dorsal side.

Edge retouch is typically crude and irregular.  Flake scars tend to be large and widely spaced along the edge, and in three cases, retouch constitutes the removal of only three or four flakes along a section of an edge.

A scraping function is inferred for most of these implements, based on the edge angle.  Two spalls have battered and undercut edges, possibly indicating chopping.  Polish was not evident on any implement.

Raw materials are argillite (N=21), sedimentary rock (N=24), basalt (N=4), slate (N=2), and sandstone (N=1).

|          | cases | mean  | median | range       | std dev | quartiles   |
|----------|-------|-------|--------|-------------|---------|-------------|
| weight   | 11    | 183.0 | 152.2  | 36.3-522.5  | 153.8   | 85.2-177.1  |
| length   | 11    | 92.9  | 84.9   | 68.4-143.0  | 22.4    | 75.6-104.5  |
| width    | 11    | 71.8  | 63.4   | 38.7-114.0  | 23.8    | 57.0-85.3   |
| thickness| 11    | 20.3  | 19.8   | 12.9-31.6   | 5.9     | 14.6-25.5   |

**Acute Angle Retouched Spalls**  (N=11) (Plate V c-d)

These implements are thinner in cross-section than those in the previous type. They form thin, acute edge angles with retouch along the edge. In general, these tools are more extensively retouched than the steep angle retouched spalls, and retouch tends to be more regular in this type. Three implements have unifacial ventral retouch, two have unifacial dorsal retouch, and three have alternate retouch. Three have bifacial edge retouch, with evidence of extensive wear (smooth, round, polished edges). One of these has abrasion and polish on the ventral surface of the flake, indicating extensive use as a cutting implement (Plate V d).

Raw materials include sedimentary rock (N=5), argillite (N=5), and slate (N=1).

|          | cases | mean  | median | range       | std dev | quartiles   |
|----------|-------|-------|--------|-------------|---------|-------------|
| weight   | 11    | 78.3  | 81.4   | 28.5-128.9  | 31.5    | 55.1-104.7  |
| length   | 11    | 79.2  | 74.9   | 63.1-105.0  | 12.1    | 72.6-87.2   |
| width    | 11    | 61.2  | 60.8   | 40.4-81.7   | 12.5    | 52.2-69.0   |
| thickness| 11    | 14.0  | 13.5   | 10.0-20.8   | 3.8     | 11.0-15.3   |

**Retouched Cobble Flakes**  (N=30) (Plate V e-h)

These are large retouched flakes from unprepared cobble cores. Most retain some cortex, but unlike cortex-backed spalls these implements only have cortex on the striking platform area or along the proximal edges of the flake on the dorsal side (see Fig. 5.11). In addition, these flakes tend to be thicker than spalls and less uniform in shape. They most closely resemble the ecailles de galets or grande ecailles de galets from Gitaus (Allaire 1978:145-51). Functionally, they are probably consistent with the "large unifacially retouched boulder flakes" (Calvert 1968:39) from the Co-op Site (see also de Laguna et al. 1964:105).

These implements have thick, steep edges, and were probably used as scraping tools. Retouch is invariably unifacial, and generally crude and irregular. Many of these implements have edges that are extensively worn, often with polish, indicating heavy or prolonged use. Polish was evident under 10 power magnification along the edges of nine implements.

Raw materials include sedimentary rock (N=13), argillite (N=12), basalt (N=3), slate (N=1), and sandstone (N=1).

|  | cases | mean | median | range | std dev | quartiles |
|---|---|---|---|---|---|---|
| weight | 30 | 71.3 | 68.8 | 14.2-169.5 | 35.0 | 49.5-91.3 |
| length | 30 | 69.3 | 70.1 | 42.4-95.2 | 12.7 | 62.2-77.2 |
| width | 30 | 49.7 | 51.5 | 24.6-71.9 | 10.8 | 43.4-54.7 |
| thickness | 30 | 18.8 | 19.8 | 9.4-26.7 | 4.6 | 14.2-22.8 |

## Cobble Cores

**Unformed Cores** (N=20)

These cores are consistent with the "unformed cores" defined by Matson (1976:131) for the Glenrose assemblage. They lack prepared striking platforms. Reduction was unsystematic, with flakes removed at random locations around the surface of the core.

Although it is possible that any of these implements was used as a cobble tool at some time, there is no existing evidence of wear or formed edges.

Raw materials include argillite (N=11), sedimentary rock (N=7), and basalt (N=2).

|  | cases | mean | median | range | std dev | quartiles |
|---|---|---|---|---|---|---|
| weight | 20 | 110.8 | 82.2 | 21.5-271.2 | 74.8 | 58.7-166.2 |
| length | 20 | 67.5 | 65.6 | 41.4-117.2 | 17.4 | 55.9-76.1 |
| width | 20 | 49.7 | 49.9 | 25.8-90.5 | 16.7 | 37.6-57.2 |
| thickness | 20 | 27.8 | 27.5 | 14.5-46.0 | 8.0 | 20.9-32.4 |

**Minimally Flaked Cobbles** (N=8)

These are river cobble cores with only one or two flake scars. In describing similar artifacts from the Glenrose Site, Matson (1976:142) suggested that such cobbles may have had a few flakes struck off to test the nature of the material for possible use as cores. The lack of any further reduction indicates that these cobbles were rejected.

Raw materials include sedimentary rock (N=7), and argillite (N=1).

|  | cases | mean | median | range | std dev | quartiles |
|---|---|---|---|---|---|---|
| weight | 8 | 233.6 | 220.5 | 70.9-474.1 | 145.1 | 100.9-355.1 |
| length | 8 | 84.7 | 82.8 | 54.5-116.0 | 23.6 | 61.0-110.4 |
| width | 8 | 60.6 | 63.8 | 46.4-72.0 | 11.8 | 47.7-71.3 |
| thickness | 8 | 28.8 | 25.1 | 18.1-50.0 | 11.0 | 20.6-36.7 |

**Cortex-based Cores**  (N=14) (Plate V i-j)

Cortex-based cores, previously defined by Matson (1976:131), have a flat cortex surface used as the striking platform.  They are distinguished from other cobble implements, such as cobble core tools, which also tend to have the cortical surface as a striking platform, in that these cores appear to be expended remnants with flake scars all around the non-cortical surface.

They appear to have been constantly turned over during reduction, rather than systematically worked back from one end or side.  This is consistent with the description of the Glenrose cores given by Matson (1976:131).

Raw materials include argillite (N=4), sedimentary rock (N=9), and coarse basalt (N=1).

|  | cases | mean | median | range | std dev | quartiles |
|---|---|---|---|---|---|---|
| weight | 14 | 339.3 | 328.1 | 85.4-653.5 | 161.3 | 206.6-454.7 |
| length | 14 | 99.3 | 100.8 | 68.6-123.0 | 16.3 | 86.8-111.6 |
| width | 14 | 78.6 | 86.6 | 42.3-101.4 | 19.9 | 63.0-91.9 |
| thickness | 14 | 36.6 | 36.1 | 20.9-60.1 | 8.6 | 31.6-39.1 |

<u>Hammerstones</u>

Hammerstones, described on page 233, are not sub-divided into types. The metric measurements for hammerstones are given here.

|  | cases | mean | median | range | std dev | quartiles |
|---|---|---|---|---|---|---|
| weight | 59 | 606.4 | 511.1 | 23.4-1975.5 | 441.3 | 248.5-876.4 |
| length | 59 | 108.8 | 106.2 | 45.3-267.0 | 39.0 | 83.4-126.1 |
| width | 59 | 72.2 | 74.9 | 22.8-111.0 | 20.5 | 57.4-88.4 |
| thickness | 59 | 44.7 | 45.7 | 11.4-76.4 | 14.8 | 35.3-55.0 |

## Saws and Sawn Fragments

**Saws** (N=8) (Plate VI a-b; Figure 5.15)

Stone saws include small flakes, larger cortical spalls, and one very large cobble fragment. They have acute edges with extensive polish, in one case extending 7 mm from the edge (Plate VI a). In each case, multiple striations exist along the edge, running parallel to the edge, thus indicating a sawing rather than scraping action.

Two implements have further evidence of modification. The large cobble fragment has extensive unifacial grinding indicating alternate use as an abrader (Plate VI a). Also present on the "saw edge" of this tool are a series of nicks and striations at right angles to the edge, indicating that this implement may have served alternately as a scraping plane.

Another implement has unifacial retouch on the edge adjacent to the "saw edge" (Plate VI b). Abrasion and polish are evident along the retouched edge and on the high points between the flake scars. Evidently, the edge was retouched and then used for sawing. The retouch may have been intended to straighten the edge to better facilitate sawing.

Raw materials include heat treated argillite (N=2), coarse granular sedimentary rock (N=2), red argillite (N=1), and green schist (N=3).

|  | cases | mean | median | range | std dev | quartiles |
|---|---|---|---|---|---|---|
| weight | 6 | 101.3 | 56.1 | 26.3-357.9 | 126.5 | 38.4-141.3 |
| length | 6 | 79.9 | 72.0 | 57.4-136.9 | 29.7 | 57.6-96.9 |
| width | 7 | 49.5 | 48.4 | 30.4-80.0 | 16.0 | 35.0-54.0 |
| thickness | 8 | 12.3 | 12.2 | 3.4-25.3 | 6.9 | 5.8-15.5 |

**Sawn and Snapped Fragments** (N=6) (Plate VI c-d; Figure 5.15)

These are thin tabular flakes, each cut by a deep groove, indicative of sawing along one lateral edge. In one case, a linear groove has been cut down the middle of one face of the implement. This may have functioned as a "shaft smoother" (see Ackerman 1968:63).

These flakes were not sawn through completely. Rather, they were sawn through partially (in one case sawing was bifacial) and then snapped. Each implement has evidence of some facial and/or edge abrasion subsequent to sawing.  These appear to be fragments of unfinished groundstone implements, sawn and snapped into a rough shape and then incompletely ground.

Raw materials include slate (N=2) and poorer quality shale and schist (N=2), one heat treated fragment of argillite, and sedimentary rock (N=1).

|  | cases | mean | median | range | std dev | quartiles |
|---|---|---|---|---|---|---|
| weight | 2 | 13.6 |  | 8.9-18.2 | 6.6 |  |
| length | 2 | 51.2 |  | 43.0-59.3 | 11.5 |  |
| width | 5 | 27.4 | 27.6 | 14.0-41.7 | 10.0 | 19.0-35.8 |
| thickness | 6 | 8.0 | 7.6 | 6.2-10.2 | 1.7 | 6.6-10.0 |

## Ornamental/decorative Objects

A general description of this class was given in Chapter 5.  It includes a variety of carved, incised and pecked and polished items.  There are five spherical stones, one of which is pecked but not polished.  The latter is partially covered with a red stain, and may have been used to crush pigment (Plate VII e).  The other four stones are polished, although they may have been naturally spherical in shape.  Two of these are likely hematite, and are quite highly polished (Plate VII a-b).  The other three are argillite.

One tabular schist fragment has been unifacially ground and incised with numerous crossing lines (Plate VII i).  It resembles the stylized anthropomorphic representations of spinal column and ribs described by MacDonald (1983:101) for items from Prince Rupert Harbour.

One polished slate disc bead was recovered (Plate VII f).  It is quite small; 0.2 grams, and 6.6 mm in diameter.

Two small polished fragments of mica and serpentine were recovered. The latter has been polished to a very high finish (Plate VII g-h).

A segmented or ribbed stone, similar to those described by H. Stewart (1973:95) and MacDonald (1983:114), was recovered (Plate VII k). Manufactured from sandstone, it includes four straight parallel incised lines.

Finally, a bird effigy, carved from a soft green stone, was recovered (Plate VII j).  It shows the head of a bird with a long pointed beak (raven?).  The base of the beak is marked by a series of six hatched incisions, stylistically similar to the segmented stone.

## Pointed Groundstone Tools
### Pointed Ground Schist Implements  (N=10) (Plate VIII k-m)

These are pointed implements manufactured from green schist.
Although all bear evidence of grinding, there is a great range in the
extent of grinding.  For example, two implements are only ground on the
edges near one end.  At the other extreme, a complete bi-pointed implement
has been ground extensively and bifacially (Plate VIII k).  Shape also
varies.  Two implements, including the one mentioned above, are symmetrical
bi-points.  Two are roughly leaf-shaped, with wide rounded bases.  One
small point has a long contracting stem (Plate VIII m).  The other
implements are broken fragments, one of which is unique in that it has been
notched on either side, 14 mm from the tip (Plate VIII l).

Despite this variability in form, these implements all have in common
lateral edges that have been ground blunt or flat rather than sharp or
bevelled.  As a result, they do not closely resemble groundstone points
from other Northwest Coast assemblages.  For example, the finished bi-point
described above resembles a "Type 1" bi-point from Component II at Hidden
Falls (Lightfoot 1983:68), but the Hidden Falls point is lenticular in
cross-section, becoming hexagonal near the tip.

The use of green schist as a raw material is also unusual, although
Allaire (1978:122) describes two ground schist points from the Kleanza
Complex at Gitaus.

|  | cases | mean | median | range | std dev | quartiles |
|---|---|---|---|---|---|---|
| weight | 4 | 8.0 | 3.5 | 1.8-23.4 | 10.3 | 2.2-18.5 |
| length | 4 | 51.3 | 47.0 | 39.3-71.8 | 14.9 | 39.8-67.0 |
| width | 9 | 19.8 | 18.3 | 12.9-31.6 | 5.7 | 15.9-23.6 |
| thickness | 10 | 4.8 | 4.3 | 2.3-9.2 | 1.9 | 3.6-5.6 |

### Ground Slate Drills  (N=2) (Plate VIII j)

Both implements taper to long "drill" points, circular in
cross-section.  One is long, slender and well finished (Plate VIII j).  It
is rectangular in cross-section, becoming circular at the point.  It
resembles the "pencil-like points" from zone II at Co-op (Calvert

1968:36). The other implement is a smaller unfinished fragment. It has a deep groove, indicating a saw cut along one edge, and has been partially unifacially ground. The point has been rounded and polished through use.

The raw material is slate in both cases.

## Ground Slate Points  (N=7) (Plate VIII a-g)

Included here are finished and unfinished ground slate points. Unfortunately, all are broken fragments with bases missing. All but one of these implements are thin, flat, and hexagonal in cross-section. Lateral edges are bifacially bevelled. They are consistent with those from Prince Rupert Harbour (MacDonald and Inglis 1981:51; Calvert 1968:36).

One implement appears to have had a long contracting stem, but the extreme distal end of the stem has broken off. It closely resembles the "Type 3" ground slate points from Hidden Falls component II (Lightfoot 1983:71).

Allaire (1978:122) describes four ground slate or schist points from Gitaus, but only one is complete.

An unusual feature among the ground slate points from the Paul Mason Site is that four have grinding only on one face. There are two possibilities to explain this. One is that the implements were unfinished or broken in manufacture, which is probably the case for three of these points (Plate VIII b, d, g). The other implement retains a bifacially ground edge, but the remainder of one face has been removed (Plate VIII c). This tool was evidently heat-treated, and it is possible that fire-spalling occurred, removing one face of the implement.

## Ground Slate Preform  (N=1)

This implement is a large, thick preform, roughly triangular in shape, and flat in cross-section. Bifacial flaking and some grinding is evident along both edges. Both faces have been ground. The distal end has broken off. The implement is 73.6 mm in width and 14.3 mm thick.

## Ground and Chipped Bifaces  (N=2) (Plate VIII h-i)

Both implements are manufactured from slate and show evidence of grinding and bifacial chipped retouch along one edge. Both are thin in cross-section and have acute edges.

Grinding on one implement has formed a shallow concave depression (Plate VIII h). This may be a re-modified abrader fragment. The bifacially flaked edge is slightly convex. The raw material is slate.

The other implement, also made from slate, is leaf-shaped and probably formed a point at one end (Plate VIII i). However, the tip has broken off. The edge opposite the flaked edge has been bifacially ground to form a sharp bevelled cutting edge (see Figure 5.16). There is a continuous series of nicks and small flake scars along this edge. The flaked edge also has some evidence of abrasion, which may be the result of use. This implement probably functioned as a knife. It is similar to two chipped and ground stone fragments recovered from the Co-op Site (Calvert 1968:43), which have alternate grinding and chipping along an acute edge. Calvert (1968:43) suggests that they functioned as knives.

|  | cases | mean | median | range | std dev | quartiles |
|---|---|---|---|---|---|---|
| weight | 1 | 66.2 | | | | |
| length | 1 | 117.0 | | | | |
| width | 1 | 50.7 | | | | |
| thickness | 2 | 8.5 | | 7.0-10.0 | | |

## Blunted Groundstone Implements

### Thick Flat Groundstone Implements  (N=4) (Plate IX k, o-q)

These are long groundstone fragments, thick, and rectangular in cross-section. Two implements (both slate) were thinned at one end. They may have been used as crude celts. The other two implements (sandstone and green schist) defy functional description.

|  | cases | mean | median | range | std dev | quartiles |
|---|---|---|---|---|---|---|
| weight | 0 | | | | | |
| length | 0 | | | | | |
| width | 4 | 25.8 | 25.8 | 20.8-30.6 | 5.2 | 21.0-30.5 |
| thickness | 4 | 12.3 | 11.2 | 8.7-18.0 | 4.0 | 9.2-16.5 |

### Pencils  (N=5) (Plate IX a-f; Figure 5.17)

Drucker (1943:57) defined pencils as "slender rods of ground slate, usually hexagonal or octagonal in form". These implements are found along the Northwest Coast from Alaska to the Gulf of Georgia. MacDonald (1969:251) applied the term to slate artifacts of rod-like shape, recovered from the Period I and early Period II levels of the Prince Rupert Harbour Sites.

Pencils from the Paul Mason Site range from oval to multifacetted in cross-section. All but one are broken end fragments. Two fragments each have extremely blunt or rounded tips.

De Laguna et al. (1964:127) suggest that pencils from Yakutat Bay may have been used as stone awls. They also state (de Laguna et al. 1964:129) that in most areas of the Northwest Coast where slate pencils are found, analogous forms also occur in bone.

Raw materials are sedimentary rock (N=1), argillite (N=2), and slate (N=2).

|  | cases | mean | median | range | std dev | quartiles |
|---|---|---|---|---|---|---|
| weight | 1 | 14.0 | | | | |
| length | 1 | 57.0 | | | | |
| width | 5 | 15.8 | 15.5 | 12.0-19.9 | 2.9 | 13.4-18.4 |
| thickness | 5 | 9.5 | 9.8 | 6.8-11.5 | 1.8 | 7.9-11.0 |

**Long Flat Groundstone Implements** (N=11) (Plate IX g-j, l-n)

These implements are similar to pencils, except that they are flat in cross-section, and the lateral edges are ground flat.

One complete implement is long and narrow in shape, and forms a blunt tip at one end (Plate IX j). Two others may have formed points but the tips are broken off.

The raw materials are slate (N=4), green schist (N=4), and sedimentary rock (N=3).

|  | cases | mean | median | range | std dev | quartiles |
|---|---|---|---|---|---|---|
| weight | 2 | 15.7 | | 11.5-19.9 | 5.9 | |
| length | 2 | 82.6 | | 64.1-101.0 | 26.1 | |
| width | 7 | 18.4 | 17.8 | 15.6-21.9 | 2.2 | 17.0-20.5 |
| thickness | 11 | 7.4 | 6.8 | 4.3-13.9 | 3.0 | 5.0-9.5 |

## Miscellaneous Groundstone

**Acute Edge Utilized Slate Pieces** (N=5) (Plate VI h-1)

These are thin slate flakes with very acute edges, and evidence of wear on one edge. The utilized edges are straight to slightly convex. Given the thinness of the flakes and the extremely acute edge angles, it is likely that these flakes served as unfinished knives or cutting implements.

**Steep Edge Utilized Slate Pieces** (N=4)

These are large pieces (each weighs roughly 150 grams) of sawn or snapped slate, with evidence of abrasion or use along one or more steep edges. Two implements are long and narrow, and multi-facetted in cross-section. These may be unfinished pencils. One implement has polished lateral edges, and some unifacial abrasion.

**Edge Ground Slate** (N=3)

Included here are large, thick, tabular pieces of slate have been sawn or snapped. In each case, there is evidence of grinding or polish on the broken edges.

**Unifacially Ground Slate** (N=3)

These are snapped or sawn tabular pieces of slate with rough abrasion and numerous parallel striations on one face. These implements may have been used, however briefly, as abrasives.

**Miscellaneous Ground Slate** (N=9)

This type includes small, thin pieces from ground slate implements that lack diagnostic attributes.

**Miscellaneous Groundstone** (N=5)

Included here are a variety of small, thin, irregularly-shaped pieces with some evidence of facial or edge grinding. They are distinct from the above class only in the fact that they are not manufactured from slate.

**Acute Edge Groundstone**  (N=1)

This is a broken piece of ground phylite.  The modified edge is straight, acute, and has been bifacially ground.  Numerous striations are visible near the edge, running parallel to the edge, suggesting a sawing function.

Unshaped Abraders

**Unifacial Tabular Abraders**  (N=7) (Plate X g-h)

These are thin and roughly rectangular in cross-section.  Abrasion is present only on one surface.  Most are of irregular shape.  Raw materials include sedimentary rock (N=6) and sandstone (N=1).

|  | cases | mean | median | range | std dev | quartiles |
|---|---|---|---|---|---|---|
| weight | 7 | 19.7 | 22.1 | 7.7-31.6 | 25.2 | 14.6-27.1 |
| length | 7 | 54.9 | 53.1 | 49.4-60.4 | 8.6 | 51.5-57.6 |
| width | 7 | 36.3 | 32.5 | 27.5-48.9 | 11.2 | 29.1-41.4 |
| thickness | 7 | 9.8 | 9.8 | 3.5-15.6 | 4.5 | 4.3-13.8 |

**Cobble Core Abrader**  (N=1)

This is a cobble core of red argillite, weighing 337.7 grams.  Cortex is present, with large flake scars covering much of the remainder of the core surface.  One large flaked surface area, intersecting the cortex was used as an abrading surface.  It has been ground flat and smooth.

**Cobble Abraders**  (N=9)

These are river cobbles that have been used as abraders with little or no modification.  Seven implements have been split, and the ventral surface has been used as a natural abrading plane.

Two abraders are unmodified discoid-shaped cobbles.  In each case, one face has been used as a natural abrading surface.

One implement is pitted on the abrading surface, and may have also seen use as an anvil.  It resembles the "anvil stones" described by Matson (1976:141).

The size of these implements varies, but none is so large that it could not have been hand-held.

Raw materials include sedimentary rock (N=4) and argillite (N=5).

362

|           | cases | mean  | median | range        | std dev | quartiles   |
|-----------|-------|-------|--------|--------------|---------|-------------|
| weight    | 9     | 450.5 | 394.8  | 130.0-1000.0 | 278.8   | 256.7-572.7 |
| length    | 9     | 109.3 | 110.4  | 58.3-163.6   | 33.3    | 83.7-130.2  |
| width     | 9     | 66.7  | 63.3   | 41.1-109.7   | 22.2    | 49.1-79.4   |
| thickness | 9     | 39.1  | 34.7   | 26.7-60.0    | 10.3    | 31.9-45.3   |

## Unshaped Bifacial Abraders  (N=5)

These implements are flat or tabular in cross-section, and have extensive abrasion on both faces.  There is no indication of edge modification.

Raw materials include sedimentary rock (N=3), green schist (N=1) and slate (N=1).

|           | cases | mean  | median | range      | std dev | quartiles   |
|-----------|-------|-------|--------|------------|---------|-------------|
| weight    | 5     | 245.8 | 228.6  | 70.1-421.5 | 62.1    | 131.4-303.0 |
| length    | 5     | 96.8  | 110.5  | 79.5-114.0 | 56.3    | 86.7-112.8  |
| width     | 5     | 69.7  | 51.9   | 40.5-116.7 | 41.1    | 46.3-80.0   |
| thickness | 5     | 15.9  | 11.3   | 4.1-35.2   | 12.3    | 6.4-27.7    |

## Reworked Unifacial Abrader  (N=1) (Plate X f)

This unusual implement appears to have served multiple uses.  It is a long thin fragment of slate.  One face has been extensively ground.  One very acute edge has been bifacially retouched.  This edge forms a curving "S-shape", convex at one end and deeply concave at the other end. Undoubtedly, this was a cutting edge, although the functional importance of the curve is unknown.  The opposite edge is straighter, unretouched and inclined at an angle of roughly 45°.  Nicking and tiny flake scars along this edge suggest use as a scraper.  The raw material is argillite.  The implement weighs 66.3 grams.

## Abrasive Slabs  (N=4)

Mitchell (1971:125) divided abraders from Montague Harbour into abrasive slabs and abrasive stones, based on their relative size.  A similar distinction is used here.  Abrasive slabs from the Paul Mason Site were probably too heavy for comfortable use in the hand.  During use, these slabs were probably set in a stationary position, while the object to be

363

shaped was rubbed along the abrading face of the slab. Each slab appears
to be broken or conchoidally fractured, so originally they were probably
even larger (the weight of the largest fragment is 1.36 kg).

One implement also has a steep (45°) unifacially retouched edge, that
does not articulate with the abrading surface. This implement may have
doubled as a massive chopper or scraping plane.

**Thick Unifacial Abraders**  (N=9)

These are thick, irregularly-shaped abrader fragments. All are
manufactured from argillite. One was extensively heated; another is
covered with red and yellow pigment stains.

|  | cases | mean | median | range | std dev | quartiles |
|---|---|---|---|---|---|---|
| weight | 9 | 60.9 | 38.2 | 32.8-111.8 | 44.1 | 34.5-101.2 |
| length | 9 | 78.4 | 83.2 | 54.5-92.9 | 16.7 | 61.1-91.5 |
| width | 9 | 40.0 | 46.8 | 22.0-54.7 | 14.1 | 25.2-51.6 |
| thickness | 9 | 25.3 | 26.6 | 15.4-38.7 | 7.1 | 19.2-29.3 |

**Small Abrader Fragments**  (N=7)

These are small, irregular-shaped abrader fragments, with evidence of
unifacial abrasion. Although they are classed here with unshaped abraders,
these are small fragments, so it is possible that any of these are from
shaped abraders.

Raw materials include sedimentary rock (N=5), green schist (N=1) and
sandstone (N=1).

Shaped Abraders

**Trapezoidal Abraders**  (N=11) (Plate X a-c)

These are thin, flat abraders that contract in width slightly at one
end. Lateral edges are straight to slightly convex, and convergent toward
one end. Abrasion is bifacial, and all edges have been ground flat.
Abraders of virtually identical shape were first noted at Gitaus in the
Kleanza Complex (see Allaire 1979:44). Elsewhere on the north coast,
trapezoidal abraders are reported from Hidden Falls II (Lightfoot 1983:54),
and from Prince Rupert Harbour (all components, but most common during the
later middle and late periods) (MacDonald 1969:251). Farther south, on the

central coast, Chapman (1982:88) reports trapezoidal abraders from the O'Connor Site.

| | cases | mean | median | range | std dev | quartiles |
|---|---|---|---|---|---|---|
| weight | 3 | 40.6 | 43.2 | 32.8-45.2 | | |
| length | 3 | 99.5 | 102.2 | 82.7-113.6 | | |
| width | 5 | 57.1 | 55.8 | 43.9-71.6 | 9.9 | 49.4-65.4 |
| thickness | 11 | 11.5 | 9.9 | 2.9-22.5 | 6.0 | 7.0-17.0 |

**Edge Rounded Abraders** (N=2) (Plate X d-e)

These implements are tabular fragments with abrasion on one face. In both cases the abrasion extends on to one edge, forming a rounded or rolled edge, so that the implements are roughly elliptical in cross-section. One implement has been pecked along the edges and on the face opposite the abrading surface. The raw material is slate in both cases.

Abraders of roughly similar shape and cross-section are reported from Namu by Luebbers (1978:44, 49).

**Shaped Bifacial Abraders** (N=13)

These are irregular pieces of abraders that are flat or tabular in cross-section. Only one implement is complete. All have evidence of extensive abrasion on both faces and on atleast one edge, such that the abraded edge is at right angles to the abraded faces.

The complete implement is flat and thin (5.9 mm) in cross-section. One face has been extensively abraded; the other face, less so. All edges have been ground flat. The implement is three-sided; two edges intersect at right angles and the third edge is convex.

Another fragment was broken or snapped along two opposed sides. There is light unifacial retouch on both edges.

The raw materials include argillite (N=6), slate (N=3), schist (N=1), and sandstone (N=1).

| | cases | mean | median | range | std dev | quartiles |
|---|---|---|---|---|---|---|
| weight | 1 | 22.7 | | | | |
| length | 1 | 86.8 | | | | |
| width | 3 | 58.4 | 65.9 | 34.3-75.0 | | |
| thickness | 12 | 14.8 | 13.5 | 5.9-27.5 | 6.2 | 10.2-19.6 |

**Shaped Unifacial Abraders** (N=8)

These implements are tabular in cross-section, and with one exception are quite thin (less than 10 mm). All are broken fragments. They have been abraded extensively on one face, and shaped or ground along at least one edge. The abraded edges are straight to slightly convex, and have been ground flat and at right angles to the abraded face. In two cases, there is evidence of abrasion along two edges that intersect, at right angles.

Raw materials include sedimentary rock (N=5), argillite (N=1), and green schist (N=2).

## Grinding Stones

Grinding stones, described on page 247, are not sub-divided into types. The metric measurements for these implements are given here.

|           | cases | mean  | median | range        | std dev | quartiles    |
|-----------|-------|-------|--------|--------------|---------|--------------|
| weight    | 3     | 370.0 | 379.5  | 302.8-427.6  |         |              |
| length    | 3     | 121.2 | 122.5  | 103.0-138.0  |         |              |
| width     | 5     | 100.7 | 99.2   | 90.9-117.0   | 10.0    | 92.9-109.2   |
| thickness | 5     | 22.2  | 23.6   | 17.1-25.4    | 3.2     | 19.1-24.6    |

## Chipped Stone Tools

### Formed Bifaces

**Chipped Bifaces** (N=12) (Plate XII a-i)

These are well-made tools formed by bifacially removing flakes from the periphery of the object. The implements generally have numerous flake scars, originating from the edge of the implement, and crossing the ventral and dorsal surfaces (thinning flakes). Two implements were manufactured on flakes that were already quite thin (Plate XII c-d). Thinning flakes are not in evidence across the dorsal and ventral surfaces. Modification constituted bifacial edge retouch to form the edge.

Five bifaces are complete (Plate XII b, c, e, f, h). The others are large fragments that are nearly complete. Four of the complete implements are leaf-shaped bifaces, roughly oval in outline, converging to a point at one end and rounded at the base (Plate XII b, c, f, h). They are generally similar in form to leaf-shaped bifaces from Prince Rupert Harbour (MacDonald and Inglis 1981:45), and to leaf-shaped bifaces from the Skeena

366

Complex at Gitaus (Allaire 1978:86-87, 99).

Raw materials include argillite (N=2), red argillite (N=1), obsidian (N=3), sedimentary rock (N=1), basalt (N=2), slate (N=2) and grey-brown chert (N=1). Green chert, which was so prevelent at Gitaus in the Skeena Complex, was not in evidence in biface manufacture at the Paul Mason Site. The chert biface has extensive polish covering both faces (Plate XII h). One proximal fragment of vitreous basalt is very well-made, and forms a sharp point (Plate XII a). It is too thick in cross-section however, to have been a projectile point. Two implements, manufactured from red argillite (Plate XII d) and obsidian (Plate XII i), appear to have been broken in the final stages of manufacture. The obsidian implement is almost complete. Triangular in shape, it was broken near the base in an apparent attempt to remove a small, remaining patch of cortex.

| | cases | mean | median | range | std dev | quartiles |
|---|---|---|---|---|---|---|
| weight | 5 | 15.5 | 12.4 | 0.3-38.6 | 14.7 | 3.7-28.3 |
| length | 6 | 53.5 | 45.9 | 19.3-98.8 | 30.9 | 27.3-85.5 |
| width | 10 | 26.5 | 28.2 | 6.2-47.0 | 12.0 | 17.2-35.7 |
| thickness | 11 | 7.4 | 7.2 | 2.7-12.1 | 3.0 | 4.7-9.9 |

**Irregular Bifaces** (N=8)

Matson (1976:106) used the term "large crude bifaces" to describe implements with a roughly leaf-shaped outline that were relatively thick in relation to their length and width. The irregular bifaces from the Paul Mason Site conform to this description, except that they vary in size. These implements were formed by the removal of fewer flakes than the previous type. Three implements have water-worn cortex remaining on one or both faces.

Matson (1976:106) suggested that the implements from Glenrose were probably blanks or preforms rather than finished objects. This is probably also true of the Paul Mason Site implements, although one implement has a dark stain along one edge that might be pitch or charcoal, indicating that the implement may have been used in woodworking.

Raw materials include sedimentary rock (N=2) and argillite (N=6).

|           | cases | mean  | median | range       | std dev | quartiles   |
|-----------|-------|-------|--------|-------------|---------|-------------|
| weight    | 8     | 122.9 | 71.2   | 4.9-311.8   | 121.8   | 30.9-263.8  |
| length    | 8     | 85.1  | 90.2   | 47.1-120.9  | 23.3    | 64.7-100.2  |
| width     | 8     | 45.1  | 40.3   | 17.5-77.8   | 21.0    | 29.6-67.1   |
| thickness | 8     | 20.8  | 20.2   | 6.3-33.2    | 10.5    | 12.1-31.1   |

**Unilateral Backed Bifaces**  (N=3) (Plate XII k-m)

These implements have one bifacially retouched edge; the opposite edge is thick or "backed". The size of the implements varies, but all are roughly similar in outline (semi-ovoid). The retouched edges are slightly convex; the backed edges are thick and straight. Although the largest of these implements is relatively thick, they all have acute retouched edges, and probably functioned as cutting tools. Two of the implements were used extensively, with a high degree of polish along the cutting edge. The closest parallel to these implements is the bifacially flaked knife recovered from the Co-op Site (Calvert 1968:67).

The raw materials are sedimentary rock (N=2) and schist (N=1).

|           | cases | mean | median | range      | std dev | quartiles |
|-----------|-------|------|--------|------------|---------|-----------|
| weight    | 3     | 79.8 | 55.6   | 6.5-177.3  | 87.9    |           |
| length    | 3     | 78.2 | 82.6   | 47.7-104.2 | 28.5    |           |
| width     | 3     | 36.7 | 36.9   | 20.5-52.7  | 16.1    |           |
| thickness | 3     | 14.2 | 12.5   | 4.2-26.0   | 11.0    |           |

**Steep Angle Biface**  (N=1)

This implement, manufactured from chert, is small, thick and roughly circular in outline. It has been regularly bifacially retouched around most of the edge. On one face, blade-like flake scars extend back steeply to a high ridge. The edge angle is greater than 45°; a scraping function is suggested. The implement weighs 10.3 grams.

**Spokeshave**  (N=1)

This bifacial implement, manufactured from obsidian, is roughly crescent-shaped in outline. It resembles a "spokeshave", and was probably used as a woodworking implement. Spokeshaves are rare from most Northwest Coast sites, although Ackerman (1968:64) reports two from the late

368

component at Groundhog Bay 2. He suggests that they may have been used to trim and smooth wooden shafts.

## Edge Fragments with Bifacial Retouch (N=8)

These are small end and edge fragments of implements that were bifacially retouched. The pieces are generally too small to predict the original form of the implement. Edge retouch is regular in all cases. One fragment of obsidian was removed by a force directed along the length of the edge, either a result of manufacture or use. It resembles a "ski-spall" as described by Smith (1974:351) and Fladmark (1983:301, 303) (Plate XII j).

The raw materials include obsidian (N=3), basalt (N=3) and quartz crystal (N=2).

## Formed Unifaces

## Steep Angle Formed Unifaces (N=3) (Plate XIII a-c)

These are unifacially retouched implements with edge angles greater than 45° (see Sanger 1970:76; Pokotylo 1978:220). One, manufactured from obsidian (Plate XIII a), is a circular scraper. Another, also manufactured from obsidian, is a roughly square-shaped scraper fragment, that may have been hafted along the edge opposite the scraping edge (Plate XIII b). The third implement is manufactured from argillite (Plate XIII c). It may have formed a point at one end, but the tip has broken off.

Although few in number, the small, circular to square-shaped implements are consistent in form and size with scrapers from Gitaus (see Allaire 1978:325). Farther north, Fladmark (1982b:328-33) reports 66 small end and side scrapers from the Mt. Edziza area. These were manufactured primarily from obsidian.

|  | cases | mean | median | range | std dev | quartiles |
|---|---|---|---|---|---|---|
| weight | 1 | 0.6 | | | | |
| length | 1 | 13.1 | | | | |
| width | 3 | 19.9 | 14.8 | 13.1-31.7 | 10.3 | |
| thickness | 3 | 3.9 | 3.8 | 3.3-4.5 | 0.6 | |

### Core Scraper (N=1)

This implement, manufactured from obsidian, is a re-modified core, with a steep unifacially retouched angle along two edges. Flake scars on the opposite edge appear to be related to the implements use as a core.

Fladmark (1982b:333) reports 11 core scrapers from the Mt. Edziza area.

### Perforators (N=6) (Plate XIII d-e)

These are thin, flake tools that have been unifacially retouched to a long slender tip. They do not appear to have been used as drills. There is no evidence of concentric wear around the point. They were probably too fragile to have been used as graving tools.

Obsidian (N=5) and chert (N=1) are the raw materials.

|  | cases | mean | median | range | std dev | quartiles |
|---|---|---|---|---|---|---|
| weight | 5 | 0.8 | 0.6 | 0.2-1.4 | 0.6 | 0.3-1.4 |
| length | 5 | 20.7 | 19.9 | 15.6-25.6 | 4.1 | 17.1-24.8 |
| width | 6 | 12.0 | 11.4 | 7.6-21.6 | 5.1 | 7.8-14.5 |
| thickness | 6 | 4.4 | 4.9 | 1.2-6.2 | 1.9 | 2.6-6.0 |

### Scraper Re-sharpening Flakes (N=3) (Plate XIII f)

In addition to the scraping tools recovered from the Paul Mason Site, three obsidian re-sharpening flakes were also recovered. Scraper re-sharpening flakes have been described by Frison (1968) and Shafer (1971). They are essentially the scraping edge of the implement, removed by a blow struck either transversely or parallel to the edge. This leaves a clean edge on the old implement for further modification. The re-sharpening flake usually shows extensive wear and undercutting along the old scraping edge.

The presence of scraper re-sharpening flakes is consistent with the extremely small obsidian scrapers recovered at the site. Obsidian, which is not locally available, was probably maintained and curated much more than locally available lithics, to the extent that obsidian scrapers were reduced through continual re-modification to very small sizes.

|           | cases | mean | median | range | std dev | quartiles |
|-----------|-------|------|--------|-------|---------|-----------|
| weight    | 3     | 1.0  | 1.1    | 0.5-1.3   | | |
| length    | 3     | 17.3 | 16.2   | 16.0-19.8 | | |
| width     | 3     | 8.5  | 8.9    | 6.7-9.8   | | |
| thickness | 3     | 4.7  | 4.2    | 4.1-5.9   | | |

## Retouched Flakes

**Regular Steep Angle Unifacially Retouched Flakes**  (N=31) (Plate XIII h-m)

These flakes are based primarily on obsidian (N=16) and chert (N=9).
Green chert occurs once.  Quartz crystal (N=2), basalt (N=3), and red
argillite (N=1) were also used.

Most of these implements are quite small, especially the obsidian
flakes.  A similar tool type was defined by Matson (1976:119).  The
implements are typically made on thin flakes with one or more edges
regularly retouched to form a steep angle.  The shape of the retouched
edges ranges from slightly convex to well-rounded.  The extent of retouch
also varies.  In some cases retouch exists along the entire length of the
edge, while in other cases it is localized to short sections along the
edge.

These implements were probably used as scraping tools.

|           | cases | mean | median | range | std dev | quartiles |
|-----------|-------|------|--------|-------|---------|-----------|
| weight    | 31    | 2.0  | 1.2    | 0.3-8.3   | 2.1 | 0.7-2.9   |
| length    | 31    | 19.4 | 17.4   | 8.7-40.0  | 8.1 | 14.5-22.3 |
| width     | 31    | 14.4 | 12.7   | 6.7-24.5  | 5.5 | 10.1-18.7 |
| thickness | 31    | 4.4  | 4.1    | 2.2-10.2  | 1.8 | 3.1-5.3   |

**Irregular Steep Angle Unifacially Retouched Flakes**  (N=13) (Plate XIII n-p)

These are large thick flakes of argillite (N=3), sedimentary rock
(N=3), poor quality chert (N=3), basalt (N=2), obsidian (N=1), and quartz
crystal (N=1).  In general, retouching of these tools was limited to the
removal of three or four large flakes along one edge.  Some implements are
"backed"; the opposite or unretouched edge is thick and has been truncated
by a parallel or transverse blow.  It is not clear whether this is a
functional attribute of these implements or the result of accidental
breakage.  Use wear, in the form of micro-flaking and undercutting, is

371

present on all retouched edges.  Three implements have edge polish, indicating extensive use.

These implements may have been used in heavy-duty scraping activities, where minimal retouch was required and extensive wear resulted.

A similar tool type was defined by Matson (1976:122).

|           | cases | mean | median | range     | std dev | quartiles |
|-----------|-------|------|--------|-----------|---------|-----------|
| weight    | 13    | 9.0  | 3.7    | 0.5-39.2  | 12.1    | 1.5-12.6  |
| length    | 13    | 32.0 | 33.8   | 13.2-51.6 | 12.7    | 18.5-43.5 |
| width     | 13    | 25.6 | 22.7   | 8.0-45.1  | 11.6    | 16.4-33.0 |
| thickness | 13    | 8.2  | 6.4    | 2.6-15.2  | 4.1     | 5.3-12.7  |

**Denticulated Unifacially Retouched Flakes**  (N=3) (Plate XIII g)

These implements have unifacially retouched edges with a series of spurs or notches at intervals along the edge.  Flake scars along the edge are large and widely spaced; this creates the spurs between the flakes. The retouching is regular in each case.  Describing similar artifacts from the Glenrose Site, Matson (1976:122) states, "the edges are usually regularly retouched, so that the notches are not merely large flakes struck off, but formed by a number of flake scars".

The raw materials include chert, obsidian and milky quartz.  These flakes may have been used as graving or slotting tools.

|           | cases | mean | median | range     | std dev | quartiles |
|-----------|-------|------|--------|-----------|---------|-----------|
| weight    | 3     | 9.1  | 11.2   | 1.1-15.0  |         |           |
| length    | 3     | 32.0 | 29.8   | 18.3-48.0 |         |           |
| width     | 3     | 27.9 | 27.0   | 17.2-39.6 |         |           |
| thickness | 3     | 9.3  | 9.2    | 4.7-13.9  |         |           |

**Regular Acute Angle Unifacially Retouched Flakes**  (N=12) (Plate XIII q-s)

These are small thin flake implements with regular acute angle retouch along one or more edges.  They were probably used as cutting tools.  Once again, the shape of the edges ranges from straight to slightly convex.  Well-rounded acute edges are rare.  The general preference seems to have been for rounded scraping edges and straighter cutting edges.

Raw materials include obsidian (N=5), chert (N=2), green chert (N=3), and quartz crystal (N=2).

|           | cases | mean | median | range     | std dev | quartiles  |
|-----------|-------|------|--------|-----------|---------|------------|
| weight    | 12    | 1.4  | 0.7    | 0.2-5.1   | 1.7     | 0.4-1.9    |
| length    | 12    | 19.2 | 16.4   | 10.2-38.6 | 8.2     | 13.1-22.8  |
| width     | 12    | 14.9 | 12.9   | 7.7-23.0  | 5.4     | 10.2-19.8  |
| thickness | 12    | 4.1  | 3.8    | 1.9-8.1   | 1.7     | 2.9-5.0    |

**Irregular Acute Angle Retouched Flakes**  (N=12) (Plate XIII t-u)

These are large flake tools of varying thickness, manufactured from poor quality raw material, including argillite (N=4), basalt (N=2), sedimentary rock (N=1), green schist (N=1), and slate (N=1).  Three obsidian flakes are also included.  Generally, retouch is located along a relatively straight or slightly convex section of the edge.  Retouch is typically of poor quality, although in some cases this may have more to do with the quality of the raw material than the quality of workmanship.

These implements were probably used primarily as cutting tools, although four implements are in excess of 50 grams, and may have doubled as crude scraping implements.

|           | cases | mean | median | range      | std dev | quartiles  |
|-----------|-------|------|--------|------------|---------|------------|
| weight    | 12    | 17.1 | 14.9   | 0.2-91.5   | 24.9    | 1.3-19.8   |
| length    | 12    | 46.6 | 46.3   | 11.7-105.4 | 29.3    | 20.9-58.9  |
| width     | 12    | 26.7 | 26.2   | 8.4-51.8   | 13.9    | 15.5-36.9  |
| thickness | 12    | 8.4  | 7.7    | 1.7-18.2   | 5.0     | 4.7-12.2   |

**Regular Bifacially Retouched Flakes**  (N=4) (Plate XIII v-w)

These flakes have extensive bifacial retouch along one or more edges.  The retouched edges are acute, although in two cases they approach 45°.  Two small obsidian flakes each have regular bifacial retouch on one edge.  The other two implements are larger, thicker flakes of argillite.  Bifacial retouch is extensive on both and quite regular.  Both have thick edges that may have been suited to both cutting and scraping tasks.

|           | cases | mean | median | range     | std dev | quartiles  |
|-----------|-------|------|--------|-----------|---------|------------|
| weight    | 4     | 18.2 | 13.9   | 0.3-44.7  | 21.3    | 0.6-40.1   |
| length    | 4     | 38.5 | 32.5   | 13.0-76.0 | 28.0    | 15.2-67.8  |
| width     | 4     | 28.9 | 27.0   | 10.0-51.6 | 19.2    | 11.6-48.1  |
| thickness | 4     | 7.9  | 7.7    | 2.8-13.3  | 4.8     | 3.3-12.6   |

**Irregular Bifacially Retouched Flakes** (N=2) (Plate XIII x-y)

These are thick argillite flakes. Both have irregular flaking along one steep straight edge. Extensive wear, in the form of micro-flaking, is evident along these edges. Polish is evident along the edge of one flake (Plate XIII x). The angle of the retouched edges, and the extent of wear, suggests that these implements may have been used in heavy-duty scraping tasks.

|  | cases | mean | median | range | std dev | quartiles |
|---|---|---|---|---|---|---|
| weight | 2 | 20.3 | | 16.7-23.8 | | |
| length | 2 | 59.7 | | 39.8-79.5 | | |
| width | 2 | 33.5 | | 28.4-38.6 | | |
| thickness | 2 | 14.3 | | 12.8-15.8 | | |

## Chipped Cores and Pieces Esquillées

**Chipped Cores** (freehand percussion) (N=19) (Plate XIV j-l)

These are extensively reduced cores of obsidian (N=2), quartz crystal (N=6), basalt (N=1), chert (N=3), green chert (N=1), argillite (N=5), and sedimentary rock (N=1). Chipped cores are distinguished from cobble cores on the basis of extent and quality of reduction. The cores included here are consistent with the nuclei polyhedriques from Gitaus (Allaire 1978:119).

A green chert core is particularly interesting (Plate XIV j). It is by far the largest piece of green chert recovered from the Paul Mason Site. It is roughly keel-shaped, with regular unifacial retouch along one very steep edge. In contrast to the Skeena Complex at Gitaus, where green chert is abundant, this core and four retouched flakes are the only modified pieces of green chert recovered from the Paul Mason Site.

|  | cases | mean | median | range | std dev | quartiles |
|---|---|---|---|---|---|---|
| weight | 19 | 24.5 | 8.0 | 1.6-159.6 | 38.6 | 3.1-27.4 |
| length | 19 | 35.8 | 31.8 | 14.8-76.0 | 17.7 | 20.4-50.5 |
| width | 19 | 23.5 | 20.3 | 8.8-57.8 | 13.3 | 11.7-30.9 |
| thickness | 19 | 17.5 | 16.3 | 6.6-37.5 | 9.0 | 10.0-23.1 |

**Bipolar Cores** (N=6) (Plate XIV m-n)

These are extensively reduced cores with evidence of bipolar flaking in the form of crushing or battering at opposed ends. There are three obsidian cores, and one each of quartz crystal, chert and argillite.

One of the obsidian cores has a series of three parallel blade-like scars at one end (Plate XIV n). This may be a microcore fragment. It is roughly keel-shaped. Unfortunately, it is very small, and appears to have been split along the face adjacent to the flake scars. Its assignment as a microcore is uncertain, and as the bipolar technique is in evidence, it has been included here.

|  | cases | mean | median | range | std dev | quartiles |
|---|---|---|---|---|---|---|
| weight | 6 | 6.7 | 2.2 | 1.0-23.9 | 9.0 | 1.4-13.2 |
| length | 6 | 22.9 | 18.6 | 12.7-45.5 | 12.3 | 13.8-32.2 |
| width | 6 | 19.0 | 14.1 | 11.6-37.8 | 10.4 | 11.9-27.9 |
| thickness | 6 | 10.7 | 10.7 | 6.0-15.6 | 3.2 | 8.3-13.1 |

**Pieces Esquillées** (N=16) (Plate XIV a-i)

These are thinned bifacially flaked implements with parallel sides, showing crushing on opposed ends. The latter resulted from a bipolar flaking technique. In general, these artifacts have been extensively flaked. MacDonald (1968:88) states that pièces esquillées were probably multi-purpose tools, functioning as stone wedges, or as grooving or "slotting" tools for bone, antler and woodworking. Matson (1976:128) states that pièces esquillées from Glenrose were used as wedges to split bone and antler. Hayden (1980:3) also argues that pièces esquillées were probably used as wedges for splitting bone.

The raw materials include basalt (N=2), argillite (N=6), sedimentary rock (N=4), obsidian (N=2), and quartz crystal (N=2). Many of these implements have extensive polish, derived through use, covering both faces.

|  | cases | mean | median | range | std dev | quartiles |
|---|---|---|---|---|---|---|
| weight | 16 | 18.1 | 7.3 | 1.3-96.2 | 25.0 | 2.0-25.7 |
| length | 16 | 36.6 | 32.8 | 19.3-71.0 | 14.7 | 24.7-49.7 |
| width | 16 | 27.7 | 24.7 | 11.3-53.1 | 13.7 | 16.3-39.6 |
| thickness | 16 | 10.4 | 9.0 | 4.8-20.0 | 4.6 | 6.8-13.9 |

## Microcores and Microblades

### Rejuvenation Flakes (N=2)

These flakes are described in detail on page 259. The metric measurements are given here.

| | cases | mean | median | range | std dev | quartiles |
|---|---|---|---|---|---|---|
| weight | 2 | 1.4 | | 0.8-2.0 | | |
| length | 2 | 17.0 | | 13.8-20.2 | | |
| width | 2 | 14.8 | | 11.6-17.9 | | |
| thickness | 2 | 4.8 | | 4.8-4.8 | | |

### Microblades (N=116)

Microblades were described in detail on pages 259 to 264. Metric measurements are presented in three tables here: unmodified microblades, retouched microblades, and microblades with edge wear but lacking flake retouch.

| Unmodified Microblades | | | | | | |
|---|---|---|---|---|---|---|
| | cases | mean | median | range | std dev | quartiles |
| length | 5 | 19.2 | 17.9 | 17.5-24.0 | 2.7 | 17.6-21.5 |
| width | 55 | 5.9 | 5.8 | 3.3-9.8 | 1.4 | 5.0-6.8 |
| thickness | 55 | 1.6 | 1.5 | 0.8-3.4 | 0.6 | 1.1-2.0 |

| Retouched Microblades | | | | | | |
|---|---|---|---|---|---|---|
| | cases | mean | median | range | std dev | quartiles |
| length | 1 | 24.5 | | | | |
| width | 4 | 6.7 | 7.1 | 4.0-8.4 | 1.9 | 4.8-8.1 |
| thickness | 4 | 1.5 | 1.2 | 1.1-2.5 | 0.7 | 1.1-2.2 |

| Utilized Microblades | | | | | | |
|---|---|---|---|---|---|---|
| | cases | mean | median | range | std dev | quartiles |
| length | 10 | 20.7 | 19.8 | 9.6-34.1 | 7.2 | 15.5-25.3 |
| width | 57 | 6.5 | 6.6 | 4.0-10.4 | 1.4 | 5.4-7.3 |
| thickness | 57 | 1.7 | 1.6 | 0.7-3.5 | 0.6 | 1.2-2.1 |

## Table II.1
## Artifact Type Distribution at The Paul Mason Site

| Artifact type | Component I | Component II | Component III | Site total* |
|---|---|---|---|---|
| **I-A Cobble Tools** | | | | |
| steep angle cobble core tools | 86 | 41 | 33 | 166 |
| acute angle cobble core tools | 10 | 8 | 4 | 29 |
| cobble choppers | 49 | 31 | 13 | 107 |
| split cobble tools | 13 | 9 | 9 | 37 |
| pebble core tools | 6 | 3 | 2 | 20 |
| pointed cobble tool | 1 | 0 | 0 | 1 |
| **I-B Utilized Flakes** | | | | |
| large utilized spalls | 53 | 14 | 3 | 72 |
| small utilized spalls | 12 | 6 | 0 | 20 |
| large acute angle utilized flakes | 28 | 7 | 4 | 45 |
| small acute angle utilized flakes | 26 | 7 | 2 | 41 |
| large steep angle utilized flakes | 21 | 6 | 2 | 32 |
| small steep angle utilized flakes | 2 | 1 | 1 | 5 |
| **I-C Retouched Cobble Flakes** | | | | |
| steep angle retouched spalls | 6 | 2 | 1 | 11 |
| acute angle retouched spalls | 8 | 1 | 1 | 11 |
| retouched cobble flakes | 22 | 3 | 2 | 30 |
| **I-D Cobble Cores** | | | | |
| unformed cores | 9 | 5 | 3 | 20 |
| minimally flaked cobbles | 4 | 2 | 1 | 8 |
| cortex-based cores | 8 | 3 | 2 | 14 |
| **I-E Hammerstones** | 41 | 12 | 6 | 59 |
| **II-A Saws and Sawn Fragments** | | | | |
| saws | 7 | 1 | 0 | 8 |

**Table II.1** (continued)

| Artifact type | Component | | | Site total |
|---|---|---|---|---|
| | I | II | III | |
| sawn and snapped fragments | 5 | 0 | 1 | 6 |
| **II-B Ornamental/ decorative** | 7 | 1 | 0 | **8** |
| **II-C Pointed Groundstone Tools** | | | | |
| pointed ground schist implements | 5 | 2 | 1 | 10 |
| ground slate drills | 2 | 0 | 0 | 2 |
| ground slate points | 5 | 2 | 0 | 7 |
| ground slate preform | 0 | 1 | 0 | 1 |
| ground and chipped bifaces | 1 | 0 | 0 | 2 |
| **II-D Blunted Groundstone Implements** | | | | |
| thick flat groundstone implements | 3 | 1 | 0 | 4 |
| pencils | 4 | 1 | 0 | 5 |
| long flat groundstone implements | 9 | 1 | 0 | 11 |
| **II-E Miscellaneous Groundstone** | | | | |
| acute edge utilized slate pieces | 3 | 1 | 1 | 5 |
| steep edge utilized slate pieces | 2 | 1 | 1 | 4 |
| unifacially ground slate | 2 | 0 | 0 | 3 |
| miscellaneous ground slate | 5 | 3 | 0 | 9 |
| miscellaneous groundstone | 3 | 1 | 1 | 5 |
| acute edge groundstone | 1 | 0 | 0 | 1 |
| **II-F Finished Ground Slate** | 2 | 1 | 0 | 3 |
| **II-G Unshaped Abraders** | | | | |
| unifacial tabular abraders | 4 | 3 | 0 | 7 |
| cobble core abraders | 0 | 1 | 0 | 1 |

Table II.1 (continued)

| Artifact type | Component | | | Site total |
|---|---|---|---|---|
| | I | II | III | |
| cobble abraders | 4 | 2 | 0 | 9 |
| unshaped bifacial abraders | 2 | 1 | 0 | 5 |
| re-worked unifacial abrader | 1 | 0 | 0 | 1 |
| abrasive slabs | 3 | 0 | 0 | 4 |
| thick unifacial abraders | 7 | 0 | 0 | 9 |
| small abrader fragments | 5 | 1 | 0 | 7 |
| I-H Shaped Abraders trapezoidal abraders | 10 | 0 | 0 | 11 |
| edge rounded abraders | 2 | 0 | 0 | 2 |
| shaped bifacial abraders | 11 | 1 | 0 | 13 |
| shaped unifacial abraders | 6 | 1 | 1 | 8 |
| **II-I Grinding Stones** | 4 | 0 | 0 | 5 |
| **III-A Formed Bifaces** chipped bifaces | 10 | 1 | 0 | 12 |
| irregular bifaces | 7 | 0 | 0 | 8 |
| unilateral backed bifaces | 2 | 0 | 0 | 3 |
| steep angle bifaces | 0 | 1 | 0 | 1 |
| spokeshave | 1 | 0 | 0 | 1 |
| edge fragments with bifacial retouch | 6 | 0 | 1 | 8 |
| **III-B Formed Unifaces** steep angle formed unifaces | 2 | 0 | 0 | 3 |
| core scraper | 0 | 1 | 0 | 1 |
| perforators | 4 | 1 | 0 | 6 |
| scraper re-sharpening flakes | 2 | 0 | 0 | 3 |

**Table II.1** (continued)

| Artifact type | Component | | | Site total |
|---|---|---|---|---|
| | I | II | III | |
| **III-C Retouched Flakes** | | | | |
| regular steep unifacially retouched flakes | 18 | 8 | 3 | 31 |
| irregular steep unifacially retouched flakes | 9 | 1 | 1 | 13 |
| denticulated unifacial retouched flakes | 2 | 0 | 0 | 3 |
| regular acute unifacially retouched flakes | 7 | 3 | 0 | 12 |
| irregular acute unifacially retouched flakes | 5 | 2 | 3 | 12 |
| regular bifacially retouched flakes | 2 | 0 | 1 | 4 |
| irregular bifacially retouched flakes | 2 | 0 | 1 | 4 |
| **III-D Chipped Cores and Piecès Esquillées** | | | | |
| chipped cores | 13 | 3 | 2 | 19 |
| bipolar cores | 2 | 2 | 2 | 6 |
| piecès esquillées | 10 | 3 | 3 | 16 |
| **III-E Microcores and Microblades** | | | | |
| microcore rejuvenation flakes | 0 | 0 | 2 | 2 |
| unmodified microblades | 11 | 4 | 34 | 55 |
| retouched microblades | 0 | 0 | 4 | 4 |
| utilized microblades | 14 | 4 | 36 | 57 |

* Component totals based on Floor 2, 9, Excavation H, J.

Site totals based on all excavations.

APPENDIX III

Faunal Analysis

Faunal material from the Paul Mason Site was analyzed by L. Roberts
(1984). This summary is based on her report. Samples were analyzed from
floor 2 (A2, A11), floor 9 (C2, C5), and Excavation J. All but one of the
samples were taken from hearth features (see Table 1). All samples were
taken from within the upper dark brown soil zone, representing the Paul
Mason Phase.

A total of 3675 small pieces of bone were analyzed. The total weight
of the sample was 26.84 grams. At least 98 percent of the bone was charred
or calcined.

A total of 21.18 grams (79.7 percent of the total sample) was
designated "class uncertain". The most specific identification possible
was the Salmonidae family, based on teeth and vertebrae fragments. There
was a second kind of fish present in the assemblage, which was
unidentifiable based on a few tiny non-Salmonidae vertebrae.

All recognizable skeletal elements were noted. Only three fish teeth
and one pharyngeal were identified. All other identifiable pieces were
infra-cranial, and consisted mainly of vertebrae and rib and ray fragments.

Mammal bone, much of it from deer-sized animals, weighed 4.08 grams
(72.1 percent of the total identified fraction); bird, 0.80 grams (14.1
percent); and fish, including the Salmonidae, 0.78 grams (13.8 percent).

Of the total 21.18 grams of class uncertain, material 20.50 grams
(96.7 percent) appeared to be fish, based on the general morphology of the
bone. Only 0.68 grams of the class uncertain material is likely mammal.
Distinctions at this level were very difficult because the bone was small,
much of it passing through 4 mm mesh. If the class uncertain totals are
added to the identified fraction, fish clearly becomes the dominant element
in the assemblage, constituting 21.28 grams (79.9 percent of the total
assemblage). Mammal constitutes only 4.76 grams (18.1 percent). This
large difference suggests that the economy of the people of the Paul Mason
Phase was oriented strongly toward fishing.

Table III.1
Faunal samples and provenience

| provenience of sample | identification | mammal | medium to large mammal | fish | salmonidae | bird | class uncertain |
|---|---|---|---|---|---|---|---|
| Trench A Unit 2 (hearth) | count | | 30 | 49 | 2 | 27 | +1570 |
| | weight (grams) | | 2.25 | .24 | .02 | .77 | 11.24 |
| Trench A Unit 11 (no hearth) | count | | | 2 | | | 62 |
| | weight (grams) | | | .02 | | | .20 |
| Trench C Unit 2 (hearth) | count | 4 | 12 | 18 | 3 | | +800 |
| | weight (grams) | .03 | 1.55 | .10 | .10 | | 3.44 |
| Trench C Unit 5 (hearth) | count | 1 | 1 | 31 | 2 | | +862 |
| | weight (grams) | .02 | .23 | .18 | .04 | | 5.56 |
| Excavation J (hearth) | count | | | 15 | | 1 | 121 |
| | weight (grams) | | | .08 | | .03 | .74 |
| SITE TOTALS | count | 5 | 43 | 115 | 7 | 28 | 3477 |
| | weight (grams) | .05 | 4.03 | .62 | .16 | .80 | 21.18 |

## 1980

95. Marois, Roger J.M., editor. "Archaeological Survey of Canada Annual Reviews 1977-1979." 106 p., 32 figures. (on request/sur demande).

96. Marois, Roger J.M., éditeur. "Commission archéologique du Canada, rapports annuels 1977-1979." 109 p., 33 planches. (sur demande/on request).

## 1981

107. Arnold, Charles D. "The Lagoon site (DjR1-3): implications for Paleoeskimo interactions" 223 p., 29 figures, 23 tables, 14 plates. (on request/sur demande).

## 1982

108. Finnigan, James T. "Tipi Rings and Plains Prehistory: A reassessment of their archaeo-logical potential." 295 p., 24 tables, 48 figures. (on request/sur demande).

110. Lennox, Paul A. "The Bruner-Colesanti site: An early Late Woodland component, Essex County, Ontario." 178 p., 35 tables, 35 figures. (on request/sur demande).

112. Trodden, Bonnie Joy. "A radiographic study of the calcification and eruption of the permanent teeth in Inuit and Indian children." 136 p., 14 tables, 22 figures. (on request/sur demande).

113. Murray, Rebecca A. "Analysis of artifacts from four Duke Point area sites, near Nanaimo, B.C.: an example of cultural continuity in the southern Gulf of Georgia region." 369 p., 71 tables, 46 figures. (on request/sur demande).

## 1983

115. McGhee, Robert, editor. "Archaeological Survey of Canada Annual Reviews 1980-1981." 92 p., 14 figures; and "Commission archéologique du Canada, rapports annuels 1980-1981." 99 p., 14 figures. (on request/sur demande).

116. Morrison, David A. "Thule culture in western Coronation Gulf, N.W.T." 365 p., 24 figures, 25 tables, 35 plates. (on request/sur demande).

117. Molto, Joseph Eldon. "Biological relationships of southern Ontario Woodland peoples: the evidence of discontinuous cranial morphology." 396 p., 13 figures, 23 tables, 5 appendices. (on request/sur demande).

118. Bernick, Kathryn. "A site catchment analysis of the Little Qualicum River site, DiSc 1: A wet site on the east coast of Vancouver Island, B.C." 368 p., 44 figures, 29 tables, 4 appendices. (on request/sur demande).

## 1984

120. LeBlanc, Raymond Joseph. "The Rat Indian Creek site and the late prehistoric period in the interior northern Yukon." 504 p., 75 figures, 99 plates, 133 tables, 3 appendices. (on request/sur demande).

121. Lennox, Paul A.  "The Hood site: A historic Neutral town of 1640 A.D.; The Bogle 1 and Bogle II sites: Historic Neutral hamlets of the northern tier." 289 p., 82 figures, 75 tables, 2 appendices.  (on request/sur demande).

122. Patterson, David Kingsnorth, Jr. "A diachronic study of dental palaeopathology and attritional status of prehistoric Ontario pre-Iroquois and Iroquois populations." 428 p., 38 figures, 14 plates, 105 tables, 4 appendices.  (on request/sur demande).

123. Pendergast, James F. "The Beckstead site -- 1977." 240 p., 10 figures, 15 plates, 59 tables, 1 appendix.  (on request/sur demande).

124. Warrick, Gary A. "Reconstructing Ontario Iroquoian Village Organization." 180 p., 21 figures, 36 tables; Dodd, Christine F. "Ontario Iroquois Tradition Longhouses." 257 p., 28 figures, 7 tables, 3 appendices. (on request/sur demande).

125. McGhee, Robert.  "The Thule village at Brooman Point, High Arctic Canada." 151 p., 34 figures, 26 plates, 2 tables.  (on request/sur demande).

126. Johnston, Richard B., editor.  "The McIntyre Site: Archaeology, subsistence and environment." 189 p., 42 figures, 43 tables.  (on request/sur demande).

127. Marois, Roger.  "La céramique préhistorique canadienne: essai de systématisation de L'analyse de la décoration."  363 p., 45 figures, 5 planches, 3 annexes (sur demande/ on request).

128. Janusas, Scarlett Emilie. "A Petrological analysis of Kettle Point chert and its spatial and temporal distribution in regional prehistory." 109 p., 24 tables, 34 figures, 3 appendices. (on request/sur demande).

129. Katzenberg, Mary Anne.  "Chemical analysis of prehistoric human bone from five temporally distinct populations in southern Ontario."  145 p., 16 tables, 10 figures, 2 appendices.  (on request/sur demande).


1985


130. Finlayson, William  D.  "The 1975 and 1978 rescue excavations at the Draper site: Introduction and settlement patterns." (with an introduction by Bruce G. Trigger). 625 p., 137 tables, 90 figures, 2 plates, 5 appendices.  (on request/sur demande).

132. Roberts, Arthur C.B. "Prehistoric occupations along the north shore of Lake Ontario." 247 p., 42 tables, 39 figures, 4 appendices.  (on request/sur demande).

133. Magne, Martin P.R. "Lithics and Livelihood: Stone tool technologies of central and southern interior British Columbia." 325 p., 33 tables, 75 figures, 1 appendix. (on request/sur demande).

134. Rokala, D.A. and C. Meiklejohn, editors. "The Native Peoples of Canada: An Annotated Bibliography of Population Biology, Health and Illness." 570 pp. **$14.95**

135. Sanger, David. "The Carson Site and the Late Ceramic Period in Passamaquoddy Bay, New Brunswick." 171 pp., 34 illus.  **$7.95**

136. Clark, D.W.  "Archaeological Reconnaissance at Great Bear Lake" 312 pp., 124 illus. 43 tables,  $12.95.

137. Morrison, D.A. "The Kugaluk Site and the Nuvorugmiut" 116 pp., 37 illus., 12 tables, $8.95.